boob

{True Story of a Breast Cancer Hostage}

envy

Shelly (Knowlton) Jones

boob: an idiot or someone who is the brunt of a joke. (noun) *slang* for breasts.

en·vy: [en-vee] plural en·vies, verb, en·vied, en·vy·ing. (noun)
  1. a feeling of discontent or covetousness with regard to another's advantages, success, possessions, etc.
  2. an object of envious feeling: her boobs made her the envy of her classmates.

Printed in the United States of America by McNaughton and Gunn http://bookprinters.com/

www.BoobEnvy.webs.com

Jones, Shelly (Knowlton)
Boob Envy / Shelly (Knowlton) Jones-1ˢᵗ ed.

ISBN (softcover) 978-0-615-74128-4
1. Breast Cancer
2. Memoir
3. Narrative Nonfiction

Preface

On my daughters 8th birthday in November 2010, at the age of 35, I was diagnosed with stage 3A Invasive Ductal Carcinoma. In normal-person-terms, that's breast cancer. It was advanced, aggressive, and scary as HELL. I had NO CLUE. I wasn't sick. I wasn't aware of it. I didn't have any sixth sense. When the lump was found-I mourned. I knew my life was going to go straight downhill. Quickly. Things moved so fast-within the week I was admitted to the hospital & was having a bilateral radical mastectomy. I had lymph nodes removed; I lost a chunk of my chest wall muscle; and worst of all I awoke without my double D's ☹

After getting over 12,500 hits on my CaringBridge journal and MUCH encouragement from friends and family, here it is. The whole naked story. I want the whole world to know the hell of cancer, and raise AWARENESS. Inform EVERYONE I can and get it all off my chest. (Haha-literally!)

I found myself looking for ANY source of information for someone in my predicament-a married, young(ish) Mom of three kids, ages 8, 4, and 10. I work full time, I know NOTHING about breast cancer, I am lower middle class. I live in a small community and do not have the resources that exist in large cities. I read lots of books from celebrity stories to self-published non-fiction. I looked for support groups tailored for people my age...my stage of life. No luck. I searched the internet for sites that were a perfect 'fit'. Found maaaaaaybe one. Possibly two. But nothing 'WOW! That's me!'

I have been subjected to MUCH pain and agony...and have been scared shitless. But I came through the other side. I'm still HERE. This book will hopefully shed some light on the whole breast cancer experience for other women. I tell all the grim details....from my mammogram diagnosis (holy FUCK---are they SURE?????) all the way through to my new foobies {fake boobies} I am 100% honest in my accounts, and hold NOTHING back. There is a lot of 'too much information' and a lot of make-you-squirm. In it I discuss every test I had. Every procedure I had. Every medicine I tried. Every side effect. Everyday life while living with my cancer. If I can help/inform/give peace of mind to at least ONE person....then I went through this hell for a reason.
For You.

I'm tired of crying.

I'm tired of yelling.

I'm tired of being sad.

I'm tired of pretending.

I'm tired of being alone.

I'm tired of being angry.

I'm tired of feeling crazy.

I'm tired of feeling stuck.

I'm tired of needing help.

I'm tired of remembering.

I'm tired of missing things.

I'm tired of being different.

I'm tired of missing people.

I'm tired of feeling worthless.

I'm tired of feeling empty inside.

I'm tired of not being able to just let go.

I'm tired of wishing I could start all over.

I'm tired of dreaming a life I will never have.

But most of all, I'm just tired of being tired.

Table of Cancer Costs

September 2010...$0.00
October 2010..$476.25
November 2010...................................**$96,928.15
December 2010..$149,474.56
January 2011...$188,201.31
February 2011..$217,147.06
March 2011...$282,801.81
April 2011...$329,571.56
May 2011..$341,332.56
June 2011...$354,986.56
July 2011...$356,542.31
August 2011...$378,094.24
September 2011...$385,156.24
October 2011...$386,304.24
November 2011...$389,904.24
December 2011...$423,127.24
January 2012...$449,165.30

*(I'm sure the total was much higher, but this was all I had
documentation for at the time I compiled all this!)*

***even I couldn't believe the jump in this monthly total-so I rechecked it.   YUP.
A $96,000 month. Each consult was $571. Hospital room was $35,000+.
The Plastic Surgeon was over $18,000. Mammogram, etc. was over $6000
after the biopsy and pathology...*

Dear Readers:

Welcome to my hell. This is my journal of my life through breast cancer. There is 'text language'; there are abbreviations that may or may not make sense. There are typos and emoticons. I do not comprehend how to segue... I have ADD and can NOT concentrate on ANYTHING. Chalk it up to Chemobrain or old age or just being a dumbass. For that I apologize. You may or may not finish this book with a headache. That's ok. Just go take a nap. Get over yourself. Did you know that there are such things as RUB ON NIPPLES? Yeah, me either. Until now! I don't suggest you Google them either. All kinds of crazy shit will pop up! There's rub on nipples, nipple tattoos, stick-on nipples *(which kind of blows my mind? I mean how many of us spend every stiff breeze crossing our arms to HIDE our NIPPLES??? Don't you frickin' LIE...you do TOO! Unless you're one of those hoochie mamas. Then you tend to let those nipsters fly.)* And there are bras that have built in nipples. Then they also make prosthetic boobs with and without nipples. I guess that's kind of nice, 'cause, say, you WANT to be a hoochie mama this weekend... then throw in your nipple prosthesis'. Go to the Fireman's picnic, dance your ass off, and fly those nips. But what if you only need ONE built in nipple? And what if it is NOT in the same position as your 'natural' nipple??? Then they're like lazy eyes (lazy nipples??!!) ...one's hunting one's fishing...going their separate ways...maybe not such a great choice after all, but then - BUT THEN! You could just stick in a bottlecap or something to try to get it to match the store bought nipple. Or cross ONE arm. Or pull out the prosthesis with the nipple---oh. No. Then not only would you be flying one nipple flag, but also only ONE boob, leaving all the drunk men (and some ladies...face it we all have our version of penis envy! oooHHH!!! BOOB ENVY! That would be a GREAT title!!) at the picnic staring at your UNIBOOB bouncing to and fro. Ugh. Now I have a headache with all this NIPPLE talk. Just make a pitcher of margaritas and put the booze in first so your minion children can't snitch any from you. It's ok. Everybody does it that way. (nobody does it that way, you fucking alcoholic!!) While editing I TRIED to put this all in some sort of order. I say tried. Again, if you have a headache... stop whining already! Jeez. You paid for the headache if that makes you feel any better?? It's almost like you asked for it. There are entries named 'Guestbook Comments:' that are actually from people that signed my guestbook on my blog. I put them all in where they belong, which was a lot of damn work! They were all bunched up in the end originally, kind of a mismatched chapter that made no sense. So I inserted them after each day/time so that THEIR comments made sense with MY comments. Make sense? I hope you appreciate all that I do for you...God, get off my BACK already! Did I ever tell you about the time I ran over the grill? Twice? See the entry for May 8th 2011...and the photo on the back page. Crap. There I go giving away the ending of that chapter... J/K ← see that???? T-E-X-T L-A-N-G-U-A-G-E. It's all the rage these days-all the tweens are doing it. Crap...the kids want supper. I'll stop listening to you complain now and pretend I'm listening to them. Fucking whiners...all of ya. Drink up. Enjoy laughing at my life. Your snorts will cover up the tears. Over.

 ♥ Shelly

For My Lobster...

It's Time to Kick Cancer's Ass.

The Beginning.
Tuesday, November 2, 2010 3:35 PM, CDT

Last week Tuesday, October 26 was a typical morning in my house. I woke up with Andy's hand on my boob. (That's my husband.) While trying to cop a feelski, his thumb brushed across my skin and he asked, "What is that?" Of course I was half asleep. I had NO IDEA what he was talking about, but was convinced he was trying to get lucky. He proceeds to tell me there's a 'lump'. So I sat bolt upright and felt for myself. Sure enough- towards the top of my right breast there was a NOTICEABLE lump. And it was tender. I undressed to look and could see the bulge....but still had no clue what it was. I thought that maybe it was a blocked duct or an infection or a fatty tumor... they happen...so I did what all girls do. I put on my medical professional hat and decided to call my best friend Jenny. "SHE will tell me it's nothing and reassure me." Well, Jenny

1

did NOT do that. She told me that I would have had her ass in the car already, driving her to her doctor. Ok. I admit it-all true. I would have. So I continued to put off calling the doctor by chit chatting with her about anything and everything. Finally she told me "CALL" So I did. I called the nurse and told her that I found a lump on my breast. They got me in within 2 hours. I had the physician's assistant do a breast exam and she too could feel the mass. She voiced that she remembered *after* I left yesterday that she should have done a breast exam. I had been in for a pre-op physical the day prior. Not that any of that would have mattered-the lump was big enough to palpitate, and 24 hours couldn't make much of a difference. Her opinion was that I should go in for a mammogram & possible ultrasound. Her nurse made me an appointment for a diagnostic mammogram on Monday November 1 at 9 a.m. in Sheboygan-a city about 12 miles away. She also put me on antibiotics in case it happened to be an infection. I had another six days to wait...and in those six days, I couldn't keep my hands off of it. Once I knew it was there I kept feeling it, and messing with it. I spent the next 6 days not really thinking about it. At this point I truly thought that I had an infected duct. The day of my imaging I was supposed to go to work. I had let my manager, Leigh, know that I would be coming in late; that I had a mammogram, and HAD to go. She is a young breast cancer survivor, and completely understood. The ironic part of this all is a coworker ten years my junior was diagnosed with breast cancer 2 weeks earlier. We had literally spent every day that we worked together talking about what she was going through. I was unusually intrigued with all she had to tell. I asked more questions than I normally would. I talked with her about her lumpectomy, future treatments, nipple tattooing you name it. I also had just done a 'Breast Cancer Awareness' display at work since October is National BCA month. Now, looking back on

2

it, I'm sure there was some divine intervention preparing me for what was to come. Monday rolled around, and I was mostly looking forward to going to work late! I don't know if I had told anyone other than Andy or my friend Jenny about what was going on. Quite possibly Betsy, but I know for a fact I didn't make too much out of it. I truly did not think this was a big deal. Mammogram Monday came and I was there early. Early as in "let's get this nonsense over with because I do NOT have time for this." I was scheduled to have a hysterectomy 2 days later, and all I could think was "I swear if this fucks up my surgery I'm going to be so pissed. I have been waiting FOREVER to have this done. I have 3 kids at home; no time for 'down time' and I'm starting medical leave on Wednesday, and and and..." Well, you get it. Those who know me.... REALLY know me...know how I am! Just walking in to the mammography section of the clinic is a bit unnerving, I'll be honest. We all have a preconceived notion of the torture chamber known as the mammogram-the pain; the SQUISH. Having had one in the past, I knew that it was uncomfortable at worst. I still at this point was not shaken. I wasn't afraid; I wasn't dreading it. It felt mostly like it was just a routine follow up to finding a lump. A waste of money; to do testing that wasn't necessary. That's what I was thinking, anyway. I was called in to the imaging waiting room and given a cape to put on after undressing above the waist. They have a few areas in there that are partitioned off with curtains and lockers to stow your things. Once in there I realized the 'cape' barely closed in the front and was only about 12 inches long!!! There was a nipple sticking out from under the bottom right and belly fat showing EVERY-WHERE and the left boob is popping out where my arm should be. ARGH!!! After locking all my modesty and personal belongings into my locker, I had to open the curtain and have a seat in the waiting area. There were two other women in this room-both senior citizens-paging through magazines. NO WAY!! I'm sorry, but I was afraid to take a deep breath in fear my juggs would just pop right out; much less calmly read a magazine about Snookie's latest escapades! For Pete's sake, you get a bigger 'cape' when getting your frickin' HAIR cut! I was called in by a very polite and friendly nurse. She made small talk, and we briefly discussed why I was there, and what she would be doing. The room was warm, silent, and dimly lit. The machine itself was very large, white in color, and moved up, down and sideways. So I have the mammogram. No biggie. She has me lift my boob up onto the 'plate'. Then she positions it so that it's within the correct 'field'. She then squishes it flat like a pancake. She also squishes it vertically. Then she checks the computer to make sure they received images that were clear. There was a door leading out of the room in the back and the nurse goes out through that, telling me that the radiologist would be reading the films right away, as is standard practice. Within moments she's back. She tells me that the doctor thought it necessary to do an ultrasound today as well. I am sent back into the waiting room while they prep the ultrasound room across the hall. I was suddenly nervous. Very nervous. Five minutes later I'm on the ultrasound table with the 'goo' everywhere from my chin to my belly to my armpits, being scanned. My left breast was done first as a base to see what my 'normal' breast looked like. Then she had me roll to the right and started to check the side with the lump. She spent a LOT of time measuring the lump-but only half as much time on the lump side as she spent on the healthy breast. *Hmm. This could go either way.* No sooner did I think that, than she tells me "He's going to want to biopsy this." Ok, I thought, this is NO good. I wondered how long it would take to get in for another appointment. I thought about my surgery scheduled for Wednesday. I thought "how the fuck am I going to be able to afford THIS bill???"

I wondered if Andy could get off of work to go with me for the biopsy-when right then in walks the doctor with his biopsy tools. *HOLY SHIT. Really??? Right here on the ultrasound table while I'm still full of goo?* Yes. Right there on the spot. Since the entire day was NOT enough fun, he was straightforward and told me flat out that he was certain that this was cancer of the breast we were dealing with. I think he may have introduced himself first, but I couldn't even be certain about that anymore. All the air in the room was sucked out. All the light in the room disappeared. Inside my chest all I could feel was my heart breaking. All I thought of was my babies, my husband, and dying. And all I could hear was........

B-R-E-A-S-T C-A-N-C-E-R.

OHMIGOD. Did he seriously just use the 'C' word???? I drove here alone-I was expecting to be at work within the next hour-I was thinking that I'd stop at Taco Bell on the way in to work-I was NOT NOT NOT NOT NOT NOT NOT thinking that I had cancer-I didn't know of ANYONE in my family that had breast cancer-didn't that ONLY happen to other people??? Seriously.. I am only 35 years old and no WAY can I have cancer?????? I ALWAYS thought I'd die from ovarian cancer like my Mom-I had that carved into my brain for the past 15 years. Who IS this guy???? How does he know that it is "likely" cancer? Is he even the radiologist? Or is he just the doctor that reads ultrasounds? Are they the same????? Holy shit, it must be advanced since he can tell its cancer just from the mammogram-before he even saw me, or felt it, or met me. Does he KNOW I'm 35? That I have three kids??? That I have a pretty chaotic life already???? Maybe he's mistaken. Maybe it was a bad image. MAYBE this is all a nightmare and I'll wake up with Andy's hand still resting on my boob...

OHMIGAWD.   CANCER???????????????????????
WHAT THE FUCKKKKKK ?????????
WHAT DO I DO??????
I DON'T WANT TO DIE??????

I was cleaned up, sterilized, and injected with something to numb the area in my right breast. Yes, needles right into my boobie. YOWZERS. Hasn't he heard of that awesome shit the dentist uses on the Q-TIP??? Jeez, man. When the numbing medication started to work a minute later, he told me to face away from the site, towards the wall. He suggested I do not look and that I breathe slowly through my nose. I just remember being in that dimly lit room, facing the wall while he cut a one fourth inch hole in my skin with a scalpel. He inserted the biopsy tool through that incision and took 3 'core' biopsies. (From researching on the internet about core biopsies, I found out that they use a 16-, 14-, or 11-gauge hollow core needle. No clue-I did NOT look.) I could hear the click of the tool he was using to remove pieces of this tumor. It hurt A LOT, and there was a LOT of pressure. And tugging. Not a fun process. They put the 'samples' into sample cups, and labeled them with my name. (What do they actually write on there??? 'Shelly Jones' right boob CANCER-BEWARE'??) The doctor told me that the pathology on these 3 biopsies would be back late tomorrow or early Wednesday. Then we would know what kind of cancer it is and what would be the next step. I was doing okay-if that was possible-and trying to

6

process this whole crazy past hour. Now I know that I was in a state of shock. He asked if I was okay-that I was being "very stoic". Then it hit me...all at once. I totally was just told I have breast cancer. That knocked the wind out of me. Tears started streaming down my face and before I knew it I was sobbing.

As you can imagine your whole life flashes before you. Childhood memories; moments in time from high school; loved ones lost; your wedding; the birth of your children; amazing things that have occurred throughout your life. Then you are faced with your own mortality. And gut-wrenching horror.

He continued talking while I wrapped my head around this. He told me he would call my gynecologist to inform him of this new 'discovery' (his words) and put my surgery on hold. He would also call upstairs to make an appointment for me to meet with a surgeon to discuss the pathology report, surgery options, etc. I was handed a card for an appointment with a surgeon on Wednesday November 3rd--two days later.

I have no recollection of walking out of that room. I have no recollection of gathering my clothing and changing. Nor do I have ANY idea how I got out of the clinic and walked all the way out to my van. I do remember wondering why the hell I left my cell phone out in the van-I needed to call Andy the SECOND I was able to.

I was sobbing this whole time, yet somehow I managed to call my husband's cell phone, reaching him at work. When he picked up, he asked "Hey, baby, how ya doing?" like he usually does. I don't think either of us discussed the appointment that morning; I don't believe he recalled that was where I was that morning. So when I answered him with a very shaky "it's NOT GOOD." I think he was momentarily confused. He asked me what was going on, and I had to tell the Love of My Life that I was just diagnosed with breast cancer. After that, it's a blank. I don't know what he said other than "I'm coming home." That was exactly what I needed to hear. All I wanted at that second was for him to wrap his arms around me. To tell me it would all be ok. To say I love you. To hold me until I woke up from this nightmare. While he drove home from Milwaukee, I needed to drive myself back to Plymouth. About a 15 minute drive. All I could think about on my ride home was my children. How in the HELL do you tell your babies that you have cancer?? I could barely wrap my head around it, how could I expect them to??? While driving home, I knew that things needed to be done swiftly-I had child care all set up for my hysterectomy; I had my LOA set up for it as well. I had rides set up to and from school for the kids. So if that surgery wasn't going to happen, then I needed to start somewhere. My next thought was my Dad. Thinking about telling him was almost more heart wrenching than it was for me to tell Andy. We barely survived my Mom's death together...how could I tell my Daddy that I had cancer now too???? WHAT parent should ever have to bear that heartache? Of course, when I am finally calm-ish, and get to his house, he is NOT HOME- Grrr! I call his cell phone and reach him-asking where he was. I was evasive in telling him that I wanted to talk to him and would he please meet me at his house. After he pulled in the driveway, I pulled in right behind him, and I could tell when he got out of the car that he wanted to know right away what was going on. I kept it together until we got in and sat down at the kitchen table. Impatiently he says "yeah?" and then I started bawling. "I just found out this morning that I have breast cancer. There was a lump and I had to go in for a mammogram and the doctor told me

8

it was breast cancer." "WHAT?????" he said, his voice going up 2 or 3 octaves...Oh My God...my heart shattered into a million pieces having to say that out loud. His voice was cracking, and I was sobbing. He asked me questions. I don't remember what they were. He brought up my Mom-but about what I don't know. He was visibly shaken and aged 10 years in those 10 minutes. Since I didn't know anything beyond that, there wasn't much else I could share with him. I just ended it with "my surgery's off for now, and Andy will be home soon so I need to go home." I've only seen my Dad cry once before this.

Andy and I both arrived home within a few minutes of each other. I got out of the van and started picking up garbage and sticks around the yard and driveway, not even making eye contact with him. Silently we both worked independently, until there was nothing left to pick up or throw out. There were no excuses left to not go into the house, to discuss this; face this. So we went into the house.

Andy and I graduated from high school together in 1993. We started dating in 1994 and got engaged in 1997. We have been through hell together. Early in our relationship my Mom passed away. In fact she was already sick when we started dating. Then my Grandpa passed away. Then his Mom. Then my Grandma. Then we went through a miscarriage before welcoming our son Josh in 2001. Then another miscarriage. Then along came Ilyssa in 2002. We lost Andy's brother the next year-in 2003. In 2005 Josh was diagnosed with a form of autism-Asperger's syndrome. In 2006, while I was pregnant with our third child, Andy's father died. After Alaina was born in 2006, I opted to have my tubes tied. That was done in May 2006. From August to September I had one constant period. HEAVY period. Yes, we all know that having a baby messes

9

the whole cycle up-but this? This was waaaaaaaay worse. This was like hemorrhaging. I went to my OB-GYN 4 or 5 times. I was put on several different kinds of birth control pills to even out the periods. I was never once given a pap. Or an ultrasound. Or any respect. One time I had even asked if there was a chance I could be pregnant?? My doctor <u>literally</u> laughed at me; ASSURED me that " he is capable of performing a successful tubal ligation. And no <u>way</u> could I be pregnant--the chances are like 1 in 1800." Well 3 weeks later on Friday the 13th while I was at work I was cramping like crazy and just felt <u>horrible</u> so I went to the bathroom to hide out. While in there I passed a HUGE amount of tissue, along with massive amounts of blood. When I got to the ER, the nurse practitioner was feeling my pelvis, and told me that my uterus felt like a pregnant uterus. Ultrasound confirmed that there was an unviable pregnancy in my uterus. Urine and blood tests also confirmed that I was about 11 weeks pregnant at the time. The baby had no heartbeat-so I had to go in for a D&C since my body was not expelling it. Instead of trusting the tubal ligation any further I opted to have my fallopian tubes removed at the same time. (That doctor is no longer employed at that hospital for multiple fuck- ups during surgeries. Malpractice. Go figure?!)

Back to our crappy life: in 2007 Josh was diagnosed with Celiac disease after being VERY sick for a very looong time. (He will need a life-long gluten free diet =$$$) In 2008 Andy's business became another casualty of our worsening economy. He closed the doors in July and was unemployed for months before landing another job in Milwaukee. Financially, that was devastating for us. He was not eligible for unemployment compensation. We had 3 small children, I was only working part time, and he had to take a HUGE pay cut. The tough decision was made to put our house up for sale; to

10

downsize; to try to save money somehow. We didn't in a million years imagine that it would take until April 2010 to sell it. The market sucked; we barely got enough out of it to pay off our mortgage-and the buyers expected the world. It was then that we decided we would relocate back to Plymouth, where I grew up and we had family. And a WHOLE lotta friends! Within the next three and a half weeks, we needed to get the kids signed up for their new school, find a place to live, and I needed to find a new job or get a transfer. Magically it all came together and in May 2010 we moved in to our new rental house. The kids had about 2 1/2 weeks of school in Plymouth before summer break came...meeting some new friends and learning their way around. I started at my new job location a week later. Finally, after a rough decade, things were settling down. We were comfy in our house, the kids had met and befriended all the neighborhood kids; work was going well; Andy continued at his job in Milwaukee.
Life was good. ☺

That evening I remember hiding out upstairs because I didn't want the kids to see me crying and crying and crying. My body hurt. My eyes felt like 2 piss holes in the snow. The pain from the tiny incision they made to do the biopsy was moderate. I think that I was actually sore from the tugging of the biopsy, not the actual cut. It was so small that they didn't need to do any stitches- just slapped a Band-Aid on there. I was scheduled to work 8 to 5 but had called and spoken to my assistant manager-telling her I wouldn't be in. I told her that I had just found out that I had breast cancer. She asked how they knew? (She was a young breast cancer survivor herself) How could they just 'know' from a mammogram? And I tried to explain to her that they did the whole works that day-ultrasound and biopsy, and preliminary pathology. She was very

11

caring and supportive. She told me not to worry about work and let me know what I needed to do as far as paperwork.

I do not remember calling my sister-or if I told her in person or what. I truthfully dreaded that call as much as telling my Dad-my sister and I are still really affected by my Mom's death. I'll have to ask her if she remembers how I told her...

Betsy called me that evening, asking how it was going, etc. I just blurted out "I found out today that I have breast cancer." I can't remember specifics but I don't think she believed me or maybe didn't hear me? So I said "No. Seriously." Well, by this time she was already ringing my doorbell and came up to support me and listen to me ramble. I don't know if I fell asleep from exhaustion or what but I was out quickly that night.

>>>>>>Fast forward to November 2, 2010<<<<<<

I stopped in at work to pick up the new set of paperwork for my leave from our personnel department. I was scheduled 11-8; didn't go, didn't call. I told them yesterday I would probably not be in, and I am 'off' starting tomorrow since I was to have my hysterectomy.

I spent hours and hours wandering around like a zombie-not knowing what to think, what to do. I couldn't think straight. I couldn't stop crying. All I could think about is that THIS is what heartbreak felt like. I did not have the slightest idea how I was going to go on. How to stop the hurt; how to face myself in the mirror...I remember undressing, and looking at my body in the mirror with disgust. With hate. With sadness. I was already bruising from the biopsy.

I was full of self-pity.
I was already broken.

Wednesday, November 3, 2010 3:30 PM, CDT
The doctor just called with my pathology report. Just as we suspected, I most definitely have breast cancer. No big surprise there. He explained to me that they were unable to "type" the cancer & that once they removed it they could do further characterization tests to determine what kind of breast cancer it is (there are various kinds). He mentioned that there were 2 types of invasive cancer-one being invasive ductal carcinoma and the other invasive lobular carcinoma. He said he *did* know that it was invasive. So I take this to mean that it is either in my ducts or lobules? I will try to figure out more tomorrow. I'll admit I was hoping to find out 'kind' so I could start researching like a maniac.

I also received a call from a woman from the clinic-I believe she said she was a Care Coordinator? She will meet us at our appointment with the surgeon; she asked how I was doing & feeling. I told her OK, but SORE and both breasts were tingly and hurt. She said that was most likely from the mammogram and biopsy. The swelling and bruising would go away eventually. She asked how Andy was doing and I told her ok-that we were both still in shock. She discussed how spouses really get affected by breast cancer too-not being able to "fix it" or do much about it. She will be my personal helper through this all-setting up my appointments, walking me through 'what's next' etc. Now to wait for my appointment with the surgeon.

Wednesday, November 3, 2010 4:45 PM, CDT

Information overload. Andy took a half day off work to go see the surgeon with me. We waited for what seemed like EVER--I literally thought I was going to THROW UP. Once we were called back to 'the room' I was a little freaked out. It was like a surgical procedure room with an adjustable table in the middle of it and huge lights hanging from the ceiling...and a little computer desk in the corner. No big oak desk with a box of tissues or a bowl of mints or those 5 silver balls that you swing back-n forth so they clack-- nothing I expected. The Doc came in and introduced himself, along with the BCCC (breast cancer care coordinator). He loaded up the images of my mammogram and ultrasound on his computer and talked with us about my family history. I told him that my mom found out she had stage 4 ovarian cancer in 1993 when she was 46 and passed away from it in January 1996 at age 49. I also shared with him that yesterday I found out my maternal grandfather possibly (?) had breast cancer at some point in his life. I had no idea. So while telling him my history he revealed that this was cause for us to be aggressive about this situation (the cancer). Considering my age-35-and family history I was probably genetically predisposed to this happening. I wanted to do the BRCA testing a.s.a.p. (*BRCA testing is a blood test to see if you have a mutation in either the BRCA1 or BRCA2 gene. If you do, you are predisposed to get breast and/or ovarian cancer.*) I will meet with a genetic counselor at a later date to have this testing done. We are waiting for the results of the estrogen/ progesterone receptor test on the tumor biopsies. If the results are positive, that means that the cancer responds to or feeds off of those hormones, and we will need to suppress them. Another test that we will do after surgery is the HER2 test. (*HER2 is a gene that sends control signals to your cells, telling them to grow, divide, and make repairs. A healthy*

14

breast cell has 2 copies of the HER2 gene. Some kinds of breast cancer get started when a breast cell has more than 2 copies of that gene, and those copies start over-producing the HER2 protein. As a result, the affected cells grow and divide much too quickly.)

It helps check if the cancer has spread. Further tests need to be run once the tumor is out. I did not find out what 'type' of breast cancer I have, but I did find out that:
- it's aggressive
- we did *not* catch this early
- it is a star shaped tumor approximately 0.98" long
- it is a Grade 3 'poorly differentiated cells'

(Poorly differentiated means that cells have changed-and not in a good way)
- that there is evidence of vascular invasion. (Lymphatic or vascular invasion means that the tumor cells have acquired the ability to invade the walls of these channels and may spread to the lymph nodes or beyond)

At this point the Dr. told me he had lined up 3 options:
1) lumpectomy (the tumor plus some healthy surrounding tissue would be removed) followed by radiation
2) a single mastectomy followed by reconstruction and chemotherapy
3) bilateral mastectomies with reconstruction; testing of the lymph nodes. If more than 4 nodes are positive for cancer, then the whole cluster will be removed; radiation is then needed to kill any leftovers; followed with bi-weekly chemo.

Less than a heartbeat went by and I decided that option #3 was what I wanted to do....don't just take out the tumor....you know that will just INVITE more cancer to that breast. Don't take just one

15

breast and in 6 months have to start over again when I find it in the other one. Let's just get it all over and done with...take away the chance of any remaining tissue getting cancer. The doctor COMPLETELY agreed that was what he would recommend since the younger you are the more aggressive breast cancer is and the more likely you are for it to reoccur. He also told me that he felt it in my best interest to continue with the plan of having a hysterectomy with the complete removal of the uterus, cervix, ovaries and fallopian tubes. During the surgery I will either have immediate breast reconstruction where they remove fat and muscle from my belly and 'build' breasts...or I will have tissue expanders put in and gradually over 6 months they will expand my muscle enough to have implants put in. That is what we will meet with the plastic surgeon about tomorrow and from that appointment decide what needs to all be organized for my surgery. From what I understand there will be 2 surgeons. I guess I'll learn more tomorrow. ♥S

Thursday, November 4, 2010 8:02 AM, CDT
Got some wonderful meds from the doctor to help me sleep and calm down. Lorazepam-tiny little things, but they really helped me last night. Now I'm working on making it through the day until my appointment in 3 hours with the Plastic Surgeon. ♥S

Guestbook Comment: Thursday, November 4, 2010 8:48 AM, CDT
Thanks for sharing this-this cancer doesn't know who it's messing with!!! You are gonna kick some ass!! I'll be thinking of you today. Stay strong my friend. Kim

Guestbook Comment: Thursday, November 4, 2010 9:02 AM, CDT
Shelly, this is a fantastic way of keeping everyone informed, so you don't have to call or text everyone. Thanks for all the updates. I

think you could totally turn this into a book. You are a great writer with added humor. You are a smart woman and you will pick the right decisions what to do. Your family will be in our prayers as you go through this tough difficult time... Love ya, Joey

Guestbook Comment: Thursday, November 4, 2010 9:28 AM, CDT
Shelly, I'm keeping you in my thoughts and prayers. You have always been a strong, independent, fun and humorous person. All those qualities will help you pull thru this. One of my favorite self-affirmations is "God will never give me more than I can handle" and I firmly believe in this. (Even though sometimes I've wished He didn't think I was quite so strong!) I was so glad when we reconnected this past month after so many years. We've shared so much laughter and tears in the past and I want to share those in the future too. Call me if you ever want to talk, yell, scream, cuss, laugh or cry. I'm here for ya. Sending love, Amy

Guestbook Comment: Thursday, November 4, 2010 9:36 AM, CDT
Hey Girl...GREAT IDEA...as usual!!!! I feel a little special my name is even in your story!!! LOL! On a serious note...you know what you have to do and you WILL do it!!! You are going to kick some serious BUTT!!!! I know I don't have to say this but...you know I am here and will be here for you and for your family! Anytime, anywhere, anything. Love ya! Jenny

Guestbook Comment: Thursday, November 4, 2010 9:49 AM, CDT
Hey there...I thought about doing something like this but never got around to it. It's great to keep track of your progress anyway you can. I write notes in a little notebook. Hang in there & just take it one day at a time or you will overload! Lisa

Thursday, November 4, 2010 2:15 PM, CDT

First, I have to say, going to a plastic surgeon for treatment of breast cancer is very intimidating. I know they deal with this stuff routinely, but to me it was just scary. I had to remove my shirt and bra, and they took pictures of what my breasts look like pre-surgery. I am proud to say that I have made it 35 years without anyone ever taking naked pictures of me! (Now let's just hope they don't hit the internet!) This will give him reference to rebuild and reconstruct after the mastectomy. I did have some questions. I wanted to know how reconstructed breasts vs. implants would be affected if I needed radiation (it will discolor the skin, and possibly alter the tissue). So he likes to do the actual implants after all cancer treatment is ceased. I also wondered what tissue expanders were and how they worked. They pulled out an example of one, and showed me. They're actually pretty cool; they are implant size 'bags' made of God knows what kind of plastic. They have a circle (the port) in the front of them with a metal backing and a magnet in it. This is so that they can find where to insert the needle when they fill the expanders. The metal backing is there so that they do not puncture the back of the expander or a lung! All of this is under my skin and in between the layers of my pectoral muscles. After at LEAST 4 months and after chemotherapy, then we'll decide how big we're gonna go and will put the actual implant in. After all the swelling goes down and the implants have settled...then we start on the cosmetic stuff. Nipples. He takes a piece of skin from your groin, cuts the circle for the areola, and sews it into your skin. Then he takes a second piece of skin folds it up all origami style and makes a nipple. That is also sewn on. A different option is tattooing. He can tattoo the nipple and areola right onto the flat skin on the breast-coloring and shading it in for depth and appearance. He told me that I was not a candidate for same day implants-I am too big

18

chested. He also told me I was not eligible for the surgery that takes tummy fat and muscle to build new boobs. There goes my free tummy tuck!! So tissue expanders it is. They will go in during the surgery. ♥S

Guestbook Comment: Thursday, November 4, 2010 3:34 PM, CDT
Praying for you and asking God to care for you.
Love you always! Andrea

Guestbook Comment: Thursday, November 4, 2010 5:00 PM, CDT
Hi, Honey. You weren't kidding with the "information overload". Do you have someone to be with the kids all day Monday? Does Andy have someone to wait with him at the hospital during your surgery? We'll talk more tomorrow night. Call me before then if you need a good cry (or bitch) session. Love ya Bets

Thursday, November 4, 2010 5:38 PM, CDT
Ok, I was rushing before to get some ZZzzzz's...and did leave out some info, as all my text-a-holic friends let me know! The WONDERFUL nurse that works for the plastic surgeon just called me and asked if I would be willing to take a surgery opening MONDAY morning-4 days from now. I told her "YES!" the sooner the better. I need this alien OUT of me like yesterday! She said the plastic surgeon didn't think I'd take it-that it was too soon. Hell, yeah I'll take it! She also discussed with me the fact that I will NOT be having the hysterectomy at the same time. They cannot do a non-sterile surgery (hysterectomy) at the same time as a sterile one (removing cancer). Obviously breast cancer takes priority here....but I'm worried about how long it'll take for me to be healthy enough to get that done...and what bad things are lurking in that region as well. Oh well. Bring it on! I do not yet know what time the surgery is

going to be. They didn't tell me how long the surgery will last. But I will be in the hospital 2 days. ♥S

<u>Guestbook Comment:</u> Thursday, November 4, 2010 5:42 PM, CDT
Shelly, I just wanted to tell you again how sorry I am that you have to go through all of this. I will be praying for you!! I wish I could be with you to support you. Please call me if you want to talk! Love you, Charity

Thursday, November 4, 2010 9:46 PM, CDT
I just got back from a last minute hair appointment with my friend Kim. I wanted to get in for a quick trim before surgery, and get a cut that was easy peasy so while I am in the hospital and at home sick I could just leave it sit. I had to get the brows waxed too...I was starting to look like a Russian Dodge ball Tournament Participant! I was sooo glad I brought along my friend Sarah. It was a good night of laughs, tears, and being me for a bit. I also got to inform two very special people in more detail about what I'm going through and some of the things that no one realizes are happening. I even let them cop a feel (sorry boys, no video cameras allowed!) Because I can guarantee you that this lump/tumor/alien in my breast feels NOTHING like what I thought a cancerous lump would feel like. They were also both surprised at how it felt, and I don't think ANY of us would have thought it was 'something'. Kim gave me some wonderful info on a program she participates in once a month-first Monday of the month-in Sheboygan at one of the cancer clinics. It's a night of beauty for cancer patients....you get to play with makeup and are shown how to apply it-say if my eyebrows fall out, something I have <u>never</u> thought about. They'll show me how to make them look natural. She offered to help with wigs, you name it. LOVE YOU Kim! ♥S

Friday, November 5, 2010 8:47 AM, CDT
So, I read your entry from last night, and there was one comment
that really struck me. It was that Kim and Sarah felt your lump
and they were both surprised at how the tumor felt. If no one
knows how it feels it's no wonder so many cases go undetected for
so long, or tumors are not detected at all! How the hell are women
really supposed to know what going on in there before it's too late?
I'm pretty consistent on self-exams, and because I'm no Dolly
Parton, I don't think I'd be able to tell the difference between a
tumor and a milk duct/gland, or one of my damn boney ribs under
there. Is this one thing that is lacking in the education of breast
cancer awareness? I've never had a mammogram. I've scheduled
and cancelled my appointments so many times because I was afraid
to go in and get my itty bitty titties smashed in a vice. I saw no
reason for it because of my age, even though my older sister is a
survivor herself. She also had both breasts removed at our age.
As soon as I am done typing, I am going to schedule an appt.
AND KEEP IT! Betsy

Saturday, November 6, 2010 8:02 AM, CDT
WOW!! What an uplifting day yesterday!!!! Sarah took a half day off
of work to hang with me-which to her couldn't have been that much
fun-but to me it was so great. In the morning I had to drop into
school and talk to the kids' teachers and tell them 'you know what'.
I just wanted them to be aware in case the kids acted any different.
We'll be having many different people helping out on different days
and that may be confusing for the kids. I later stopped at St.
Vinny's to look for some double sheets for the bedroom that we will
be setting up in the lower level of our house for me. I also found a
cute winter jacket for Ilyssa. Her BRAND NEW one from last year
is OF COURSE too small. UGH. The one kid of mine that actually

grows NORMAL! So that is taken care of...just need some dang
SNOW BOOTS!!! While I was there my BCCC called with the details
of my surgery. I will need to be at the hospital at 7:15 a.m. Monday
morning. At 7:30 I will have the sentinel lymph node test done in
nuclear medicine. Today I need to run to Sheboygan to pick up some
numbing cream, because you can just about guess where they're
going in through...yep more needles in the nipple. >>shiver<< It will
take a while to get the pathology back on the nodes so my surgery
isn't until 11:15 a.m. It will take approximately 3-4 hours, and I will be
sent home the next day. Wow. She also told me to start stool
softeners Sunday and get some Senokot in case I get constipated
after surgery-pretty common, I guess. She noted my Vicodin
intolerance in my chart. I will be coming home wearing a brace and
a drain or two on each side. I called Lesley at work to fill her in
on what is going on and to request some info on the kinds of
medical leave I am eligible for.

I took a power nap and later spent a few hours with Melissa and
Betsy (also known as Princess Consuela Banana Hammock and Fifi
and the Flower Tots-lmao). We went for dinner in Sheboygan and
enjoyed food, laughs, and chit chat. Gotta run for now. Our sitter
is coming so Andy and I can get away for a while before telling the
kids...UGH. Wish us luck. Love you all ☺ ♥S

Guestbook Comment: Saturday, November 6, 2010 8:56 AM, CDT
Shelly, I've been thinking about you every day since we first heard
about this. I've been praying for you every day. I've watched my
close friends go through this and was strong for them. It's a bit
harder when I think of you. My friends were older, their kids were
older. It brings me to tears to think of you & your young children.
Usually my way of helping would be to cook, bake, etc. I have a

friend with celiac disease and I know about reading labels and the special foods department with gluten free products. But I'm sure there are other things you will need. Please know that Uncle David and I are here to help in what ways we are able. Just please let us know. God Bless you with the strength you need, God bless you with family and friends to help support you and God bless your husband and your three beautiful children. Love, Aunt Elaine

Guestbook Comment: Saturday, November 6, 2010 11:50 AM, EDT
Dear Shelly, you're in my thoughts and prayers daily. I know the importance of taking control of your cancer with positive thoughts, a proactive game plan and a caring support group. You have caring family and friends that are here for you. Count me in on doing whatever I can to help you through this. Rick

Guestbook Comment: Saturday, November 6, 2010 2:35 PM, CDT
Hey Shelly, you've got a good sense of humor. That's a good thing and you show it well in your blog. You are constantly in my thoughts. Expecting the best for you. Love always. Roberta

Saturday, November 6, 2010 7:04 PM, CDT
What a spectacular day today!

♥I got up early and accomplished a lot around the house
♥an outstanding young woman came to babysit our kids so we could get out just the two of us (thanks KASIE-and your chauffeur TYLER!!! I know teenagers are allergic to getting up early.....but THANK YOU)
♥thanks to Sarah and Mike who made me smile at Kwik Trip today ☺
♥PINK KAYAK WARRIORS: yes, you know who you are! That was me, the crazy woman yelling out the window of the silver van..."THANK

23

YOU LADIES" It means a LOT to me....I recognized a few of you but my crazy hubby was driving too fast to see you all!

♥thanks to the huge church on PPP in Falls for having the rummage sale today...lots of work went into it and we found multiple treasures for our family on a budget ☺

♥my nieces found out 'the news', and took it ok. (Don't worry Boo, I'll never back down, I'm gonna show *it* who's BOSS. And Alex...I am EAGERLY WAITING to see what's on that dry erase board!)

♥Andy & I sat the two older kids down and had 'the talk' that I have breast cancer. It went well, we kept it light, and we had multiple books from the public library to back us up; let the kids browse through and read to us.

♥Amazing Betsy sent me a text asking Josh to come over to help Miranda rake. He was excited to do it, worked together with M, and got to get his mind off things. THEN sneaky Pete came over with the rest of her family and totally took charge and helped us clean out the office, set it up as a bedroom, and Larry helped Andy haul all the crap to the garage! What would have taken him (and weak ME) all weekend was done in hours...while Brynn and Davis kept the other 2 kids outta our hair ☺

♥THANK YOU Jerry for the file cabinet! It's already full of crap lol

♥I enjoyed a long nap in the recliner this afternoon, only woken up a few times by the kids fighting

♥cleaned, organized, scanned, printed, and filled out many community care programs, financial assistance for medical bills, and all that jazz. Wish me luck with that! We enjoyed a family dinner (our daily tradition-we always eat supper together) and now the kids are coloring. Josh is asking a LOT of questions about Veterans, war, Vietnam, and the war in Iraq. It's great to see him interested in world events. ♥S

Saturday, November 6, 2010 8:22 PM, CDT
Shelly, just wanted you to know that I'll be praying for you and your
entire family on Monday. May God guide the surgeon's hands and
may the surgery be a huge success. Remember, call if you need
anything. Love, Kerry

Saturday, November 6, 2010 9:30 PM, CDT

I am so grateful for all the offers of meals, food, child care,
transportation, margaritas, and housework!!! Anyone that knows me
well, knows how uncomfortable that all makes me! But THANK
YOU. There are so many offers of meals that it is overwhelming!
If you need to get ahold of us please email or call Andy's cell. Please
be patient with him/us while this week progresses....he will be BUSY
taking care of me, the three kids, and going to work. As of now,
Andy is taking off of work Monday, Tuesday, and a half day on
Wednesday. We have ALL child care needs met for those 3 days.
Starting Thursday and Friday we will hopefully be having Miranda
come over after school at 3:50 to be here and care for the kids
until Andy gets home. Hopefully she can work on making them snacks,
help them get homework done, and start supper if needed (right,
M?!?!?) Our neighbor Lisa will be driving the kids to school in the
mornings. (((((THANK YOU)))) I seriously cannot say that enough. ♥S
p.s. I'm still waiting for those IV bags of margaritas...

Saturday, November 6, 2010 9:53 PM, CDT
So I got to 2nd base with you. It was easy too!!! Just kidding.
Anyhow I think I've always had this idea of what a lump felt like and
I'll tell you that was most certainly NOT what I had in my mind AT
ALL!! It wasn't the hard pea, or woody rough feeling small little
lump. I would call it more of a firm bump. Not really firm either.
Kind of more of a swelling like when you get stung by a bee, but not

25

quite that hard. And Betsy, I think it's funny that you say because 'your girls' are small you're not sure what it would feel like and I can say exactly the opposite. Being big I feel like there is not a chance in hell that I would find it. Scares the daylights out of me!!! I think after learning of this I will be a lot more pushy when I do go in for my checkups. I also agree that we all need to be more proactive in learning what a lump feels like~ why aren't they teaching us about this??? Hope this helps. Thanks again for the feel. I've learned lots! Love ya, Kim

Guestbook Comment: Saturday, November 6, 2010 9:57 PM, CDT
Hey Guys, I know that this is going to be a difficult time, but hang in there and be strong. We will help you any way that we can. If you need anything at all, please don't hesitate to ask... Dave and family

Guestbook Comment: Saturday, November 6, 2010 10:17 PM, CDT
I want front row seats to watch you kick this cancers ass so hard it will be afraid to even look at you! Sara

Guestbook Comment: Saturday, November 6, 2010 10:18 PM, CDT
Just a note to let you know that your website has brought tears to my eyes. I look forward to reading about your courageous fight, I admire you so much and you are such a strong person. Since the day I met you, I learned that you go after what you believe in. All the hours of research and calling doctors and doctor appointments in Madison and Milwaukee for Josh, you just stayed on top of it and you got answers. You know how to go after and get what you want, and I know with your positive thoughts and your willingness to never ever give up, you will come out of this like a true star. You have forever changed my perspective on life-when I think I have a bad day or I can't handle it another minute, or I am feeling sorry for

myself and I know it is sad that it takes something like this to change people's life, but you have truly changed my life. We are praying for you and your family and wishing you the best. Hang in there, if anyone can do it, the Jones Family CAN! Love & Prayers, Joey & family

Guestbook Comment: Saturday, November 6, 2010 10:29 PM, CDT
I thought that I signed this already but I need to tell you, I'm home most every day and if u need to drop the kids off for the day, please don't think you're intruding! We are here for you sister. Sara

Guestbook Comment: Saturday, November 6, 2010 11:22 PM, CDT
You will be in my thoughts, keep looking at the positive side of things and you'll be fine. Mike

Guestbook Comment: Sunday, November 7, 2010 6:30 AM, CST
thanx aunt shelly for the message u wrote 2 me!!!! Brittany

Guestbook Comment: Sunday, November 7, 2010 5:39 PM, CST
Shelly, I want to let you know that you are in my prayers. If you need anything please let me know. You once said that Sandi and I were like sisters, well that goes for you too, Sister. Your family means the world to me and I will be there for everyone. I was reading something and they said that the Big C means CURE! I will be watching for your updates and your way to recovery. God Bless you and your family. I will be saying extras prayers. Love you Pam

Guestbook Comment: Sunday, November 7, 2010 6:10 PM, CST
Hey Shelly I'm so sorry to hear about this. You are a great person and I know you will pull through all of this. I just want you to know

you have a ton of people by your side for anything you need. I wish you the best tomorrow and my thoughts & prayers will be with you! Best of luck & love, Paula

Sunday, November 7, 2010 6:49 PM, CST

12 hours and counting.....I am going to totally lose it if I stop cleaning, rearranging, cleaning, eating and/or cleaning! I know it will be a 'no sleep' kind of night; I already am prepared for that. I got the chance to be my sons' hero tonight. He had been playing outside with some of his friends and his FAVORITE gun was left in the grass. Ultimately leading to the guns death.....CRUNCH. Anyone and EVERYone that knows Josh knows that it's ALL about the army guns! So after all our guests left...I drove him to Fleet Farm and let him pick out ANY gun he wanted. No, our children are not spoiled...we do not ever just buy what they want. BUT tomorrow is my surgery. I needed to make him happy, before he becomes sad due to me. We had a house FULL of family today! ☺ Wish it didn't take cancer to have a fun Sunday football party at my house!! Tim, Sara, Lily and Chelsea popped in for a visit.....with enough supplies for a WHOLE spa WEEKEND! LOVE YOU GUYS! You somehow knew exactly what we will need.....and stocking up now is THE way to go. Awesome! Sandi, Adrian, Brittany and Alex popped in to pick up supplies for my kids coming over tomorrow and Tuesday.....mostly the Gluten Free food along with the keys for the house and van. Brittany made me an amazing picture/get well card and Alex even made me a 3-D card! I love you two GIRLS!!!!!!!! (*I have started putting together a 'Strength Wall' in the downstairs bedroom. I need something to stare at while I am an invalid for a while! So I put up a large strip of white wrapping paper, and have begun taping up all the cards and artwork I've been receiving. They have been coming in daily-in the mail, in person, homemade, from my nieces, etc.*)

28

Next Dad popped in to just hang out and help keep my mind off of things....mostly by screaming at the STUPID Vikings!!!! Ugh! And they *had* to win! (Oh well, Andy deserves *SOME* good news this week!!!) Candice and Jake popped in and I got the most thoughtful card and beautiful bracelet of COURAGE from their family. I will wear it with PRIDE, knowing that you feel I am one COURAGEOUS chick! Signing off for now, hoping to speak to you all soon...with ONLY good news. Love from us ALL,
♥Shelly, Andy, Joshua, Ilyssa and Alaina ♥

Guestbook Comment: Sunday, November 7, 2010 8:06 PM, CST
Ok...so even though I have read every entry when you make it I haven't signed the book yet because I just get emotional every time. I even signed up to get a text when you make a new entry, just because my family, even ones I don't get to see that often, mean everything to me. I am praying for you every day. Since you do have Phillips blood in you I know you are a fighter. I will be thinking of you tomorrow. Hang in there! Love, Karen

Guestbook Comment: Sunday, November 7, 2010 9:22 PM, CST
Good luck tomorrow Shelly. You are in my prayers. If you need anything, just let me know. Susan and family

Guestbook Comment: Sunday, November 7, 2010 10:31 PM, CST
Good luck tomorrow. Be strong. Michael

Guestbook Comment: Monday, November 8, 2010 2:48 AM, CST
I have been thinking about you since you broke the news to all of us. Today you will hold a special place in my heart. I am wishing you an uneventful surgery and complete recovery.
Take care of YOU! Tracy

I have mourned the loss of my breasts. I have swallowed my pride
and asked others for help. I have made peace with the people in my
life; the people I have shut out of my life; the people no longer in my
life. I have asked God for forgiveness for my sins. I have
prayed, and sworn, and screamed, and cried more than I have my
whole life combined. I have asked God to spare my children the pain
of this. I have begged for Him to watch over my children. Me.
My husband. Our Medical Team. I have accepted the sorrow that
has settled into all my bones like a cold draft. I will come out the
other side of this. There IS no other choice. There is NO WAY I
will curl up and die. I. Will. Beat. THIS.

Monday, November 8, 2010 4:35 AM, CST

HUGE EXHALE........Grab your Kleenex or Puffs, or a roll of toilet
paper. NOW. Seriously get up off your chair and grab some sort
of absorbent material and get comfy. This is gonna be sad...
I think the scariest part for me, right now, is that I feel absolutely
fab. Knowing that in a few short hours my world will be turned
upside down....it's just crazy. It's not like when you go to have a
baby...sure there are nerves, and uncertainty...but THIS? There's no
happy ending and I don't get a little bundle to focus on and enjoy
(...well they BETTER not send me home with a little bundle!!!!!) I just
can't wrap my head around how B-I-G this is...and that this is truly
happening to ME. Within one week (last Monday I was told at my
mammogram/ultrasound/biopsy that "this definitely was a cancer") my
whole world has changed. Not visibly, not physically (yet) but there's

30

this whole other level of emotions that no one knows about, the thought process becomes more than just "Oh, shit, cancer." It becomes "what if's?" What if today of all days is my last day on this earth? What if I will never see my kids, or husband, or family or loved ones again? What if the cancer is just everywhere? How in the hell do I tell my kids? They are so young and so little; I just couldn't do it to them. How do I look them in the eye this morning and tell them it'll all be alright when I have no CLUE that is even close to what will happen?!?!? God needs to be shining down some kind of spotlight today and sending me PEACE. No matter what happens today, tomorrow, or 6 months from now, I love you all... that's why you're here checking up on me, right?!?! And I can NOT do this without you. ♥Shelly

p.s. Not that anyone wants to think about it, but if anything happens to me today or tomorrow or next year............stick with Andy... he's amazing, and will need UNBELIEVABLE amounts of help to deal with our kids....they're NUTS!!! Like me, he'll NEVER ask, but will need the strength to help the kids grow up. He is my life, my best friend, and my Lobster ('Friends' reference!) I am so afraid of what will happen to him when I die.

Guestbook Comment: Monday, November 8, 2010 5:38 AM, CST
good luck aunt shelly!!!! u will be on my mind all day!!!!!!!! Brittany

Guestbook Comment: Monday, November 8, 2010 5:44 AM, CST
Ok, so I guess it's my turn to tell everyone how easy it was to get to second base with Shelly, lol! Finally! What our hubbies have been joking around about for years came true, but there weren't any cameras to catch it. At least I don't think there were only Kim knows for sure! But when I felt this "lump", I couldn't believe how

31

much it didn't feel like a lump. To me it was more of a "thick patch of skin". It was maybe an inch in diameter and nothing at all what I had expected. If it was me, I probably would have thought nothing of it. I would think I'd see how it is next week and go from there, knowing I'd probably be saying that for many weeks. Truth is you can never be too paranoid with feeling anything that you don't think is right. Thank God you went in when you did Shelly! I've been thinking of you nonstop since last Monday, Shelly. You have shown great strength and courage so far & I know you will continue to do so. We've been through so much so far & we'll get through this also, you are one of the toughest chicks I know & I know you'll kick this cancer so far it won't know what hit it!! I'll be praying extra for you today & thinking of you during your surgery. It's going to be difficult to concentrate on anything until I hear you've come out of surgery with flying colors. Let me know if you or Andy or the kids need anything at all. Love you lots & I'll see you real soon!! Sarah

Guestbook Comment: Monday, November 8, 2010 7:56 AM, CST
Sending lots of prayers your way today!!! You are such a strong woman who's gonna kick cancers butt!!! Love ya! Jen

Guestbook Comment: Monday, November 8, 2010 8:10 AM, CST
Good luck today! I'm thinking of you and praying for you!!!! Stacey

Guestbook Comment: Monday, November 8, 2010 9:09 AM, CST
Heavenly Father, we look to you today to keep Your hand upon Shelly and her family. Wrap Your comforting arms around them as they face these trying times. We pray to You for Shelly's recovery and healing. You alone are God and through you all things are possible. Be with Shelly's surgeons today and guide their hands so that they

may give her the best care possible. Thank you for our friendships, God. Give us all strength that we may be there in the coming months for the Jones family. Help us to see their needs and be strong for them in their days of sorrow and weakness, and that we may also be there to rejoice with them in their small victories as Shelly heals. We pray this wholeheartedly in Jesus' name. Amen. ~Betsy

Guestbook Comment: Monday, November 8, 2010 9:22 AM, CST
Shelly, I prayed last night, until I couldn't pray anymore and fell asleep. I prayed the first thing when I woke up this morning. And again after Karen and I talked this morning. Then I cried when I read Betsy's wonderful prayer that said it all so beautifully. I'm going to keep praying all day until we hear something about how you are doing. I pray He will send you peace and confidence that He is in control and He will keep you in his loving care. And yes, I am also praying for your family. They are so precious! You have a wonderful group of friends. Gather strength from their support. We love you. Aunt E

Guestbook Comment: Monday, November 8, 2010 9:33 AM, CST
Keep the faith, Shell. Love you. Roberta

Guestbook Comment: Monday, November 8, 2010 12:49 PM, CST
GOOD LUCK!!!!!! I'm here and hear you. I have faith and you should too. I'll pray for you and your family tonight, even though I had knee surgery I'll still kneel before I go to sleep and pray. Denise

Guestbook Comment: Monday, November 8, 2010 3:47 PM, CST
Sending love and prayers your way. I am in MN for the week so I won't be crashing your party in the hospital. Looking forward to

hearing another post from you about how you and the family are holding up. Love & Hugs, Amy

Guestbook Comment: Monday, November 8, 2010 4:50 PM, CST
Continued prayers for you AND Andy and the kids today... and I will not stop praying! You aren't alone in this Shelly...you've got all of us but God IS with you too! Don't forget that! XOXO Charity

Surgery info:

The day of my surgery, I went to the hospital at 7:15 a.m. We registered with the front desk, then with the ladies in the room off to the side. They double checked our insurance information, address, phone number, and put on my ID bracelet. ((As if someone would WANT to be me today.)) I had been given numbing creme with lidocaine to put on my skin 45 minutes before the procedure; covering it up with cling wrap (seriously.) to keep it on my skin, and where it needed to be. Let's just say it did not help with any of the pain. We were then taken to nuclear medicine where the 'sentinel node' test would take place. The folks in NM are the warmest people...but man, that place is a torture chamber. The first thing you have to do is lay on the table, then they inject your areola with 4 or 5 shots of radioactive dye that will go to your lymph nodes and make them blue. That way, during surgery they will know where the sentinel node is. While there, they are able to monitor the movement of the dye on a screen (looks like a fishing doppler) to be sure it is moving-and moving where it needs to go. I was a **snibbling mess** during the procedure. First off, you're a bag of frazzled nerves.... because "hello!" You're there because you have CANCER. Then there's the fear of the unknown, and the icing on the cake...the PAIN. Two hours later I needed to go back to nuclear medicine for more pictures. The camera they use to monitor the dye is called a

Geiger Cam. It works like a Geiger counter. They put a lead square over the injection site (otherwise THAT area would show up the brightest) and look on the monitor for the brightest areas. That shows the sentinel lymph node. That little guy will come out first, and if it's positive for cancer...the whole first cluster of nodes will be taken out. After that procedure I was sent back up to the room to wait for a bit before my surgery. I don't remember much of it at all; thankfully I had kept a journal. There was an ID check, they listened to my lungs, heart, blood pressure, checked my temperature, heart rate, put an IV in my left hand, took my history and talked about what would be going into the IV. I remember my plastic surgeon coming in and drawing all over my chest and stomach with purple marker to mark where he'd be cutting, etc. Little did I know that marker would be on there for WEEKS! It ended up being glued into some of my incisions, and stayed there until the glue wore/washed off. My BCCC was in and told me that I did test positive for the ER/PR-GOOD NEWS! That means the cancer is sensitive to estrogen and progesterone hormones in my body; and I can be given a medicine to block it!! That's great news for my daughters too! Even though I know that there will be HUGE advancements in medicine before they have to deal with this. I remember being scared shitless going in, but trying to be brave for my family that was there. I even think I was joking around as I was being wheeled out of the room.

Monday, November 8, 2010 9:34 PM, CST
Andy filling in for Shelly for this update
Shelly's surgery went well. The doctor checked the lymph nodes in her right armpit and unfortunately the first one did show cancer so he removed the rest of the lymph nodes in that cluster and then did the double mastectomy. The other doctor then came in and did the

35

reconstruction and put in the tissue expanders. Shelly was very sore and in tons of pain coming out of surgery so she got a couple hits of morphine to ease the pain and let her rest. Let me say that there is nothing worse than seeing the one you love with all your heart crying because she is in so much pain. It just tears your heart out because you are so helpless and can't stand to see her hurting. Fortunately the morphine kicked in fast and sent her to lala land. The doc came in and talked with her about the surgery and then she went back to sleep. She slept till 8 p.m. when I was getting ready to leave and we talked for a while. I was stalling about leaving but she told me to get my ass out of there and get the kids. (That's my wifey!) The doc sent orders for her to have the self-medicating button for the morphine so that when the pain got too bad she could get some relief. As I was leaving, the nurse came in to check to make sure she was peeing (catheter-yep she was peeing!) and to dump the drain tubes from her breast incisions. She seems much more comfortable and able to get some actual rest now. I will try to update more in the morning after I go to see her.....knowing her, she will get online and beat me to it!! Thanks so much to Betsy and Sandi for staying with me through the whole day until Shelly got back to the room. You also made sure she was comfortable before leaving. You have NO idea how much that means to Shelly and I. Thanks also to everyone for the texts, voice mails, messages and best wishes. We love you all so much! Thanks to ALL for helping keep Shelly's spirits up before her surgery! It helped make it easier for her to deal with everything. Talk to you all soon and will update again! Andy

Betsy journaling for Andy & Shelly: 11-08-2010

5:20 p.m.-dose of morphine which isn't quite kickin' the pain, so at 5:40 had a 2nd dose. Nurse went to check with doctor to see how much and how often Shelly could get pain meds. Now at 6:00 she is finally resting. Nurse came back in and said doctor is having her hook up a morphine pump so Shelly can administer pain meds as needed. I wish I could take this all away from her. ☹ I can't believe that she would actually go home tomorrow! When the Doctor stopped in this evening he said they would re-evaluate tomorrow. This shit sucks! Or as Shell would say: Shit with a capital "S"! I love you guys! ♥Betsy

Guestbook Comment: Monday, November 8, 2010 6:36 PM, CST
Hi everyone...Andy just called me and wanted me to let everyone know that Shelly's surgery went well. The first part of the surgery was 2 hours and the reconstructive part was another 2 hrs. She was in quite a bit of pain so they gave her morphine and hopefully she will be able to rest. Andy will try to update later on. He doesn't know when he will be going home tonight-it depends on how Shelly is doing. Jenny

Guestbook Comment: Monday, November 8, 2010 7:09 PM, CST
Praying that everything went as well as possible and that your recovery is swift. I pray for God's healing hand to reach down on you and give you comfort and strength through all of this. Praying for your family and that the Lord will keep them safe as well. 'So do not fear, for I am with you; do not be dismayed, for I am your God. I will strengthen you and help you; I will uphold you with my righteous right hand. Isaiah 41:10' Jennifer

Guestbook Comment: Monday, November 8, 2010 7:13 PM, CST
Elaine & I have you in our prayers. We think of you often & I believe Elaine will have some baking to do for you to help out. Try & relax & get your rest. Uncle David

<u>Guestbook Comment:</u> Monday, November 8, 2010 10:34 PM, CST
You don't have to tell me how great ANDY is. He's a great guy. I see the love he has for you every time I see you together. He would walk to the end of the earth and back for you. Shelly you are a fighter and always have been. I am praying for you every day. Please remember that I am here for you too. West Bend is not far away, and I can be there in a moment's notice. You mean a lot to me too. Love to you, Andy and the kids. Pam

<u>Guestbook Comment:</u> Tuesday, November 9, 2010 6:40 AM, CST
Good Morning Guys! What a great morning to get up and read that all had gone well!!!! Prayers do get answered. Thanks Andy for filling us in, it means so much to me to be a part of the 'family'. I know you all are in God's hands and He will be sure you're taken care of. Love to you all and continued prayers for a speedy recovery. Love Ya, Cyndi

<u>Guestbook Comment:</u> Tuesday, November 9, 2010 6:46 AM, CST
Thanks for the updates Andy. I know how hard that can be when all you want to do is take care of your family. Thank you to Betsy for being there to represent all of us and support you. That hospital would never be big enough to hold all of us that love you both. I'm glad to hear that Shelly got the button; nothing like waiting around to get relief to make you feel worse. I hope today brings more pee and trips to lala land can sometimes be a good thing ☺ Love ya, Mary

<u>Guestbook Comment:</u> Tuesday, November 9, 2010 7:35 AM, CST
Andy it's good to hear the surgery has gone well. Shelly and your family are in my thoughts daily. Say hi to her from me when you see her. Take care! Richard

Tuesday, November 9, 2010 8:30 AM, CST
So glad to hear you are on your way to healing. Andy your comment
about seeing your loved one hurt made me tear up. You are doing
everything you can by being by her side. You are healing her in
ways the doctors can't. Leave the narcotics to them you got the
good stuff. Love. Praying for you guys. Love, Kim

November 9, 2010 Journal entry-after the fact, but squeezed in
here so it all makes some sort of sense in a twisted journal/memory/
memoir/online/word processing doc king-of-way! Here goes:

I barely remember being wheeled into surgery yesterday. Just the
ugly green walls and yellow tiles everywhere. Of course, the next
thing I remember is moaning and groaning in recovery. There was
a LOT of pain. There was a lot of pressure in my chest from the
tissue expanders. The surgery was over 4 1/2 hours long. That is
insane. In surgery they started with the nodes-pathology takes a
while. While waiting for those results, they started the mastectomy.
I did not have what is called a skin sparing mastectomy; I had all of
the breast tissue and most of the skin removed, along with the
nipples and areolas. We did not want to give cancer a chance at
continuing to live in my chest!!! They also had to remove a portion
of my chest wall muscle on the right side; the cancer side. Two and
a half hours in, the first surgeon came out and reported to Andy.
Since the pathology came back positive for cancer in that 1st lymph
node...they went and took out a whole cluster. His portion of the
surgery went well. I would start chemo approximately 4 weeks
after surgery. The plastic surgeon had decided (along with me) to
start reconstruction instantly-he surgically placed the tissue
expanders between the layers of pectoral muscles, put an initial

amount of saline in them (150 cc's) and closed up my chest slowly and precisely. My old breast weight was approximately 650cc's (each).

HOLY MOTHER OF GOD WHAT A LooooNG 24 HOURS.

Before I knew it, I was back in my room. When I saw Andy sitting there, waiting for me to wake up, it was a huge relief! He told me that the doctor had been in to talk to me, discussing the surgery-I didn't remember much of that. The first words out of my mouth were "did it spread??" Unfortunately Andy had to tell me that yes, it had spread to my lymph nodes...but pathology on the cluster wouldn't be back until tomorrow. The next time I woke up was to tell him to GO HOME!!!! His day was longer than mine...I got to sleep through most of it. The kids needed to see him and know that Mommy was ok. He was so torn about leaving, but I insisted; thinking of my babies first. I knew I'd just spend the night drugged up and dozing. Amongst being woken up for vitals and meds, I was also woken up to have my drains emptied and the output measured. When they did the surgery, they had to cut my chest both horizontally and vertically. The horizontal incisions were roughly 11" long each, with a 4 inch break between the two. The vertical incisions were of course MUCH smaller, they were about 5 inches long. At the end of my horizontal incisions out on the sides there were 2 drains on each side. The drains themselves look like grenades. There was plastic tubing coming out of my skin, about 2 1/2 feet long, ending in a JP bulb. Measured on the bulb were notches of CC's. The output had to be under so many CC's before they would remove them. These kept the wounds on my chest draining and helped them heal better since they didn't have to work on reabsorbing all that nasty. The nurses decided that MIDNIGHT would be a good time to remove my catheter-whose bright effing idea was that?!?!? Once that was out they cleaned me up some since I had my period-OF COURSE. Then they had me sit on the edge of the bed and try to stand-DIZZY. When morning arrived, the surgeon popped in to see me. He gave me some info on the tumor. Here's the **FINAL DIAGNOSIS**:

T(tumor) **3**: refers to the size and extent of the primary tumor
N(node) **2**: refers to the involvement of regional nodes
Stage 3 cancer=YIKES.
The left breast tissue showed NO CANCER. Some fibrous changes but that was all. YAY!!!! ♥S

Guestbook Comment: Tuesday, November 9, 2010 8:32 AM, CST
I didn't hear from Andy this morning, so I hope that means he had a good night's sleep and all went well with the kids this morning. I'm praying the doctors and staff decide they should keep Shelly at least one more night. Yesterday we were told if she does go home today, it would be later afternoon or early evening. I think if nothing else, she should at least stay so they can help her manage the horrible pain she's in. Andy couldn't be more correct in saying it's the hardest thing to watch someone you love and care about suffer so much, and yet be so helpless. It hurts for Shelly to even breathe right now. I can't imagine trying to get her in a car and drive all the way back to Plymouth. Every bump in the road is going to be torture. By the way...those nurses REALLY need to learn how to "drive" those hospital beds better! I think if Shelly could have, she would have jumped up and slapped the crap out of the nurse who rammed her into the wall AFTER SURGERY a few times! Andy couldn't even hold on to her bed rail because she felt every time he moved his hand. Glad we were able to get her a morphine pump last night. It pays to be persistent! I have a noon meeting, so I will stop up at 1:00 to see her today. I will give her all the love and

41

support shown here from her WONDERFUL friends and family the past few days. I'll let her know of the prayers and caring thoughts you all are sending. Keep 'em coming! Andy and Shelly SOOOO appreciate it! Betsy

Guestbook Comment: Tuesday, November 9, 2010 10:05 AM, CST
Ah, you have a "magic button" to push. Good deal. This is when drugs are good. Still holding you all close to our hearts. Roberta

Guestbook Comment: Tuesday, November 9, 2010 10:39 AM, CST
Prayers are wonderful and answered! You are on your way UP! When I'm not doing anything else I say or talk to God-it's great that there is no busy signal to heaven. Thanks Andy for your updates. Sending you all my love for a speedy recovery. Give the kids a hug for me. Keep some for yourselves as well!!!!! Kathy

Guestbook Comment: Tuesday, November 9, 2010 2:22 PM, CST
Okay, update on our girl...I just came from the hospital and Shelly is looking pretty darn good! (Feeling good, too, from all her drugs!) The nurses are now giving her Percocet to try to wean her off the morphine. She hasn't used her pump since before lunch, so that's a good sign. At least if she does okay w/ the Percocet, she can manage her pain at home, hopefully. They are still talking about sending her home tonight after supper. Don't get me wrong, Shelly is still in major pain, but she seems to be in a much better place than last night. She was sitting up having her lunch of dry toast while I was there. Shelly received a larger bra/band around her chest today and that has helped her feel better. She can breathe now without feeling as though a big fat cat is sitting on her trying to smother her! Shelly and Andy were also shown how to change the dressings and empty the drainage. They both said her incisions

look really good. I think they were both pleasantly surprised. I was relieved to hear that today. Her plastic surgeon did say last night that everything looked great and Shelly has really good skin, which is going to help in her healing. In about a week, Shelly will have a PET scan done to be sure the cancer has not spread to any other areas of her body. This is one of our biggest fears right now, of course. One of her cancer advisors came in and talked with Shelly about that this morning. She told Shelly her type of cancer would most likely travel to her bones if it had spread. I guess this was "good" news as the bone cancer would be easily treated. Shelly and Andy have so many worries now. They are so grateful to all of you for your prayers and support. They send their love and appreciation to all. P.S. Shelly wants ice cream!!   Betsy

Tuesday, November 9, 2010 5:34 PM, CST
shell here. typoing on phone while cranked up on percocet and can't focus is not fun. THNX 4 all prayers...got up n walked b4 w/ a walker. NOT FUN. Holy shit. ♥S

Guestbook Comment: Tuesday, November 9, 2010 6:02 PM, CST
So glad to hear things went well. You have constantly been on my mind & in my prayers. When you are feeling up to it I will bring you that ice cream! Lots of love! Karen

Tuesday, November 9, 2010 6:09 PM, CST
Staying another night at the hospital=GOOD NEWS! ♥S

Guestbook Comment: Tuesday, November 9, 2010 6:45 PM, CST
So, Andy's post brought me to tears ... your love for each other really shows. I hope that you are able to sleep and that your pain is being managed. Will keep you guys in our prayers each and every

43

day. Hugs, Kerry

Guestbook Comment: Tuesday, November 9, 2010 8:30 PM, CST
I'm certainly happy to know that you are spending another nite. Take
all the help you can get. My prayers are still being sent to God. I'll
try to see if you need anything tomorrow. Luv, Kathy

Guestbook Comment: Tuesday, November 9, 2010 8:33 PM, CST
So glad you are staying another night. Also glad that the pain is
subsiding a little bit. Betsy, thanks for the awesome updates. Sleep
good, Shelly. Kim

Guestbook Comment: Tuesday, November 9, 2010 9:33 PM, CST
Shelly, you are one young vibrant tough woman! You'll get through
this sweetie, I know you will! Many thoughts, love, & prayers to you
& your family. Jane

Guestbook Comment: Tuesday, November 9, 2010 9:49 PM, CST
Thank you so much for the updates. I can't express to you the
range of emotions that I have felt in the last week!! I can't even
begin to imagine what you have been feeling or going through
yourself along with your family! Know that I will always be here for
you whenever you need me & more! love you! Melissa

Tuesday, November 9, 2010 10:04 PM, CST
Andy updating for Shelly
Shelly is doing so much better today! She was still in quite a bit of
pain this morning and giving the morphine button a workout. Her
favorite line today was "GREEN MEANS GO!!!" referring to the button
lighting up green when she could push it to get more morphine. It
was funny when they were weaning her from the morphine IV to

44

the Percocet pills and she had both in her system. She had some interesting questions and thoughts at this point, even asking if she had brought Ilyssa's school treat in today. Lala land must be a great place! This afternoon she ate soup and toast and then was able to get up and do a lap down the hall and back. She then slept more and got up to eat some dinner. Shelly decided to stay one more night at the hospital since she was having a little bit of weakness, dizziness and lots of pain. I think they will be releasing her shortly after breakfast in the morning as long as she is still doing well. It's gonna be a long road, but the hospital stage is almost behind us! Thanks to ALL for the support and kind words. They mean so much to Shelly and I. She is going to need lots of support to help her get through this. She is a tough old broad, but still scared under all her armor. I'm not sure how soon she'll be able to get on the computer to update everyone after getting home. Also, I'm not sure about visitors for tomorrow. I would call her cell and see if she's up for a visit or not. Thanks again everyone! ~Andy

Guestbook Comment: Tuesday, November 9, 2010 10:34 PM, CST
Thanks so much for the updates Andy! So glad to hear Shelly is doing so well and really glad that she is staying another night. Hugs and more Hugs. Jenny

Guestbook Comment: Wednesday, November 10, 2010 6:46 AM, CST
Glad to hear you have some good drugs for the pain! I thought about you all day Monday and I'm so glad to hear you are doing as well as you are! I'm keeping you in my prayers each day, your story is so inspiring, stay strong girl! Stacey

Wednesday, November 10, 2010 07:00 AM, CST 7am. Sitting up-feeling better. Still lots of pressure when I breathe and of course where

the expanders are. I think the sites where the drains come out are pinching me the most. Here's "what's next" as I remember:
*16th?? Meet with both doctors for follow ups
*wait for pathology to come back on tumor.
*1-3 weeks PET scan??
*DRAINS OUT
*after 1 month start chemo
*one (week?) meet with oncologist

7:30 a.m. Plastic surgeon was just in-took a peek and asked if I had any questions. I didn't. He left.

11 a.m. Sent home. Lost my cell at hospital somewhere. UGH!! Alaina came to the hospital with Daddy to pick me up! It was GREAT to see her! Andy changed my drains before we left the hospital. We had to stop at Walgreens for my pain meds and antibiotics. Once home Dad and MaryAnn were waiting for us. Andy checked my drains before he left for work to make sure they're not overfull yet. MaryAnn stayed to bbsit me and keep Lainey out of my hair! She's been real silly & not sure what to make of it all. I slept.

Guestbook Comment: Wednesday, November 10, 2010 9:00 AM, CST
So glad to hear you are on the road to recovery! Will continue to pray for your pain to go away and quick healing so you can continue fighting! Nicole

Guestbook Comment: Wednesday, November 10, 2010 10:06 AM, PST
You are one strong chick! I just read your journal entries, my Lord girl, you are amazing. My Grandmother had a double mastectomy years ago. She is doing great and recovered fast. I can only hope you retain that strength and fight, even when all the hoopla settles

and the calls recede. I hope you continue to journal your thoughts; it makes all of us 'under 40' chicks realize that it can happen at any age and that we should take our health serious. And until it happens to someone of our age, we see it as a Grandmas cancer! God bless you, your amazing hubby and your adorable children. Tracy

Wednesday, November 10, 2010 12:48 PM, CST

Andy here again Shelly is home - we lost her phone at the hospital so call my cell if you want to talk to her. She is doing awesome. No visitors today please as she still needs rest, but she should be up for visitors tomorrow. I would ask that you call before stopping to visit just to make sure she is up for it.

Wednesday, November 10, 2010 1:25 PM, CST

I'm home. And I'm actually ok so far. Sleepy and uncomfortable but not from the surgery. Mostly from laying in the recliner vs. being in a hospital bed for 2 1/2 days. MaryAnn is here helping me and keeping Lainey outta my hair, while Andy had to go to work this afternoon. I of course forgot MY phone at the hospital, and am hoping it turns up sometime today so we can pick it up tomorrow. I will meet w/ the oncologist (Kumar) tomorrow at 11:00. I've heard he's excellent. Please keep up the kind words, I ♥ to hear from ya! ♥S

Guestbook Comment: Wednesday, November 10, 2010 1:27 PM, CST
Hip Hip Hooray she is home!!!! Great news. I'm sure it feels great to be home. Please don't overdo it and take it easy. I know how you are. Many, many naps coming your way. Prayers still coming for a speedy recovery. Love ya babe! Jenny

Guestbook Comment: Wednesday, November 10, 2010 4:10 PM, CST
Great news...that you are home! I would like to be of help if I can.

Not sure what I can do but willing to give it a try. Sending more prayers for a speedy recovery and a good report from the DR. Love you all. Kathy

Guestbook Comment: Wednesday, November 10, 2010 4:18 PM, CST
Hi Shelly, so glad you're home and I'm so glad Mary Ann can help you, she would make a good nanny, praying for you and hope you have good news when you see the doctor, take care of yourself, let me know if I can do anything for you, Love Judy K.

Guestbook Comment: Wednesday, November 10, 2010 4:32 PM, CST
As long as the oncologist's assistant isn't a guy named Harold! Adam

Guestbook Comment: Wednesday, November 10, 2010 4:52 PM, CST
Hey Girl! So happy to hear you felt well enough to go home today. My prayers are with all of you, so take care of each other... Good luck tomorrow ☺ Cyndi

Guestbook Comment: Wednesday, November 10, 2010 5:51 PM, CST
I know u want to visit with everyone but take a day or two for yourself to sleep and sleep and lay around with ur family! Too many visitors too soon will exhaust you! Love you! Sara

Guestbook Comment: Wednesday, November 10, 2010 6:11 PM, CST
WOW Shelly! Way to go. No grass growing under your recliner. Don't overdo. Glad to know you have friends to look in on you and help out. Friends are life's greatest treasure. Love always. Roberta

Guestbook Comment: Wednesday, November 10, 2010 7:49 PM, CST
Hey Shelly, I'm so glad that you were able to come home today, hope

all is going well. I am sure it is a relief to be with your babies and your husband. Anxiously waiting on the doctor's report tomorrow. Take it easy and don't overdo it, REMEMBER YOU COME FIRST!!!! If you aren't up to visitors then just say NO!!!! I heard every time you tell someone NO you are telling yourself and your family YES!!! REST and RELAX the best you can, and let everyone else do everything else for you!!!! Hang in there...Love and prayers sent your way....Love, Joey

<u>Guestbook Comment</u>: Wednesday, November 10, 2010 8:46 PM, CST Thinking of you lots Shelly. Hoping you heal fast. Keep up the good spirits, you have so many friends that care about you and are pulling for you. Love ya hon, I'm sure each day you will feel a little better! Candice

Wednesday, November 10, 2010 9:29 PM, CST

Andy here-update time

I had to work this afternoon, so I'm sorry for no update other than she was home. Big thanks to Mary Ann for hanging with Shelly till I got back. First, we have good news. Pathology is back and of the 17 lymph nodes in the cluster that were removed from her right arm pit, only 4 of the 17 had cancerous cells. This is good because the nodes act as a filter and if they are not all affected, this may mean that the cancer has not spread beyond the lymph nodes. Unfortunately, due to their involvement, the cancer is at Stage 3. Second, the left breast had a couple areas that had fibrous changes (Shell can explain better) but there was NO cancer in the left breast at all. The cancer is diagnosed at stage 3. Stage 1 and 2 refer to the size of the tumor. Stage 3 says the cancer has spread to the lymph nodes. Stage 4 means the cancer has spread to other parts of the body. SHE IS NOT STAGE 4. So, even though

49

she is stage 3, the fact that only 4 nodes showed cancer is good news! We meet with the oncologist tomorrow to discuss more of this and to figure out what the next step will be. Hopefully Shelly will be able to update by herself tomorrow; she does a much better job than I do. Thanks again for all the kind words and support everyone. We appreciate it soooooo much! ~Andy

<u>Guestbook Comment</u>: Thursday, November 11, 2010 8:00 AM, CST
So glad to hear the good news! I will keep praying for you that all is well! Take it easy!! Stacey K.

<u>Guestbook Comment</u>: Thursday, November 11, 2010 10:26 AM, CST
Thinking of you this morning and hoping things are getting better day by day!!! Rest lots...Kim

<u>Guestbook Comment</u>: Thursday, November 11, 2010 10:46 AM, CST
Hola Chica!! I'm glad I had the chance to see you for a little while last night. Anytime you need me to come over and help you or the kids just let me know, I'm there for ya!! I hope everything goes ok for you today and you are feeling a little better. Take care and talk soon. Love ya!! Sarah

<u>Guestbook Comment</u>: Thursday, November 11, 2010 10:49 AM, CST
Good news Andy reported today. Time for good news! Hang in there, Shelly. There's a lot more stars to wish on and hugs to receive. And, probably crap to endure, too. Thinking of you with love and smiles. Roberta

Thursday, November 11, 2010 11:02 AM, CST
Hi guys, it's Shelly. Thanks to MaryAnn, Sarah, Dad, Sandi, Miranda, Davis and Cody for all your help with me, the kids and the household.

Of course thanks to Andy--who had to drop me off at home from the hospital, go to work in Milwaukee and come home to hell---the kids were tired/nuts/naughty... Homework and tears to take care of, showers and hair to untangle...teeth to brush and also to take care of me. ♥I LOVE YOU♥ I just got 'up' for the first time today. Washed up, walking around, now off to the Chemo Doc. I have felt like absolute SHIT all day...so sore and wiped out, but took a good nap, and feeling better. Now off to get in the car with Andy...GOD HELP ME!!!! We all know how HE drives!!! Not sure what the deal is for today, if it's a consult or if we're actually setting up chemo appointments? ♥S

Thursday, November 11, 2010 4:13 PM, CST
Met with the oncologist today at 12. We did not find out anything new or surprising vs. what we were already told. The plan as of today is to heal. November 16 we will meet post op with both surgeons. December 2 I'll have a PET scan to check to see if/where the cancer has spread. Then the week after that I will have a total hysterectomy to remove my ovaries/uterus/cervix. I no longer have fallopian tubes. The reason I was to have this surgery done before all hell broke loose was because of my mom's history of ovarian cancer and also my own dysfunctional menstrual periods and ovarian cysts. More later, I need to work on some stuff. ♥S

Guestbook Comment: Thursday, November 11, 2010 4:51 PM, CST
Hi Shelly thanks for the update. I like the idea of healing one day at a time. Some days you think you're not healing and then you will start to feel stronger, and it will happen slow but sure, just take it easy and do not overdo anything, take care of Shelly! Love Judy k

Thursday, November 11, 2010 10:16 PM, CST

Ok. More time now. Lovely Ms. KT borrowed me her laptop so that I can update a bit easier and more often. AND now that I know what kind of cancer I have I can research research research. At the oncologist today we were told I have Stage 3 Invasive Ductal Carcinoma. IDC is THE most common type of breast cancer THANK GOD, cause there is one kind that is rare, and I thought for SURE I'd have that one!!! Just seems to be my luck. I was again told that I am T3 N2...the size of the tumor at officially 3.2cm...1.26 inches. There is a third classification of M-of which my test results came back neutral. They are doing more in depth testing in the lab to give me the M number. M will refer to if I am HER2 positive. That is another way to find out if the cancer has spread outside of my breast. My left breast tissue came back ok, with no cancer but some fibrous changes. The PET scan will be coming up soon, which is a 'picture' of my whole body showing any "hot spots" where cells are using up glucose faster than elsewhere or multiplying faster than they should be. THAT will be a bad thing. Breast cancer usually spreads to your brain OR bones OR lungs OR liver. The kind I have is most likely to spread to the bones...which sounds AWFUL but is more treatable.....so they tell me. Sometimes I feel like they're blowing smoke up my ass. The PET scan will show us. THAT is the ultimate DREADFUL test. I'll start chemo right around Christmas. I'll do 12 weeks of chemo then probably radiation as well since the lymph nodes had cancer too. After the radiation I will think about the implants and have that surgery. UGH.

This week I am still down and out...completely immobile from the pain. I spend all my time sleeping and resting on the couch/recliner. It is hard to not let this get to me and drag me down. I already have struggled with depression for years and

52

years and every Fall/Winter I get the whole 'seasonal depression' thing. I'll have to up my Vitamin D by a million units!!! It gets me down just sitting and watching life pass me by-while my kids are still playing; fighting. Andy's doing the grocery shopping and the daily routine is still going on without me. My body is hurting, but my mind is not in the same place. It's still sharp- thinking, planning, and searching for ways to get around this 'illness'. I can NOT believe this is happening to me. In less than a week my world has gone from trick or treating with my kids to frickin' CANCER. It's still shocking to have to tell people....I could not have imagined the outpouring of support and well wishes and PRAYERS that have come from SO many for me. I am getting emails from people that I haven't talked to in over 20 years wishing me well; telling me how good of a person I am; how this is unfair. I guess it is true-I believe in Karma...not in the unfortunate cancer part of this whole mess, but the "do good unto others..." part of karma. I have HUNDREDS of people praying for me; having their churches pray for me, their youth groups; their families who don't even KNOW me. I'm putting my life in God's hands, trying not to be pissed at Him, and I will learn from this experience as well....once it's over. ♥S

Guestbook Comment: Friday, November 12, 2010 6:19 AM, CST
Shelly, I have never personally been where you are, but maybe it could help by thinking of this time as not passing you by, but a chance to take it all in. You are able to see clearly what you are fighting for, Andy and the kids. We all know how strong you are, but don't be discouraged by the days when you just don't feel like being super woman. We all know she is still in there. Mary

Guestbook Comment: Friday, November 12, 2010 9:46 AM, CST
Good morning Shelly. Just read your update; I appreciate how you

are able to share this process and your feelings with everyone. That'd be hard for me to do. I keep you close in heart. Watch some funny DVDs-guaranteed to help with the healing. Hugs. Roberta

Guestbook Comment: Friday, November 12, 2010 4:00 PM, CST
Hey Babe...it was GREAT seeing you today! Thanks for allowing me to visit. Sorry we didn't stay very long, but I didn't want to overdo it and tire you out. Either next week or the week after I would like to come again. Stay strong and beautiful! Love ya lots! Jenny

Guestbook Comment: Friday, November 12, 2010 5:44 PM, CST
Hola gorgeous! I have so much fun stopping over after school. Really it's fun, mostly because I love your kids & I also love you: anytime during the day and you need me, weekends, anything I can be there. I don't have school next wed. or fri. so I can stop over anytime you need me for whatever you need me for. Miranda
P.S. I'll tell Cody to get on buying that new broom lol

Guestbook Comment: Friday, November 12, 2010 9:25 PM, CST
Shelly I am glad to hear you are at home. I am praying for you all the time. Thanks for the update. This is also to let you know that I was thinking of you today so I wore PINK in your honor. Pam

Saturday, November 13, 2010 10:47 AM, CST
Well, this sucks. I KNOW I typed a huge journal entry yesterday...but I guess it disappeared??? Maybe I closed the window before it loaded?? Bummer. I know I'll forget lots, but will try to sum up the last few days: So, I've been sitting in this recliner. The End. At least the oncologist appointment is still on here, I don't know if I could recall all that info! Thank God my BCCC has been writing it all down for me in my notebook! Of all the

54

things Aurora offers, I'm most impressed with that-the Breast Cancer Care Coordinator they give you. She makes all my appointments, keeps things moving along, gets me info I need, like the "how to tell my kid" books from the Vince Lombardi Cancer Clinic. She asks the questions before I do, and answers them thoroughly.

Yesterday was really a great morning. I spent time with my nieces (who were babysitting ME for once!) until MaryAnn could be here at 9:30. Just hanging out and being in the same room is so much help--just being there for me when I have something to say, something to gripe about or just can't lift my damn arm high enough to grab the remote--Andy's WORST nightmare!!! My wonderful adopted sister Jenny came into town from Horicon with her Mom, Diane just to clean my house...seriously, who could ask for ANYTHING more?! When someone asks "do you mind if I clean your toilets" who would say no, right?! So they cleaned and scrubbed and disinfected the bathroom and kitchen. ☺ They also brought TONS of food, and meals (THANKS to JOEY as well!!! Great lasagna!!!) and just plain ole' stocked us up! Dad came to visit too, asking if there was anything we needed.

Fish a.k.a. Ryan popped in next with some McLovin' from McDonalds. Anytime you show up with comfort food--you're in. Come in, stay awhile, and make yourself comfy. XOXO He really cheered me and MaryAnn up and made me laugh a bit too much!! My incisions were sore afterwards!

Then even with all THREE of us here, we STILL managed to forget to be outside to get Alaina off the bus (yikes!) so she got to take an extended trip around town on the bus and they dropped her back off an hour later...she was M-A-D at me!!! My Dad came back with

TONS of groceries and milk and all kinds of necessities like RASPBERRIES! YUMMY!!! Around 1:00 my 'good day' went totally SOUTH and I kicked Fish and Dad out so I could CRASH. MaryAnn stayed to babysit me (lol) and Lainey and I crawled into the spare bedroom downstairs and CRASHED. While I was in a Percocet coma, Miranda stopped in to see if I needed any help, then Sandi came to take over for MaryAnn. Lisa brought the kiddos home from school for me. (THANK YOU!!!) And Sandi helped drag my sorry ass outta bed when naptime was over! Going from sitting in a semi reclined position for a week to lying flat in a BED was NOT a good move! I was so unbelievably sore after my nap you wouldn't believe!!!! I literally could not even sit up by myself. But putting it off any longer was not an option since my bladder continues to work like a CHAMP! Sandi also helped prepare one of the meals Jenny had brought so that when Andy got home he could just make the GF meal and feed the chicklets.

After supper Betsy called and volunteered to pick up my girls and do something special with them! They went to Sheboygan with her 3 daughters to get their nails done. From there they went and did a bit of shopping. My girls came home with pens and notebooks-which my kids LOVE! Betsy even bought me some great things as well-some kick ass breast cancer charms for my Italian charm bracelet and a few silicone bracelets about BC and surviving. Love you BETS!!

While the 'Drama-Twins' were out and about with Bets, Andy got to spend some MUCH NEEDED one on one time with Josh building and playing Legos. He really is stretched for time lately, and Josh has been increasingly emotional...so I think some 'normalcy' is what he needed. I got to enjoy the peace and quiet while catching up on some of my DVR'D shows that I can't always watch with the kids around

56

like House, Grey's Anatomy, and Sons of Anarchy. Too much blood and gore on them lately. I also looked up and researched some cancer stuff while sitting here. Didn't really learn much new...

Andy got to give me a sponge bath--not fun in the LEAST!!! And for the first time ever I got to SEE what was done to me, and not just feel the pain. It is ugly and scary and waaaayyyy worse than I thought it would look like....but at the same time I have to remember this is the beginning of a new kind of body, and there needs to be some ugly to make room for the new perky implants I will have. LOL. It felt so good to get clean, since I can't shower, but it also was TOO MUCH all at once. I started blacking out and got dizzy, sweaty, thought I was gonna puke, and/or have the diarrhea...so I quick sat on the toilet, and Andy got me the bucket..He got the thermometer to MAKE SURE I don't have a fever....because right now fever is the worst thing I could get....that would mean infection in my incisions or internally. I took a few minutes to calm down, warm up, gain my strength back, and Andy finished stripping my drain tubes and measuring the fluid in them...and I went to the recliner! I felt really weak the rest of the night and crashed for a few hours. When I woke up at I a.m. I was hungry, needed pain meds, and went right back to sleep. This morning I woke up feeling sooo much better and Andy got to wash my hair. Make that career opportunity #2 that he is NOT cut out for!! Hairdresser and NURSE! In the hospital he was bumping my IV, smacked my arm, and tugged on my drainage tubes...you name it. If he didn't love me so much, I'd think he was MEAN!!! But all accidental. I know he's trying hard to just help me with whatever I need. The kids this morning have been helpful with cleaning up and getting the mail and helping me do stuff around here while Andy does the 'big' stuff like laundry and dishes. Josh is finally at the age where he is able to help with bigger stuff than the girls -

he is stronger, more responsible, and a bigger help. He just got done enjoying some 'BOY TIME' with his buddy Dustin. They played ARMY and Legos and kick 'n catch. Alaina is busy combing out my hair for me. My hair used to be really long and it is THICK, so having her brush it was always painful. Now, since it is so short and fresh outta the sink washed, she isn't ripping it out of my head! Ilyssa is enjoying some Daddy time just watching TV together. Melissa and Kasie will be here shortly...I can't wait to see them! Thanks to Jamie and Stacey for the flowers yesterday too-WHAT A SURPRISE. It's amazing to have soooooooooo many people from all aspects of my life praying and thinking of me. I need every single thought you send up to God....truly. ♥S

<u>Guestbook Comment:</u> Saturday, November 13, 2010 1:16 PM, CST
Happy Saturday Shelly; what a marvelous writer you are to tell it like it is. Minus the scary parts, I think you are making a fabulous mend. Thank God for all your wonderful friends who live around you. Everyone is priceless. Keeping you and your family close in our hearts. Hugs. Roberta

<u>Guestbook Comment:</u> Saturday, November 13, 2010 3:47 PM, CST
Hey Shelly, I think not being able to reach the remote is a guy's second worst nightmare. Not being able to reach something else (nameless body part) would be their actual WORST nightmare. Lol! Love ya, Mary

Saturday, November 13, 2010 8:53 PM, CST
Ugh. Talk about a total 180. I felt so great yesterday, and all day today I have been feeling so mediocre. I'm continuously discouraged with how little I can do at this point. I really am so uncomfortable and thought for sure by now I'd be doing some light duty around

the house. Andy is a Saint. He keeps reminding me that while my body is NOT cooperating, it is mending. That while I sleep and rest and watch 6 straight hours of TV, my body is mending. He reminds me that what I had done just FIVE days ago is so 'BIG'. So much more than just a quick biopsy or an in and out surgery. I had a flippin' bilateral MASTECTOMY. My body cannot just bounce back from this which I am so used to with any past medical procedures. Having your tubes tied is soooo not on this same level. He also reminds me that not only is my body healing from the surgery, it is mentally healing (REELING!!!) from a CANCER diagnosis, and the emotional damage that has brought. Within 18 days life has just gone thru a tornado!! So I thank GOD for Andy who is my rock, and my 'rubber band on my wrist' to snap as a reminder that even Wonder Woman has off days. Effing Lynda Carter. ♥S

Guestbook Comment: Saturday, November 13, 2010 10:01 PM, CST
Hey Shelly.....Glad you liked the lasagna and extra glad you told me you do not like cottage cheese, more for me and my BUTT!!!! Jenny and I are going to hopefully come up next week with the kids, but if it is too much, we will just make it a drop off time. I thought the kids could play with Lainey, they just love her and then we can just drink margaritas. You like me and Jen think you can do it all and it must be so frustrating not being able to. Let everyone help you and stay resting as much as you can. You need to build up your strength for your next big step. Stay strong and lots of prayers and love are sent your way. Love ya, Joey

Guestbook Comment: Saturday, November 13, 2010 10:04 PM, CST
Well, none of us wives want to admit it, but Andy hit the nail right on the head. You just went through something physically and emotionally draining and your body IS healing. Listen to it and don't be

discouraged. From the sounds of it you are doing WAY more than I thought would be possible. Rest well my friend. Tell Andy to keep his day job, you already have a hairdresser! When you're up to it we'll get you to the salon for a kick ass shampooing, but in the meantime if you need help with that at home I have shampoo and will travel. Love ya, Kim

Guestbook Comment: Sunday, November 14, 2010 6:30 AM, CST
Andy is so absolutely right! Listen to him. This is time off for you. Relax and enjoy your family from the new perspective of the recliner. It may give you new insights to capitalize on later. In the meantime your body and mind can heal. And I hope you didn't get any of the Minnesota snow; we didn't but I get a little nervous when they talk about flurries...Love, Roberta

Guestbook Comment: Sunday, November 14, 2010 6:42 AM, CST
Shelly I know we don't want to ever think that our husbands are right, but Andy is exactly right! You had two MAJOR surgeries not just one, but two! Give yourself some time...I know I can easily just sit here and say that, but it's true. Every day will get a little better. Sure some days will not get better and you may even feel like you went backwards, but they WILL get better! Things will never be the way they were, but they will be better in a new way! You are one of the strongest, most positive, caring women I have ever met and I KNOW without a doubt that you will take on anything and everything that is handed to you with a smile on your beautiful face! You amaze and inspire me every single day! I feel blessed to call you my "friend" Jenny

Guestbook Comment: Sunday, November 14, 2010 7:11 AM, CST
Morning Shelly, You are very blessed to have Andy, you have to be

patient with your recovery, one day at a time, and sometimes one hour at a time. God heals all and just take it easy you have a good reason to be a couch potato for now. You are in my prayers and just remember to call if you need anything. Love, Judy K

Sunday, November 14, 2010 9:42 AM, CST

I feel like I fought in an MMA fight all night! I just can't ignore these damn drain tubes!!!!! I saw pictures of my friend Lisa's on her page, and she has hers all taped up and covered, and gauze over them....mine are not covered at all, and the brace rubs on them. Very painful. I'm not sure if covering them up would help or hurt. Roberta--you always have something great to say at the right time. Thank you. ♥S

Monday, November 15, 2010 2:21 PM, CST

Well, today was 'catch up' day at my house! I did some light housework & worked on sorting some papers that have been piling up. I also returned a million phone calls-the work stuff, the disability stuff; the doctors that have left messages, nurses, friends and family from here to Texas. AND I got some questions answered that had been on my mind.

I had been worrying about limited range of motion in my arms, due to the tugging of the pectoral muscles and the lymph nodes being taken out. My triceps area is 'waking up' and tingling....some pain here and there with that. YIKES. So I called my BCCC and asked her some of those questions. I asked if I should be doing any exercises now while at home to keep my arms moving and she said no, that tomorrow at my appointment with the plastic surgeon I should bring that up and ask. She would hate for me to do anything to compromise where I am at this time. (And NO ONE wants me to

accidentally tug these tubes out less than I DO!!) I also prodded her about my disability papers that have not been completed...here's hoping that she figures out which Doctor's desk they're sitting on and gets them to fill them out!   I asked her what to expect at the appointment tomorrow...she took the measurements that I've been emptying outta the drains and told me I *might* get one out...and that it is unpleasant. Woo hoo. More unpleasant. Can't flippin' wait!!   He may also inject some more fluid into my tissue expanders to start the 'expansion' and I asked if they numb you. NO. Yes, you read that right, they stick needles into the freakin tissue you just had operated on WITHOUT NUMBING IT AT ALL. Flippin' sadists. Would he like me to stick needles into his nether regions without anesthetic?!?!?!? Nope. Bet not. So a million phone calls later, here I am, having some down time while Mary Ann, Lizzy, and Lainey are upstairs. Just about time for pain meds and a siesta.
Love you all. ♥S   p.s. DAVE M. (((I love ya)))

Guestbook Comment: Sunday, November 14, 2010 3:07 PM, CST
Shelly I was glad I was able to talk to you today even for a brief moment. Please remember, it's all about you. You have to take care of yourself. When you say you are not up for company, you are not being rude. We need to realize that you come first. We all want you to beat this. Know that I love you just like my little sister (now I have 2). All my love to you, Andy and the kids. Pam

Tuesday, November 16, 2010 4:43 PM, CST
Update: I had both doctor appointments today. The plastic surgeon said everything looks AMAZING. I say gross. He says amazing. Hmpf. I guess he knows what he's talking about. ☺ The wounds are looking good. I had one drain taken out. HOLY MOTHER OF ALL THAT IS HOLY DID THAT HURT.   FUCK.

62

I could have seriously passed out. Ugh. The doc told me it wouldn't hurt. There I was lying on the procedure table; he put one hand against my ribs & used the other to pull that f*cker out. YOWZERS! I have three more to come out. We will go day by day on the other ones; see when they slow down to less than 30 cc's per day per drain. I then went to my regular surgeon for a post op appointment. He didn't look at or do anything since I had just met with the PS, just asked me if I had questions and talked about when we'll put the port in. It'll be after my hysterectomy, but of course b4 chemo. So between December 8 and December 20 I'll have ANOTHER surgery. Jeez!!! Tired, lazy, and sore today...too much go go go. But we got all of it done...except paying bills....that I can put off forever, right?? ♥S

Guestbook Comment: Sunday, November 14, 2010 5:25 PM, CST
Hi Shelly, Have been thinking about you so much and hoping that each day gets just a little better. You must be an amazing person to have so many people who care about you. I will certainly do my part by being there for Alaina and taking care of her while she's with me (she's so easy to love!) Sending my best wishes for a full recovery.
Fran

Guestbook Comment: Sunday, November 14, 2010 9:26 PM, CST
Hi, Shelly! I thought of you all day today and blew you a kiss down the street. The girls will be over tomorrow after school. Let them know if you need them to run to the store or anything.
Love you! Betsy

Guestbook Comment: Monday, November 15, 2010 12:32 PM, CST
Hey woman, I hope you're getting some rest while you can! Kasie was so glad to see you yesterday!! Of course I love seeing you! I think

she felt relieved to see how well and good you truly are doing! We all see and know your strength! You are an inspiration to so many women and men! My family and I will continue to pray for you, Andy and the kids! I love you babe! Melissa

Guestbook Comment: Monday, November 15, 2010 2:30 PM, CST
Just poking in my head to say "hey" and hoping this is a much finer day than most of those before. Here's a riddle you can try out on your kids: You use it between your hands and toes. The more it works, the thinner it grows. Have you guessed what it is? If it slips by you, let me know and I'll tell you the answer. Hugs, Roberta

Guestbook Comment: Monday, November 15, 2010 5:44 PM, CST
Was just thinking about you today and it sounds like you are up and moving around. I pray for you, Andy and the kiddos every day and hope that your appointment tomorrow goes well. I'm up next week in Plymouth and would love to stop by and see you. If you guys need anything let me know and I can bring that as well. Kerry

Guestbook Comment: Monday, November 15, 2010 11:11 PM, CST
Don't worry Shelly, you won't feel the needles, you don't really have any feeling left in that area. Drains coming out is a bit uncomfortable, mostly because you are scared sh**less, but nothing like the pain you have been going through. Also, if they fill you and it is too uncomfortable, which it can be, you can ask them to take some out to relieve you! In terms of pain, it is all downhill from here!! Amy

Guestbook Comment: Tuesday, November 16, 2010 4:26 PM, CST
Hi Shelly! It's Tuesday and wintery looking where I am. I've just spent time with best friends for our going away meal together as

Richard and I leave the day after tomorrow for the west coast. My time with friends reminds me of how precious friends are and how glad I am you have good friends around you! Hope this day has gone well. I suspect you may be exhausted by time the day is done. Rest well, Roberta

Guestbook Comment: Tuesday, November 16, 2010 6:11 PM, CST
THE CANCER CHANT, I WILL RANT.
Cancer I did not give you the right,
To invade my body and take a bite.
This is my body with all my might,
I will prevail with one hell of a fight.
To the cancer inside, I will battle and kill.
For that is my body's God given will.
To my cancer, these words I do send.
Your life is short and near the end.

(A poem contributed by a visitor of Healing Cancer Naturally)
Love you Girl; Joey

Guestbook Comment: Tuesday, November 16, 2010 6:22 PM, CST
It was great seeing you today Shelly. You look great even though I know you feel like crap. I can't begin to understand how you are feeling right now but I just wanted to let you know I think you are one of the bravest people I know and you are handling all this crap with such dignity...oh and even though it hurts to laugh you still have your sense of humor! Keep your chin up, keep laughing and you along with your friends and family by your side will kick this cancer's ass!!!! Love ya girl...hang in there. Candice

Tuesday, November 16, 2010 6:43 PM, CST

In the last two days I have had the wonderful opportunity to speak person to person with two of my favoritest family members. My Uncle Rick and my cousin Luke. Ok, technically 2nd cousin, but we still love him...My Uncle is going through cancer treatment himself. He was diagnosed with Hodgkin's lymphoma earlier this year. He had become very ill, to where his son needed to take him to the hospital. There he was in ICU for what seemed like ever. They were trying to stabilize him. He is still going through chemotherapy, which will be followed by radiation. I don't think I've seen him since 1996 when my mom passed away. My heart breaks that he is going through this, and I hope we can comfort each other during this shitty time. Luke, on the other hand, is NOT sick! He is doing well, busy being a Daddy to his two girls and a hubby. He has been affected by the economy as well in his teaching position, so now he has been helping out children that have developmental disabilities. What a rewarding job for him, & I can see him doing VERY WELL in that career! Again, it has been YEARS since I have seen or talked to him, since he used to live with my dad. His family has moved up north near his Dad. I'm hoping next summer we can plan a get together & I can meet his wife and children!

I have had so much support from everyone-friends AND family, but these two phone calls really meant a lot to me. Both of these men have shown me that we all have our struggles, and even though they're all different struggles, they're still pretty much the same in the end. They affect our job; our home life with our spouses/ significant others; our relationships with our children. They affect our outlook on life and what truly is important. We've all had to struggle with health issues, whether it is our own, or our parents, or our step parents, possibly even our children's'. And we've all had struggles with jobs in this economy-either slowing down towards a lay off or being downsized; not making it and closing up, or even just reduced hours REALLY affects all of us. NO ONE plans on their income just being GONE. And truthfully, who is even prepared for that?! Having a savings account is one thing, but being able to sustain your current lifestyle without the current income--not gonna happen! Christmas is drawing near and I'm worried about how we're going to swing it. The kids are all about quantity at this age. Us? Nope. I feel they should focus more on giving, and the reason for Christmas. It's a hard age to try to teach them that, but also a crucial age. I'm hoping they are thankful for what they do get, and can accept that. I'm just hoping they are healthy, happy and we all get to be together. I would rather have cancer 50 times than have my children EVER have to go through any of this pain, emotional or physical. I know what is important in my life. I know that it is NOT the clothes you wear, or what you spent on a prom dress, or what car you drive or even where you live. It is ALL about family and nourishing that family so that they too will grow up into decent people that care about their kids and like spending time with them...teaching them what matters-what is right and wrong, teaching them NOT to lie, sneak, steal, or bully. All kids wander off the path....but GOOD parents have kids that wander back...I just hope that all my family/friends/acquaintances.....make it through all the tough times with a support system like mine. I mean holy shit...over 840 people have visited my caring bridge site just to check up on ME. THAT is huge to me. And I hope you feel like an amazing person for being a part of my life because you ARE amazing to support our family. Life's tough......but guess what? I'm waaay tougher. And I know you would be too in my situation. Love ♥S

Tuesday, November 16, 2010 7:10 PM, CST
Hola chica! Your last post brought tears to my eyes, again. You really nailed it on what is most important in life (obviously the car I drive isn't the most important thing in my life!) Your family will get through all of this; you have an amazing support system with all your friends and family. Don't be afraid to ask any of us for anything, we're all here to help. (and Katie hasn't asked for her laptop back, so don't feel guilty about using it longer!). Kris Green and Sharon L send their love and prayers for you. I'll see you soon when I'm sure my house is germ free! Love ya babe!!! Sarah

Tuesday, November 16, 2010 10:05 PM, CST
♥Thank you. You know who you are. ♥S

Wednesday, November 17, 2010 6:01 AM, CST
Hey Girl...has anyone ever told you that you are amazing? Well...get ready...YOU ARE!!!!!! Every day YOU amaze ME with your strength, sense of humor, and by telling it like it is. That is one thing I love about you Shelly you...tell it like it is...no sugar coating it, but the God's honest truth! You thank all of us for helping you thru this, but I think that ALL of us should say "THANK YOU" for helping us!!!!!!
Love Ya! Jenny

Wednesday, November 17, 2010 10:27 AM, CST
Ah Shelly, you have become so wise. You teach and remind us all. Thanks! Love you. Roberta

Wednesday, November 17, 2010 7:32 PM, CST
The most uncomfortable part of this darn surgery/cancer is the crapass itchy brace/support bra thing they stick on you. Clearly invented by MEN, they Velcro straight up the front....with the stiff

itchy part of the Velcro in towards your skin, and the soft plush part away from your skin. I need to reinvent these things...or at LEAST write the company that made them! Any time it shifts or overlaps the scratchy part rubs your skin raw. Grr. So I spend more time stuffing gauze in behind there than I do on the actual incisions! I had Ilyssa help me empty my drains last night. For anyone that has not seen what these things look like, go look on the net after this update. Basically it's 2 clear plastic hoses coming outta each of my sides, connected to what looks like a plastic clear grenade with a valve on like an inner tube lol. You squeeze the grenade, and plug the valve, creating the suction you need to pull the drainage outta the wounds. We empty them about twice a day, each time getting anywhere from 10 cc's to 35 cc's from each grenade. Once I have less than 30 cc's out of each one for 24 hours at least, then I'll have the others removed. One was taken out yesterday-BLECH. That can totally bring down a grown woman! While Ilyssa (she's 8) was helping me empty the drains last night, she got an accidental sneak peek at a few of the incisions....and she handled it really well. Better than I did the first time!!

Pretty much everyone is curious about what they did, how it looks, and what the process will be of getting the tata's back! I will describe it best I can.

What they did on me (everyone's different) is they made an incision across the bottom of each breast from under the arm (the side of the ribcage) towards the breastbone. Probably about 10 inches long on each side. Then they made an incision up in the middle of that first one to the top of what was my breast, so I have an upside down T on both sides. Then I have an incision between the top of the breast and my armpit where they took out my lymph nodes on

69

the right side. That area is what is causing me the most pain these days. It feels like I have bruised or burned or skinned the inside of my upper arm--from the nodes being taken out--but there is nothing on the outside bruised or red or anything. It's just all my nerves coming back alive after the surgery and the inside being angry about the nodes coming out! Don't get me wrong-I still can't freakin' stand the area where the tubes come outta my ribs...you can't imagine how many times you bump that area when you don't notice-every time you put your elbows down, or lean over in the recliner or even try to freakin' wipe!!!!

Taking a shower is a total thing of the past. I'm not allowed to take one until the drains are all out and the incisions are healed over. That gives us another obstacle. Shaving. I've been unable to shave since last Sunday before the surgery--ugh! Still can't shave the pit on my right side. I am unable to lift my arm high enough, as well as the fact that it is all still numb and I'm afraid of slicing my skin! I know, I know, more information than any of you want to know...but this is my journal and BELIEVE ME I **am** censoring it!!! There are many, many more icky things you don't want to know!!!!

Today my Dad came over for one last visit before he took off up north for his deer hunting trip. Thankfully he will not be going alone and is still able to go to do something he really enjoys. Sandi also popped in while I was in the middle of my Percocet coma...I feel guilty when people are here and I'm all doped up, but my alternative is PAIN. And let's just say I'm not a fan. Everyone's been extra helpful with making sure we're taken care of, the kids have some extra attention, and helping with grocery delivery.

Jenni came by today as well, for the first time since this all started. I don't think I've seen her since August? It was so nice to catch up and nicer that she is such a close friend that I can doze off and not feel uncomfortable or guilty...she just grabbed a blanket and snuggled up on the couch too! She helped make lunch, helped keep Alaina from making bad choices, and just hung out with me and Miranda. Today has been a total lazy day, not a lot going on. Watching movies (Grown Ups, and Charlie St. Cloud) and sleep sleep sleep. ♥S

Guestbook Comment: Wednesday, November 17, 2010 10:02 PM, CST
If only people knew ALL the details, lol! Just wait til you start expanding your boobage and people want to see what everything looks like! Oh it's so fun to watch people's faces...it's kinda like the car accident thing they don't wanna look but they can't look away. LOL. Not being able to shave my pit is also a BIG problem for me. I hate that I can't and then you have doctors looking in there and you're all hairy. Ick. One positive of chemo and radiation is no need to shave. Have you noticed a strong smell from your incision pit? No matter what it won't go away! One lady told me to try a vinegar wash but I haven't dared since my incision is still healing. Do you have stitches or did they glue you back together like me? Hang in there lady one day at a time. Lisa

Guestbook Comment: Thursday, November 18, 2010 7:06 AM, CST
So that's where I need to come to catch a nap?!
Love ya, keep up the good work. Mary

Guestbook Comment: Thursday, November 18, 2010 7:48 AM, CST
Wow Shelly, that last post was interesting to say the least. I had no idea how they did that. Just wish you weren't the one to inform the rest of us! I had Percocet after my C-sections-that is some

71

goooood stuff! Glad to hear you are taking time for a nap and had a lazy day. You need to rest even though you clearly would rather not be! Stacey K.

Thursday, November 18, 2010 2:56 PM, CST
Happy Birthday to my Mom! It's been a long, sad 14 $^{1/2}$ years since she went away......She would have been 64 this year. It's hard to believe she's been gone since 1996. ♥S

Thursday, November 18, 2010 3:08 PM, CST
WOW!!!!!!!!! Almost 1000 visitors on my CaringBridge site! Amazing. Thanks for trying to keep up with me. ♥S

<u>Guestbook Comment</u>: Thursday, November 18, 2010 4:15 PM, CST
Miss you! Jenny

<u>Guestbook Comment</u>: Thursday, November 18, 2010 8:21 PM, CST
Hi Shelly. Was thinking about you today. Actually, I think of you all the time. You are a very brave woman. Went to church this weekend and said a few more prayers for you and your family. Just know that I love you like my sister. I am just a phone call away, so please don't hesitate to call. That goes for Andy too.
Love ya, Pam

<u>Guestbook Comment</u>: Thursday, November 18, 2010 11:54 PM, CST
Shelly, you are lifted up to God in prayer! Stay strong. He has you in his loving arms. Dawn

Friday, November 19, 2010 7:19 AM, CST
Yahhhooooo!!!!!!!!!!!!! I slept in a BED last night!!!! HOW AWESOME!!!! I woke up sore as hell but I sure slept like the dead!! My chest

muscles and rib muscles were ANGRY but within 5 minutes I was feeling better once I was up and moving. What a great day for no school. It's ugly outside. Well, it looks that way from in here, anyway! And all the kids: Joshua, Ilyssa, and Alaina are awake/semi awake and all snuggled in their quilts I made them last year for Christmas. I hope the day continues to be a quiet lazy day with no fighting or yelling...I should get a few wishes, right?!?!?!?! I've received some amazing emails in the last few days (thanks Pat and Dawn!) It really helps build my strength knowing that so many people have me in their prayers. I spent yesterday lounging with Jenni, talking about the old days, watching TV and dozing. She was gracious enough to run me to McD's to pick up lunches for the kids and took me to Parkview to eat with them. Ilyssa had been asking me FOR WEEKS! So it was a nice surprise for her and for Alaina who was done with 4K right when we got there so she didn't have to ride the bus; she enjoys sitting with the 'big' kids at lunch and eating McD's! We sat with Ilyssa's friends...two cuties that are always polite and happy to see us. Then we 'table-hopped' over to the 4th graders to eat with Josh. He sometimes wants me there and other times not so much...but he was very happy to see me yesterday. We even sat at our 'own' table, since I didn't want any kids bumping my incisions or drain tubes. It went well, and he even listened when I told him he HAD to wear his jacket outside, even though 'no one else is wearing one' and he went to go get it. We spent the rest of the day chillin'... and dozing....watching TV and keeping Alaina entertained..... which is NO easy feat! Heehee!

A friend of mine, Kate, and I had a little chat online about how I can benefit from massage therapy and the holistic part of my healing, including getting my lymphatic system in gear to flush out the chemo once we get to that point.

73

I did more research on places that have grants, financial assistance and aid for people going through cancer (and NOT WORKING!!) hoping once the bills start ROLLING in, we can qualify for something, since we still need to pay the rent, the car payment, etc.!!!

Tonight Melissa is coming over and we're having a comfy pajama night...since I'm ALWAYS in pj's these days....she didn't want to be over dressed lol! Kasie is coming too. Maybe Betsy can pop in as well! We're ordering pizza from DeO'Malleys and I'm so excited! LOVE my friends and love me some pizza!!! Ok, off to OD on Taylor Swift music (with Ilyssa), DORA (with Alaina) and Josh playing ARMY with shooting sounds included. ♥S

<u>Guestbook Comment</u>: Friday, November 19, 2010 6:18 PM, CST
love ya aunt shelly. Brittany

<u>Guestbook Comment</u>: Friday, November 19, 2010 7:18 PM, CST
Just wanted to let you know how much I love 'just lounging' with you!! I can't wait to do it again!!! It's so great being able to spend time with you! Love ya!! And as always you're in my prayers!!!! Jen

<u>Guestbook Comment</u>: Friday, November 19, 2010 8:26 PM, CST
Wishing we lived closer so we could just pop in and give you hugs! We all miss you the kids have great memories of your kids. Have a relaxing weekend and rest and relax. Love ya lots!!! Joey

<u>Guestbook Comment</u>: Friday, November 19, 2010 8:33 PM, CST
i miss you aunt shelly. hopefully i get to see you pretty soon. love,alex
ps i made lots of faces for you ;) ;(,o:),and i saved the best for last and how i really feel <3.

Friday, November 19, 2010 10:45 PM, CST

Healing in leaps and bounds today! ☺ I spent a good part of the morning and all the way through lunch up and about in the house! I made spaghetti for the kids and Miranda and had the girls do clean up. After lunch I zonked out big time, waking up to 2 GOOFY girls!!!! There was flatulence involved, and TONS of giggles. That's all I have to say. This afternoon I received some special gifts in the mail-- THANK YOU Sharon! Sandi brought me over 2 Piggly Wiggly gift cards from her and Kay-a HUGE thank you to you both; we need those more than you know!!!!! It filled up our pantry this afternoon and stocked up our freezer some too! She also drove me to the clinic to sign more medical release forms for work-let's hope I get at least one disability check before I go back to work!!! Then we went to Wal-Mart for my VERY FIRST TRIP out ever without Andy!! It was short and sweet I got what was on the list and THAT WAS IT! By the time we got to Pig, I just sent her in and stayed in the car, I was too tired. Once we got home the kids put all the groceries away and we ordered up some pizza for our movie night in with Melissa and Kasie! Around 7:30 the doorbell rang and we got the most pleasant surprise EVER.....some thoughtful peeps through word of mouth hooked us up with not ONE but TWO fresh turkeys!! He also brought over some fresh chicken eggs and even some turkey eggs!!! They're speckled! I've never seen turkey eggs before! I continue to be thankful to EVERYONE and You-know-WHO-upstairs....for everything given to us, brought to us, bought for us, and prayers sent. I am just moved to tears when I think about this position we've been put into; about what we have to look forward to and how absolutely lucky we are to have all kinds of wonderful friends like you. ♥S

<u>Guestbook Comment</u>: Saturday, November 20, 2010 6:30 AM, CST
hi aunt shelly !!!!!!! i miss u alot 2!!!!!!! we should chat on fb
sumtime!!!!!!!!!! lolz Brittany♥

Saturday, November 20, 2010 12:59 PM, CST
Yes, I would LOVE to see all kinds of people I know on my FIRST
outing in public...when I look like I just crawled outta bed. That just
freakin' rocks. UGH! But I did find 2 cool hats to wear when my
hair falls out. ♥S

<u>Guestbook Comment</u>: Saturday, November 20, 2010 3:43 PM, CST
Hi, Babe! Hope you had a great night with the girls last night! It's
just what you need to keep your spirits up. Wish I had been able to
be there. Sounds like you had a great surprise last night! A couple
of turkeys for a couple of turkeys HAHA! I have you in my
prayers as always; see you at 9 a.m. tomorrow!! Betsy

Saturday, November 20, 2010 4:00 PM, CST
Andy's heading out to his buddy's tonight for a sausage party.... any
girlies wanna come over and hang out....head on over. ♥S

<u>Guestbook Comment</u>: Saturday, November 20, 2010 5:13 PM, CST
Hey you should get your first disability check issued on day 14 after
being out. Disability should contact you telling you when ur payment
will be issued and for how much. You did call disability directly
though, right!? Lisa

<u>Guestbook Comment</u>: Saturday, November 20, 2010 7:36 PM, CST
nice to see you today aunt shelly. luv ya lots, alex

Guestbook Comment: Saturday, November 20, 2010 8:06 PM, CST
Got your message~ I'll be there at 9 tomorrow   Have a great
night!! Kim

Guestbook Comment: Saturday, November 20, 2010 9:35 PM, CST
Hi Shelly. I haven't vanished and you continue to be in my thoughts
while we've been on the road will make it to Anna's tomorrow for
brunch and stay 8 weeks, more or less. Usually try to hit a motel
before dark, but today took us longer (avoiding snow predictions for
tonight in Flagstaff and made it to Phoenix). Anyway enjoyed a
gorgeous sunset over the mountains with pink in the sky, blue clouds
looked so fake but it was real! Glad to learn Josh has a good
teacher this year. That helps a lot! Keep up your good work. Love
reading your journal. Roberta

Guestbook Comment: Saturday, November 20, 2010 10:10 PM, CST
Hey Shelly, Sharon told me the news and we are going to come visit
you soon. We are hoping to give you a little time to heal before we
overwhelm you with hugs!! lol We need to see pictures of that cool
hat too. Glad to hear you are feeling ok and I truly hope and pray
that road continues. Keep the FAITH, HOPE, AND COURAGE! I will
let you know when we are thinking of coming to make sure you are
home. Take care girly and stay strong! Annie

Saturday, November 20, 2010 11:03 PM, CST
Today I could be the poster child for a PROZAC commercial. I'm
just blah. Frustrated by not being able to do my 'normal' stuff. I
can't REALLY go bummin'. I tried to today; we went into Kohl's and
ShopKo and Wal-Mart. That completely wiped me out. I slept for
over 4 hours when we got home. I can't imagine how bad chemo will
affect me. I guess once I get these drains out AND stop the pain

77

meds AND can DRIVE again....maybe I'll start cheering up. The girls and I and Sarah did nail polish (yes, I am SPARKLY!!) and they played with Sarah's hair....she looked BeauTIful with 45 different barrettes in! Tee hee! We had ice cream (YUMMY Dilly Bars, Sarah!!!!!) and watched Tinkerbell then Shrek 2. Sarah played games with the girls which means a LOT to me, since I'm not up to sitting on the floor. Or moving all over doing board games. UNO is about as 'hands on' as I get these days. So they got some great one on one time with a mama figure. Hoping my hubby comes home soon....I sure am missing him. ♥S

Sunday, November 21, 2010 3:48 PM, CST

Stuck in the middle of the waiting game....waiting to feel better, waiting for my next appointment, feeling like I have nothing else on my calendar BUT the PET scan....it's just looming ahead of me. I know one thing-I HATE THIS RECLINER!! ♥S

Guestbook Comment: Sunday, November 21, 2010 6:11 PM, CST
Hi Shelly, thinking about you again today. Tell Andy I was sorry to hear about the Viking game. NOT! Anyway, I just wanted to wish a HAPPY THANKSGIVING to YOU AND YOUR FAMILY. Love you. Pam

Guestbook Comment: Sunday, November 21, 2010 7:37 PM, CST
I was emailed your website today and had the opportunity to check it out. Here is what I first say, "You go girl and kick the cancer's butt." You keep your head up girlfriend! Just step back and look at how far you have come already. You have the best friends and family there for you. Just keep letting them in. To the woman that I look up to; you are full of the strength, love and courage to fight this. You keep going full force. We wish you the best!!! Lots of love, Jen S.

78

<u>Guestbook Comment</u>: Sunday, November 21, 2010 9:38 PM, CST
You looked great today. I know you don't feel it, but you look it!!!
Sleep well tonight. Kim

Monday, November 22, 2010 6:52 AM, CST
WHY does pain have to be the first thing I feel when I wake up in
the morning??? Boy, I can't believe how much I miss the good ole
days where my bladder felt like it was gonna explode and THAT woke
me up. ☹ ♥S

<u>Guestbook Comment</u>: Monday, November 22, 2010 10:08 AM, CST
It's like too much ice cream or too much sunshine or too much lazy
resting, it gets old and we want no more. BUT keep the focus, let
yourself get stronger. Envision the time down the road just enjoying
good times with your family. Thinking of you from Sunny Southern
California where they forgot to tell us the temps would be in the 40's
this morning! Roberta

<u>Guestbook Comment</u>: Monday, November 22, 2010 12:25 PM, CST
Hey there. Unfortunately the painful mornings will continue...especially
with doing the stretching exercises. That was a 'wonderful' surprise
for me when I went from waking up with little pain to 'OMG WTF!'
But once you actually GET UP it subsides, it's just the getting up part
that you don't wanna do. Hang in there though. Each day is a better
day even though some days it doesn't feel like it. Mine suck when I
get the implant filled cause then my chest feels like it's gonna
explode from the new pressure but after a day it starts feeling
better again. All these mountains we have to climb and I don't know
about you but I definitely wasn't a hiker! Just gotta remember once
we hit the top of the mountains, there's that 'soothing' walk down..
Lisa

Monday, November 22, 2010 4:47 PM, CST
♥Thanks Kim for the awesome pedicure yesterday! ☺
♥Thanks Elaine and Karen for popping in to say hi...what a lovely surprise!!!!! ☺
♥Thanks Toni and Sarah for the time spent visiting today ☺
♥Thanks Mike and Amy for the card...so wonderful of you. I really love you guys. ☺
♥Thanks Braunie and Jake for entertaining my boys for a night this weekend. They both really needed it!!! ☺
♥Also thanks to Judy K., Toni and Sarah for the card....love you guys too! ☺
Anyone else I forgot....just know it is NOT forgotten! ♥S

Guestbook Comment: Monday, November 22, 2010 8:00 PM, CST
Hello, my Lovely! Kim is right you did look great Sunday morning! Any other pampering you need? Let me know. If you are up to it one of these days I will come "play" with your hair for you! You are fabulous and inspire me every day with your strength and perseverance. You will make it through this even though the road seems awfully long right now. I'll be there for you no matter what you may need! Can't wait to get "out" with you Friday night before the parade. Betsy

Guestbook Comment: Monday, November 22, 2010 10:03 PM, CST
Hi Shelly, Thought I would pop in to see how things were going. You are such a trooper! You just amaze me in every way. Tracy W-D.

Guestbook Comment: Monday, November 22, 2010 10:26 PM, CST
Ok Shelly! You are way too nice and you know what I'm talking about!!! What a nice surprise! I saw Ilyssa at school today when I dropped Ray Ray off after her dentist appointment...what a nice

smiley face she has! She gets it from you and hubby! Keep looking up! Love and Prayers! Dawn

Tuesday, November 23, 2010 9:25 AM, CST
Good Morning Shelly. Any living, breathing morning is a GOOD morning. San Diego Chargers won last night. Cheers for a wonderful day for you. Love, Roberta

Tuesday, November 23, 2010 9:47 AM, CST
In general, I am not a person who is weak. I never ask for help...I am Wonder Woman (underoos and all) and can do it myself. BUT you all have been UP MY BUTT about letting you know what we need. And we appreciate it all so much. From the tips of my beautiful pedicured tootsies, all the way up to my heart. I love you all. Thank You. ♥S

Tuesday, November 23, 2010 10:02 AM, CST
The hardest part of each day is accepting help. Having to ask (out loud) for someone (whoever is here) to help me get up outta the chair or to reach the blanket that fell or to please get the clothes outta the washer because I cannot reach all the way down into it. I feel helpless on a good day.

BUT. I chose this. I chose this course of treatment. And that's what it is-treatment. I could have had just a lumpectomy, but then what??? A month later have a mastectomy? 6 months later find cancer in the other side? I chose to have a complete hysterectomy in 2 weeks to throw myself at 35 years old into menopause, with no chance of using hormone replacement therapy to help with the hot flashes, or mood swings, or night sweats.... because that HRT would feed the cancer, and possibly bring it back. Andy is

81

behind me 100%. He knows what he's in for....YIKES....and is ok with that. He in no way wants to be a widowed father of our 3 kids and knows that in my choosing this aggressiveness course of treatment that it is what we NEED to do for our family. Hopefully the menopause will be short lived (yeah, right lol). But also hopefully being this aggressive will boot the cancer to the curb forever. ♥S

Tuesday, November 23, 2010 10:26 AM, CST
I do not live in a state of perfection. I live in a constant state of CHAOS!!

Tuesday, November 23, 2010 11:38 AM, CST
If you see me in the store, and I and/or my 3 kids look like white trash....realize what we're going through, and just be thankful they're dressed-and that I remembered them all! ♥S

Guestbook Comment: Tuesday, November 23, 2010 7:46 PM, CST
hey aunt shelly we've got really bad colds mom, Brittany and I have one; mom's the worst Brittany's the 2nd worst mines the 3rd. mine was gone but then it came back. love alex (ps xoxoxo and i miss you ALOT. and i had my first basketball practice.)

Guestbook Comment: Tuesday, November 23, 2010 8:40 PM, CST
Hey Girl, seven more days and I finally get to see you!!!! Can't wait....Hang with you and get some work done for you. Love and miss you! Joey

Wednesday, November 24, 2010 5:59 AM, CST
I've received some amazing cards in the mail the last few days...thanks guys, I am so lucky to have you. I've gotten to catch up on the phone with Tessa, a friend I've known since I was

six. I really enjoyed my visit with Kerry, a true, kind, giving, genuine person that I have known since 6th grade.....can you believe that is TWENTY FOUR YEARS?!??!?!?! Kerry you are AMAZING! You took my mind off of what has been going on with me, and it was so amazing seeing you as a Mom.....you are an Angel. THANK YOU. I am tearing up as I type this just thinking of your kindness and generosity. I love ya. Enjoy your family this week...and I can't wait to see you again. Who knows, once I feel better, I may be up to a road trip! Reading the guestbook here from the beginning is such an eye opener. Thanks for all the support, friendship and love. ♥S

Wednesday, November 24, 2010 12:37 PM, CST

Grumble grumble gurgle ROAR. I had called in my numbers this morning to the Doctors office--they are not dropping off as quickly as I had hoped in order to get the drains pulled. But 'Awesome Kim' my PS's 'woman in charge' talked to him, and he decided to have me come in today at 2:00. I am of course TERRIFIED and excited with the idea of being free of yet another drain tube. It's great when it's out, but hurts like a BITCH getting there. Dad's taking me and I'm really sad that Andy can't be with me. Being brave is sucky when you're chicken. Last time he assumed 'the position' next to my head and just let me squeeze the shit out of his hand. But this time I'll be alone. I'm hoping not to pass out if one does come out! I had called the other day to inquire about getting some kinda numbing magic the next time I came in for this and basically they could numb the skin BUT the 8 inches of flexible catheter looking tube on the INSIDE is basically growing to my skin....and that is why it's so painful when pulled out. Now if that didn't just give you the freakin' WILLIES....you are much braver than I. I do not have a strong stomach when it comes to medical stuff...I don't watch them draw blood...I cannot look at my incisions for more than a quick glance. I don't like things that make my stomach flip flop...such as the nasty thought of having these plastic drains growing to my tissue inside of me and then having to YANK it out. FFFFFFFFFFFFFFFfff-ah-CK!!!!!!

p.s...I can't even watch my kids pull their teeth out. I'm a wuss, I know. ♥S

Guestbook Comment: Wednesday, November 24, 2010 1:15 AM, EST
Shelly your postings have really opened up my eyes to what goes on. Because of you, I have finally scheduled my first mammogram (I'm 41) and have made an appointment for a full physical that is about 4 years overdue. Keep up the good work and live every day to its fullest. Many, many thoughts and prayers to all of you. Riquie

Guestbook Comment: Wednesday, November 24, 2010 9:42 AM, CST
It was so nice talking to you on the phone yesterday! Hang in there WONDER WOMAN!!!!! I CANNOT wait to see you on Tuesday! PLEEEEEASE start making a to-do list for Joey and I. We are ABLE and WILLING to do whatever you need done. Have a wonderful Thanksgiving with your loving husband and 3 beautiful children! I will be THANKFUL this Thanksgiving for my AMAZING friend Shelly!!!! I love you! XO Jenny

Guestbook Comment: Wednesday, November 24, 2010 10:44 AM, CST
Happy Thanksgiving Eve! We do have much for which to give thanks, big and small. I cherish the memory of the time your mom stopped overnight with us in Maryland when she was on a road trip. It will be good for you to have family around you tomorrow. Love, Roberta

Guestbook Comment: Wednesday, November 24, 2010 2:19 PM, CST
I can't take the loose teeth either. Couldn't they give you some of
that great sedation stuff they use at the dentist? It's not like you
are driving anyway. I hope it wasn't too horrible. Love ya! Mary

Wednesday, November 24, 2010 9:13 PM, CST

Today went well. Thanks for all the follow up questions regarding my
doctor appointment. I ended up only getting one drain taken
out. But on the up side, it didn't hurt at all. Unfortunately it's the
holiday weekend and I'm stuck with 2 left in until Monday at least.
I have once again been blessed with my Fairy Godmother Betsy's
generosity-she swooped in and cleaned my house and helped me out
with getting the place ready for Thanksgiving....thanks again for the
millionth time. Love You!!! NOW I'm home alone with the kids:
whining, crying annoyed...and that's just ME. The kids are kicking my
ass, and they are an hour past bedtime, but NO ONE is tired. Just
ask them. YEAH, right. Now since you are all reading this and have
been sending up prayers and prayers and prayers....I need to ask
even ONE *more* favor. A best friend of mine is going through a
horrible divorce. She has been treated poorly (read: shitty), walked
all over, and verbally brought DOWN. She is one of the STRONGEST
women I know (and that says a LOT) and does NOT NOT NOT NOT
NOT deserve this. Please pray for her too. She needs the strength
to keep her head up, KNOW she is in the RIGHT, and not let her be
beaten down. ♥S

Guestbook Comment: Wednesday, November 24, 2010 10:27 PM, CST
Your friend is being prayed for as are all your helpers. So glad
this trip to the dr. went much better. Happy Thanksgiving and I'm
so glad you and your family came into my life. I don't have your

address or your phone # only Andy's is it all right to call him? Luv
Kathy

Thursday, November 25, 2010 4:22 AM, CST
Happy Thanksgiving Everybody!!!! You would think that I'd be down
this year, with not a lot to be thankful for, since, y'know, the big 'C'
word. And it's not that I am thankful for *having* cancer-that would
be insanity. I am so unbelievably thankful for everyone that has
been newly brought into my life; past friends that I've been lucky
enough to reconnect with; and family that I haven't been all that
close with in a while have been back in my life, and I've been
enjoying every second of it!!!! Catching up with everyone has been
so much of a 'stress reliever' that it truly keeps my mind off of all
the bad things that we've been going through.

For all of you I am thankful.
We also had some huge successes this year. We sold our home in
Horicon which definitely helped us out with our goal of moving back to
Plymouth.   It was a struggle; we miss our loving neighbors and
friends like crazy. The good thing is that when we moved here we
fell right into having great neighbors again. The decision to relocate
was both difficult and easy. We had a beautiful home, a great fenced
in yard, and we could walk to the pool and park in less than 3
minutes. One of my best friends lived just around the corner...and
we were surrounded by great loving neighbors. AND who can leave
out the Ice Cream Station?!?!? Yummy. But I am definitely
THANKFUL that here in Plymouth we were lucky enough to find a
great place to rent that is JUST PERFECT for our family. We have
all kinds of great people in our neighborhood as friends and plenty of
kids for OUR kids to play with. ☺   It really is great for us where
we 'are' in life right now. (Can I still bring up Chester's in

November?!??! Hell yeah, I can!)

My dad and sister are also in the area to help us out. They have most definitely come through, and I just can't thank them enough. I mean, really, my Dad took me to the BOOB doctor yesterday LOL! ((he did wait in the car though--haha)) Sandi has been helping with the kids, groceries, chauffer service-you name it. Thank God for you guys.....

I am THANKFUL that here we have HUNDREDS of friends-not just 4. They have come through in leaps and bounds. Food/meals, shelter, rides, gifts, groceries, flowers, phone calls, visits, housecleaning, childcare--even boxes of GF cereal left in my door --- TOTALLY help us out. Having three kids and cutting down to half my income is such a struggle.

I am THANKFUL that I had the opportunity last March to become a full time employee again, after 2 years of being part time. That opportunity brought with it the chance to pick up life insurance, short term disability, short term plus disability and LONG term disability. Being able to keep getting 50% of my pay with my STD+ at this point (for 26 weeks) is a blessing. Imagine having NO pay while going through cancer. Yikes. There are so many 'extras' needed that you don't even think about-mainly the gas money needed for daily trips to the local clinic, the lab, the hospital, the cancer clinic. You also need to stock up on medical supplies like gauze-every size and shape you can imagine-medical tape, Neosporin, laxatives, Imodium, Tylenol, prescriptions, copays, coinsurance amounts, payment plans for 5 different places...thank God for my benefits through work! There is more cost involved with someone being home all the time (the utility and water bills) more groceries to feed everyone that is coming in and out. I've needed some new clothes to wear so that they're loose against my painful areas. All those little things that creep in. Along with Andy missing some work. He does not get paid when he's not there. Nor does he get vacation time.

Today on Thanksgiving I am thankful for the life I am living...it's a fucked up one right now, but it's all mine ☺ I do still have my health—I have cancer, but it is not right now affecting me. I feel fine, I can function (minus the pain—which we'll just ignore for today) and I can finally drive again! YAY! I have been able to play with the kids again...even if it's only Uno (only a MILLION times!) Even just watching iCarly sitting next to each other on the couch really counts to them. I've been isolated in the recliner for weeks, not allowing anyone to sit on me, but now we're slowly working back into snuggling. ☺ I've invented a 'birdie nest' for the kids...while I am sitting up in the recliner with the foot rest up— I make a little nest with a blanket between my knees—and let the girls snuggle in there. They love it!

I have the BEST HUSBAND in the entire Solar System. Andy and I have been through EVERYTHING together—the worst of the worst. We've also been blessed to witness all of our friends get married--and each time has been so much fun, so much happiness. We've also welcomed many new babies into our 'group' of friends... both here and in Horicon/Beaver Dam. It's amazing the dynamic of the kids...from Tyler who is SEVENTEEN already (driving, and dating, and talking college!)!?!?!?!?! To Lillian, who at 5 months old is the youngest (right now!) It's wonderful to be able to know so many people in all kinds of different life stages. It's amazing to think that Andy & I have been together since the beginning. Sixteen YEARS!! For over half of my life I have been with my best friend. There

88

have been struggles, but there are so many good times. Just ask Andy about my special laugh. LMFAO. Happy Thanksgiving all; we love you. ♥S

Guestbook Comment: Thursday, November 25, 2010 5:55 AM, CST
Happy Thanksgiving my friend! I am blessed to call you my friend and right now I am missing you like crazy! Your last journal entry is so true! It takes a strong person to see past the "C" word and to be truly thankful for what you are going thru! Even though I miss you sooooooo much and when I drive past your house twice a day I think of you. I know that it was a blessing for you to move back to Plymouth. The support and outreach that you have gotten is amazing. Now show the world what kind of person YOU really are! Love ya!!! Jenny

Guestbook Comment: Thursday, November 25, 2010 10:25 AM, CST
Happy Thanksgiving to you and all the Wisconsin Phillips family. I need your current mailing address, please and thank you. Keep up your football spirit- there's lots today. Love you, Roberta

Guestbook Comment: Thursday, November 25, 2010 6:56 PM, CST
Hi Shelly. I just wanted to pop on here and wish you a very Happy Thanksgiving! I am so thankful for your journal here so I can keep up to date on how you are doing. I read EVERY entry and continue to pray for you and your family. Will be praying for your friend as well! Wish I lived closer so I could do more! HUGS! xoxo Charity

Friday, November 26, 2010 4:18 AM, CST
Ok, I just need to BITCH. Yeah, that's right, I said it. Bitch. Not complain. I found out Wednesday that my insurance will not cover a

PET scan for me. It's not that it isn't medically necessary.....any time there is lymph node involvement the doctor says it is medically necessary. But my insurance still won't cover it. Period. Millions of people have cancer every year so how can you tell me that they are denied a PET scan? The scan that will show if the cancer has spread or not...where it is; where it's at. I'm pretty ticked.

So instead of a PET scan on 12/2, I'll be having a bone scan along with a CT scan. I've been trying to do research to see if those 2 tests together are equivalent to a PET, but am having a hard time finding data. If you or someone you know has any input on this subject, I would LOVE to hear it! I'm doing all that I can with research, but really wish I could find someone that would tell me "yes, it will give you the same results." or "no, those tests aren't even CLOSE to what you need". My care coordinator told me that we WOULD get the same results with the 2 tests instead. But I still have the doubts. Ok, bitching over, back to your regularly scheduled blog. ♥S

Friday, November 26, 2010 9:50 AM, CST
You know exactly who loves you when you have cancer. ♥S

Guestbook Comment: Friday, November 26, 2010 10:13 AM, CST
Yeah, me too, I read every journal note. Hang in there. There's no promise of an easy life, even when we do good. Love you. Roberta

Friday, November 26, 2010 1:24 PM, CST
This was the first year in FOREVER that my Dad was home for the Thanksgiving holiday. It turned out that his friend that he goes hunting with wanted to be back for Turkey Day, so he decided that he would come home too. There were other factors as well; unfortunately I was a main reason. Always sweet, but not when it

boils down to having cancer ☹ It was a really nice day...Sandi came over around 9 a.m. to start getting the bird ready and all we had to do was stick it in the oven at 12.   NO PROBLEM!!! Dinner was at 4:30 so Sandi & Candice jumped into the kitchen and made it all happen! The bird was done and we did the quickest easiest sides we could. Instant potatoes, frozen veggies, canned cranberry sauce, stove top stuffing and brown-n serve rolls....IT WAS DELICIOUS!! Oh yeah, and canned gravy. I'm sure my grandma is rolling over in her grave with all the corners we cut but trust me, it all tasted the great!!! They worked hard and it paid off. For dessert we had cherry and pumpkin pies with Cool whip! After that we all took some quiet time on the couch/recliners....and relaxed. The kids played amazingly well all afternoon & into the evening, with the exception of minor whining from my 8 year old 'teenager'.   Andy did the dishes and cleanup and we still got to enjoy some quiet time later in the evening. The kids all passed out early and slept in the living room with me.

I hope you all had a wonderful Thanksgiving Day, and survive the black Friday shopping/shoppers/drivers. Today the kids and I are watching movies on TV, hanging out...doing nothing. The best kind of day! ♥S

Guestbook Comment: Friday, November 26, 2010 2:11 PM, CST
That's the one thing with the holidays. Who cares what you eat or where you go as long as you are with the people you love. My family always ate out for Thanksgiving. Some people get kind of 'disgusted' that we don't do the 'traditional' Thanksgiving, but who gives an F! We didn't have time for all that prep being on the farm and my mom wasn't willing to do it anyways so why not let someone else do all the work and hey no clean up afterwards! Same goes with Christmas.

91

It's about being with family, not what you eat! Lisa

*I remember that Betsy had been trying to get me to come
downtown to watch the Christmas parade and then meet up at
Antonio's for a warm-up cocktail. It was so terribly cold out that I
decided no, I wanted to stay home. I also was still sore and
miserable from my past few weeks.*

Friday, November 26, 2010 8:45 PM, CST

I was sitting on the couch hanging out after a long day-after-
Thanksgiving when the doorbell rang. In walked Betsy and Davis
and Miranda, so I thought that her family was just popping in to say
"hey." Well, she continued crossing the living room, and then I saw
Fred and Shawn and Sandi and Adrian and Dave and Mike and Angie
and Kelly and Larry and Brittany and Alex and more and more and
more people kept walking through my living room lining up!!! I'm not
sure who was all there (please don't be offended....I was drugged up!)
but there must have been 20 people there, easily. I got this whole
nervous feeling...wondering **WTF??** So, once everyone had piled in,
Betsy leads the group in telling me how much they all love me. How
much they all care about me. How they know that what I am going
through is a horrible thing, and that they know we could use some
support. It turns out that together they have secretly been
meeting up and planning a benefit for us! At that point Betsy turns
the foam board that she was holding around so I could see, and in
her hands she was holding a printed advertisement for the 'Better
Boobie Benefit' in my Honor. The butterflies in my stomach started
dancing around! I started shaking and crying! I had to make

some bad jokes in my nervousness-to take some of the tension out of myself! She continued talking about the secret meetings; the work that has already gone into it; the AMAZING donations they had already received; all the people that are involved. What an amazing feeling!!!!! I couldn't believe that she kept this from me! What a stinker!!! I hope I never have to reciprocate (for like reasons) but you all know I would do so **in a heartbeat**. I had a hug-conga line going on as everyone filed back out...leaving me in the shock of it all!

Joan & Crew: THANK YOU! You made our evening! Caroling and cookies go together like peanut butter and jelly...yummmmm! You are a blessing to our family. Thank You.

Thank GOD I have a strong heart....too many surprises in one evening and you guys may kill me!!! ♥S

<u>Guestbook Comment</u>: Friday, November 26, 2010 9:27 PM, CST
Hey Girl, it only took about 15 minutes to look for the recipe for our all-time favorite mint patties that you gave us. It's funny, I always know what type of paper the recipe is on, but it still takes me about 30 minutes to go through the box. Then, after we found it, we had to laugh because it is on white paper that is thinner than 'normal' paper -because that is the paper you used! I should've known that if it was from Shelly it would not be NORMAL paper lol! Then of course I have about 9 different kinds of chips from milk chocolate to white chocolate to cinnamon to butterscotch, but you got it...NO semi sweet chips so we couldn't make them today. Anyways, we got 2 kinds of cookies made and a grand total of 445 cookies, and that is what is frozen, we had more, but we also had 8 munching children and 2 munching mommies. So excited to come see you on Tuesday!

Glad you had a great Thanksgiving. Your positive attitude inspires me every day. We are so blessed to have you in our lives! Love ya lots, Joey

<u>Guestbook Comment</u>: Friday, November 26, 2010 10:13 PM, CST
Shelly I was glad to read you had a nice Thanksgiving. You can be sure you will see me and John at your benefit. I would not miss that for the world. I said an extra Thanksgiving Prayer for you and your Family yesterday. LOL Pam and John

<u>Guestbook Comment</u>: Saturday, November 27, 2010 9:17 PM, CST
Hey Shelly, I check your Caringbridge site daily for updates so thanks for keeping up with it. I just want you to know that you have my love, support & prayers daily. I'm lifting your name to the Lord for healing for you and strength for you and Andy as you fight this. I wish we lived closer together so I could pop in with a nasty casserole! From one TTC Mama to another ~ a million hugs. Love you bunches! Sheri

Sunday, November 28, 2010 2:28 AM, CST
You know what's amazing? Being able to spring up outta the chair at 2 a.m. to help Ilyssa who is having growing pains and needs Motrin. The key word in that sentence is SPRING!!!! Can you believe it folks?!?! Being able to get up outta the chair, and walk straight into the kitchen to GET the Motrin. Not cringe or flinch or need a minute to let everything be *less mad* is a big step for ME!!!! We've never gotten a family portrait professionally done just the kind where I set the tripod up. I have a friend whose daughter does photography on the side. I had contacted her to set up a time that worked mutually for us. Today she emailed me to say that she could do it TODAY at 1 p.m. I'M SOOO EXCITED!!! I'm not sure where

we'll be going to do them, since it is so effing cold out! But I'm sure she has some amazing ideas. I just really have a bug to do this before my hair starts to fall out and I get *sick*. I'm sure my football fanatic hubby will be ecstatic lol...he may be missing from the family pictures! (It's SUNDAY) ☺

Yesterday was a pretty good day! I did some Christmas shopping with my sister; Alaina got to see SANTA at the mall and we got an amazing picture of them together; I took a THREE hour nap which is becoming normal for me, probably since I'm up at 2 or 3 a.m. every damn day!!! When I woke up I spent some time with the kiddos and then Betsy and I went to DQ with her 2 littles, and my Ilyssa. Everyone got special time with Mommy and even Daddy had some time without the kids (playing POKER with the guys!!!) He had a good time, and I'm so glad he went! DQ was yummy like always, nothing better than a blizzard when it's winter! Life is Good. ♥S

Guestbook Comment: Sunday, November 28, 2010 6:36 AM, CST
2 days!!!!!!!!!!!!!!!!!!!!!!!!! Can't wait to see you! Jenny

Guestbook Comment: Sunday, November 28, 2010 8:59 AM, CST
Life IS good Sheri

Sunday, November 28, 2010 9:07 AM, CST
I have been super private (in real life-NOT ON HERE OF COURSE!) about my diagnosis for many reasons. As I have said before I look at this as a weakness. I feel like my body has betrayed me, and it's hard to share that with the world. Anyone that knows me knows that I just do NOT show weakness....and all this craziness and helplessness pisses me off. I can't believe all that I have yet to endure....more mental anguish with the bone scans/CT

95

scan on Thursday...and wait wait wait for the results. Then a few days later an oophorectomy hysterectomy-removal of uterus/ovaries/cervix. When I wake up I will be straight into menopause. I know we all have preconceived notions of this 'M' word...but from reading and researching...there's the night sweats, the hot flashes, the mood swings, the bone loss, the list goes on and on and on.....shortly after I have my stomach cut into and while I am still recovering from the damn mastectomy...I will be starting chemo. We all know what chemo does to you ☹ I will be given a regime of two chemo medicines. Adriamycin and Cytoxan. While doing some research I found out that Adriamycin is nicknamed 'The Red Devil'. Together they are mean, strong, and evil. THAT does not sound like fun. Yikes. I turned down the clinical trial.....you have to be post op for 28+ days before starting chemo/trial drug...and I just don't want to wait that long. I don't want to put off what needs to be done any longer. Let's get this ball rolling!!!!! I have been reading a parallel story online of a woman, age 30 with a like cancer diagnosis, and it is just so amazing what different doctors do. She's in PA, and her Doc did chemo first, then pet/bone scans...THEN removal of both breasts. She then has to take Tamoxifin for 5 years to fight the estrogen receptors. TOTALLY ass backwards from what my team is doing. I just find that so weird!! She is negative for the ER/PR and BRCA testing...so she gets to keep her ovaries, but chemo can also put you into early menopause; they give you shots to shut down your ovaries. So I guess my story and hers are semi-same.....in the end we both have the same symptoms and ending. She started this journey in March, so she's done with chemo, done with surgeries, and moving on with her healing. Let's hope I can inspire someone in 8 months when MY journey is complete....and pray it goes fast! ♥S

Sunday, November 28, 2010 10:17 AM, CST

Family pictures are on hold until next Sunday. She had something come up. No worries! That gives me more time to talk the family 'into' it lol. ♥S

Guestbook Comment: Sunday, November 28, 2010 10:42 AM, CST
Hey there I'm glad I checked in. Was looking for your # on here to call you. I just noticed that pictures are on hold. I can certainly get you guys all spiffed up. Let me know what works best for you. Give me a call since I'm still unable to find your #. I called Andy's phone but didn't leave a message. We'll chat soon.... Kim

Guestbook Comment: Sunday, November 28, 2010 7:36 PM, CST
You are truly amazing...still having a sense of humor after everything you are going through. I hope you realize how special of a person you are and I am so fortunate to call you....friend. You and your family are in our thoughts and prayers. Sincerely, Angie

Guestbook Comment: Monday, November 29, 2010 11:19 AM, CST
Marilyn Monroe said "Everything happens for a reason, people change so that you can learn to let go, things go wrong so you can appreciate them when they're right, and sometimes good things fall apart so better things can come together." Hope this is a good week. Love, Roberta

Guestbook Comment: Monday, November 29, 2010 3:36 PM, CST
"The Lord will guide you continually, and satisfy your needs in parched places, and make your bones strong; and you shall be like a watered garden, like a spring of water, whose waters never fail." Isaiah 58:11 Our continued thoughts and prayers. Uncle David & Aunt Elaine

Monday, November 29, 2010 5:25 PM, CST

I got the drains out!

I GOT THE DRAINS OUT!

I GOT THE DRAINS OUT!

I GOT THE DRAINS OUT!

Holy crappers, what an R-E-L-I-E-F!!!!!!! You guys can't imagine what a huge comfort it is to have them damn things outta my SIDES! My arms bumped them all the time, I couldn't sit in the recliner w/o bumping them, and every time I moved they pulled! THANK YOU KIM!!! You saved the day, made my day, and I hope I enlightened YOUR day by dropping an F bomb on the doctor!

...as he was yanking on it all I know is my leg came up and I said through clenched teeth... "You're a FUCKING liar! That hurt like a BITCH!" (((I can't believe I dropped the f bomb at my plastic surgeon!))) Haha!

I have now joined the "club" where other cancer victims feel the need to show me their foobs (fake boobs.) Not sure how I feel about that! Not that I'm comfortable whipping out my ta-ta's... anywhere, anytime, OR online....I'll admit that we've been taking pictures throughout this journey. Nothing nasty, no worries. And don't go look on FB, they're NOT there lmao. BUT it was nice to see my PS's "work". Turned out lovely....and let's hope my journey is less than 10 months long...Tomorrow I start advancing on my reconstruction ...it will be the first time I have a 'fill'. Now if you haven't asked or read what this all entails....when I had my bilateral mastectomy they inserted tissue expanders between layers of my pecs. YOWCH. These expanders have a self-sealing 'port' with a

98

metal backing & a magnet in it so that it they can 'find' it right away. Every so often-starting TOMORROW AT 9 a.m.-they will stick a needle into my ta-ta's and inject saline (?) every so often (weekly? Bi weekly? I dunno) for 4-6+ months; until I'm done with chemo and/or radiation. Once I'm 'full up' we'll switch out the expanders with the implants. I'm excited/nervous to do this (of course no one wants to feel pain) but also to move forward and get going with the repair this damn cancer has done to my body. ♥S
p.s. Paula-I love you

Monday, November 29, 2010 5:40 PM, CST

Ok, I know I *just* updated, but I have another weird thing that has been going on since my surgery. I get goose bumps ALL THE TIME. Like, we're talking dozens and dozens of times a day. I'm not cold. I'm not standing outside....I'm sitting in my 70 degree house under blankets, totally snuggly...and I get goosey's starting at my right shoulder blade, all over my back....then to my arms. A few seconds later it goes away. SOOOO weird. I wonder if it has something to do with anything. Maybe it has been caused by nerve damage/sensitivity/misfiring? I have a definitive line on my right torso from it! Maybe I'm just freakin' weird. Probably. ♥S

Guestbook Comment: Monday, November 29, 2010 8:00 PM, CST
...it's one of those 'weird' things we get to experience. Basically because they severed all of the nerves in your chest they are over-firing cause messages aren't making it. One night I had goose bumps and it was funny cause you could see where I had no nerves on my foob cause there was a 'line' on one side where I had goose bumps & on the other nothing. That was weird! Lisa

Monday, November 29, 2010 11:47 PM, CST

It seems my insomnia has taken a turn for the 'different'. Now I can't fall asleep at night. WTH?!?! I have lots going thru my head, from kid stuff to house stuff, to health stuff, to CHRISTMAS which is freaking me out that it is so close! Maybe I just need to work on turning my brain off at night.

I did finally get 'the call' from my disability company that my last 3 weeks' worth of checks are on their way. Hopefully I can have them in time to pay the rent!!!! It will be nice to get that out of the way and then work on Christmas shopping for the chicklets! Each year as they get older it gets soooo much harder to shop for the little stinkers!! Josh is all about the Legos......every damn year. His whole room is stocked with them, and I am constantly stepping on THEM! UGH. Ilyssa has never been a 'toy' kid. She always wants them, and asks for them, but once she has them.....she forgets all about them. She really likes music, and dancing, and playing school. That is extremely hard to shop for!!!! She has a desk, a huge dry erase board, and notebooks up the wazoo! So we're going to have to improvise! She also has asked for a Nintendo DS--but not sure what games she would like? Any suggestions? I don't know where to start. Alaina is the typical 3rd child. Hand me down clothes, hand me down toys, & hand me down books so she literally needs NOTHING. Imagine how well THAT would go over Christmas morning!! Haha. She is really into those 'squinkies' toys....she has just always loved the little trinket type toys. I did get a kick-ass gift for Andy that he'll love...I can't wait to surprise him! Well, I guess I can't go to sleep if I don't get OFF OF HERE!!!!!!!! Night all! ♥S

<u>Guestbook Comment</u>: Tuesday, November 30, 2010 8:19 AM, CST
So bummed that I can't come today to see you! I sent some things

100

with Joey for you. I know there will be another time, but I was so looking forward to coming today. Damn pneumonia!!! Oh well...there will be another time! Love ya bunches and miss you! Stay positive! Jenny

Guestbook Comment: Tuesday, November 30, 2010 5:25 PM, CST
I'm glad to see they have a website like this to share your story with everyone. You and your family are in our prayers! Stay strong, keep up the fight, and kick this cancer's ass! We love you guys! Joel

Guestbook Comment: Tuesday, November 30, 2010 7:59 PM, EST
Hey Shelly, I finally got hooked up with your caring bridge site. I gotta tell ya, I have colleagues that have had breast cancer, but oddly enough I have never had a friend my own age with it-so how you are dealing with it is inspirational, at least to me, and I am sure to other people who love you too. I am sure you have bad days, and stressed out days, and just plain scary days but from the posts you put on FB you are just carrying on with normal life. It's amazing how your kids are probably a good distraction. I want you to know that when I say that I am thinking about you, I mean it truly! Love ya and am looking forward to your next update. Ann

Guestbook Comment: Tuesday, November 30, 2010 8:16 PM, CST
Shelly, had a great time visiting you. Man you look so amazing. I know that you don't like people saying that because you think we all think you look like "death" but girl you are beautiful! I think you look better today than you looked this summer, just saying positive energy and thoughts and gratefulness all shows in you I hope we didn't wear you out too much, you had 2 doctors' appointments and then had to be our direction lady to get around your town. Try to get

some good sleep tonight, and oh by the way did hubby get the garland up yet? I always found it helpful to place the things you want done on their bed, because, they all like to sleep....lol! Wish we could have done more for you. I am so in *awe* at what your 'circle of friends' have been doing for you.....you have such a wonderful support group and they are sooo amazing!!! They really know how to get things rolling and that is fantastic! Love you much!!!!
Rest tomorrow....Love, Joey

Tuesday, November 30, 2010 11:13 PM, CST

What an L---O---N---G day. No sleep last night and no rest for the wicked all day long. I started out by running the kids to school...of COURSE there had to be drama! No one could find their hat. No one could find their assignment book. No one could find their take home folder. Once we finally got past all that drama we got to school and JOSH can't get his glove on. Whatever dumbass company these shitty gloves came from decided to make them where the lining does NOT attach to the outer material. SO when my 9 year old takes his gloves off, the lining pulls outta the fingers, and next time--you guessed it--he can't get the darn things on!!!!! SO here we are at the curb at school, he's breathing down my neck yelling at me to "HURRY UP! I'm gonna be late!!!" While I'm cramming a pencil into each finger to fix them... .finally with one more to go he said something to tick me off, so I said "I'M DONE. Get out." He said ok, and left. I left with high blood pressure...and he was all happy. URGH! I threw those fuckers right out the window. If you see them outside the school FUCKING LEAVE THEM THERE! They are straight from Hades.

From there I ran to the PS for the 2nd day in a row. Today was my first experience getting the ta-ta's filled up. NO, they're not 'topped off! It's gonna be slow going. After my double mastectomy they had 120 cc's of saline in. Today they added another 100cc's to each side. All I can say tonight is Owwwww. Having ANYthing placed UNDER your chest wall muscles is not nice. And now we're not just expanding the tissue...we're expanding the pectoral muscles too. So once again, every move, every turn, is slow going. I also had some stitches removed today. I thought I was all Franken-glued together, but apparently I had a few stitches at the 'intersection' of the 2 incisions down at the bottom, so those all came out today. It didn't hurt; no worries. Neither did the insertion of the needle on the cancer side. I don't really have any feeling in that side. The "good" side was just uncomfortable. The process for the fill was nothing special. (I'm typing this well after my reconstruction has been completed...so bear with me!) First I got to gown up, and talk shit with Kim. Then I lie on the table, lean back, and get sterilized with that brown stuff...iodine? I air dry, then Kim gets out the magnet-it's a chain (think dog tag chain) with a small cylinder magnet at the end of it. She swirls that over my expanders until it focuses in on the port. Then she loads up her HUMONGOUS syringe with sterile saline from a bottle, and the doc sticks it in, and it feels as you would imagine...you can feel the thunk of it hitting the port (the metal back protecting my expander and lung) and the heavy hard pressure of the saline going in. I was able to tilt my chin down to watch my tiny little mounds fill up. And then when it was all in, or I felt too much pressure they stopped, covered the hole up right away, and put squares of gauze over it...taping it in place. Then on to the left side. That side did smart quite a bit! Same routine, but feeling that thick needle go in even just that tiny bit into the port-ouch. I wish there was a way to attach video!

While I was there Awesome Kim told me about an AMAZING deal she got on black friday at Goodwill.....apparently a retail truck smashed a crapload of 'Go Go and Me' doggies.....and they gave them to GW and were selling them for $20!! (Ok, 19.99!) But they're normally $59.00 I think? It's one of those fur Real pets. Any who....I ran over and scored one! Awesome! Alaina has really wanted one for like 2 months. Mommy is EXCITED!!!!

I sped home to see my wondermous friends Joey and Julie. They buzzed over from FDL and Horicon to see us; helped us clean and organize; filled my freezer and put up my Christmas decorations! It was so hellamazing; the friends I have are the best! It really sucked that Jenny couldn't make it but her little guy has pneumonia.... and between his not feeling good, her lack of sleep, and my iffy immune system...it was just better this way. But I'll see her soon, I just know it. My kids were so excited to see the holiday decorations up when they got home-they just loved it!

Once my friends were safely on their way home, Lainey and I once again headed back to the doctor's office. This time for my pre-op checkup for next week's surgery. *Sigh*. The doctor looked so sad when she came in and had tears in her eyes. Let me tell ya that is NOT an encouraging feeling for ME!!!!!!!! She was just floored with what has been going on (she gets faxed all my records) and really was interested in how I was *doing* and I told her pretty good. I feel I am in a good place for what I am going through....the added stress of being a mom of 3; not working (still no disability check......) and my health. She also really stressed my genetic counseling appointment set up for Dec 13. I am very adamant about going....I would not avoid doing it....but she is pretty concerned about my daughters' and nieces' future. Well, I most certainly am as well. If

104

they can pin this darn gene and give them blocking meds to keep from getting this 'C'...that would be kick ass. I can't lie and say that I go a day without crying AT ALL. At some point in every day I have a break down. I get overwhelmed by fear and pain and uncertainty for my children's future. Once we both had a GOOD CRY, and hugged out some emotions...we did the pre op, and I was set to go. After the Doc appointment, I had to run to Wally World for pull ups and soda and socks (how do all 3 of my kids LOSE so many damn socks? They just NEVER turn up again?) I ran into Paula, my dear friend from long ago. I told her to pop in some day...I'm always home for Pete's sake! After WM Lainey and I went to school to pick up the big kids then FINALLY we went home. Joey had already put our supper into the oven, so that was taken care of. Ahhhh. We got the new flyers for the benefit and Andy changed the wording a bit to remove the 'boobies' verbiage to please everyone. No worries. We even had some people come by and pick them up already! So crazy! The planning committee is soooooo wonderful! ♥S

Guestbook Comment: Wednesday, December 1, 2010 10:16 AM, CST
Good morning Shelly (it is morning here in CA.) Hope your day is good; every day has a twinkle of good in it. It will only shine brighter. Love, Roberta

Wednesday, December 1, 2010 12:56 PM, CST
A-W-E-S-O-M-E Kim...Bless You. You, too, are a part of my healing...and I hope I NEVER have to share you with any of my friends--on a professional level. On an everyday level---you'd fit RIGHT IN. Bless You...♥S

Wednesday, December 1, 2010 5:00 PM, CST

T-minus 14 hours until I have to be at the hospital to check in for my scans. I do NOT understand why my insurance will not cover a PET scan for me. I have stage 3 cancer. I am young. There is no goddamn reason not to. But apparently they don't cover them for people that do not medically need one. You know, like me. Because, y'know, being 35 and having stage 3 breast cancer means I don't need any fancy dancy testing to see if the cancer is anywhere/everywhere else. 10 year old technology will do just fine. Yeah, thanks assholes. Glad I pay my premiums every week so I can get screwed by the company that should be *making* me take these kinds of tests to catch it before it gets any costlier! Argh. SO I am writing my letter to appeal that bullshit right now. I'm not sure if it will help, since my other scans are tomorrow already but I can't imagine that in the future I wouldn't need a PET to see if the treatment is working, or effective, or whatever the hell. Blech. Because I just don't have enough to do. I forage onward and upward. ♥S

Guestbook Comment: Wednesday, December 1, 2010 10:54 AM, CST
Hello, my lovely Petunia! Just wanted to let you know I am still thinking of you☺. Hope you are having a somewhat stress-free day! I reminded the girls to stop in just in case you need any little errands done or laundry or anything. I pray to God every day to heal you and give you strength. I know you have your moments, but trust in Him. He will comfort you. Psalm 30:10-12 'Hear, LORD, and be merciful to me; LORD, be my help. You turned my wailing into dancing; You removed my sackcloth and clothed me with joy, that my heart may sing Your praises and not be silent. LORD my God, I will praise You forever.'
I love you and am ALWAYS here for you. Betsy

Guestbook Comment: Wednesday, December 1, 2010 6:26 PM, CST
OK so I'm FINALLY catching up with all your entries since I got
back home. WOW a lot has happened. Yay the drains are out you
must be feeling so much better. OMG I can't believe you are having
PET scan issues. I am so sorry. Hopefully your appeal letter will
help them see the light. Can your doctor write something for you as
well to include with your appeal? Major prayers coming your way
about the CT/Bone scan tomorrow. Let us know how it goes.
You're on my mind...hugs and prayers. Love Kerry

Guestbook Comment: Thursday, December 2, 2010 1:24 AM, CST
That is a bunch of crap!!!!! Amy and I hope everything is well.
Our well wishes are with you. Mike and Amy

Guestbook Comment: Thursday, December 2, 2010 5:16 AM, CST
Hey girlie, best of luck today! We have you & your family in our
prayers. Jen

Guestbook Comment: Thursday, December 2, 2010 5:49 AM, CST
Hey girl...you are in my prayers today. Hopefully everything will come
back clean and you will be on to your next surgery! You continue to
inspire me every single day! Love and miss you! Jenny

Guestbook Comment: Thursday, December 2, 2010 10:26 AM, CST
Good luck today!!!! I'm thinking about you and praying for a clean
scan!!!! Stacey

Guestbook Comment: Thursday, December 2, 2010 12:45 PM, CST
Wishing you the peace and comfort you need for today. Anna says
your doctor should be able to address the PET scan issue with your
insurance company and resolve it. That's her perspective from

working in insurance claims for several years. Love you, Roberta

Thursday, December 2, 2010 2:17 PM, CST
After 7 hours, both scans are done. I'm home relaxing. Alaina is zonked out on the couch, and I think she has the right idea...♥S

Thursday, December 2, 2010 8:12 PM, CST
This morning the evil alarm clock was ringing at 6:15 a.m. I was told to be at Memorial Hospital at 7:30 a.m. for my CT and bone scan. So I dragged my ass out of bed, bundled up and headed out into the freezing cold morning. (Does ANY of this sound like fun yet????) I was told that I could drive myself NO PROBLEM, so I sent Andy off to work and the kids to the neighbor's house to go to school. Ok. I had a CT scan this summer on my stomach so I knew what to expect...drink 2 bottles of NASTY crystal light with the contrast powder mixed in slowly over an hour. So here I am at 7:45-all checked in-when they ask why I haven't had my creatinine checked? How the fuck do I know?!? I just had my pre-op 2 days ago and they did a CBC but that was it. She sends me to the lab; they draw my blood. They sent me back to start sipping the contrast and I start getting the willies from how freakin' nasty this stuff is. Word to the wise....if you ever think you need a CT scan....try to AVOID it!!! The scan itself is nothing...you lay on a table and it slides you thru an upside-down U shaped machine (the scanner). You have to take a deep breath and hold; take a deep breath and hold; take a deep breath and hold. It checks for more of the anatomical abnormalities... where the bone scan checks the make-up of the bones, looking for abnormalities there. Before you can be scanned they hook up an IV in your arm, send in some saline, and then put in the dye-which causes a weird taste in your mouth and a warm feeling all over...settling in your bladder & making you feel like you wet

108

your pants!!! After that the worst is over 'if' it is not excruciating
to hold your arms up over your head. Which, in my case, it
is. Yowch. So then the evil, evil man with the needles (from my
LAST trip to nuclear medicine the morning of my last surgery)
shows back up and inserts some crazy meds into the IV before I
go, and tells me to return to nuclear medicine at noon (this is at
9:30) for my bone scan. Ugh. I thought that both tests would be in
a row. My first thought was shit, what am I going to do about
Lainey? She gets off the bus at noon! So I quick call Andy, let
him know, I quick call Dad, to see if he could come over and watch
her, and quick call Betsy.   Half way home, I still had not heard
from Dad, so I called Jenni and she was able to help me out.
YAY!!! I headed back home to relax for an hour and then right
back to the hospital....with Betsy driving me. She managed to strong-
arm me into letting her take me lol! I'm glad I did...I went through
the first test of the day alone, and didn't realize how emotional the
day would be. We literally got there at 12:02, and by 12:04 I was
on the bone scanning table. Again, you lay on a long table, this time
under a big camera. You slide halfway into a tube, up to your hands
(feet first) Then the camera part slides over your head and comes
down real close....for 4 1/2 minutes. Then the camera slides down
your body and stops again, for 4 1/2 minutes and keeps going until it
gets to your feet. By 12:30 Betsy and I were out the door. I
got home around 1; Jen left around 2; at 3 my friends came from
Fond du Lac Wal-Mart to visit; at 4 I brought the kids home; at
4:30 Nikki & Sarah headed back, and by 5 I had a migraine from
hell....brought on by ONE NAUGHTY CHILD (mine!) and too much
radioactive juice pumping through my body. By 5:30 when Andy got
home, I felt like absolute shit, and my head was POUNDING. I had
to cancel on Sarah who was gonna come visit with Alex... .but I had
such a crazy day I just wanted to cry....so I did. I took a one

hour nap and woke up feeling much, much better. Now I'm just emotional.... hot...and still sleepy. But I still have lots of water to drink to flush this crap outta my system. What the heck is the chemo going to do to me when I feel this shitty from just the stuff for the scans? I hate to even think about it... ♥S

<u>Guestbook Comment</u>: Thursday, December 2, 2010 8:46 PM, EST
Hey Shelly! Here's hoping for a clean and speedy report on your scan!!!! Ann

<u>Guestbook Comment</u>: Thursday, December 2, 2010 9:12 PM, CST
Hey girl, don't worry about tonight. Just take care of yourself first and try to get some sleep. You really are one of the strongest people I know. We'll see each other soon. Love ya lots!! Sarah

<u>Guestbook Comment</u>: Thursday, December 2, 2010 10:41 PM, CST
Hang in there honey. I can be a driver and companion for you any time until Jan. 3. I'm leaving for Az. for a mo. or so. I remember taking my husband for all his treatments so just let me know. Luv, Kathy

Friday, December 3, 2010 6:13 AM, CST
Roberta & Anna: we did go back and forth with the insurance on the PET scan. In fact the hospital I go to gives you a personal coordinator to help with all that stuff. She said initially they denied it, but thought that when the oncologist called them to talk to their 'guy' that does the review of necessity she felt it would go through. It didn't. I then called BCBS and asked WHY it was denied and was told they have *very* specific guidelines for how a PET scan will be allowed and under what circumstances. She then asked me why I needed it and I told her that I was dx with a late stage aggressive

110

breast cancer and they needed to check if it had spread....so they could alter my course of treatment to fit. Apparently that is too vague and I don't get one?? BUT she was very cool and told me to appeal that decision....and gave me the scoop on who to appeal to, what to all send along, things that will help like letters from my doctors, research showing how a PET is 15%+ more specific than the combo of a CT/bone scan. So we'll see what good that will do. ♥S

Friday, December 3, 2010 11:09 AM, CST
Feeling much, much better today! (Except for the nasty kink in my neck and shoulder) I no longer am feeling like I have been poisoned! THAT is cause for celebration lol! ♥S

Guestbook Comment: Friday, December 3, 2010 5:43 AM, CST
Clean Scans Clean Scans Clean Scans!!!! Can you hear me chanting!!! Love You! Jenny

Guestbook Comment: Friday, December 3, 2010 11:19 AM, CST
That's terrific that you have a personal coordinator! A great asset for sure. Glad you are using her and she is helping you through the grid. It is never easy. Hoping for good reports. Roberta

Guestbook Comment: Friday, December 3, 2010 9:31 PM, CST
It was great seeing you tonight. I'm so glad you guys came. Wish we could have chatted more. If you want me to style the girl's hair Sunday I can do that too. See you at 9! Love, Kim.

Saturday, December 4, 2010 11:04 AM, CST
No results yet-I'm antsy for MONDAY already. ♥S

Monday, December 6, 2010 9:47 AM, CST

I know, I know, nothing new all weekend...I'm the worst blogger
EVER!! Lol! This weekend was amazing... (p.s. NO results yet)...I had
some generous and amazing visitors. When you feel the world is just
not going your way, something spectacular comes along and makes
the world right again. We were chosen to 'Shop with Santa' at
Kmart here in Plymouth this past Saturday. The kids were each
allowed to shop for themselves with an adult partner and truly loved
it. They had a nice time, picked out GREAT toys, and really felt
blessed. My aunt & uncle came by later in the day, bringing with
them a very sentimental card and a fruit basket---and if that wasn't
thoughtful ENOUGH, they also threw some GF cookies in the fruit
basket!!!! Thinking of Josh specifically to make sure he is included in
the 'gift' is fantastic. Those things touch your heart, y'know???
Thank you David and Elaine...I love you. Saturday afternoon was nap
time......until 3 or so when I got up and ready to go to the ballet with
Melissa! Kasie was once again performing in The Nutcracker @ the
Weill Center. She and the WHOLE dance company did amazing! It
was beautiful and definitely something I will always remember. Before
and after the recital I got out to do some Christmas shopping, last
minute stuff I needed for our next day family photos and I found

112

Andy a NEW wedding ring! I have been saving up since AUGUST when he lost the darn thing while we were swimming in Long Lake! It's hard to shop for one when he's not here. BUT while I was at Kohl's I saw 'the' perfect one, silver and black, simple and beautiful. (And the $75 price tag didn't hurt either) I surprised him with it the next morning while the kids were opening their surprises from St. Nick (and the WILTZIUS'...naughty naughty, naughty.) He says he really likes it, just hard to get used to wearing one again. I told him GET USED TO IT BUDDY! Your single days are OVER!!!!!! Haha! Sunday we went to see Kim again. Josh got a haircut and the girls got their hair "prettied up" for our 1 p.m. photo shoot ☺ Thanks again, Kim! At one o' clock we went to Sarah M's house (who so graciously offered us the use of her home to do our family photos) and her daughter Brenda (www.brendakayphotography.com) did our family/kids/couple shots. Brenda, who is as friendly as she is amazing, did a wonderful job as ALWAYS and I just can NOT wait to see the pics! I'm sooo excited! (But, then again, I've always been an instant gratification kinda person! That's why online shopping is NOT for me!!!) Thanks again, Brenda and Sarah!!! After we got back (35 minutes was all we were gone!!!!) Andy & I crapped out in a dead sleep for a few hours....

Sarah T. popped in to visit and to chitchat....we sucked her into our Harry Potter marathon...hehehehe....then later Dad came to visit...and Sandi....and Cory......then Sarah just couldn't stay away-she came back for more! Lol! But the house was full, and since we were also putting up our Christmas tree...she headed out. I slept in an actual BED for the 4th night in a row....what a relief!!! BUT lying flat on your back with pillows and towels and blankets propping you up all over is NOT comfortable any time after 5 a.m. There's only SO much 'back' sleeping one can do!!!!

Today I have a million and one errands to do (phone, email, and stores) so I'm heading out....throw in 2 kids' doctor appointments and paperwork pickups....UGH. Tomorrow kid #3 has to go to the dentist....her spacer broke in her gums....and she is in a lot of pain. Poor baby. Dentist couldn't get her in today (PISSES me off-but whaddaya do? Right?)

Hi ho hi ho.....waiting for that DARN oncologist to CALL! ♥S

Guestbook Comment: Monday, December 6, 2010 9:50 AM, CST
The sunrise over the mountains this morning was spectacular reminded me of how spectacular you have been through these weeks of ups and downs. Keep on keeping on. Thinking of you today. Roberta

Monday, December 6, 2010 10:34 AM, CST
One result in: the HER2 neu that we had done on the tumor the day of surgery came back neutral...so they did more in depth testing...and it is NEGATIVE!!!! THAT IS GOOD! Positive would mean that it is a 'more' aggressive cancer, and 'more' likely to come back. NEGATIVE IS AWESOME! Also, the bone scan results are in, but the CT scan has not been dictated yet. They will call me later in the day to sum up both reports. We hope. ♥S

Guestbook Comment: Monday, December 6, 2010 1:40 PM, CST
Yeah for good news!!!! love ya! mary

Guestbook Comment: Monday, December 6, 2010 1:47 PM, CST
That is just wonderful news!!!! I couldn't be happier for you. Recovery baby!!!! Suck it cancer! Kim

Monday, December 6, 2010 2:14 PM, CST

Today is the day for GOOD news! First, the HER2 test is negative (see prev. post) NOW....drum roll...please.......the scans are clear, and nothing crazy showed up! (No 2nd head hiding up my ass or anything either! Andy still debates that...) ♥S

Guestbook Comment: Monday, December 6, 2010 2:42 PM, CST
Doing the happy dance for clear scans!!! Woohoo!!!! Karen

Guestbook Comment: Monday, December 6, 2010 2:51 PM, CST
Time for the Alleluia Chorus tis the season too!!!!! Roberta

Guestbook Comment: Monday, December 6, 2010 3:17 PM, CST
I'm so happy to hear all the good news!!! Cancer has messed with the wrong chica this time! Sarah

Guestbook Comment: Monday, December 6, 2010 3:51 PM, CST
You are in my thoughts more than you can know. I barely had a chance to even know you (FDL WM bakery) and now you are going through this terrible time in your life. You are in the biggest fight of your life, but you will win. I have read your journal and know how strong and brave you are. You have family and friends that support you in so many ways. Remain positive. I wish the very best for you & your family. Barb

Guestbook Comment: Monday, December 6, 2010 5:59 PM, EST
AWESOME NEWS SHELLY!!!!! Ann

Guestbook Comment: Monday, December 6, 2010 5:14 PM, CST I can't tell you how relieved I am to hear the good news!! This is fantastic!! I am sending you all my best wishes and prayers. Uncle Rick

Guestbook Comment: Monday, December 6, 2010 6:58 PM, CST
YEAH!!!!! AWESOME!!!!!   Glad to hear the good news!!! Jen

Guestbook Comment: Monday, December 6, 2010 7:16 PM, CST
Prayers answered! So glad Shelly! Candice

Guestbook Comment: Monday, December 6, 2010 8:20 PM, CST
HIP HIP HOORAY!!! I'm doing a dance right now! Love You! Jenny

Monday, December 6, 2010 10:16 PM, CST

Wheeeewwwwwwwwwwwwww. That's me, finally exhaling after 5 weeks.
Andy asked me tonight why I was so *eh* about the news when I
told him....I told him I guess it's because it is FANTASTIC news....
but...I still have cancer. ☹ Now, don't mistake this for a pity party,
cause believe you me....I was smiling EAR to freakin' EAR when I
got the news, and couldn't call everyone FAST ENOUGH!!! I even
called my Dad during his 'nap' which is like poking a BEAR during
hibernation! But he was relieved and happy for me/us! I think when
I told Andy I was still semi shocked! You know--expect the worst,
so you won't be disappointed when it's the best? Kinda like that.
Today I really am seeing a light at the end of this tunnel....even
though it's farther away than warm weather...it'll come. Tomorrow is
another crazy day. Thank goodness I have surgery on Wednesday
so I can get some REST.

I gotta get up and be beautiful so I can feel good about all life has
to offer...run the kids to school, head to Sheboygan for my 2nd 'fill',
run back to Plymouth, grab Ilyssa from school, and get her to the
dentist. After that, back to school, back home to pick up Lainey
once the bus brings her....then a bit of rest, and at 2:15 I have
physical therapy to get my arms/shoulders muscles working how they

116

should again. The PT herself is 'the best' which makes me happy. I know that at some point I'm going to have to go back to work and my job decorating cakes will be SLOW GOING until I get my strength and range of motion back. It's not like I can just NOT squeeze the pastry bags lol! After that, back to pick up the kids from school and head home for an 'Eclipse' party just me and Ilyssa ☺ She's Team Edward...I'm Switzerland. Andy received something AMAZING today from his friend/client Michele. HUMONGOUS HUGS coming your way, babe!!!! And I know you've been reading this. We Thank God for you!

Well, I've been playing Donkey Kong Country for HOURS now, time to head up to bed. And I hope to sleep past 5 a.m.! ♥S

Guestbook Comment: Tuesday, December 7, 2010 5:29 AM, CST
YAY for you!!! We are SO happy for you and your family!!! You keep kicking ass Shelly!!! You are one strong lady! Jen S

Tuesday, December 7, 2010 5:32 AM, CST
I slept sooooo great last night!!! I truly think that being in my own bed is helping me heal! I'm comfy and cozy and love my BED!!! I still woke up at 4:52 a.m. UGH. But was able to wake Andy up early so he could head in to work early to make up some of the hours he'll be missing. He luckily is able to take off Wednesday and Thursday to be with me in the hospital even though he is out of PTO (paid time off) and they don't offer 'vacation' there. His employer has been amazing through this all, and I just can't thank them enough. This morning is warm and quiet in the house....Andy fell asleep with me last night, and left the whole downstairs up and running (oops!) and the thermostat up. So it's nice and 70 in here now. If only the darn hallway could warm up! Ok, off to enjoy the quiet with an ice cold

117

mountain dew b4 the kids wake up! ♥S

Tuesday, December 7, 2010 11:24 AM, CST

Crazy morning....took kids to school, ran to Sheboygan, got to see
Kim my new bff lol! She just makes my day when I go there for all
kinds of medieval torture (yeah, right!) So I left smiling! ☺ "The
girls" got their 2nd fill up today...only 75cc's though...100 was too
UNCOMFORTABLE. And by uncomfortable, I mean it *hurt like a
bitch*. Now I gotta stretch out those damn chest muscles some
more.....deep breaths are now considered exercise. Ugh. I picked Lu
up from school and took her to the dentist...she has a spacer in to
keep her molars from moving around until her missing tooth comes
in (around age 12) and the damn thing BROKE OFF. There is a
spike that goes down into the gums to anchor it...and it broke. It
was stabbing her, so she got it taken out today, and they didn't even
charge me! THAT is so rare......and wonderful. Thank you!! I take
back the complaining I did about not getting in yesterday! I took
her back to school and who is in a line in front of the door?
ALAINA! I got a quick warm hug from her...my favoritest little ray
of Sunshine! I had to run Josh's lunch in to him, he forgot it, and
when I peeked in the classroom he looked like SHIT. He teared up
and said he wanted to come home. So I took him home with me.....
with a stern warning that he will NOT be playing outside at all today.
He was cool with that...so I know he isn't feeling good. I may cancel
PT today now..... ugh. ♥S

Tuesday, December 7, 2010 12:11 PM, CST
Perseverance is the watchword with the good news in the bag. Next is the daily grind with all you'll need to do to forage ahead. Life will not always be easy, but it will provide growth in character of which I have no doubt you will excel. I'm proud of you. Roberta

Tuesday, December 7, 2010 9:05 PM, CST
You are such an inspiration to me! I have no idea how I would be if I were in your situation, but reading your story inspires me. You have been through a lot already, more than you should have, and are enduring more procedures than a young mother can imagine. I continue to pray for you and know you will kick this cancer's ass, as you say. Way to think and stay positive! Good luck with your next surgery! You will get through it with flying colors! Katie

Tuesday, December 7, 2010 9:23 PM, CST
Oh MY. "The Girls" are ANGRY!!!! Maaaaaaaybe a bit too much saline on the right side. With every breath my under-boob hurts down by my ribs. BUT on the flip side, I'll be in the hospital tomorrow overnight with the "good" drugs ☺ so hopefully all those muscles will be stretched out by the time I am back to normal! I did end up cancelling my physical therapy appointment today...Josh was just feeling cruddy, and I did NOT want to take both sick him and tired Alaina to the clinic...I'm sure they appreciate that! Ok, off to watch Eclipse w/ the hubby! Keep us in your prayers tonight. ♥S

Wednesday, December 8, 2010 7:03 AM, CST
Thinking of you today babe! You are in my prayers. Get some rest while you are there! Love You! Jenny

Wednesday, December 8, 2010 7:18 AM, CST
I'll be thinking of you today. Just one more step towards recovery.
Hoping for a super quick recovery! Love, Kim

Wednesday, December 8, 2010 7:21 AM, CST

I gather just as much strength from my 'guestbook' on here as I
do the phone calls/cards/visits! Keep it up!!!!! Today is crazy. Josh
is still sick, so he isn't going to school today. Also his ADHD meds
are GONE (NO!!!!) and the prescription they gave us on MONDAY of a
long acting version wasn't covered by insurance. So I called and
they said they'd have the doc call me back. WELL, of COURSE she
was off yesterday. SO now, before I go to the hospital, we need to
pick up the script, fill it, and get it to him. HOW??????? Today is
my hysterectomy. I will finally have my uterus, ovaries and cervix
removed. My fallopian tubes were removed a few years ago. Pray
for great results, and that there is no cancer found. My sister
Sandi is watching the kids for us-GOOD LUCK SCHNEIDER'S! PRAY
FOR THEM! Haha! ♥S

Wednesday, December 8, 2010 11:50 AM, CST
The sun comes up and the sun goes down and the world keeps
turning round and round. I think you're making every moment
count in these days. Good for you! Just keep holding on to the
brass ring. Roberta

Wednesday, December 8, 2010 3:15 PM, CST
...prayed surgery went well, can't wait to hear that it did! I'm glad
you will be able to get some good sleep today maybe they can send
you home with some morphine. You are strong, hang in there!!!
Love ya, Joey

Wednesday, December 8, 2010 3:21 PM, CST
Hi Shelly, Hope your surgery went well today, it's one less obstacle you will have to face. Praying for you. Take care of yourself; hopefully I will get to visit you next week. Love, Judy K.

Wednesday, December 8, 2010 10:31 PM, CST
Update from Andy.....Shelly is doing *well*. She was able to get up and walk to the bathroom twice with little problems. She has some discomfort from the air pumped into her abdomen during her surgery. I figure a couple of good farts and she'll be good to go. Just kidding Shell! She was able to eat dinner without feeling sick to her stomach. She was feeling well enough to flip me the bird and yell at me a couple times. She should be getting out sometime tomorrow, probably around lunch time. Thanks everyone for your well wishes and prayers. ~Andy

Thursday, December 9, 2010 6:58 PM, CST
Josh went to school yesterday thank goodness. I got home from the hospital at about 11:45 am, just in time to get my little Sunshine off the bus. ☺ She was sooo happy to see me! Love that smile of hers. The *Biggs* on the other hand...played outside in the snow with the neighbors for the longest time.....but now that it's time to come in and do homework and supper----holy beasties. I am S-O-R-E. My stomach feels like I'm in labor...even though it's probably just the gas they fill you up with during surgery. I'm finally uterus free! The surgery went very well, and there was nothing scary in there that they could see off the bat. Everything is being sent off to pathology.....let's keep our fingers crossed. Hoping I can sleep tonight, the Percocet doesn't seem to numb the pain so much. UGH. This is my life????? ♥S

121

(Love from my husband...)

'Hey Baby,

I know this is a shitty time for you right now, but I think it's the perfect time to tell you just how much I do love you. We have our ups and downs like any married couple; but that doesn't change the way we feel about each other. You are the one I love with all my heart and soul. I couldn't imagine what life would be like without you by my side. You are my shining star, the gravy to my mashed potatoes, the yin to my yang and every other dorky saying!

I love to see how excited you get when you get good news. I love your 'tard' laugh. I love to see you get goofy and chase the kids or scare the crap out of them! I love your sense of humor, no matter the situation. I love how your eyes sparkle as you watch the kids being goofy. I love it when you get riled up/annoyed. I love your beautiful eyes; I have never seen eyes so striking. I love how you 'pop' one eye open to stare/glare at me when I think you're sleeping! I love your goofy sock fetish and your Chester's fetish. I love your caring heart and the joy you get out of life. I love how you text like a teenage girl!

There are so many things that I love about you but the two that stand out the most is the love you have for our children and the love we share together. You are the love of my life and my partner. So, no matter how shitty things seem with the whole cancer situation, know that I am and ALWAYS will be right by your side and together we will get you through this and we will grow to be old farts together.

I love you.
Your Hubster,
Andrew Jones'

**(when Andy and I were dating, he would sign EVERY card with his last name as well-LOL-as if I had dozens of 'Andrew's' in my life!!

122

Guestbook Comment: Thursday, December 9, 2010 9:44 AM, CST
Hi, Shelly! Thinking of you always and praying for you! I really
appreciate the call from Andy yesterday after your surgery. Even
though my head feels like it's ready to explode, I couldn't stop
worrying about you until I had word from him. Hope you are feeling
a little better each day. As soon as I am feeling better, call on me
for ANYTHING you may need. Even if it's just to get the kids out
of the house for an hour or two so you can rest. Davis and
Miranda are available, too. They tell me every day they just love you
so much! It's great now they have 2 moms nagging them instead
of just me! Take care, and don't be afraid to call. By this weekend
I should be A-Okay. If you can take on cancer like a super hero,
I can take on this itty bitty cold! Love you!!!! Betsy

Guestbook Comment: Thursday, December 9, 2010 12:13 PM, CST
Glad to hear surgery went well. Still thinking of you. Let Andy know
if he needs anything to give me a call. Kim

Guestbook Comment: Thursday, December 9, 2010 8:30 PM, CST
Glad everything went well. Thinking of you and praying for a speedy
recovery. One more step in this mess is done. Keep your chin up.
We are all here if you need anything. Keep smiling babe...we love you!
Candice

Guestbook Comment: Friday, December 10, 2010 12:11 AM, CST
Shelly!! Sorry this took so long....I thought I needed a "special"
password to log onto your site!! Yeah....I'm still blonde!! Even though
this is so late in coming, I've been praying for you and the family
CONSTANTLY!!! You are SUCH a WARRIOR!! Seriously....the fact that
you keep going with such ferocity while keeping your fantastic sense
of humor is truly inspirational!! If there is ANYTHING I can do for

you, Andy, Josh, Ilyssa or LaineyBug please don't hesitate to let me know!! I'll be sending all my positive energy your way!! Love ya!! Lynn P.S. I can't believe you don't have flamingos on your site!!

<u>Guestbook Comment</u>: Friday, December 10, 2010 5:12 AM, CST
Hey Shelly, Glad to hear your surgery went well. Praying for you and your family. Jen S

<u>Guestbook Comment</u>: Friday, December 10, 2010 5:48 AM, CST
Glad you are home and everything went great! Get some rest. Love ya! Jenny

<u>Guestbook Comment</u>: Friday, December 10, 2010 11:03 AM, CST
Glad surgery went well! One more step up the road. Roberta

Friday, December 10, 2010 8:50 PM, CST
Today was mostly spent in lala land to avoid the pain, and sleeping. Dad hung out with me all day and I guess I was pretty boring! So like they say, if you can't beat 'em, join 'em! We were napping a good portion of the afternoon! My incisions are annoying at best... most of the pain is crampy; like menstrual cramps (without the UTERUS!!!) but I'm guessing that is from the gas they use to pump up your belly. It's trying to work its way out. While in the hospital I asked when I can expect the menopause symptoms to appear (since we removed both ovaries too) and they told me it'd be awhile, since my body has to use up what's in there. Awesome. I continue to be tired, weak, and sore. But my chest doesn't hurt as much when I have pain elsewhere! Good trade off? Hmmm. ♥S

<u>Guestbook Comment</u>: Friday, December 10, 2010 9:28 PM, CST
Glad to hear it went well. You are holding so strong through all of

this, you are an amazing woman. Angie G.

<u>Guestbook Comment</u>: Friday, December 10, 2010 11:01 PM, CST
Shell, so I emailed you the recipe while sitting in the hot tub but
don't know if it sent so I will do it on here becuz I will be gone for
most of day tomorrow. First of all I hope you have a baker coming
over to do it! You should be RESTING!

<u>MELTING MOMENTS</u>
2/3 cup cornstarch
1 cup flour
1 cup softened butter
1/2 cup powder sugar
1 1/2 tsp vanilla
Cream butter and powder sugar. Add vanilla and cornstarch. Drop by tsp and
bake 325 for 15 to 17 minutes. Frost when cool.

<u>Icing</u>
1/4 Cup soft butter
1 1/2 Cup powder sugar
1 Tablespoon Almond extract.
Mix together, tint with food coloring. I doubled the recipe and got 180 cookies

Enjoy girl. Love ya, Joey

Saturday, December 11, 2010 10:28 AM, CST
LOVING that my hubby took all 3 kids with him to Sheboygan to see
Santa @ the Harley store, while I enjoy the peace and quiet. I think
its nap time. ♥S

<u>Guestbook Comment</u>: Saturday, December 11, 2010 4:54 PM, CST
I guess there is peace on Earth! Enjoy!!!! mary

Saturday, December 11, 2010 9:35 PM, CST
Thanks Mary for the packages in the mail and the steady stream of
cards....I love ya. ♥S

Sunday, December 12, 2010 3:52 PM, CST
Four days POST op for this darn hysterectomy and I'm still so sore!!! WOW. My lower back is ANGRY!!! The incisions are simply irritating and luckily that is the only actual 'pain' I have from the surgery. Monday I am to be back in Sheboygan at 9 a.m. for my appointment with the genetic counselor... ♥S

Guestbook Comment: Sunday, December 12, 2010 4:53 PM, CST
Hope you are feeling better. I got your envelope in the mail; do you want them posted at both schools? I hope that all your baking turned out good-I am completely baked out! Hugs and love from snowed in me! Love, Joey

Guestbook Comment: Monday, December 13, 2010 8:05 PM, CST
Hi Shelly, just a note to say I am thinking of you. My sisters, Deb and Becky, and Mom are also praying for you. I keep them updated as to how you are doing. They are on the sidelines cheering for you to kick this. Pam

Monday, December 13, 2010 9:56 PM, CST
Can't sit at the computer very comfortably so here I am typing on my cell. lots of typos im sure but deal lol! today has been challenging. what should have started out as a quiet day turned to chaos! ♥S

Monday, December 13, 2010 10:02 PM, CST
ugh. cell phone wont let me typo more at one time. update tmrw. ♥S

Guestbook Comment: Tuesday, December 14, 2010 8:48 AM, CST
Hi Shelly, Hope you have a good day today and your pain lessens. Thinking of you! Dawn

Tuesday, December 14, 2010 2:31 PM, CST

Ok, Alaina is sleeping, and I am feeling ok enough finally to sit up at
this darn computer. I wish laptops weren't so damn expensive!!!!! I
haven't felt up to updating. Not just because I'm not a whiner....but
because when you're blah why share that right?!?!?!! So I spent the
weekend in my trusty old recliner snoozing and pain free thanks to
my good ole friend Percocet. Today I'm finally not in enough pain to
take it! Yesterday, like I started to say, was HECTIC! I had all
3 kids set up to start going to the in-school daycares ...the older
two would go in the morning until school started, then again after
school until 5:30, when Andy could pick them up. Then 'A' would go
before 4K until it starts, and ride the bus home at noon, to continue
napping with me. Wednesday she has NO 4K so she is signed up to
be at daycare all day.

Sounds like a perfect plan, right?????

Bring on Monday. It started with a 2 hour weather delay; morning
4K was completely cancelled. So now what?!?!? Andy called the big
kids' daycare, and they were still open. They could go until school
started at 10:45. BUT since Alaina had NO SCHOOL, we just kept her
home. Crazy. SO at 7:30 Andy took the big kids to school daycare.
That changed my morning a bit. I had a 9:00 appointment with the
genetic counselor in Sheboygan at the Vince. My Dad came at 8 to
pick me and Lainey up-the roads were HORRIFIC! I think we did
30 mph the whole way there. This is going to be a long few months

127

going to Sheboygan every few days for treatment!!!!! We arrived there safely and I got all checked in. Once I went in and met her, we sat down and got right to it. She informed me of all the percentages, statistics, options, etc. Basically she just needs to inform me before I do the BRCA genetic test. I have to sign consent and go over pricing....$3,350 for ONE blood test! We are not sure if my insurance will be covering it-it is no longer a medically necessary test since I had both of my chesticles removed along with my uterus and ovaries. I already reduced my risk of ovarian and breast cancer as much as I could! We're going to try to run it through the insurance company...and hope it goes thru. Tomorrow I will hear from the lab out in Utah either way-they call if my portion is anything over $325. Then I have to set up payment, or pay over the phone, or cancel. Of course I won't cancel. I'd like to know the results for my daughters, sister, & nieces. Basically if I'm BRCA1 positive, my sis probably won't be. Hopefully that's the end of the 'cancer' line. But she can still get tested if she'd like; her insurance will have to cover it-but then it'll only be about 1/10th of the price....because then they can test for only the one gene that I am positive for. After that we did the blood draw and the 3 of us headed home. When I got home the phone was ringing....it was the big kids' daycare... yikes! She let me know the kids did really well, and had a nice time....but she was surprised to see them. I was blindsided...I asked why? She explained that when we had set up our day care days and hours, that she had let me know that the morning group was too full to allow our kids, but afternoon was no problem. OOPS!!!!!! I apologized profusely...I guess I just got all mixed up between that day care; Alaina's daycare. She could only go in the morning, not afternoon, and they could go afternoon, and not in the morning....I dunno. I have so much going on, I think I'm just losing it. So today I drove them to school (I know I know, I'm not supposed to drive for another week but couldn't find anyone else last minute). We kept Alaina home, and will just send her a full day on Wednesdays. Ugh so much to orchestrate! I'm hoping by having all 3 kids set up to be in day care every Wednesday til 5:30 that can be my chemo day. Otherwise I just have to scramble around finding care for the kids. Miranda came over yesterday after school THANK GOD!!!!!! I just had to sleep! I could no longer watch Alaina- she was hell on wheels all day, and didn't wanna nap. ☹

Guestbook Comment: Tuesday, December 14, 2010 3:04 PM, CST
I'm ready for a nap just reading that......sounds like you could use a personal assistant! Stacey K.

Tuesday, December 14, 2010 5:38 PM, CST
Can I just say how GRATEFUL I am to Miranda and Davis????
These girls come over and help cheer me up telling me stupid and hilarious stories of their childhoods!!! They help clean, straighten up, fold laundry, haul stuff upstairs, and vacuum. They load the dishwasher, play with Alaina, and make me laugh.
THANK YOU ladies ♥S

Guestbook Comment: Tuesday, December 14, 2010 9:35 PM, EST
Hey Shell, thinkin' of you every day, wishing I could help you and the family out. I see your requests and it just annoys me that I am so darn busy getting my kids all over the place. Keep asking people though...I am sure I am not the only one who has these thoughts. As for those Christmas cookies, could I help out there? I am a baking fool lately anyways. LMK, Ann

Tuesday, December 14, 2010 11:53 PM, CST
This Weeks' Top 10 List:

10. Thank God for the internet.
9. Christmas decorations/Christmas trees make the house sooo much more warm and cozy and comfortable.
8. My 2 older kids went to bed without much of a hitch tonight ☺
7. Good night kisses from my 4 year old are magical (and she's great at wiping tears.)
6. Friends that come over just to sit and stare at the TV with you are about the best friends a girl can have.
5. The kids are enjoying the daycare center. But bitch about going.
4. Fairy Godmothers DO exist.
3. I've been getting a steady stream of cards in the mail...and that _really_ brightens my day while I am on "house arrest" (hint hint...KEEP IT UP!!!)
2. Christmas cookies from anonymous coworkers make EVERYTHING better.
1. I have slept on my SIDE for 2 nights in a ROW!!! WAHOO!!!! (But I still miss tummy sleep though!) See...I can find good things in my day! ♥S

Guestbook Comment: Wednesday, December 15, 2010 11:00 AM, CST
Hi Shelly, we're off today to San Juan Capistrano to meet my cousin on my mom's side...one of only two. We've lived far apart as adults but have that instant connection when we get together. She's an R.N. and teacher. I'll share your story with her; she may have some insights into life interrupted with the "big C". Hope today is a restful day. Roberta

Wednesday, December 15, 2010 2:11 AM, CST
Our heating element went out on our stove tonight (in the middle of a batch of Christmas cookies!) So any Christmas cookies that show up at my house are ALWAYS welcome lol. ☺ ♥S

Wednesday, December 15, 2010 6:41 PM, CST
I spent the morning running errands with my Dad and then we went out to eat at Tiffany's Waldo café YUUUUMMMMMMMMM. I went to get the heating element for the stove that was $60!!! I also did some retail therapy... Christmas shopping, stocking stuffers, crafty shit...you name it, I bought it! Then we had Pizza Hut for supper (whoa tummy☺). Too much junk food today! And I did it!!! I haven't napped at ALL today!!! Here's hoping I can sleep tonight! ♥S

<u>Guestbook Comment:</u> Wednesday, December 15, 2010 9:09 PM, CST
Hi Shell, You are a busy, busy bee lately!! I'm glad that you are getting out and about, I can't believe after just one week from a major surgery you are out and about and driving. You bad bad girl lol! Miss you & the kids like crazy. Love ya, Joey

<u>Guestbook Comment:</u> Thursday, December 16, 2010 8:02 AM, CST
Good Morning Shelly! While I was driving to Falls to pick up the boys this morning, I noticed how beautiful the snow was on the trees as the sun was rising. The snow was drifting in the fields and the icicles were glistening in the sun. It was so peaceful. Just minutes before I was freezing cold getting gas and almost slipped on the ice swearing I hate winter.....lol. I hope you find something good in the bad today like I did! Have a good day Shelly! Stacey K

<u>Guestbook Comment:</u> Thursday, December 16, 2010 12:07 PM, CST
Hi, Babe! It was SOOO good to see you yesterday! The week I was
sick seemed extraordinarily long since I couldn't come visit. I'm
Glad you are able to find the great little things in your life that make
you smile. I don't know if I could be as strong as you. Isaiah
40:31 'But they that hope in the Lord shall renew their strength,
they shall take wings as eagles, they shall run and not be weary,
they shall walk and not faint.' So, I'm wondering if D told you how
she used to try to put things in her bellybutton. Like books? LOL!!
Please let us know if there is anything else. The Littles will be at
Larry's moms on Friday night-I may have to come pester you again
& play Legos! Bets

<u>Guestbook Comment:</u> Thursday, December 16, 2010 12:43 PM, CST
The Isaiah 40:31 reference Betsy W. quoted below was a favorite of
your Great grandma Bertha Jaquette Phillips. She wrote it in my
autograph book when I was a child. Finding good things in each day
is a great focus. It makes for happy memories for everyone. R.

Friday, December 17, 2010 12:48 PM, CST
We had the kids' Christmas concert last night at the high school...we
ended up sitting in the balcony. The VERY top row. Not that I
care...but SOME people aren't all 100% healthy...and most definitely can't
do stairs that well yet--MAYBE all the 100% healthy people could
mosey THEIR asses UP......so that us people could sit down on the
ground floor-and not do 150 stairs!!!! The concert went WELL and
even after a rocky week with Josh getting the boot out of music
class....he did AMAZING! A little talking, but he WAS NOT the only
one! Ilyssa spent more time giggling & chatting lol! Great concert,
Mrs. Scudella! You brought back great memories of my elementary
school years! ♥

Guestbook Comment: Friday, December 17, 2010 8:22 PM, CST
Hey Shell! Parkview had an awesome Family night tonight. I would have sooooo made you go with us. They had Santa there who gave us a book mark to pick up a free book; they had arts and crafts (bookmarks) they had reading with the DOGS (yes 3 real ones that are trained-super cool!) A station to write Santa a letter, decorate your own cookie, play a game on the smart board, listen to Christmas stories and last but certainly not least....EAT free pizza, salad, fresh fruit, fresh veggies, stuffed bread sticks with cheese and juice boxes and chocolate milk. Yes, my love for food is the same! The teachers asked about you and are still praying for you. Hang in there girl... love and miss you. Love, Joey

Guestbook Comment: Saturday, December 18, 2010 5:50 AM, CST
Hi...haven't talked to you for a while. Miss you! Sounds like you are up and about which doesn't surprise me at all! Mike is doing ok. He is only working half days because he is so tired and still not feeling great. He is done with the belly shots and now just on Coumadin. The dr. took him off the antibiotic early because it was making him feel yucky. Did more blood work- his liver tests came back high. Don't know why. Rechecked them and they are even higher. He is scheduled for an ultrasound on Monday to see if that will tell us anything. Other than that I've been trying to get ready for Christmas. Stay strong, you inspire me every single day! Love You & Miss You! Jenny

Guestbook Comment: Saturday, December 18, 2010 1:48 PM, EST
Well....I am just glad you were able to go to the concert and enjoy it and still find the humor of all the "little" things the kids do during the big concert. Jack never looks like he is actually moving his lips, he

looks wooden while singing, but I try not to say anything, cuz he is so proud of himself. So are we! Ann

Sunday, December 19, 2010 8:16 AM, CST

Got to spend time shopping yesterday w/ my hubster...ALONE!! (Well, if you don't count the other 500 people in the store!) We got most of our Christmas shopping DONE! Woo hoo! Ran into some old friends in the process.....it was really nice to see them and see how fast their kids are growing! Unfortunately the day ended with a BLINDING headache for me....and I spent the rest of the day in the recliner. ☹ That'll teach me to 'forget' to take my meds.....Just when I am feeling a *bit* better.....I gotta take two steps back. Tomorrow is 'the day' I meet with the oncologist at the Vince Lombardi Cancer Clinic. It's set up as a consult, so I would assume since he's been on vacation for a few weeks that we'll go over the results from my CT and BONE scans (which again were C-L-E-A-R!) Yahhhoooooey! My guess is we will also be setting up my chemo schedule. That's what he told us @ our appointment in November anyway. I hope and pray I can have them push back chemotherapy until Christmas is done. I could give a crap about New Years'...I'm not a big party animal. I just want to be able to enjoy my kids this holiday. I'm gonna try to fit in another 'fill' this week. I skipped out last week since I just had the hysterectomy....I figured that was enough pain for one week. I'm missing me some Kim though....so I need to get in there for a good laugh!!! I also need to get my butt in gear and call to schedule physical therapy for my arms. Not everyone 'gets' why I need this...I've had to explain it a few times. When I had my surgery that pulled and messed up all my muscles across my chest and in my armpits. Also, when they removed the lymph nodes under my right arm there was internal issues and

134

trauma, causing tightness and pain. I've spent the last 5 weeks trying *not* to put my arms up and over and/or around. The first few weeks were a struggle with getting my shirt on and off and showering....now I'm pretty self-sufficient I guess. I still have to wear loose t-shirts and a sweater that closes in the front so I can get it all on myself. Showering still sucks, I have to duck my head down to wash my hair, and FORGET sleeping with my arms up....I have to sleep like a dead person.....flat on my back, arms straight down....may as well put a rose on my chest lol. I'd probably look like Dracula! I've lost a lot of muscle, range of motion and strength... SO.... considering my job requires me to have actual arm strength and mobility (I decorate cakes for a living- including wedding cakes) I better get my ass in PT...so that I can get outta this damn house!!!!!! I know my work buddy Sarah is missing me! ☹ Andy and I are going to the meeting today for the planning of the BB benefit....and it may seem strange...but I had NIGHTMARES about it all night long! I dreamed we had the actual 'benefit' in the garage like a rummage sale, no one showed; it was disorganized, and I stepped in dog shit. Not cool. Andy didn't show up to the 'garage sale benefit' so we called and called, and he was still in bed sleeping-- and said he'd be "right there" to help haul my scrapbooks outta the garage....and never showed. He went back to sleep. Grrrr. (Now Bets, you KNOW this is not me doubting you-just my irrational fears creeping through my drugged up haze lol!) Betsy has strong-armed me once again into going to this next meeting and I told her how WEIRD I felt about going... uncomfortable, and, I dunno, greedy. But we'll be there to see everyone which I'm EXCITED AS HELL about!!! I haven't seen any of them in over a month!! It'll be fun. Dad's following us to Kiel so he can find his way....and Kasie will be watching the kids for an hour so we can have some peace and quiet. Ahhh. ♥S

Guestbook Comment: Sunday, December 19, 2010 2:25 PM, CST
MERRY CHRISTMAS SHELLY TO YOU AND YOUR FAMILY. I AM
OFF THE WEEK AFTER CHRISTMAS. 26Th to 31st. I WILL CALL
YOU TO SEE IF YOU ARE UP FOR COMPANY. PAM

Guestbook Comment: Sunday, December 19, 2010 5:27 PM, CST
It is raining in Paradise (aka CALIFORNIA) and it is predicted for
a week- must be liquid sunshine or something. I know snow and cold
is the alternative...hope this is a great day for you and the family. Six
days until Christmas. Roberta

Sunday, December 19, 2010 9:00 PM, CST
I am again BLOWN AWAY by the stamina my friends/family have
shown while planning this benefit and helping out our family! I know
I have been to a meeting or two before tonight, but DAMN! It is
so incredible! Jenny: HOLY SHIT...I am just beyond words.
Blessings to you and ALL of the employees at Kurtz!! ♥S

Guestbook Comment: Monday, December 20, 2010 2:57 PM, CST
u should check with ur cancer center.. my PT is actually part of the
cancer program...she only works with people who have cancer and
are/were going through treatment plus it's free or as my man would
say it's somewhere in the billing :p my PS hooked me up with her.
Maybe you have something different out by you but thought I'd let u
know. Lisa

Guestbook Comment: Monday, December 20, 2010 4:13 PM, CST
Hey Shell..... Hoping all is as well as can be expected. My 3 older ones
were just shoved outside to get their energy out and Marissa was in
her room for throwing a fit after she hit me with her shoe....needless
to say she got out of her room with the door shut and the gate off

the ground 3 inches, she is reminding me more and more of Lainey and Houdini.....from clothes, to shoes to escaping and EVERYTHING!!!! I was hoping for a late start tomorrow, but after I got everyone picked up from school, I am hoping that we at least have school!!!! Just wanted to say hi, and have been thinking about you every day. Love, Joey

Monday, December 20, 2010 6:32 PM, CST
I have sooo much to update, and don't feel at all like typing. I need that program where I speak and it types!!! The kids are busy playing the Wii FIT plus game we received last night as a gift from all the wonderful people at the benefit planning meeting. THANK YOU! It most definitely is something we can all benefit from! Alaina and Ilyssa have already started playing.

*A HUMONGOUS GIGANTIC MONSTROUS THANK YOU to Jenny S. and Kurtz manufacturing...All I can still say is HOLY SHIT. You really truly have no idea how much that benefits us and helps us with our medical bills! I hope I never have to return the favor, but please know I would in a HEARTBEAT!

*Betsy-you are truly a selfless person. xoxo

*Carol-you sneaky little thing you-and my money's on KIM knowing about this too! Wow. Thank you from the bottom of my heart. You are definitely making this experience easier to handle...and the holidays....thank you, VLCC.....

*Thanks to everyone helping out with the benefit, getting donations, baskets, gift cards, you name it. We really appreciate the time you are all putting into this!! ((And STOP making me freakin' CRY!!!!!))

*Thanks Kasie for watching the kiddos!

*Thanks Sandi for taking me to my appointment today!

*Thank you Uncle Rick for the fun card in the mail...I feel like that Doggie most days...and you bet your ASS I'm using this opportunity to eat anything I damn well please! Haha!

*Thanks Uncle David for bringing over the weights ☺

*THANK YOU VAL & SARGENTO R&D!!!!!!!!!!! I think you blew me away. You'll have to come over next week with Michelle...I'll bake something with my new mixer!! Love you.

*Thank You to BCBS for paying my medical bills!!! ♥S

Monday, December 20, 2010 6:43 PM, CST
The Big 'C' Update:

Met with the oncologist today. He examined my upper surgical sights and voiced that I am healing well. He then asked me if I'm ready to go on to the next step/process. "OF COURSE I AM" I said, so tomorrow (yes, I know there's crappy weather coming our way) I have to be at the hospital at 10:30 a.m. for a NOON surgery to have my port-o-cath put in. I'll be there for a few hours and head back home the same day. Yippee. Thursday I am scheduled to have an echocardiogram to make sure my ticker is in good enough shape to go through chemo. And the answer to the BIG question everyone has been asking...I will start chemo next week Wednesday the 29th at 2 p.m. It'll last maybe 3+ hours. This will be the mix of Adriamycin & Cytoxan that they nicknamed the 'Red Devil ' because it's red and makes you feel like shit. I will do that every other week for four treatments (8 weeks total) then I will do a different chemo called Taxane every other week. At the end of those 12 weeks I will be the happiest bitch you ever met. Just pray that God gets me through all these procedures and treatments. ♥S

138

Monday, December 20, 2010 6:55 PM, CST

I never heard from the insurance company about the payment for the genetic test (GOOD NEWS!!!!) So that means they're paying for it!!!! One week until I get the results! ♥S

Guestbook Comment: Monday, December 20, 2010 7:19 PM, CST
WOW. That's all I can say of everyone's generosity. You all are so giving from the very bottoms of your BIG hearts! I could never have imagined that Shelly's benefit would have grown to be what it is. It's only possible because of ALL OF YOU out there helping in every way. THANK YOU doesn't even cover it. And to all of you working on the side to make sure the Jones family has what they need-GOD BLESS YOU! This has been a remarkable experience. Shelly you are loved!! Hebrews 13:16 ...'And do not forget to do good and to share with others, for with such sacrifices God is pleased.' Betsy

Tuesday, December 21, 2010 7:58 AM, CST
Ugh. I'm sick. Effing sinuses. ♥S

Tuesday, December 21, 2010 8:12 AM, CST
Just called to see if I am still able to have surgery since I'm sick. Good news the surgery is still on!

Guestbook Comment: Tuesday, December 21, 2010 10:35 AM, CST
Just popping up to say hi. I'm delighted to read your posts and see that you are managing to do what you must and meeting each new step with humor and courage. Ah, you come from good stock. Oh, in case you haven't heard of the unusual rain in Southern CA, it has been coming down for 4 days straight; we are not floating away yet...and we have power. It's just that the solar clothesline isn't working! Roberta

Tuesday, December 21, 2010 11:03 PM, CST

Surgery went well. I was out like a light then back awake in the room within the hour. They made an incision on my chest (upper left) and inserted a central venous (CV) port to allow easier access while administering chemo and other meds. Chemo can be very hard on your veins, causing them to collapse. There is a cathedar like hose that they snake into your vena cava so that there is a direct line of meds going into the body. Once it is in, there is a small lump under the skin that you can slightly feel. After healing, there is no maintenance needed. They can also use it to do blood draws, eliminating that extra poke. During chemo appointments the nurse will swab the area with alcohol before inserting the Huber needle. The needle is attached to the tubing. Chemotherapy is administered through this tubing. The nurse flushes it with an anticoagulant medicine, such as heparin to clear the lines and dissolve any blood that has clotted. Once blood work is drawn and the chemotherapy is administered, the nurse flushes the port again and removes the needle. Right now I am sore sore sore sore sore. I once again got an Rx for Percocet....man, how do people FUNCTION on this shit?!?!??! I feel soooo drunk right now and I've been on it more than off it for the last 6 weeks; but NEVER have I felt like this before. Thankfully there was nothing eventful in the hospital (well, ONE thing with a med mix up, but no worries). One more thing crossed off my list of things to do before Christmas! ♥S

Guestbook Comment: Wednesday, December 22, 2010 11:39 AM, CST
Hi, Shelly, I hope today finds you a little less sore than yesterday. I'll call this evening to see if there is any last minute holiday "stuff"

with which we can help. Take care. I pray for you every day that God gives you the strength you need, both physically and mentally, to win this battle. Love you lots! Bets

Wednesday, December 22, 2010 1:22 PM, CST
Jesus....how much feeling like shit can one person put up with??? I can't believe it's been 6 weeks and 2 days since this hell began. It feels like I've been going through it for MONTHS. I'm sick of feeling shitty, hurting, not being able to do jack shit, and sick of not working or making money for our family. And I'm sick of staring at the 4 walls.....AND I'm sick of winter. Stepping off of my self-wallowing soapbox now. The end. ♥S

Guestbook Comment: Wednesday, December 22, 2010 2:53 PM, CST
Yeah I hear ya. We wish we could take the pain away and all that goes with it. It's too blasé to say "this too shall pass" except that it will. We've had a week of rain here 24/7! Now this afternoon clouds are breaking up and we've had 5 minutes of sunshine twice. So welcomed! Hang in there Shelly. Love you. R

Guestbook Comment: Wednesday, December 22, 2010 3:00 PM, CST
Christmas is only a couple days away.....that morning, watching the kid's open their gifts will make all the pain go away, at least for a little while! Stacey K

Guestbook Comment: Wednesday, December 22, 2010 7:32 PM, CST
You are welcome to come feel shitty here next Tuesday if you want, and I'll even come get all of you. Let me know. Love ya, Mary

Guestbook Comment: Wednesday, December 22, 2010 7:32 PM,
Thought of you all day today Shelly. I wish I could take your pain

away...hopefully you will feel up to us visiting on Sunday but if you're not, that's ok too. Merry Christmas girl! We all love you and are praying for you. Love, LOVE, love your family portraits, what a great looking family. Well besides Andy. Kidding! Merry Christmas, Candice

Guestbook Comment: Wednesday, December 22, 2010 8:36 PM, EST
You are right Shelly....about it all! The frustration of the whole thing is enough to try the patience of anyone! Hopefully, watching your children enjoy Christmas will help alleviate the negative at least for a couple moments. ♥ Ann

Thursday, December 23, 2010 2:57 PM, CST

My un-lucky rabbit's foot is still working. ☹ I went in today for the echocardiogram (an ultrasound on your heart) which *should* have been just easy peasy. Of course it wasn't. Having tissue expanders threw it all for a loop. She couldn't see what she needed to...unless she CRAMMED the Doppler into my 'under-incision' from my mastectomy. And by cram I mean 'what-the-fuck-do-you-think-you're-doing?????' She then decides that she needs to try using a shot of 'contrast'. Oh, and by the way, we can't put it in through my brand new shiny PORT. That's too close to my heart. We have to start an IV in my hand; get the contrast in and flowing and then re-CRAM that Doppler into my boob pit. Which *still* does not help. She is unable to get the image that she wants, so she tries going from above the TE. Which is exactly where the incision is for my new port. OWWwwwww. At long last she throws in the towel, telling me that she isn't sure she got anything that was useful. Grrr. I didn't cry. I was very proud of myself! But I did want to. Is everything from now on going to be painful and suck????? It also doesn't help that I am eternally exhausted. I can't sleep. As in

AT ALL. I feel like a little kid on Christmas Eve EVERY NIGHT. I am anxious and just can't calm myself. Sigh. ♥S

Guestbook Comment: Friday, December 24, 2010 11:38 AM, CST
I wish I could take away the pain for u. My heart aches for you. I'll say some stronger prayers and believe He'll hear them. I know that it's hard to have faith at a time like this, but God is listening. My favorite verse is: Faith is being sure of what we hope for and certain of what we do not see. Hebrews 11:1 Honey, please try to have a wonderful Christmas. Let the joy in the kid's faces lift u up. Luv, Kathy

Friday, December 24, 2010 11:44 AM, CST
Christmas Eve!
THANKS Gentine's
THANKS Sargento R & D
THANKS Val ☺
THANKS Mary
THANKS Shirley L.
THANKS Parkview SCHOOL
THANKS Sipple's!!!!
Thanks to you also, Jenny & Joey.....sure miss you two. ♥S

Friday, December 24, 2010 6:17 PM, CST
Thanks Toni ☺ A nice relaxing day at home while the kids drive us nuts and I nap! Yay for the Holidays! ♥S

Friday, December 24, 2010 8:27 PM, CST
I may be fighting cancer, but my children are happy and HEALTHY and ANXIOUS for that fat man to show! They're curious though-- since we don't have a fireplace this year, where will he come in?!?!?!

Ho ho ho.....happy holidays to you all...Christ the Savior is Born.... ♥S

<u>Guestbook Comment</u>: Friday, December 24, 2010 8:45 PM, CST
Oh Shell I too wish I could take the pain from you for a day or
maybe two? I am not nearly as strong as you to take it for much
more. You are dealing with all this crap and for you to say anything
remotely positive just reminds me why I am so blessed to call you
my friend! Wishing you and your family the BEST EVER Christmas!!!!
Because of you, I have so much more to be thankful for! Love ya
lots and Miss you TONS!!!! Joey

<u>Guestbook Comment</u>: Saturday, December 25, 2010 5:54 AM, CST
A very Merry Christmas from Rick and Jordan to Shelly, Andy and
their wonderful family. Richard

<u>Guestbook Comment</u>: Saturday, December 25, 2010 8:33 PM, CST
Merry Christmas to you and your family. We hope you had a
wonderful day filled with laughs, presents and lots of food. Praying
for you and your family. Love ya- Jen s.

<u>Guestbook Comment</u>: Saturday, December 25, 2010 8:57 PM, CST
Hi how are you doing? Thinking of you and hoping I have time to
come to your benefit on Saturday. Talk to you later. Bette

Saturday, December 25, 2010 10:50 PM, CST
Merry Christmas!!!! The kids woke up at a NORMAL time this year---
last year was 3 a.m. This year was 6 a.m. Whew! By about 6:20 I
was awake enough to harass Andy awake and headed down to set up
the video camera. I like to get the 'shot' of their faces when they
first see the tree full of Santa's treasures! By about 7 we were
rolling along pretty well! Everyone took turns and waited 'sort of'

144

patiently. We were all wowed by everything all the SECRET SANTA'S sent over, dropped off and snuck in-between our doors. Ilyssa's BIG surprise? A Nintendo DS....she'd been asking for one for TWO years. After I had already bought one, a gentleman Andy works with said "really? My daughter has one and she doesn't use it....want it?" So now we have 2...but shhhh...that's still a surprise. We gave her the one we bought on eBay and 7 games altogether! SHE WAS BLOWN AWAY!! Josh's big gift was a Lego Star Wars M-TT ship full of droids ☺ He kept saying "you guys did NOT! You did NOT!!!!" Ohhhh YES we did!!! Andy found it at SVDP for EIGHT DOLLARS this summer!!!!!!! What a steal! It sells for $216 online! We're only missing about 6 pieces. Thankfully we can go on to Lego.com and have those sent to us for FREE! Wahoo!! Alaina's big deal was the Go-Go and Me white puppy that walks and yips. She LOVED it! I am so thankful that I am able to spend another Christmas with my family. Lulu just showed up crying with a tummy ache. Ugh. Signing off for tonight. Andy & Lainey are sleeping. Back to MOM duty. ♥S

Sunday, December 26, 2010 5:08 AM, CST
It ended up being a harder holiday than I thought it would be. Emotionally.....my own mortality HIT ME like a ton of bricks. Maybe it's the menopause, maybe it's the fact that I didn't take any pain meds so I wouldn't sleep the whole day away.....maybe it's just the fact that I'm a realist-and I do realize that this may very well be my last Christmas. No one knows which way things will pan out. My health could tank. I could get in a car accident.... you name it. This breast cancer wasn't caught 'early' and it is still a cancer. I could die from this. Wow. Just saying that out loud is insane. Now don't get me wrong, I'm not one to wallow...to feel sorry for 'poor me' and succumb to this. But again, in MY head I know this year may

145

be the *last* of many things-holidays, birthdays, vacations, teacher's conferences, you name it.

It really HIT me.

That's all I'm sayin'. We had a nice Christmas at my sisters'. The kids were all good and played nice. Dad got his suspenders snapped by Alaina a few times and he even liked his "TOUGH GUYS WEAR PINK" T-shirt that I made him! I made ones for the kids too...my girls and my nieces got pink tees that said 'Wearin' PINK for my Mommy/Aunt Shelly!' I made them by making an image on line of a peace sign made out of flowers. Then there was an image of a stick girl on there, of course wearing a pink ribbon! I made Andy one too...it was pink and said Tough Guys Wear Pink. ☺

Even though I was in a ton of pain from my port surgery and everything else, I made it through the day with only some crying.

Guestbook Comment: Sunday, December 26, 2010 7:36 AM, CST
Merry Christmas my friend. I know everyone says this to you, but I'm going to say it too...I too wish I could take some of this burden and pain from you. For some reason you are the "one" that has to go thru all of this, but know that you are not alone. Even though I may not be there with you or talk to you every day PLEASE know that you are in my thoughts and prayers EVERY single day! It sounds like the kids had an awesome Christmas. Mine did too. Natalie and Emilie got a Nintendo DS to share and they LOVE it! Mike and I play it too when they go to bed. HEHEHE! They all got pillow pets. Steph got fur real penguins and puppies that make noise. Rocky got cars, cars, and cars! He loves them. Take care, my dear friend. Love you and miss you! Jenny

Monday, December 27, 2010 6:54 AM, CST
T-minus 2 days.....let's get the ball ROLLING already! ♥S

<u>Guestbook Comment:</u> Monday, December 27, 2010 7:09 AM, CST
I tried rolling the ball, but it didn't budge!   Not til Wednesday. Love
Ya! Jenny

Monday, December 27, 2010 9:16 PM, CST
Got my genetic testing back.....
*BRCA 1 NEGATIVE.
*BRCA 2 NEGATIVE.
********WTF!!!!!!!!!

Such a history of cancers...yet no mutations? She advised me that
it's possible that the technology just hasn't advanced to the point
where they can 'find' my mutation...such as 5 years ago you could
have been negative, but now would be positive.....better testing, better
technology. So what's this mean?? Nothing. For me nothing
changes regardless.

Sandi will have a harder time getting services for her to get
checked frequently enough...and possibly not ever get this.

As for my daughters...they'll need to technically start being tested at
age 25 (10 years younger than I am now) BUT on a side note-I
can guarantee they'll be diligent sooner than that. Like age 18. If I
have anything to do with it!!! SO. More knowledge that is good.
Ish. ♥S

Monday, December 27, 2010 9:21 PM, CST
...should've added that the genetic counselor chick is BLOWN AWAY

that I have no mutations......she was 99.9% sure I had BRCA 1
mutation. But like I said, maybe they just haven't 'found' the
technology. ♥S

<u>Guestbook Comment</u>: Monday, December 27, 2010 10:12 PM, CST
Hi Shelly, Glad to learn of the good reports from the tests. Take it
for what it is and be thankful for now. Sounds like your children
had an awesome Christmas. All the best, R.

<u>Guestbook Comment</u>: Monday, December 27, 2010 10:24 PM, CST
Glad to see the goodish news, not that I understand any of it, to
me it's a foreign language. I am slowly understanding bits and
pieces and I am learning more talking to my now 2 high school
friends who have parents with cancer. Praying and thinking of you
daily! Love and Hugs. Joey

Tuesday, December 28, 2010 3:24 PM, CST
I just made the call to the Doc to see if I can get some sleep
meds. I'm sick of not sleeping! It's my FAVORITE activity!
Tomorrow is the big day....my first chemo ☹

<u>Guestbook Comment</u>: Tuesday, December 28, 2010 10:42 PM, CST
Sweet dreams tonight; sleep well. R

<u>Guestbook Comment</u>: Wednesday, December 29, 2010 5:57 AM, CST
I hope today goes by quick and smooth for you. Sending extra
prayers and positive thoughts your way. Don't be afwaid!!! Sarah

<u>Guestbook Comment</u>: Wednesday, December 29, 2010 6:10 AM, CST
Stay strong today like always...I will be thinking of you...Love Ya!
Jenny

Wednesday, December 29, 2010 6:12 AM, CST

Word to the wise: take Ambien while already in bed all comfy cozy...
'cause otherwise you'll fall right over! I slept like the dead for the
first time in 7 weeks. Yahooooo!! I spent some MUCH needed time
'out' with Sarah last night....only a true friend knows how much you
need ice cream when it's still 24 degrees out lol! Brrrrrrr... but
so yummy! I tried a strawberry CheeseQuake blizzard--delish!
Sorry Betsy-I wasn't screening my calls...I just was not home!
Hoping to talk today. Looking forward to Melissa coming over to visit
today and trying to keep my mind off what I have to do today. ♥S

Guestbook Comment: Wednesday, December 29, 2010 12:28 PM, CST
Thinking of you. Roberta

Guestbook Comment: Wednesday, December 29, 2010 10:45 PM, CST
Thought of you all day today. Hoping it went well for you. Are you
feeling up to a cut tomorrow? Kim

Guestbook Comment: Thursday, December 30, 2010 9:14 AM, CST
Hi Shelly, I am so sorry, I had no idea you were going thru this!!! I
got the info for your benefit in my son's Friday folder last week. I
look forward to seeing you there. I want to tell you a story... 1 yr.
ago today my cousin (age 29?) was diagnosed with stage 4 Hodgkin's
Lymphoma. Today she is in remission...SHE BEAT IT... I know you
can too. I have read many of your journal entries, and you have
already been so amazingly strong. My thanks goes out to your
friends and family who are helping you so much, and especially to
Andy. You are very lucky to have such a wonderful husband. I
want you to know you are in my thoughts and prayers! I will keep
reading your entries, thank you so much for posting them. Jen B

Thursday, December 30, 2010 11:25 AM, CST

Ok. Day 1 after Treatment 1: Yesterday I went in for my first treatment at 2 p.m. I had the initial blood draw done to see where my blood counts are at. Then they made sure my heart function test came back ok. (I did chemo, so I assume it did??) She used my port for the first time ever-what a horrific nightmare. ☹ It was the most horrendous pain EVER. I don't think any words that I type could EVER describe it. The RN told me that some people have no problem with it-that it doesn't hurt them in the least. Then she said that others are almost hypersensitive there, hurting more than it should. And by God, which one do you think I ended up being???? It sure couldn't have helped that I just had the port put in a few days ago-so that whole area was sore. The needle they use is HUGE and felt like someone was stabbing me with an awl. I then got hooked up to the pre-bag-fluids, anti-nausea meds and got 2 shots in my port IV to relax me, and swallowed a Benadryl. The first chemo drug was the Adriamycin-the bright red one that makes you pee orange (lol). She administered it through 3 tube-like syringes into my port IV (the medicine looked like frozen juice pops) then talked to us more about what to expect, what to look "forward" to...etc. Also when I should take my anti-nausea meds. One of the anti-nausea meds I was given is Emend. I need to take one the morning after chemo, and one again the following morning. Studies have shown that the combination of Emend with this chemo regime basically eliminates all nausea complaints (WOOOO HOOOO) so it's very important to follow through with meds. I am actually NOT a good medicine taker--I always forget!!! I'll have to get a watch that has an alarm! Maybe even a digital one so I can read it thru my Percocet haze. Then I was given a bag of Mesna (SP?) to protect my bladder. Chemo is notoriously tough on your soft tissues....from your lips all the way through your stomach, intestines, and you can

150

imagine where it all exits when flushed out......so I have to try to drink 1+ gallons of water a day to keep flushing that crap outta me (thanks for the heads up Rick!!) Then I had an IV bag of the 2nd chemo drug-Cytoxan-that lasted about an hour. Then more Mesna... protecting that bladder. I had to wait another 1/2 hour or so to finish off the pre-bagged fluids and then got to go home. We made a quick stop at Walgreens to pick up my 3 anti-nausea meds. One was the previously mentioned Emend (1 pill for each of the 2 days after chemo) that cost $899.90-that's for 8 pills total for the whole chemo schedule!! Then I got Zofran to take as needed @ $39.99... and then Compazine $499.99. (More than I make in 2 months!!!!) Thank God my insurance out of pocket is MAXED out, and I had to pay ZERO!!!! Once we got home, I was woozy. I think it's from the Benadryl. That always makes me feel loopy. I like to think it wasn't from the toxic chemicals they poured into my body!!! I headed up to bed early and slept it off. ALL THREE KIDS WOKE UP WITH GROWING PAINS LAST NIGHT A MILLION TIMES---UGH! This morning we woke up LATE...and rush rush off to the Dr.'s office to have my one week follow up from my port surgery. He said all looks good. Then at 10 back to Vince Lombardi Cancer Clinic to get my Neulasta shot--the shot I will have every 'day after' chemo to force my body into mass producing white blood cells. (**EACH** shot cost $6,870-over $1000 more than my whole chemo treatment.) Shot me right in the belly! It was that or the back of my arm, and the Oncology nurse said the belly hurts LESS. I was on it! Then sat there for 15 minutes to make sure I wasn't going to have any side effects/reactions to the shot, and off we went! Sandi was nice enough to drive me and stay in the van with the kids to keep them outta my hair! It's getting harder to find sitters because everyone's getting sick...and I can't have that come here. ☹ Right now I feel ok. No nausea, no tiredness outside the normal 'Mom-of-3' tiredness.

Josh is at a play date-THANK GOD!!!!! And another friend is taking the kids out -n about later at 3:00. Good day! ♥S

Guestbook Comment: Thursday, December 30, 2010 12:13 PM, CST
Glad to hear things are going good so far, you look good! I'm happy to take Josh off your hands for a few hours, but he might not be allowed back here...he's already showing Alex where to buy even more Legos online!!! Hahaha. We'll talk soon, love ya!! Sarah

Guestbook Comment: Thursday, December 30, 2010 1:35 PM, CST
Stay strong! Thinking of you! Hugs! Jenny

Guestbook Comment: Thursday, December 30, 2010 1:57 PM, CST
WOW lots of info!!!! Like always you have it all understood to a perfect T!! Glad you aren't feeling sick! Hang in there girl. Love, Hugs and Prayers sent your way. Holding my breath so you don't get my son's flu! Love Joey

Guestbook Comment: Friday, December 31, 2010 5:07 AM, CST
Hi...5:05 a.m. Friday...can't sleep...hope you are! I hope you are feeling as good as you can for what you are going thru. Wishing you a Happy New Year's Eve! Joey and I are planning on coming on Tuesday with the 3 baskets. Take care of yourself! Love Ya...Jenny

Friday, December 31, 2010 7:56 AM, CST
Day 2 after treatment 1: I woke up early, not feeling nauseous YET. I took my Zofran early, to try to 'stay off' the ick feeling. Then I made t-shirts for all my friends' kids this morning for the benefit. ☺ I made a cute image on the computer that I printed on iron-on paper. Thanks to Hobby Lobby and their cheap $5 t-shirts! They said 'Wearin' PINK for Shelly!' Just like the ones I made for

my kids for Christmas. I can't believe this year is coming to a close.....what a roller coaster. We have sold our house in Horicon, moved back to Plymouth, and it seems I've been in and out of the hospital all year! First with stomach issues....ended up being GERD, and Barrett's esophagus, (permanent damage to the cells in my esophagus) then I threw my back out 3 times, and now THIS?!?! I'm NEVER sick!!! WTF!!!! I can count on one hand how many times I've had to go to the hospital:

1. I was born.
2-4. Having all 3 kids.
5. Tubal and D & C.

This year...I quadrupled that number! UGH!
Happy Holiday...and here's to a waaaayyy better 2011! ♥S

Guestbook Comment: Friday, December 31, 2010 2:26 PM, CST
Have a wonderful New Year's Eve. Let HOPE for the New Year flood your soul. Roberta

Saturday, January 1, 2011 2:44 PM, CST
Day 3 post chemo: Zofran definitely helps more than Compazine. I've been feeling seasick all day but if that's the worst...no biggie! ♥S

Guestbook Comment: Sunday, January 2, 2011 8:40 AM, CST
Good Morning Shelly, Hope you don't get sick from your chemo. Looking forward to seeing you on January 8th. Thanks for the family picture that you sent me. I pray that 2011 will be a much healthier year for you. You will make it thru this and then it will be clear sailing for you. Love Judy k

Sunday, January 2, 2011 9:58 AM, CST
With your positive attitude still strong you are AMAZING!!!! Can't
wait to see you this week! Joanna

Sunday, January 2, 2011 10:28 AM, CST
Good morning Shelly, hope you are feeling better! I will be bringing
the "crew" (girls from work and Danny) with me on Saturday. Can't
wait to see you! I know it will be a great success! Keep on smiling
girl. We could use directions if you have an address or we could
just drive around Sheboygan and Plymouth until we find you. (We'll
have Danny with us. It could be entertaining!! lol) See ya soon! Annie

Sunday, January 2, 2011 12:59 PM, CST
DIRECTIONS to the benefit: from pretty much anywhere...
Hwy 23 to Plymouth.
Hwy 67 SOUTH into Plymouth
67 goes into town. When 67 turns to the left, go straight ahead and
you will come to a stop sign at the rail road tracks. Stop, and then
go straight. The very next stop sign (1 block) is a 4 way
stop. TURN RIGHT. (There should be a gas station on your left)
The building on the right is the building it is in. The building is divided
into 3 parts. The first is a restaurant called Antoinette's, the second
part is a bar called Antonio's, and the 3rd part is the banquet hall
called Amore'. The benefit is at Amore'; parking is available in a lot
across the street and on the street itself. ♥S

Sunday, January 2, 2011 7:08 PM, CST
Day 4 post treatment 1: Candice picked up ALL THREE KIDS at
8:30 this morning and KEPT THEM ALL FREAKIN' DAY!!!! Wooohooo!
Andy & I had some quiet time....did wash, did dishes, paid bills...you
know, all that stuff that screams "quality time". We slept on the

couch and did a whole lot of nothing after lunch. ☺

Everyone is asking how I am feeling? Well, better than I thought I would, that's for SURE. I am still queasy (on a good day) and every smell is nasty-every movement makes me nauseous, and being awake is boring. BUT. I am not throwing up, not in pain, not getting my ass kicked. YET. So suck lemons, CANCER. ☺ ♥S

Sunday, January 2, 2011 7:11 PM, CST
p.s. holy shit the Benefit is SIX days away.

Monday, January 3, 2011 10:25 AM, CST
Day 5 post treatment 1: Feeling fantabulous TODAY!!!! Weak, but ravishingly HUNGRY. I think I spent $75 on junk food at the Pig. LMAO J/K...got juice and stuff too...Maybe the fact that the kids are all GONE has something to do with it?!?! I need an extracurricular activity to keep me busy while I feel like this! Sleep doesn't count! Must be all the steroids. ♥S

Guestbook Comment: Monday, January 3, 2011 10:55 AM, CST
Loved talking to you this morning. Every time I talk to you it makes me miss you even more and makes me love being in your life even more! Can't wait till Saturday. Enjoy your day before the kiddos get home! Talk to you soon! I'm signing off...Love Ya, Jenny

Guestbook Comment: Monday, January 3, 2011 7:03 PM, CST
I would be careful what you ask for-you know Jerry does live in Plymouth. Lol! Maybe I should bring you over my pictures and albums and have you put together the kid's alphabet albums I am never going to get to. What would you charge for something like that? Mary

155

Tuesday, January 4, 2011 10:54 AM, CST

Day 6 Post Treatment 1: First ill effect from chemo: (ok, besides the fatigue) I just zipped my jacket and tore 4 of my nails. (just by then running up against the metal zipper.) I even have strengthener on.....and they ripped into the quick. YOWCH. ♥S

Guestbook Comment: Tuesday, January 4, 2011 11:36 AM, CST
My nails hurt now just reading that. Glad that you are still feeling pretty good. I said a little prayer that none of your kids or my kids get sick. STAY AWAY flu!!! Hopefully my house is done with it now and your house will miss it completely. Try to get some rest today. Love ya. Hugs! Jenny

Guestbook Comment: Tuesday, January 4, 2011 11:38 AM, CST
Hope the sun's shining where you are; it is here (finally) and it does a lot for my spirits. Thinking of you. Roberta

Tuesday, January 4, 2011 12:51 PM, CST

Yes, Roberta, the sun IS shining! I do better when it's sunny too. But I'm guessing a big difference between WI sunny, and Cali sunny right now! (It's 20 degrees here!) I hope you all made it safely through the rains and minimal if ANY damage to your loved ones' home. Enjoy yourself! ♥S

Guestbook Comment: Tuesday, January 4, 2011 4:39 PM, CST
Put your arms around yourself as much as you can (I know it may hurt a little) and give yourself a little squeeze, close your eyes, smile...that is me giving you a great BIG hug. I know this sucks and it's not fair and no one understands, but I am here and love you tons! Call me anytime! Jenny

Tuesday, January 4, 2011 9:46 PM, CST
Thanks, Jenny ☺

Tuesday, January 4, 2011 9:47 PM, CST
Wish me luck tomorrow. One week after chemo & my blood draw is
early in the morning. Send me lots of healthy white blood cells &
enough platelets! Over. ♥S

<u>Guestbook Comment</u>: Wednesday, January 5, 2011 5:57 AM, CST
Here's to healthy white blood cells and enough platelets!! Hugs. Jenny

<u>Guestbook Comment</u>: Wednesday, January 5, 2011 9:40 AM, CST
Teleporting all the health you need AND have a fun time at the Triple
B Bash on Saturday. Laughter & Love cure a lot of things! Roberta

Wednesday, January 5, 2011 2:03 PM, CST
Good news and bad news this morning. Good news? I'm handling
chemo well. Bad news? My white blood count is 1.0 K/uL (thousands
per cubic milliliter =K/uL). It should be 4.2 - 11.0 K/uL. GULP. Time
to start up the antibiotics to prevent an infection! Anyone that is
coming Saturday...wash your hands religiously! PURELL PURELL
PURELL!!! I also have low hemoglobin; need more iron. I have more
tiredness. ♥S

Wednesday, January 5, 2011 2:11 PM, CST
Found out today that I need to have a MUGA scan this Monday.
What the hell is a MUGA and will I feel violated!?!?!?!? ♥S

Wednesday, January 5, 2011 10:27 PM, CST
I have to have the MUGA (Multiple Gated Acquisition) scan to re-do
the heart function test (EKG) that FAILED 2 weeks ago.

Remember? They couldn't get a good shot of my heart because the tissue expanders (fun bags) were in the way? The whole reason for these scans is to keep an eye on the functioning of my heart..... before during and after chemo. The combination of drugs being using for my chemo are hard on your heart-they're 'cardio toxic' (and toxic for the rest of me too, duh!) So essentially they will need to monitor the 'good' functions of my heart and watch for any decline. The MUGA test is another nuclear medicine visit @ the hospital. From what I've read, they remove a vial of your blood; add to it a radioactive isotope (marker) that attaches to the red blood cells, and then inject the blood back in. Once back in, the isotope emits weak gamma rays which can be detected with a special camera positioned over me. They can follow those marked cells and watch the left and right ventricles to make sure they're pumping! As the blood fills the ventricles (or chambers) of the heart, the camera picks up a clear picture of the heart's function, creating an animated image of the beating heart which is used in diagnostics.

So that is my Monday. Wednesday is back into the "Big Chair." Not only am I the only young person in there (that I have seen as of yet) BUT my feet don't even touch the stinkin' ground in there. ♥S

Thursday, January 6, 2011 7:54 AM, CST
In need of some good, encouraging words in my guestbook today ☹

Guestbook Comment: Thursday, January 6, 2011 8:09 AM, CST
You are a beautiful and STRONG person. I have never witnessed such a determined and strong woman. It is inspiring to know you even more so being related to you! Hang in there! We all love you!
Karen

Guestbook Comment: Thursday, January 6, 2011 8:13 AM, CST
Um...let's see...good encouraging words...you are an amazing, strong, funny, beautiful, wonderful, kind, caring, super, loving, human being! I hope that these words make you smile and make you feel better. I have Roo and Jacob here because Joey has a chiro apt. and dentist appt. Lucky me! Actually they are playing good right now. Wish you were here so you could sit around with me because that is exactly what I am doing today...sitting around! Can't wait until Saturday. Call me if you need me I'm always here anytime! Love You! Jenny

Guestbook Comment: Thursday, January 6, 2011 8:45 AM, CST
Hi Shelly, just wanted to say hi. Looking forward to the benefit on Saturday! So is my son, he kinda knows your kids. He recognized them in the picture for the benefit. I explained it to him and he is looking forward to going too. I know you will have a GREAT turnout. You are such an amazing person, you have so many friends   See You Saturday!!! Jennifer B.

Guestbook Comment: Thursday, January 6, 2011 9:58 AM, CST
Hmmmmmmm... Life as Seen from the Big Chair: you could write a book; you are writing a book! What insights you are getting from us old people. Old is good. We like old. We want you to experience old! We have a friend, Jill, a young friend who developed a rare and aggressive cancer in 1985. She would NOT give in. Many treatments, many surgeries later when all of us who knew and loved her, thought it was impossible to go on, and time she let go, Jill had the determination to carry on. To go for one more treatment option. The frosting on the cake is Jill won! Five years later she threw a grand party for the doctors, nurses, caretakers and friends who had helped her through the treatments, and returned to the joy of her life: teaching children in the classroom. Stay strong

159

and determined. Your future is unfolding; this is part of your journey. Keep notes while you're in the Big Chair. You have lots to share with your world. Love you. Roberta

Guestbook Comment: Thursday, January 6, 2011 11:37 AM, CST ((SHELLY)) there is a virtual hug. Wish I was closer to give you a REAL hug!!! Please know I am praying for you and BELIEVING that you are going to get through all of us! Love you Charity

Guestbook Comment: Thursday, January 6, 2011 6:42 PM, CST Thinking of you always! I never stop praying for you either! Sending you lots of love and lots of hugs! You are an AMAZING STRONG WOMAN! And DON'T EVER forget that! Can't wait to see you on Saturday!! Jen

Guestbook Comment: Thursday, January 6, 2011 8:57 PM, CST Here is my attempt at making you giggle: what do you call a nun with a washing machine on her head? Sister Matic
What do you call a vampire that can lift up cars? Jackula
How does Posh Spice keep her husband under control?
He's at her Beckham call!
What do you call medicine for horses? Cough Stirrup
What do you call a Roman emperor with the flu? Julius Sneezer
What do you call a woman who throws her bills in the fire?
Bernadette
Love ya, Mary R.

Guestbook Comment: Thursday, January 6, 2011 10:30 PM, EST Hey Shell, hope you are doing well today and have better blood counts. We are looking forward to the party on Saturday. I am bringing my kids and hopefully my husband. We are all healthy which I know is important right now!!   I don't know about you, but I miss Christmas vacation already. Even though my kids were whining about being bored last week, I missed them all week, while I was at work. Super busy, this week. Teacher in-service's and lots of lesson planning and of course teaching. Our county-wide art show starts in a month at the John Michael Kohler Art Center, so I have to prep and matte work from 2 schools for the show. It's lots of fun and I know that Plymouth shows in the exhibit as well. Maybe it would be a fun outing for you in a month or so. I think the opening is the end of Feb or March. I am rambling here, cuz I figured you would like to read something. Another pal I have (that is a BC veteran) suggested that instead of always asking how you are, I should share about my day too. I hope that sounds OK to you...it almost feels selfish to go on about my day??? See you Saturday! Ann

Thursday, January 6, 2011 9:35 PM, CST
Hey there!!!! I'm sending a virtual hug your way. You're one strong beautiful woman. Don't ever forget that! I'm looking forward to seeing you on Saturday. Sleep tight sunshine, tomorrow's a new day. Kim

Friday, January 7, 2011 5:08 PM, CST
...massive headache alllll day. Can't function. Sorry I didn't call, Kate, I'm not feeling up to it. ☹

Friday, January 7, 2011 5:58 AM, CST
Good morning Shelly...I have to say that I am so proud of the way you have taken charge of your fight against your cancer. It's hard to stay focused on what your medical team is telling you to do while at the same time raising a family. I think you have been doing a fantastic job at both!! I am very proud of you. From one cancer

patient to another...hang in there, niece, it only gets better! Richard

<u>Guestbook Comment</u>: Friday, January 7, 2011 12:13 PM, CST
Hey Babe...can't wait until tomorrow! I'm so excited to see you! Hope
that today is better than yesterday and tomorrow even better and
as each passing day comes and goes they get better and better!
That is a major run on sentence, but who cares. Jenny

<u>Guestbook Comment</u>: Friday, January 7, 2011 12:47 PM, CST
Shelly, you have people all over praying for you right this very
minute. Open your heart and let it all in. Love & light Sheri

<u>Guestbook Comment</u>: Friday, January 7, 2011 8:38 PM, CST
Keep your chin up girl. We are all pulling for you and we all love you.
Hope your headache goes away. We will see ya Manana! Candice

Friday, January 7, 2011 9:40 PM, CST
Ok, so here's what I found out works for (part) of my triple
headache......the sinus-ey part of the headache went away when I
boiled some hot water with peppermint extract in it for 15 minutes
and turned the fan above the burner on turbo. WOOO HOOO! Called
the doctors' office about my headaches....they didn't call me back
after an hour and a half, so I called them back (5 p.m. was coming
up quick!) I was told to take Tylenol and maybe have a caffeinated
soda in case it was a caffeine headache.

REALLY. I hadn't thought of either of those in the last **FIVE
FUCKING DAYS THAT MY BRAIN WAS SWELLING OUT OF MY
SKULL!!!!!!!**
>>>>breathe in.....breathe out.....breathe in.....breathe out.....<<<<
"Um," I tell her, "I have tried that the last 2 days. I have been

162

drinking Mountain Dew the last 24 hours also-no relief." She asks if I have thought of trying ibuprofen. (See my statement above!!!) >>>>breathe in.....breathe out.....breathe in.....breathe out<<<< "YES. The previous 3 days I have used that. No relief."

Then she suggests I call my primary physician.
"ARRGGGGGGGGGGHHHHHH!!!!!!!!!!!!"
If I could reach through the phone and strangle someone-THIS WOULD BE THAT POINT. (No offense ma'am, it's not personal but pretty soon my brain is going to explode out of my skull and start dripping OUT OF MY EARS!!!!!!!!!! GIVE ME SOMETHING!) "Ok", I declare; teeth clenched and blood boiling. "I will do that." At this point it's 4:15 p.m.; I'm SURE they're not busy on a Friday night....and I'm also sure they will be PROMPT in calling me back. Eh hem. I call the wonderful nurse and she tells me I should ask my oncologist. Again, I have to use all my superpowers to not scream into the phone "I DID!!!!!!!!!" She tells me she has to talk to the doctor, and get back to me. I stress that I have **brain pain**; that this is *important*; please do not let me fall through the cracks and not get back to me. I am reassured that they will call me back. Tonight. We all know the clinic closes at 5, riiiiight? At 5:45 p.m. they call back-WHEW-and I am told to go ahead and take the oxycodone (Percocet) that I have at home to relieve it. Ah, FUCK IT. I give up. I am in so much pain I could CRY at this point.....and I did. I have of course tried taking that too-it didn't work. THAT'S WHY I AM CALLING. BECAUSE WHAT I HAVE AT MY DISPOSAL IS NOT FREAKING WORKING! I AM FAIRLY **BRIGHT** AND IF THE SHIT I HAVE DID WORK, I WOULD *BE* TAKING IT EVERY FOUR HOURS ON THE DOT-NOT CALLING EVERY FUCKING HEALTHCARE WORKER I HAVE EVER COME

IN CONTACT WITH TRYING TO FIND OUT HOW TO MAKE MY HEADACHE GO AWAY!!

AAARRRGGHHH!!!!!!!!!!!!

Ok.

>>>>breathe in.....breathe out.....breathe in.....breathe out.....<<<<

Since I haven't taken any oxycodone since 12 p.m., I open the bottle and try another (since my sinus-ey type headache went away with the yummy Dr. McGillicudy smell ☺) And-go figure-you should have seen this coming-there are only 2 left. If I wasn't a week away from being bald, I would RIP MY FUCKING HAIR OUT. Narcotics are not something you can just get a refill on...I need the Doc to give me a paper with the Rx on and physically take it to the pharm. The Rx I have is from my surgery to put in my port-- totally different doctor--so I can't get THEM to give me more.

"So, GOD, if you're reading my boring yet thoroughly entertaining blog on here...REALLY?!?!?!? Can you just throw me a bone FOR ONCE and let me wake up tomorrow HEADACHE-FREE so I can enjoy life for a brief day and go to my Better Boobie Benefit and absorb the love and support from my family and friends?!?!?! Then I promise I will go back to being sickly and boring and stationary *first* thing Sunday morning. I don't feel that is too much to ask. Oh-and if you really ARE listening...maybe not just no headache; maybe no aches, pains, or anything else...just a good flippin day."

Stepping off my soapbox. ♥S

<u>Guestbook Comment</u>: Saturday, January 8, 2011 1:20 AM, CST
Wish so desperately I could help you, Shelly! If only it were adhd
meds you needed I could fix you right up! Lol! Get some rest
(easy for me to say, I know) and hopefully all the positive energy
from today will at least help heal your soul. Love ya! Mary

<u>Guestbook Comment</u>: Saturday, January 8, 2011 6:25 AM, CST
I hope that God heard you yesterday and you wake up pain free
today. Keep fighting sista. Prayin' for you every day. Jen

<u>Guestbook Comment</u>: Saturday, January 8, 2011 6:48 AM, CST
Today is ALL about you! I hope you woke up headache free and you
are ready to party like a rockstar! So many people are praying for
you and are amazed at how you are already kicking cancer's ass!!
We'll see you in a little while. Enjoy your day-sit back and relax and
let the fun begin! Love ya babe! Sarah

<u>Guestbook Comment</u>: Saturday, January 8, 2011 6:54 AM, CST
Hoping my prayers for you today made your headache go away!
Can't wait to see you my beautiful friend...I miss you so much and
my kids are so excited to see your kids. I told Jacob he can see
his girlfriend today and he said Alaina isn't my girlfriend with a big
smile on his face! Love ya girl see you in a few hours! Love Joey

<u>Guestbook Comment</u>: Saturday, January 8, 2011 8:10 AM, CST
Hoping you woke up headache free today. I can't wait to see you
today! Kim

<u>Guestbook Comment</u>: Saturday, January 8, 2011 8:30 AM, CST
Hey Shelly I am going to try and make it today. Mike is in Boston
for a funeral and you know how it is with carting kids around. Cole

has a tourney in FDL today but I'm going to bust out early. I hope GOD heard you and you feel better today. Kate

Saturday, January 8, 2011 8:47 AM, CST
Hell, yeah, it's gonna be a good day. I think I'm ready!   Bring on the Better Boobie Benefit!!! ♥S

§§§ I walked into Amore nervous and afraid. I was overwhelmed with such a range of emotions! It was very humbling, realizing that so much effort, time, goods and services were brought to this place- this event-to help me out. My family. There were close to 50 people organizing the 'Better Boobie Benefit' for us. Never in my life (aside from my wedding) have I felt so much LOVE!! Once I stopped shaking and got over my nerves I was excited! I had just gone through two months of hell and could NOT wait to see all my friends. I love a good party!!! I felt exhilarated being there surrounded by pink balloons, pink flowers, family and friends sporting pink ribbons. Right when I walked in the door, the first person I saw was my old friend Kim, with her daughter Emberli. I have known Kim since I was 6 years old. Now she lives over an hour and a half away and made a trip HERE for OUR BENEFIT! I was so overwhelmed-again-and honored. Her familiar smiling face made all my butterflies go away. I was absolutely HONORED that she would even come. I don't believe I have even seen her once since I graduated in 1993. After hugging her and playing with her little girl I started looking around and noticing the details! There were tables and tables and tables of donated silent auction items! There were pink ribbons at the sign in table. Pink confetti, pink balloons, everyone was wearing shirts that said Save 2nd Base!. The Sheboygan County Motorcycle Club was outside cooking. Volunteers were frying, selling, mingling, organizing, selling raffle tickets. There

166

were goods for sale-some handmade, some home-made. There was a H-U-G=E bake sale. There was a table set up for Mary Kay facials. There was a DJ, Karaoke and a band. And there were PEOPLE. Lots and lots of PEOPLE!!!! Per my request there was Purell everywhere and I had to wear a mask all day to keep the germs away; I had just had my first round of chemo 10 days prior. Luckily I still had my hair at this point. It took another week to fall out. I had been really sick the week leading up to the benefit-so in truth I didn't really know how I'd feel-or if I could even go. I had been having some very intense headaches. God continues to work in mysterious ways because that day I had NO HEADACHES and felt great. I truly felt that the anticipation of seeing everyone and their hard work come to fruition made my body snap out of the funk it was in! I got to walk around the whole day hugging everyone and talking to them. I still cannot believe the crazy amount of items donated by people and businesses in our community. Did I mention the crazy amounts of PEOPLE there?!?!?? And it was not just Plymouth that jumped in to help....cities and towns throughout all of Sheboygan county rallied together to donate. And possibly beyond! Even today, months later, I don't know everybody who donated. It was A LOT!! I had been invited to one of the benefit planning meetings and got to hear some of the major goodies! There were bucket raffles, giveaways, raffle items, you name it!

I made my way around the room quite a few times-taking it all in-seeing who was all there. At the end of the day-around 4:30 p.m. the bartenders estimated attendance to be around 1200!! The place was steadily packed all day! What a blessing it is to be back in this community ! Dear Plymouth, I love you ☺ ♪♪♪

I know I've been slacking on blogging BUT it's been a rough day. Emotionally, physically, and mentally. Emotionally I am so *unbelievably* humbled by the outcome of the 'Better Boobie Benefit'. Roughly 1200 people were there throughout the day!! They sold all the raffle items/ silent auction items. If you weren't there, it was INCREDIBLE! The crew had received so many donations from area businesses and people! You name it, they had it-food, clothing, movies, jewelry, booze, gift cards, EVERYTHING! They blew through the t-shirts they had made that said 'Save Second Base'. The DJ and band was a great success, as was the bake sale! It feels fantastic to be a part of a community that comes together for such an event! Just about everything was donated, so the planning committee could keep their costs down. I had so much fun watching the kids run around, people watching, reliving memories with others, sitting and visiting with people, eating, and smiling. I cannot believe how many people from the PHS class of 1993 were there! It was really cool. There were family members there, and classmates' parents, family friends of my parents, and coworkers of mine, Sandi's, Andy's, Dad's, etc! Coworkers of the planning committee members'. Strangers. People from my medical treatment team. WOW. I played with my kids and nieces, met some people that knew me when I was young. Sat and talked serious with ex-coworkers; described some of my treatments. I had to wear a mask for most of the day. I did not want to pick up anyone's germs. After a while I took it off for photos, so I looked less like the Unabomber. I had tears in my eyes when I sat up at the bar, receiving gifts, and cards, and advice from everyone. I have no words to describe the day. Love and Light.

Guestbook Comment: Saturday, January 8, 2011 3:22 PM, CST WOW...is all I can say! All of the people that put the benefit together did an AMAZING job! I'm so glad that I got to see you and talk with you for a while. It was nice to put a face with all of the names. Everyone that was involved "thank you" for loving Shelly the way that you ALL do! Jenny

Guestbook Comment: Saturday, January 8, 2011 6:40 PM, CST
I was so overwhelmed with the turnout for the benefit, I can only imagine how you were feeling about it. I am so grateful for everyone that showed support for you and the cause today! We love you. Karen

Guestbook Comment: Saturday, January 8, 2011 8:14 PM, CST
I just want to thank you for letting me be a part of your life. We are all so blessed to be able to call you our friend. Your supports system is all because of YOU!!!!! You are a wonderful woman and for that I am a better person knowing you. The benefit blew my mind! It was so crowded, but I wouldn't have wished it any other way. The people who organized this whole thing did a fantastic job. I had a wonderful time, only knowing my sister and her family; all your friends and family made me feel at home. Best of luck to you and your family...take some medicine and get to bed you have got to be on overload and completely exhausted! Lots of love.....Love, Joey

Saturday, January 8, 2011 8:21 PM, CST
Whew! I am still reeling from today! I am too exhausted to type or let out all my appreciation here.....but please know that it is there and THROBBING to come out, but the muscles in my WHOLE body are throbbing too. ☹ Gotta take care of myself first! I am letting in the light and love from today...and my cup runneth over. THANK YOU. And you're right. I will beat this ☺ ♥S

Saturday, January 8, 2011 8:50 PM, CST
What an awesome day today!!!! I know you felt all the love that was around you today! You have an incredible support system around you. Sleep tight my friend and we'll talk soon. Kim

Saturday, January 8, 2011 10:53 PM, CST
Hey Shelly. I had a great time at your benefit. Heidi and Molly and I have decided to do the Elkhart triathlon in your honor and raise money for breast cancer. I guess I am doing the swim again and it will be cold but it doesn't compare to anything you have been thru. I just talked to Mike in Boston and he said he was really sad he missed your benefit because he was in school with you for a long time. He would probably still be there talking to everyone because he loves to talk. Hope you had a great time at your benefit. See you Tuesday! Kate

Sunday, January 9, 2011 9:12 PM, CST
My hair is starting to hurt. ☹ From the reading I have done both online and in the binder I received from the cancer clinic a lot of people report that you can feel when your hair is about to let go. From my point of view: it feels like I had my hair in a very HIGH very TIGHT pony tail for too long. And you know that feeling you have when you FINALLY take that pony tail out? That tight tingly pain? That's what it feels like. Times 1000. No one seems to know why that happens. I think it's just your hair dying at the root. Almost time to be beautifully bald....just a few more days....

Sunday, January 9, 2011 11:19 AM, CST
What good news from your benefit! Thinking of you. Roberta

Monday, January 10, 2011 8:39 AM, CST
Good Morning Beautiful! I can't stand Mondays. Finally all 3 girls
went to school with no one being sick. Just Rocky and me for a
couple of hours. I'm not feeling very good today, but what else is
new. I hope you are feeling ok. Have a great day and call me if
you want. Love Ya! Jenny

Tuesday, January 11, 2011 5:25 AM, CST
Dear Cancer,
You have put me through HELL. For the last 71 days you have
invaded my life; messed up my family; and made me cry. I think you
are a mean spiteful bastard that doesn't realize I already have
enough on my plate. My three children are high maintenance; my life
is still in chaos from relocating to Plymouth; my husband and I enjoy
boring. BUT you have taken that nice, quiet, boring life and changed
it into a world of running and doctor appointments and nausea and
pain and drugs and worry. You have made me afraid to move, bend,
think, and leave the house. You have made me quite knowledgeable in
the terminology of all things breast cancer related. The words
'Stage 3A Invasive Ductal Carcinoma' are words I never thought
would cross my lips. You traumatized me when you reared your ugly
face at my initial mammogram ultrasound biopsy. While I was there
all alone-you became my number 1 enemy. It took everything I had
to hold it together just long enough to break the news to my
husband; my family. You made my husband panic; you made my dad
relive every second of my mother's cancer in those first few
minutes after I had to tell him. You suck. You have made me go
through the absolute hell of a double mastectomy. Pain that no one
could imagine. You made me go through the hell of drains and tissue
expanders. You have made it impossible to lie on my stomach-and
that is one of the only joys in my day. Well, it WAS anyway.

171

Asshole.   You took away my happiness; you took away a chunk of
my children's innocence.   They now are aware of your name; they
are aware of words NO CHILD should have to know....things like
mastectomy, hysterectomy, drains, incisions, ports, mammograms,
menopause, chemotherapy, radiation, and BALD.   You snuck your way
into my lymph nodes causing more extensive surgery...more scars,
more worry-a lifetime of baby-ing that arm.   You have made my
upper torso a source of stiffness and pain.   You have made me go
through a second surgery to remove all my female organs-throwing
me into early menopause, causing me MORE rage and mood swings
and pain than before.   You have scarred up my body more than the
pregnancies of THREE children ever did.   You have made me go
through medical tests/procedures that 90% of people have never
even heard of and couldn't imagine.   The pain from these procedures
is unbelievable.   UnFATHOMable.   Some of the things I have been put
through have damaged my spirit.   You have made it necessary to
have a port put in so I can receive the "lifesaving" chemo.....which is
made from MUSTARD GAS.   Seriously.   You have made me go on a
crash diet.   You have made me become a 'hat person' when I have
never worn one in my life.   You have made me become close enough
to the pharmacist that we're on a first name basis.   You have
introduced me to more medications and prescriptions than I would
ever normally put in my body.   You have humbled me to have to ask
for help from people that I barely know; people that I would never
show weakness to.   You have made me rely on others for things I
would never before do.   You have made it impossible to do certain
things for myself-simple things like get a shirt on or shower.   You
interrupt others' schedule by attacking me...making my family and
friends take time out of their day or off of work to help out.   You
made me afraid; made me feel small that first day walking into the
'chemo room'.   You took away all my bravado and self-esteem; made

me feel meek and sickly. You put me through even more pain every time they access my port. You made me shake and shiver; feel nauseous and unable to be a Mom to my children. So for all of the hell you have put me through and all of the hell yet to come all I have to say to you is "bring it."

Go ahead, bring it. See, what you DON'T know about me and what not many people know about me...is that I am a fighter. This is such a small portion of my life that this isn't going to bother me long. I may be down right now and beaten up...but my Family has my back. My Friends 'got my back'. I have this humongous support group behind me EVERY STEP OF THE WAY. They are AMAZING. You see, we had this HUGE party this past weekend, and you weren't even invited. We celebrated my fight. We brought awareness to the world about you and your evil doing and will save at least ONE life telling people to get a mammogram; to see their doctor regularly for breast exams; to do their self-exams at home in the shower or in bed. WE, cancer....are onto you. You will never take these special people away from me....we will do what we can to kick you out of our lives permanently. Some of these people have been in my life since I was 5 years old. Some of them are brand new in my life and only have popped into it because of YOU. One more thing to 'thank' you for I guess. You have brought me new friends; better friends. You have brought my existing friends closer again; closer than ever before to stand beside me and fight you. You have brought people back into my life that I haven't seen in yeeeears. Some as long as 18 years ago. You see, these people came together to support me. To cheer me up. To help me. They have started getting mammograms they have been brought together to reconnect with each other. They too are making sure that you are not part of my life for any longer than necessary. We surround ourselves with light and laughter....just to keep you out. I have reconnected with 2 amazing people through all this and the two of them have become a support system beyond ANYthing I could ever have imagined. They have helped us since day one of relocating back to Plymouth and continue to give of themselves to our family. They are selfless in that they have done everything for us-from helping us move, to cleaning our toilets when I just can't. You cancer have strengthened my relationship with my Soul Sister, Betsy. You have brought me back to having her in my daily life, and you can bet your ass I thank God every day for her. Not you. So there. You have brought my husband and I closer together than ever before. You have taught him what a Moms job entails. You have taught him patience, caring, and selflessness. You have taught him that not even YOU can keep me down. You have brought out strength in him that I'm not even sure he knew about, much less me! You have brought my love for him to the surface; shown me the exact reasons I'm glad I married him. You may sometimes bring us stress, and strain, and burden. But have you met my KiDs?!?!? You got NOTHIN' on them. They have kicked my ass on a daily basis for years in preparation to fight you. They have hardened me, made me stronger, and made me who I am today....so I can take you down. You have lifted me up to a place where God is now taking over. You have brought me to His attention and He's 'on it'. You can't go up against Him and win, cancer. Not with this chick. Bring on the chemo, the sickness, the baldness, the radiation, more surgeries....you name it. I have no other choice than to go through this, so I may as well bring my A-Game...... you know the one. The one where I beat your ass and you never come back. Fuck off and Die

♥Shelly

Guestbook Comment: Tuesday, January 11, 2011 5:52 AM, CST
Your blogs are so amazing Shelly, thank you for sharing your

174

everyday moments with us and opening our eyes to the story behind it all! You are one strong lady...and determined! You go girl! Tina

Guestbook Comment: Tuesday, January 11, 2011 6:28 AM, CST
THAT's the Shelly we know and LOVE!!!! Mary

Guestbook Comment: Tuesday, January 11, 2011 7:19 AM, CST
Right on Sister!!!! Kim

Guestbook Comment: Tuesday, January 11, 2011 7:52 AM, CST
Shelly... I just read your last journal entry. It made me cry, gave me the shivers, and I laughed at the end! You are so amazing and I love your spirit. SHELLY YOU ROCK!!! Candice

Guestbook Comment: Tuesday, January 11, 2011 8:17 AM, CST
I love you! You made me laugh, you made me cry, but DAMN RIGHT! I got your back!! You are amazing and you are going to kick this shit right back to hell from where it came! I'm on TEAM SHELLY! Betsy

Guestbook Comment: Tuesday, January 11, 2011 8:53 AM, CST
You are an amazing strong BEAUTIFUL woman! Cancer should be very very afraid of Shelly Jones because Cancer has nothing and I mean NOTHING on her!!!!! Love ya babe!!! Jenny

Guestbook Comment: Tuesday, January 11, 2011 9:40 AM, CST
I just finished reading your 'dear cancer' and I'm in tears. Not sure why, but I'm weeping at the computer. I don't think its cause of the cancer and I don't think it's sad for Shelly tears. I think its happy tears. Happy that you're so strong and determined and geared up for 'The Fight'. Happy that through everything you're

going through, you're finding the positives in every day. You are an inspiration, Shelly. And you're a very special woman. Love & light! Sheri

Guestbook Comment: Tuesday, January 11, 2011 10:23 AM, CST
WOW Shell; good girl! Roberta

Guestbook Comment: Tuesday, January 11, 2011 1:22 PM, CST
That was amazing!!! Your strength is abounding an inspiring to all who know you and are privileged enough to call you friend!! I know I am!! God willing, we KNOW you will get through this!! Love you lots!!!! Melissa

Guestbook Comment: Tuesday, January 11, 2011 11:54 AM, PST
Just read your last journal entry. YOU are so talented at writing just exactly how you feel. You can make me cry and laugh all at the same time. You can put me into your shoes, if just for a bit. You can make me feel your frustration and your will. So, along with being one of the strongest women I have even known, jeez...your writing is genius!!! Write baby write!!! Tracy

Guestbook Comment: Tuesday, January 11, 2011 11:08 PM, EST
Shelly, I love the letter! I love that you share so much with all of us, and I love that you poured all of you into it! It's amazing how much I have learned from you and your posts on FB and Caringbridge. You are right about the cancer bringing all of us closer to you! I will be thinking about you as you have your 2nd chemo treatment. I hope it goes as well as I guess it can, or at least the side effects are manageable! I know....yeah right! ann

Wednesday, January 12, 2011 12:05 PM, CST
Well, kids, today was the day I got my hair cut SHORT. As in shorter than it's ever been in my LIFE! (Except maybe when I was born.....) BUT I like it-cute and sassy and easy. Kim once again did an amazing job and I got to check out her NEW salon! Beautiful work there, Kim and Greg!!! Best of Luck! ☺ Andy is taking a half day of work and going with me to chemo #2...Blech. Not looking forward to feeling like ass for the next few days. I think it's worse THIS time because I know what to expect. ☹ But all those 'C' cells need to know who is boss, and get out or DIE!

On the way there we need to drop Andy's car off to be repaired... his passenger side wiper stopped working yesterday. Thank God it wasn't the driver's side! Hopefully Sunset Auto in Sheboygan Falls can fix us right up and on the way home we'll pick his car up. Wish me luck today @ chemo.....I'm gonna need it! ♥S

<u>Guestbook Comment</u>: Wednesday, January 12, 2011 5:38 AM, CST
Shelly, you are an amazing woman. I am on "Team Shelly" too. You go & kick ass. We are all cheering you on. Love ya girlfriend!!! Jen

<u>Guestbook Comment</u>: Wednesday, January 12, 2011 6:18 AM, CST
I will be thinking of you today and wishing I could be there with you while you do your second round of chemo. Good thoughts, prayers, and hugs coming from Horicon! Love Ya! Jenny

<u>Guestbook Comment</u>: Wednesday, January 12, 2011 6:36 AM, CST
I'm thinking of you today as you go in for chemo -you show that stuff and cancer who is the boss!!! Let me know if you need anything, we're here for you! Love ya babe! Sarah

Guestbook Comment: Wednesday, January 12, 2011 12:58 PM, CST
My thoughts and prayers are with you as you go through chemo today. Hoping you feel better than last time. You need to publish your journal into a book and make a ton of moolah! You are an excellent writer! Good luck this afternoon and post pics of your new do, can't wait to see it! Joey

Guestbook Comment: Wednesday, January 12, 2011 6:29 PM, CST
Thinking of you and hoping that you are home resting and that it is all over until next time! Love Ya Babe! Jenny

Guestbook Comment: Wednesday, January 12, 2011 10:05 PM, EST
Would love to see a pic of the new hair! Hoping all is going as well as possible post-chemo tonight! Ann

Guestbook Comment: Wednesday, January 12, 2011 10:02 PM, CST
I may be a bit biased, however your hair looks great short. I hope your appointment went as well as it could have today. Let me know if you need anything. Kim

Guestbook Comment: Thursday, January 13, 2011 6:38 AM, CST
Love your sassy new 'do! I hope that you were able to get some rest last night and that you can rest some more today. Stephanie, Rocky and I are going to Joey's today so call if you would like to chat. Keep smiling! Love Ya Babe! Jenny

Guestbook Comment: Thursday, January 13, 2011 11:06 AM, CST
Sassy is right! Got the hair cut to fit your personality! Maybe I should call it a "kick ass" hair cut instead! Praying that some of your symptoms are eased and do not last as long this time around! Love ya! Melissa

178

Thursday, January 13, 2011 6:19 PM, CST

All of my friends here are soooo encouraging! Everyone has been full of compliments; telling me I should turn this into a book. I haven't the slightest clue how to do that...besides hitting PRINT and stapling it together! And I'm too OCD to do it anyway...I'd have to go back and rewrite so much lol! I did post 2 pics on CB of my new hair cut for everyone to point and laugh at (j/k!) I hate my picture being taken even MORE than I hate having cancer! (Ok, a BIT of an exaggeration, but....well....really...it's close.) At 3 a.m. I was woken up by "Mommeeeeee....I had a pee accident..." from our 4 year old. For some reason her teeny tiny bladder just can't go all night, and she needs to wear a pull-up. BUT I went to bed early and the other parental unit (names left out to protect the *innocent* eh hem) forgot to put one on her. And would he get up to help? Heck no, he just rolled into bed an hour or so before, so he was too TIRED. UGH. Hubster of the year award is OUT THE WINDOW! HELLO??!?!? I just had chemo for God's sake? So now she's clean and warm and wearing A FRICKIN PULL- UP!!! And currently has her toe in Daddy's belly button LMAO! Payback, baby! Cancer is such a RIDICULOUS expense (my first Chemo was $4800. The Neulasta shot cost $6200. HOW is chemo cheaper than ONE shot in the belly?!?!??) And I know that this is going to be a very long process before everything is completed. Guess how much my mastectomy surgery was? $69,193.88. Hoping and praying that my cancer doesn't come back or that anyone else in my family is hit with major health concerns. My lovely friend Rachel W. once told me that her mom had cancer when she was young and she doesn't really even remember it, other than her lying on the couch all the

179

time. Rach-you have NO IDEA how good that was for me to hear! Physically the week *should* have been smooth sailing. Hmpf. ←That's mom talk for BULLSHIT. Sunday was lovely, lots of relaxing and dozing in the recliner. Dave popped in for a bit and shocked us with the totals for the Benefit. WOW. I was actually SPEECHLESS, and if you even know me AT ALL that is sooooo not me lol! Then around rolled MONDAY. MUGA scan day. I was told I could drive myself no problem and that all they were going to do was take out some blood, attach a tracer to it, then reinsert it; put me into the tube to get pictures of the functions of my heart. Sounds easy, RIGHT????? Hell no, you should know my luck better than THAT at this point. Well, first off I FORGOT THE NUMBING CREME. It's lidocaine that they gave me to apply to my port area to "numb" it so when they cram in the one inch long needle it's supposed to not hurt as much. BULLSHIT. Didn't work last time I used it so I guess nothing lost, eh? I get there right at 10 and get called in right away. I lay down so they can access my port and stick in the needle. Let's just say it's a one inch long thumb tack. Ugh. So the RN missed once. Instant bawling from me....it is one of the most excruciating things you can go through. She didn't even give me a second to recover from the pain and she crammed it in again without even letting me take in a deep breath or anything. I think it's safe to say I hate her. She missed the second time as well. This was just unbearable at this point....I was hyperventilating/crying. I told her she was NOT to touch me again without numbing me or putting me out or something. She disappeared...and they were gonna go through my arm. WHEW. It took me quite a while to calm down and catch my breath again.....and right as she was going to stick the needle into my arm the Radiology tech stopped her. While calling oncology to see if they could do it that way or not...apparently they wanted one more STAB into my chest. BUT this time they put on a

180

whole tube of lidocaine and left it sit on it for 45 minutes. As I mentioned earlier, the LIDOCAINE DOES NOT DO ANYTHING FOR ME... But they are the medical professionals so once again I put my faith in them. Stupid fucking me. I wait in nuclear medicine for the 45 minutes trying to calm down and once again lay on the table. They call an RN from the oncology floor upstairs to try the access. She tells me to 'visualize' my breathing and to close my eyes. She CRAMMED the needle into me and once again, for the third time that morning, I am in excruciating pain. Tears IMMEDIATELY spring to my eyes and the hiccup breathing that comes with it. THANK GOD AND ALL THAT IS HOLY they didn't miss this time!! I think it helped that they used a longer needle. They drew the blood and then I had to wait half an hour before they could reinsert. Thankfully putting it back in was no problem. I guess just getting the blood OUT is the sucky part! FINALLY I lay down on the table to go into the tube. There was a little glitch in the reading; the metal in the port of my tissue expander was in the way this time. UGH!!!!!! Last time the echocardiogram was inconclusive because they couldn't see around my tissue expanders. BUT they did finally get what they needed, and I got to leave the torture chamber of hell. F N A. Tuesday I went in for a fill for the first time in forever....since before my hysterectomy in early December. That went ok, just more pain by sticking huge needles in my boobie areas. The only good news is I only felt pain in the left side; my right side is still numb and has no feeling since the mastectomy. I am finally a charter member of the Itty Bitty Titty Committee. Move over, Sarah! (lol! Conway Twitty..) Wednesday was Chemo day...it was at 1:45 and ONCE AGAIN turned into hell day. (As if Monday wasn't enough fun) The nurses had used some freezy spray stuff last week when they took my blood that IMMEDIATELY numbed the skin at my port, so I requested that again. THANK GOD they used it. And it worked because I felt NOTHING the first time. NOTICE I said first time. She did not get it in the right spot⊗ so the second time she had another nurse come over to adjust the needle (keeping it in, but wiggling it around) but that didn't work. Eventually they had to take it out and cram it in again. DIDN'T FEEL A THING. Then they still couldn't get a flash of blood from it, so we had to get a longer needle, and try a THIRD time. This time they resprayed and OVER sprayed so that I wouldn't feel anything. THEY WERE WRONG. I don't know if they sprayed the wrong spot or if they over sprayed it to the point of reversing it or WHAT THE FUCK. But the third time I felt every blasted thing and was sent immediately into tears. I can NOT explain how EXCRUCIATING that pain is. Why some people don't have any pain with and some do is beyond me. Maybe because my nerves are hypersensitive since the surgery?? No clue, but I can usually handle LOTS of pain -I mean I had 3 kids with NO drugs. WTF. So needless to say, this week has been hellacious-today being my first day post chemo #2 I felt really good all day....until I woke up at 5 p.m. from my nappy-poo and felt NAUSEOUS. I had to drag my butt up to Urgent Care in Plymouth to get my day-after Neulasta shot in the belly. By the time I got home I was holding back chunks, and feeling AWFUL. I put a Zofran under my tongue (the only antinausea med that is immediate) and am now feeling better. A bit queasy and FED UP with these damn kids. BUT thank God for anti-nausea meds. Thank you to Miranda for helping with Alaina even though I had to wake your ass up to watch her while I went to get my shot! And a HUGE thank you to Mary for supper tonight, I don't think I could've handled cooking anything as nauseous as I am. My friend Sarah has set up a mealtrain.com account for us. ☺ Meal train is a site where you are able to enter information for a family or individual that you would like to help. You can enter their favorite meals, days of the week they need help (i.e. chemo night!) and what time you could drop it off. You then email all your contacts a link, they can follow it, sign up to bring a meal for the intended person, and it's a HUGE help for the family. Personally it was a LIFE SAVER for us! I have been horribly ill, have no energy, and the kids gotta eat! ♥S

Guestbook Comment: Thursday, January 13, 2011 7:40 PM, CST
Wow I love your hair!!! Awesome!! Sorry you had a crappy week at the docs!! Sending ((((hugs)))) Love ya Jen

Guestbook Comment: Thursday, January 13, 2011 7:50 PM, CST
I am so sorry for your yucky week and all the pain that you had! That is unbearable and more than any one person should have to go thru. I wish that you would never have to go thru it ever again, but you have to in order to get better. It is a good thing that you are such a strong human being. The week that you have had would have brought most of us falling to our knees, but you YOU my friend say bring it! Love Ya Babe! Jenny

Guestbook Comment: Thursday, January 13, 2011 8:21 PM, CST
OMG! All your posts are true reality calls to me. You bring me right back to reality every time. I mean seriously I was mad at fb for not working, my 9yo daughter forgetting her basketball shoes for practice & the roads were complete crap & I can go on & on....I was so crabby! You are totally amazing & I love you girl. P.S. I love the hair it totally fits you! Joey

Guestbook Comment: Thursday, January 13, 2011 10:00 PM, CST
Ok Ok I admit it when I came on here there were 3,999 visits & I wanted to be 4,000 so I closed out & came back on! Jenny *(Jen-that's why I love you!)*

Friday, January 14, 2011 1:48 AM, CST

Well, here is a new one....1 a.m. and wide awake. ☹

First I wake up to Josh bumbling around, looking for a cup of water...without having any kitchen dishes upstairs, this is a problem. So I send him down to get a cup of water. Back up he comes with a bowl of snacks, no water. LOL. That's my boy!!! THEN I wake up to Miss Alaina crawling into our bed....picture a WWF wrestler bouncing off the ropes-THAT'S how she stumbles into our bed. It felt like an invasion of GODZILLA. PLOP! She drops in between us taking us all out in her bounce. Ugh. THEN as if that isn't enough to keep me from sleeping, half an hour later, Ilyssa stumbles in, crawls into bed with us. W T F?!?!?!?!?! All of this is NOT normal around here, I think it's some sort of separation thing with these 2 girls, with me being sick. Usually I only have to fight Andy for the bed! He blissfully snored through the whole thing, while I crawled down the steps with my huge bag of meds, and a puke bucket. Now I'm watching Grey's Anatomy and blogging. HOPING my sleeping pills will kick in sooner rather than later!

Friday, January 14, 2011 7:27 AM, CST

☹ ←Super super sad face......My hair has started to fall out in huge clumps. Time to go GI Jane. Heading in to see Kim...

Guestbook Comment: Friday, January 14, 2011 7:37 AM, CST
Let me know if you need to do anything about the hair. Kim

Guestbook Comment: Friday, January 14, 2011 8:37 AM, CST
Call me if you need me! Love Ya Babe!! Jenny

Friday, January 14, 2011 9:21 AM, CST
Well. As Kim put it "that was the shortest lived hairstyle"... I went in

184

this morning and had my head shaved. Very emotional morning for me. I know, I know. I said it didn't bother me. And it doesn't, not really in the grand scheme of things. BUT I didn't sleep last night...or the last 70 nights...and I feel so gross today, with the chemo running rampant in me....that all together it made it just ONE MORE THING. And that I'm afraid pushed me over the edge. I did not look into the mirror, I did not say anything, just put my hat on, and walked out the door. I would love to know what went Kim's head after I left...I did snap a shot of my bald dome with my cell....WHOA am I gray! I still have some peach fuzz-Kim didn't dare break out the straight razor with all my sobbing and sniffling....so maybe I'll be brave and post it, and maybe I'll Photoshop it into something hilarious. Who knows? So now I'm home alone to deal with this today. And let me tell ya--NOW I know why men wear hats all the time....its DAMN cold with NO HAIR!!!!! Off to glug some tepid water. Sounds so yummy, doesn't it?!?!? ♥S

Guestbook Comment: Friday, January 14, 2011 10:19 AM, CST
Hang in there chickie. It'll be alright. I finally got so sick of what little was left of my hair that hadn't fallen out that I took a razor to my head Wednesday night! Now I am balder then manager Mark! LOL. It does take some getting used to with not having any hair but REMEMBER it WILL grow back and when it does it will be BETTER than it was before and most of the time it comes back differently! Hoping mine has some curl in it when it comes back. Plus now it's so much easier to get ready...just the dreaded 'what hat do I wear today?' LOL Lisa

Friday, January 14, 2011 1:06 PM, CST
LADIES: WHEN IS YOUR MAMMOGRAM AND DO I FREAKIN' NEED TO TAKE YOU?? Get on it. NOW. Don't make me hurt you. ♥S

Guestbook Comment: Friday, January 14, 2011 2:09 PM, CST
You are absolutely beautiful bald! You are amazing and I couldn't even imagine being in your shoes but somehow God knew you'd be strong enough to handle it and for that you are BRAVE! I know you didn't have a choice and would never have chosen this but all I can do is let you know you are awesome! Ever need to talk call me!!!! Love ya lots. Joey

Guestbook Comment: Friday, January 14, 2011 4:16 PM, CST
Personally, I think you look great. Yeah, a hat really keeps you warmer. Time to get your style on!!! Think of the money and time you'll be saving on hair care product right now. Just a quick wash and rinse, a light wax and buff, and out the door!! You're doing great. Keep nagging your sister and Karen, too!! Richard

Guestbook Comment: Saturday, January 15, 2011 6:53 AM, CST
You are beautiful Shelly. Ryan and Jake made some cookies yesterday when I was at work. We are gonna drop some off for you before we go to Carissa's. Love ya babe! Candice

Guestbook Comment: Saturday, January 15, 2011 10:03 AM, CST
Working on it....checking into cost and coverage for my age. Karen

Guestbook Comment: Saturday, January 15, 2011 3:39 PM, CST
Hey beautiful...hope that you are having a good day! Love Ya Babe! Jenny

Guestbook Comment: Saturday, January 15, 2011 5:09 PM, CST
Might want to check this out:
http://www.cleaningforareason.org/cancerpatients.html

It might be worth a try. They are in the Sheboygan area. Roberta

Saturday, January 15, 2011 6:56 PM, CST

What a horrible shitty awful craptastic day. EVERYone in my house is high maintenance today! And everyone says I'M going through MENOPAUSE! UGH! Since the moment we all woke up, we have been butting heads. I literally slept the day away. Andy and I awoke at 2:30 or so with Dad and Judy in our house. So they stayed and visited for a few hours, watching some TV, looking at the photos from the BB Benefit and playing with the kids. While they were here, Ilyssa started complaining that her EAR hurt. AGAIN. So I gave her some Motrin, and after an hour, it was STILL hurting her. Andy ended up taking her up to the clinic. Yes, ANOTHER ear infection. She had tubes put in 2 years ago, but this is her sixth one this year (since last March) so I'm not sure if they are no longer working or if something else is going on but we WILL be calling on Monday to get in with an ENT to further discuss this. SO ridiculous. During her last one the tubes were still in place so who knows. They are so painful for her and I feel so bad for her when they happen....just hoping it's a quick fix.   All my kids have a 'weird' thing. Josh can't burp. Ilyssa can't blow her nose. Alaina...well Alaina is just ALL weird!!!! LMAO!

So I keep being asked how I am feeling today....well, to be honest, not great. I am cold and achy and in PAIN. My collar bone on the left side has been aching all day, both of my legs are hurting badly, and my stomach is iffy at best. (bone pain comes from my Neulasta shot) I also have moderate to severe pain on my right side where the cancer was...right around my tissue expander. In fact it's been so bad at night that I can't even sleep. It radiates from my armpit (freaking me out about the lymph nodes...) under the expander

187

to the top of it. I guess maybe I should worry about it? But I've had so much pain the last few months that I'm kinda used to everything sucking. I have been medicating with oxycodone for the pain, and alternating nausea meds for my stomach. I still have somewhat of an appetite today, which is good. Last chemo I had NO appetite. But unfortunately my sense of taste has left the building...I can't taste much of anything. UGH. And food is one of my favvvoooorrrite things! Oh well, this too shall pass, right? Right.

How do I like being bald? I DON'T!!!! It stinks! But I am thankful that this is happening now, not in summer, because my winter hats would make me stick out like an even BIGGER sore thumb! Also I love summer...so it would be awful to be stuck inside all the time feeling yucky! The kids are more likely to be indoors in winter, so I don't have to worry about where they are and what they're doing all the time like I do in summer! But I sure do miss all the neighborhood kiddos being here playing all the time. ☹ Braunie brought me some homemade chocolate chip cookies today that he & Jacob made. Thanks!

Well, I think that's about it.....we're hiding upstairs trying to avoid the FOOTBALL game going on right now....I am so not a fan! And hopefully Andy can have some quiet time while we hang out up here. Josh is playing Lego's...Ilyssa is playing her DS...and Alaina is watching Scooby Doo in bed with me ☺ I love quiet time.....when it happens. ♥S

Guestbook Comment: Saturday, January 15, 2011 10:27 PM, EST
Surprised to see the new look when I opened your journal tonight. Did you decide to do that to kind of take matters into your own hands, since it was going to happen anyway? Sorry things are

going cruddy with the kids. I think maybe lots of negative behavior cuz of cabin fever?? My oldest has his moments too. Do you want more cookies, my kids love to bake with me, we CAN do that for you. Hey, you mentioned something to me about doing something for your kids' schools as a thank you. Teachers love food! Speaking honestly, they don't want anything back from you, just for you to get well and keep being the grade 'A' mom that you are! Let me know if you want to chat more about this. Ann

Guestbook Comment: Saturday, January 15, 2011 10:45 PM, EST
Hi Again, just read your post about chemo #2. Your descriptive writing skills are amazing. I think people are right, a book would be a good outlet for you, but, however, you are way busy already with those kiddos. Back to your post, holy ouch!!! I think you made me get it just a teensy bit when you compared it to the 3 births with no meds, hot damn that's got to be mind-blowing painful! Cole was 10lbs 2 oz and 23 inches, with no pain meds and that really frickin' hurt. Your stabbing descriptions were amazing. Your blood pressure had to be topping out just from keeping yourself from punching someone. Again, you amaze me with your ability to go thru this and go home and be a mommy and wife. I know, I know....like someone gave you a choice....Ann

Sunday, January 16, 2011 2:04 PM, CST
I wish I could throw up or something to make me feel better....I'm usually against throwing up...but I'll do ANYthing to feel better. Ugh. Feeling nasty even with an antinausea pill every 4 hours around the clock...☹

Guestbook Comment: Sunday, January 16, 2011 6:50 AM, CST
Morning babe...I'm sorry that yesterday was not such a good day.

Hopefully today will be a much better day! Steph and I are up, everyone else is still sleeping. Last night Steph said her ear hurt while I was putting her to bed...ugh! But...this morning it doesn't hurt! HIP HIP HOORAY! Poor Lulu and her ears I can't believe that. That's crazy. I think a trip to the ENT is a great idea. Today I have Sunday School to teach and then a little laying around doing nothing...I hope. Probably should look at the school stuff and make sure no one has homework before tomorrow. Well...take care and I will talk to you tomorrow. Love Ya Babe! Jenny

Guestbook Comment: Sunday, January 16, 2011 8:42 PM, CST
Hoping you feel better soon. I will send healthy vibes your way, at least so you don't feel like throwing up. I hate that feeling. I hope the kids had a better day too; when it rains it pours. Here is to an awesome MONDAY........It can only get better...right? Hang in there. Love ya, Joey

Guestbook Comment: Monday, January 17, 2011 8:10 AM, CST
Thinking of you today as always... hope your Monday is better than your Sunday. Hopefully you will at least get a little rest while the kids are at school. The girls will check on you after school. Call me if you need anything! Would you like me to look into getting you a Taser?? Betsy

Guestbook Comment: Monday, January 17, 2011 12:34 PM, CST
Every day I wish I could help you, take on some of your burden, take even just a little of your pain away, anything to ease this trial for you in any way. KNOW that I will always be here for you whatever it is whenever it is! You are in my thoughts and prayers too. I love you! Melissa

Monday, January 17, 2011 1:30 PM, CST

Ahhhh. I got to feel normal today if only for 2 hours. ☺ At 11:00 I got a bug up my ass to go to Elkhart Lake to the feed mill shops to check out the GF food selection. Not really impressed. Everything they carry that is GF I can get at Wal-Mart for 15-20% less. Oh well! The roads were not all that bad, and I rolled into Plymouth *just* in time to pick up Lainey from school. She was super surprised and so was Ilyssa who was leaving the gym when I was there! Alaina's class went to play in the fresh snow for a few minutes....and I got to chat up another Mom. Wearing a hat outside (over my BALD head) is less conspicuous when it's snowing and cold! So I got to be "just another mom"!

After school we made a pit stop at GNC--holy CHATTY CATHY working there! Everything we have and deal with, so does she. HATE people that try to "compete" with your shitty life-if you want it, it's yours.

Anyhow, thanks to Mindi's advice, we picked up some melatonin, for both me and Joshua. I'm hoping it will relax him enough so that he can drift off easier! (And me too!!!) From there we ran through the snow over to Kmart, where my stalker, Kim, was waiting for me outside the restroom LOL! She looked damn cute in her hat-maybe I CAN pull it off! Haha. Picked up the necessities....TP, garbage bags, paper towels, cookies...lol....drinking water.

Alaina and I shot through McDonald's drive through looking for a healthy lunch (stop laughing.) She wanted apple dippers and I wanted a fruit and walnut salad (yyuuuuuuummmmm......) WELL. Can I just tell you that all of the items I purchased were EXPIRED!?!?!?!?!?! The fruit and walnut salad was to be used up 3 days ago......and the apple

191

dippers 4....so what a waste of $5 and my time, and now I STILL had to make lunch. PISS ME OFF. Don't they know NOT to mess with menopausal women?!?!? Home; safe and sound, car unpacked, and snoozy............ ♥S

Guestbook Comment: Monday, January 17, 2011 3:20 PM, CST
No one's shitty life can compare with yours! You have it delivered daily to your back door by dump trucks! LOL. I know what you mean, though, about people like that always trying to one up you with their sob stories and ailments. Sigh...All I can come up with is cat puke on my carpet from time to time, so I don't even try! Sounds like you had a pretty good day otherwise. Sorry the Feed Mill was disappointing.   I had heard good things about it (but that was from someone who happens to have a lot more money than us!) Missy told me Aldi's has REALLY GOOD GF lunchmeat for CHEAP that they always carry. (Her picky hubby likes it, so it must be nummy). The manager also told her they will be expanding the GF varieties because they are so in demand. I'm sure they will be much less expensive than the Mill. Bets

Guestbook Comment: Monday, January 17, 2011 7:07 PM, CST
Glad today was a little bit better than your yesterday! I just shoveled for an hour...YUCKY! I'm so sick of winter. Tell all those people that think they have it worse to eff off!!!! It sounds like you had a busy day. Hoping that you can get some sleep & that the melatonin helps both for you & Josh! Love Ya Babe! Jenny

Guestbook Comment: Monday, January 17, 2011 7:32 PM, CST
Thinking of you. Roberta

<u>Guestbook Comment:</u> Monday, January 17, 2011 10:41 PM, EST
Ironic that you mentioned the Melatonin-and I did see the
conversation between you and Mindi on FB. We just started using
that with Jack during Christmas break and it does really work! We
tried going placebo with Jack and yes we could tell a difference.
Jack has had sleep issues cuz of having the super enlarged tonsils
and adenoids for so long that now he still doesn't know how to sleep
thru the night. A seven year old who has never made it thru the
night!! Believe me we've tried it all and we're really sick of all the
well-being "help" about getting Jack to sleep, but turns out he just has
plain old sleep disorder, which may turn into sleep apnea as he gets
older, but hoping not. So, after my long story, I hope the melatonin
works for you. Tina also gives it to her kids and swears by it.
McDonald's, they don't get much right! So many times they have
forgotten things and I have to turn the van around and go in! I
have little kids that's why I use the drive thru, so I don't have to
go in with little kids! Annoying! I hope you continue to try and have
some "fun" shopping for neat hats! Are you planning to do a wig,
sorry if that's too personal, I don't know cancer etiquette very well!!
Have a good night, luv ya! Ann

Tuesday, January 18, 2011 6:26 AM, CST

Ok, so I'm not one to hold much back on here.....but some things I
don't need you all to know. ☺ What I do like to do here is spread
the word on how SHITTY going through this is...and impress on you
that you SHOULD get a mammogram and NOW. 15 minutes; no pain,
just uncomfortable. Insurance will cover it...its preventative now, and
99% of insurances have changed to cover preventative care. And if
they don't, and you have no family history of breast cancer...STILL
push for it! Jesus! Does any of this sound like fun to you?? If I
would have ever done a self-exam or had a breast exam at any of

my physicals (I should have pushed for one) I would have caught this early, and not be one step away from death.

ANYWAY. What I wanted to share today....is the horrendous mouth sores that are caused by chemo. They showed up last night. They are on my tongue, cheeks, lips, and palette of my mouth. UGH. They make it hurt to talk, eat and drink. I am supposed to do a mouth wash of BAKING SODA and warm water. Can I just stop right here and say I would rather lick FEET than swish with that concoction??? Ugh. My gag reflex is HIGH and that just sounds fucking NASTY. Ew. I am using the Biotene mouthwash that my oncology nurse recommended; HOPING it works and gets better throughout the day. Why does it wreak havoc on your mouth? Because chemo "irritates" all your soft tissue...from your nostrils (don't blow your nose too hard, you'll get a bloody nose) to your mouth (no soda or spicy foods....it'll irritate the hell outta your mouth) to your stomach (no spicy or greasy foods) and keep away from highly acidic foods (or it will irritate any ulcers/GERD/heartburn you have and make it worse). Chemo irritates your whole GI tract. So along with every other thing in my world SUCKING during chemo now I have 'that'.

I have a super funny story to tell you about what happened after my shower this morning. You all know that I'm losing my hair. I grabbed the white fluffy towel that had just come out of the dryer (ahhhh!!!) and dried off my chrome dome. My hair's all of a 1/4" long and bristly...and after I dried off my painfully fuzzy head...I started drying off my arms. After my arms are dry I look and notice that I have little pieces of what I thought was dead skin all over...since chemo dries out THAT too...to the point of looking like a MUMMY. Well, I look closer because there is a LOT of it...and here it's all my little stubbles from my head. It rubbed off onto the towel...and I just rubbed it all over myself. Ew. Back into the shower I went to rinse off! With TWO different towels this time. Anther funny....last night I was feeling sick. Like flu type sick. Chills, sweating, stomach cramps, RUN to the bathroom, sit with a bucket in my lap....the whole FUN nine yards. For about five straight hours. (ok, this doesn't SOUND funny yet, but keep reading!) So I went upstairs to bed and Andy came up to say good night. He then proceeds to tell me that he feels bad leaving me up there all alone, especially if I'm still feeling like I'm going to puke. So then I tell him that there's nothing he can do for me anyway...it's not like I need someone to HOLD MY HAIR!! Haha. That cracked him up and he felt better ditching me up there since I had my sense of humor back. Ish. ♥

Guestbook Comment: Tuesday, January 18, 2011 8:05 AM, CST
Good Morning Beautiful...You are so damn funny! It takes someone special to see the little things and to be able to laugh at them. I'm so glad that you can because that will help you get through all of the big things that are not so funny! My hope for you today is that you feel better today than yesterday even if it's just a little! Love Ya Babe! Jenny

Guestbook Comment: Tuesday, January 18, 2011 8:14 AM, CST
Only you, Babe, could put a "funny" spin on this. You made my day. I was not feeling like coming into work today & have been sitting here with the "blahs". I just need some Shelly time I think! Hope you have an okay day. Betsy

Guestbook Comment: Tuesday, January 18, 2011 1:43 PM, CST
Shelly, yes I get my mammo every May. I would rather have this exam than the other one...get in the stir ups. (Fun fun). I tell

everyone I know to get their exams. Easy and fast. YOU ARE MY HERO. PAM

<u>Guestbook Comment:</u> Tuesday, January 18, 2011 5:30 PM, CST
Thinking of you today Shelly...as I whine like a baby about my sore throat and thinking of all the things you have to deal with on a daily basis makes me feel like a big PUSS! You are so strong girl and I love that you still have your sense of humor. Mouth sores-seriously? That just sounds painful. I guess I don't know much about side effects of chemo. Keep your chin up. Love ya. Candice

Tuesday, January 18, 2011 7:14 PM, CST
Tonight I have had to lock myself in the "office" (read BATHROOM) to get some peace and quiet. We just enjoyed a delicious supper compliments of Rick & Leah....holy yum! I just had some of the chops and some potato soup for dinner and it was all scrumptious. THEN we had the 'brilliant' idea for some quality family time.....a game of UNO. How can UNO turn into psycho family time you ask??? Just let your 4 year old 'learn' to deal (by peeking at each card first) and lay back and listen to the 8 year old and 9 year old go NUTS. SO about 10 minutes into the game and enough screaming to bring down Super Nanny....I grabbed all the cards outta every ones hands, threw them down and announced IT'S FUCKING BEDTIME! Yes, it's 7:00. No I don't care. Sent their asses in to brush their teeth and up to bed. (Except Alaina, who truthfully was not doing anything wrong and if she's upstairs when Ilyssa is in a pissy mood (haha Pissy Lissy) that just leads to more drama and screaming than I can handle. So one hour and 15 minutes after the gang came home I'm fed up with them. UGH. Sometimes being a parent is harder than it looks. ♥S

Tuesday, January 18, 2011 7:22 PM, CST

Starting tonight I am at my lowest numbers (for white count and hemoglobin. This is called the nadir.) I have to start back on antibiotics for the week. The 7-10 days after chemo are the toughest. I just get dragged down and sleepy and my legs feel like they weigh 500 pounds each....and I also have to start wearing my 'creeper' mask. So if you see me around school or the grocery store or Wal-Mart....just know that I'm not wearing it because I'm sick; I'm wearing it so I don't GET sick. Tomorrow I am excited to be taking my van in to get fixed FINALLY! The damn heater has been temperamental for the whole winter and I did buy a thermostat, but I never had a chance to get it put in...and well, then my whole world went to HELL....so we're headed over to Sunset Auto in Falls (hi Matt!!) for a tune up and to check out my heating/cooling system. Another *good* note--I got my EOB from blue cross today, and the $75,000 that was pending more information from the hospital went through and was COVERED 100%! Thank GOD for out of pocket maxes! ♥S

Guestbook Comment: Tuesday, January 18, 2011 8:40 PM, CST
I know I shouldn't laugh but heehe!!! We just had a game of Star Wars Trouble (that I won at the benefit) turn out much the same way on Sunday. He only got 20 minutes behind bars though. Hope the rest of your night went smoother. Kim

Guestbook Comment: Wednesday, January 19, 2011 6:20 AM, CST
Shelly, are there any kind of creamy Popsicles you would want? Mary

Guestbook Comment: Wednesday, January 19, 2011 6:27 PM, CST
Hi girlie, finally looked at the computer today and read your journal (way back to the 8th) keep in mind honey, it's not how you weather

the storm, but how you danced in the rain. Stay strong girl and KICK IT! Annie

Wednesday, January 19, 2011 2:23 PM, CST
It's a GOOD day! A full night's sleep really makes all the difference... Had a kick ass visit with Jen today...THANKS for visiting me ☺ Also just got the call from Sunset on my van.....YAY! Good news-just a new thermostat, and plugs, along with the tune up! VERY affordable! Time to bake the boys there some more goodies!   ♥S

Guestbook Comment: Wednesday, January 19, 2011 10:21 PM, EST
Shell, you make a story out of a normal cruddy day and make the rest of us smile, that in itself makes you a hell of a woman! I feel for your son, Asperger's is rough for the kiddo to figure out; rough for parents also to diagnose, deal with and get on the right meds. Things you all know too well. I won't pretend I know on a personal level and say things I have no idea about, I only have a teensy experience from teaching.   I have had many students struggle with all the ADHD and Asperger's combo's. The great thing for me is that many times, art is often Zennish in helping to focus. All kids are different, hope he has something that helps him too. Hope the new dosage helps! Ann

Thursday, January 20, 2011 12:02 AM, CST
Mary-I love all popsicles. Hands down.
Ann-Josh is AMAZING at art...you would be blown away at what he can draw and has drawn at such an early age. I'm hoping also that tomorrow on the new meds makes all parties involved HAPPY!! Annie.... slacker!!!! Thanks again for bringing up the bus to the benefit ☺ I hope you were able to see the pictures on FB from it. Nice ones of all of us ☺ JEN & JOEY....I don't care if you develop leprosy...your

asses better be gassing up the ghetto vans. Sandi: thanks for getting *right* on it with the doctor appointments... HUGE relief for me...lots off my mind. Karen....you too...Kim...hee hee... board games should be OVERRULED. Roberta: Thank You ☺ Rick: You too ☺ Betsy BooYa....love ya too. Hoping to feel fantastic tomorrow to call you and soak up the Betsy time. Let M know I can still pick her up if she wants! Everyone else: Love ya ♥S

Thursday, January 20, 2011 12:14 AM, CST
I am officially getting a cold. NO GOOD. Today was a fantastic day, hands down. The 2nd half of the day continued to go great. I did some retail therapy (helps all sick people!) had some quick chow from the drive thru window (B-R-E-A-D-S-T-I-C-K-S!!!) and headed home to do some redecorating. Quick supper, quiet time with the kids (a total lie) and sent them to bed. MELATONIN ROCKS! All 3 were asleep by 8:15! Yahhhoooo! THANK YOU GOD. I need any breaks I can get! ♥S

Guestbook Comment: Thursday, January 20, 2011 6:42 AM, CST
Good Morning Beautiful...the ghetto van is gassed and our leper asses will be in them shortly! Can't wait! Love Ya Babe! Jenny

Guestbook Comment: Thursday, January 20, 2011 6:52 AM, CST
We are on our way with all our sickies! We are sooo excited!! See you in a few hours!!!! Love ya joey

Guestbook Comment: Thursday, January 20, 2011 11:01 AM, CST
Retail Therapy! Love that prescription...must remember to use the term...there'll be no problem doing it! Roberta

Friday, January 21, 2011 4:40 PM, CST

Easy 'cancer' 24 hours, shitty 'Mom' 24 hours. Yesterday was awesome! Jen & Joey came up first thing in the morning and spent the day here, hanging out, and helping organize and clean and clean lol! It was awesome to see Stephanie, Jacob, Rocky, and Marissa too! Man I miss them. ☹ It was nice and relaxing and exhausting all at once! BUT once the kids were home life went nuts like *every* day the last few weeks. ♥S

Guestbook Comment: Friday, January 21, 2011 5:47 PM, CST
Had a great day yesterday with you! Just for the record, I was so excited that my girls got done early and they came home & the rest was TERRIBLE!!! I haven't had an afternoon this bad in a long long time, fight fight fight....ugh! Joanna

Guestbook Comment: Saturday, January 22, 2011 6:57 PM, CST
Hey Honey! How are you? I thought I would pass on a piece of advice from my boss. She was asking how you were doing and I told her about the mouth sores from the chemo. She said that her nurse told her to drink TONS of water the day before and the day of chemo...she said it was so hard to do but she forced herself to do it. I thought I would let you know. Miss you, I will come visit soon, ended up that I did have strep throat last week so once I know my family is not contagious we will come visit. HATE FLIPPIN WINTER! Spring please come soon so we can play outside again! Candice

Guestbook Comment: Saturday, January 22, 2011 8:32 PM, CST
Hope your head isn't too cold in this subzero weather. You may have to double up if you're going out! Hope your day was good. Lunch on the 7th sounds great. We'll work out the details as it gets closer. Have a great night. Kim

200

Guestbook Comment: Sunday, January 23, 2011 12:05 PM, CST
Hey beautiful...hope your weekend is going well. Natalie has been sick since Friday night...throwing up. She threw up all night Friday into early morning Saturday, was lying around yesterday and this morning threw up again! WTF!!! She is now lying on couch and finally drinking something. Praying that no one else gets it. She obviously won't be going to school tomorrow so if you are around this area tomorrow I probably won't see you because you do NOT want this! My head still hurts with sinus pressure-I did try the peppermint extract and water on the stove and it helped so I am going to do that now again! Well, take care of you! Love Ya Babe! Jenny

Guestbook Comment: Monday, January 24, 2011 11:10 AM, CST
Hi Shelly, I am just amazed at this site. Thank you so much for sharing it with us! You truly are amazing and strong! Your strength and courage are an inspiration for sure! Although I do not visit or call often...please know you are in my thoughts and prayers EVERYDAY! You are so loved! Now go KICK SOME ASS!!!!!! Love you! XXXX OOOOO Stacey

Guestbook Comment: Monday, January 24, 2011 9:21 PM, CST
Testing the new password; good choice. Wish I knew about this site when my mom was dealing with her cancer. Michael

Guestbook Comment: Tuesday, January 25, 2011 9:43 AM, CST
Love the new picture! That we should all look that good. Just wishing laughter in your day and sunshine on your shoulder. Roberta

Guestbook Comment: Tuesday, January 25, 2011 10:18 AM, CST
Hey beautiful...wish we could have connected while you were in the area yesterday, but with Natalie being sick there was no way. Hope

201

your day was good yesterday and that today is better! Love Ya Babe! Jenny

Tuesday, January 25, 2011 8:31 PM, CST

I know, I know, I'm slacking. But no news is good news, right? The weekend went pretty well. I had tons of energy when I woke up Sunday, but once it was gone, it was GONE. I crashed hard after lunch....sleeping for about 4 hours. Today was another 'fill' day....pump up the boobies! I had to explain this to someone today so I thought I'd go over the "new boob" process one more time: the day of my mastectomy, I immediately started the reconstruction process. They removed all 'my' tissue, and replaced it with tissue expanders. Now, if you're like me you have NO IDEA that they exist OR what they look like. They go in between your chest wall muscles and gradually they stretch the skin and muscle out to prepare for the exchange surgery. After I feel that I am "filled up" enough, I will go through another surgery to exchange the expanders out for real implants. I get to decide size (not ANDY!) and the PS will work his magic. After that they make actual nipples and areolas and stitch them into place (at a later date) and sometimes even tattoo the areolas to the color you like to match skin tone etc. Right now I am extremely uncomfortable. They put in another 75 cc's on the left side and 100 in the right. In all truth I am MORE than uncomfortable, and may be going in tomorrow morning to have some taken out. Hopefully Doc is in. Tomorrow also brings round THREE of chemo. I am completely dreading it. Not the actual chemo, or the way I feel after it for 5 days, but the stab of the port needle! I had such a horrible experience last time that I literally could cry just thinking about it. I'm hoping that icing my port area and using the numbing spray will go my way tomorrow... let's all hope. ♥S

<u>Guestbook Comment</u>: Wednesday, January 26, 2011 5:11 AM, CST
Hello gorgeous. I hope you have a wonderful day. Wishing you lots
of pain-free days and plenty of sunny days. Keep on kicking
girlfriend. Jen

<u>Guestbook Comment</u>: Wednesday, January 26, 2011 8:02 AM, CST
Hey Babe, just wanted to let you know I'm thinking of you today!!
And praying for a pain free day for you!! Sending all my love! Jen

<u>Guestbook Comment</u>: Wednesday, January 26, 2011 10:54 AM, CST
EXTRA prayers for you today. Betsy

<u>Guestbook Comment</u>: Wednesday, January 26, 2011 1:10 PM, CST
Hope you have a good day today, Shelly! Thanks again for "friending"
me! Amy

<u>Guestbook Comment</u>: Wednesday, January 26, 2011 8:28 PM, EST
Hope the chemo went as well as frickin' possible today. Port pain?
God, after looking at the picture of the port, can't they just knock
you out until after you're hooked up? I mean, I know they can't,
but that looks scarier than an epidural needle. Here's hoping your
post chemo week is smooth....er Love Ann

Thursday, January 27, 2011 9:07 AM, CST

Chemo went quicker than usual yesterday; we were done by
4:40. The port access only took ONE try THANK God and the pain
was only about 70% of the usual. I had a new nurse; she used the
spray and if she would've waited one additional minute to let it freeze
I probably wouldn't have felt anything. Didn't get sleepy this time...
boo for me. I never sleep anymore these days. Even with the
valium. Ugh. White blood count was 6.6—I guess that is a good thing—

compared to ONE! Feeling shitty today; mostly just wiped out and GI issues. Thankfully the kids are all at school, and I can be lazy until noon when Lainey gets off the bus. I have 2 episodes of Bubble Guppies DVR'd for after-lunch bribery....hoping she'll nap soon thereafter. Signing off to zone out............... ♥S

Guestbook Comment: Thursday, January 27, 2011 9:36 AM, CST
So glad that the nurse didn't miss the port, mainly for her safety! I know you have a good punch! Rest today and take it easy. Jen and I are relaxing today and watching the white stuff hit the ground...we wish you were here we could use help holding the couch down!!!! Love ya, take care, Joey

Guestbook Comment: Thursday, January 27, 2011 9:46 AM, CST
Hang in there! I don't know how you do it! You are one tough cookie!!! Try to sleep whenever you can. Amy

Guestbook Comment: Thursday, January 27, 2011 9:47 AM, CST
Hope every time is easier! Roberta

Guestbook Comment: Thursday, January 27, 2011 10:22 AM, CST
Hi, Toots, hope you're catching a good nap this morning. Right now I wish I could lay my head on my desk and take one, too. Showing up to my next meeting with drool running across my cheek and keyboard imprint on my forehead most likely is NOT a good idea, however. Thanks again for the good time the other night! I soooo needed that. It's good to escape my own zoo and visit someone else's once in a while. Can't throw peanuts to the same monkeys EVERY day! I'm so glad to hear your last chemo wasn't quite as traumatizing as the previous one. Cancer is bad enough without adding all the extra unnecessary BS. We'll get the girls over one

of these days again so Josh can have some alone time with dad. I know how Buddy tires of his sisters and wants to sell them. Has Lainey been good at meals? She has that sleepover with Miranda to look forward to! Love ya! Take care and call if you need to get out of YOUR zoo and make an ice cream run! Betsy

Guestbook Comment: Thursday, January 27, 2011 10:30 AM, CST
Glad the treatment went a bit better than last time! Sleep when you can. Have a relaxing & uneventful day. Kim

Guestbook Comment: Thursday, January 27, 2011 11:34 AM, CST
Hi Shelly, Thank you for allowing me to be here with you down, this long hard road. You are so strong; you inspire me!!!! I think you are so very cute with your new "Do" I had a dream about you the other night, I hugged you so hard, and you told me "I Won!!" We cried together & I woke up. I hope that this gives you strength, I know you're gonna be okay! I can feel it! Hang in there my friend. Many hugs & kisses... Banana

Guestbook Comment: Thursday, January 27, 2011 3:39 PM, CST
I'm glad to see your strength and sense of humor are still intact! Stay strong...I am so proud of you!!! A big hug from TX, Rick

Guestbook Comment: Thursday, January 27, 2011 3:41 PM, CST
Hey beautiful...so glad this chemo went better than the last and hope the next one is better than this one. Mike and I met with the hematologist again yesterday. Pretty much everything is the same as last time. He has to have another colonoscopy in 5 years because his polyp was precancerous. His INR was 1.48 and they want it at 2.00 before he can go off the shots. So...shots morning and night still. They also upped his Coumadin to 7mg instead of 6mg.

205

They will check blood again on Monday and hopefully it will be at 2.00 so we can stop doing the shots. July 6th he has to go off Coumadin for 3 wks. and then they will do CT scan to make sure clots are gone and do blood test to see what his number is for the Protein S deficiency and then whatever that number is we will get a permanent plan. So that's what's going on over here health wise. Get some rest! Love Ya Babe! Jenny

Guestbook Comment: Thursday, January 27, 2011 7:39 PM, CST
Hoping you are feelin' ok. Want to come and see you soon now that the strep throat has passed and I am not contagious anymore! Hope you get some sleep chica, I will call you this weekend. Candice

Thursday, January 27, 2011 7:47 PM, CST

What a loooonnnng craptastic day. I don't feel like being funny. I don't feel like entertaining you. I just feel like whining, and complaining and playing the cancer card. But I can't. I have three high maintenance kids in my house this evening (unfortunately they all belong to me) and one hubby that has a chest cold, and is whining like *he's* the one with a death sentence!!! Josh is making folding a basket of laundry into TORTURE. Alaina is raging and freaking out (dare I tell you since NOON she's been a BEAST?!?!?) and quite honestly I'm afraid to say out loud that Ilyssa is amazing tonight after last night being the beast. Thank God typing is not "speaking out loud". Everyone is taking turns pissing me and/or Andy off.... eating supper is not a ONE HOUR task. It also should not include being bitched at by me to GET UP AT THE TABLE 500 times. I'm only semi joking when I say SUPER NANNY COME ON OVER!!!!!!!!!! Feeling-wise, I feel blah today; tired and fatigued and blech. I had to go up to urgent care again today and get my Neulasta shot...had the same Uber perky lady RN. Some perky people should be smacked.

206

I'm there because I have cancer; not to listen to 'perky'. I am past the point of enjoying being home all the time. It has been 12 weeks and 3 days that I've been sitting home, bored to death. It sucks even more because it's not like I'm home with a broken leg....I can't really have a lot of visitors-I can't risk all the germs and sicknesses...I can't go anywhere or do anything, I'm too weak. I can't go back to work because with chemo every 2 weeks-I feel like shit for 6 days, then crappy for 2, then good for a few...then back to the Big Chair. I have nothing to talk about on the phone with anyone....what do you talk about when all you have going on is Cancer? B-O-R-I-N-G!!!!!!! So here I sit with a God awful tummy ache (thank you Chemo, for stopping my intestines from working) I have no energy to even get up and get a drink....I seriously am going nuts just being home alone all the damn time. Well, except for when the kids are home, then I'm going nuts because the kids are home. No win situation!

THANK GOD for meal train! Mrs. Wieneke, Alaina's WONDERFUL 4K teacher brought over a huge supper tonight!!! She and Mrs. Conlin brought chili, hard rolls, GF rolls, deli meat, cookies, carrots, cheese, chips-the whole shebang!! YUMMMMMY! THANK YOU! ♥S

Guestbook Comment: Thursday, January 27, 2011 8:06 PM, CST
Sending you positive thoughts and some REM sleep! Hope the kiddos settle down and that you have a relaxing night. Can't wait to see you again in a few weeks! Hugs & Love Kerry

Guestbook Comment: Thursday, January 27, 2011 8:53 PM, EST
Never thought I would write this to you. However, I am glad your chemo went well today, or as well as it can go. Can you request that nurse again? Maybe she has a better touch or is more patient

or something? Hope the recovery time from this one goes fast... maybe feeling stronger by the weekend? Take care, hope you sleep tonight! Ann

<u>Guestbook Comment</u>: Friday, January 28, 2011 12:34 AM, CST
Just getting a chance to sign on and it looks like a good time to do it. Headed to bed early but by 11:30 my brain is up and ready to go for another day. Just trying to get tired again so I can function in the morning. Where has this cancer crap surfaced this time? I know I should remember this stuff but it just doesn't seem to want to stick until I can get it into long term memory, yet I can't hold it long enough to get it there. Doing some reading on different cancers and comparing it with what my husband went though. Think about attending some support group when you can get out. My husband never did that but I think it would have helped. You get so used to being isolated, that it becomes more natural then you can imagine. But maybe with the kids they will get you back in the mainstream quickly. We didn't have your group around, so there is a difference but yet it is nice and interesting to see how others are coping with it all. Think of you often and the family. Sorry I'm a terrible meal planner but if you like sausage and scrambled eggs, I might fit in. Anything beyond "boiling water" can be a challenge. Take care and know that people are praying. Read the 91st Psalm often.....great protection and promises. Saralie
{*Free hugs for Betsy... *}

<u>Guestbook Comment</u>: Friday, January 28, 2011 8:29 AM, CST
I will bring din din at 6pm. I am off early today so maybe I can finally get my butt in gear and get those pictures together. Hang in there. Mary

208

Friday, January 28, 2011 8:59 PM, CST

Update on health today....today is THE BEST I have felt 2 days post chemo EVER. I had a great day...I'm betting mostly because of the SUNSHINE!! I cleaned up the house, did laundry, baked 2 loaves of GF bread, and a peach and raspberry cobbler. Yum. Mary brought over a delish supper, and we all ate until we were stuffed!!! We even got dessert....the yummiest EVER!!!! Thank God for today. I sure needed it. ♥S

Guestbook Comment: Friday, January 28, 2011 10:12 AM, CST
Sounds like your days go from one extreme to the other. Way too quiet to way too crazy. Hope you get some good time in the middle. Not much of a cook to help with the meal train but I love to read and have a ton of books. If you're interested, I could drop some off. Might help pass the time during the too quiet days. Abbie

Guestbook Comment: Friday, January 28, 2011 10:15 AM, CST
Are you a reader? Sounds to me you need a couple good reads to take you off to other places when you hit the boring times. What kind of books do you like? "The Help" by Kathryn Stoclett was a good read for me. I'm trying to get ahold of "Family Meeting" by Miles DeMott (very, very distant cousin) which sounds like it could be pretty funny. Roberta

Guestbook Comment: Friday, January 28, 2011 3:51 PM, CST
Hey beautiful...hoping that today is better than yesterday and that when the kids get home it is calm. (Yeah right.) I know how it is with kids and how crazy it is. I know that after school is the worst time of the day around here and I feel bad about that because I don't see them all day. Oh well. Have a great weekend! Love Ya Babe! Jenny

<u>Guestbook Comment</u>: Friday, January 28, 2011 9:59 PM, CST
Yay! Glad you had such a great day today!! Doing the happy dance
for you!!! ☺ Charity

<u>Guestbook Comment</u>: Saturday, January 29, 2011 12:25 AM, EST
Hey Girl! Also glad you had a better day and maybe a slightly better
one with the kiddos. I too have been lookin' at the meal train
website. I feel like it might be more manageable for me if I made
ya something freezable and then you can use it when you want. I
don't know yet. Feeling like a lousy cook for my own family lately.
Very unimaginative when it comes to cooking. My own day sucked
big time today, came home to a completely dead refrigerator. We
have a side by side and the compressor is clogged or something.
Good thing its January! Food is in totes in the garage right now.
Damn it! Have an awesome weekend, hope it doesn't snow too much!
Ann

<u>Guestbook Comment</u>: Saturday, January 29, 2011 8:12 AM, CST
Thank God for good days and sunshine! Hope it's the beginning of a
streak! Roberta

<u>Guestbook Comment</u>: Saturday, January 29, 2011 8:17 AM, CST
So happy you had a day!!!! Praying for more to be sent your way!!
Love ya!!! Jen

Saturday, January 29, 2011 8:59 PM, CST
I took the girls to see 'Tangled' tonight....very cute movie. Enjoyed
some special time with them after the drama of Andy & Josh going
to urgent care. Andy has bronchitis. Then we hit Michaels and
Target---love love the clearance RACKS!!!!! I bought bunches of

scrapbook paper for 19 cents a piece! That's GOOD! Love you all, thanks for the well wishes today, yesterday, and all week. ♥S

Guestbook Comment: Saturday, January 29, 2011 11:22 PM, CST
Glad you had a good day with your girls! ☺ Hoping tomorrow is a good day for you!!! I will try to keep my kids in a bubble so I can see you Wednesday! Love ya, Joey

Guestbook Comment: Sunday, January 30, 2011 7:16 AM, CST
Hey beautiful...so happy that you had a nice day out with your girls! Hope that today is a great day. I will see you Wednesday because we are all healthy as of now and will stay that way. I need a Shelly fix! Keep staying strong like you always do. You continue to inspire me every single day! Love Ya Babe! Jenny

Guestbook Comment: Sunday, January 30, 2011 11:28 AM, CST
Just checking in on you and glad to learn the upswing is still there. Here's to the beginning of a good week. We're promised 6 inches of snow tonight -it'll look great through the front window! Enjoy it now it will be gone before we know it! Roberta

Sunday, January 30, 2011 11:29 PM, CST
Happy ONE WEEK EARLY Birthday to my Hubster! Impromptu bday party today, since I'm feeling good ☺ Hope he likes his gifts! ♥S

Guestbook Comment: Sunday, January 30, 2011 1:38 PM, CST
Have a fun party today, Shell! Glad you are feeling good! Charity

Sunday, January 30, 2011 8:46 PM, CST
Party's over; Josh is back home from fun time with Aunt Candice; nap time was had by all; and it's BEDTIME!! Ahhhhh.....can

you feel that? Yeah, I bet you can the stars and the moon and all galaxies near and far are lining up for BEDTIME. Now if I could get them to go UPSTAIRS! The only downside to late naps. ☹ Andy had a great birthday party...we ordered DeO'Malleys pizza (thank God they offer gluten free pizza!!) since his FAVORITE-Dino's-was NOT OPEN YET. Grrrr.....It was yummy and must have gone over well... since it was GONE! The kids bought him a Mario Brothers Yahtzee game; Mommy bought him an electric razor, shaver, thing-a-ma-jig. He mentioned something about making a Bonsai bush...and I tuned out LMFAO!

Sandi brought over a huge chocolate chip cookie from Wal-Mart-even though they gave her a hassle about writing his name on it at 4 p.m. WTF??? Slackers! But they did it, and it didn't end up on Cake Wrecks haha!

Like I said, today has been a pretty good day; I was pretty sleepy all afternoon but overall felt well. And in my world a good day=good news. ♥S

Guestbook Comment: Monday, January 31, 2011 5:30 AM, CST
Hey beautiful...I'm so glad that you all had a nice day for Andy's party! HIP HIP HOORAY!! You gotta celebrate those great days so the not so great days don't seem too bad. I'm not sure I will be seeing you on Wed because have you heard about the blizzard we are going to get??? Maybe they are wrong and we won't get any. I hope not because I know you have a busy week. Well, it's 5:30 a.m., Rocky got up, but is now sleeping on the couch and no one else is up...QUIET!!! I love quiet in the morning. I think I am going to go enjoy it before everyone wakes up and is is complete crazy! Have a great day! Love Ya Babe! Jenny

Monday, January 31, 2011 8:45 AM, CST
Monday, Monday; one of the best days of the week. Snow is
staring, finally. The nightly weather report led me to believe we'd
awaken to a foot of new snow. Not so! Now we'll see what comes.
Slowly getting my new computer in order after the crash of the old
one some time ago. It has been a challenge. Fortunately I'd made a
backup of the genealogy data. Other priority projects among them
"spring" cleaning; are not even happening, yet. It will take lots of
cooperation with Richard who will actually do most of the work. With
Parkinson's, I only get weaker and slower. Very annoying but I keep
on truckin' -that's all I can do. And we do what we must, right?
Roberta

Monday, January 31, 2011 10:50 AM, CST

Dishes done (the dishwasher running still counts, right???)
Laundry started (still sitting in the washer, but it's on its way,
right???) Kitchen swept (pile of crap shoved in the corner to be
dust-panned up later.) Mail retrieved and opened and filed in the
trash accordingly. Today I received the papers from work telling
me I am OUT of FMLA time and am no longer on job-protected
leave. Now I start a personal leave, hoping to be back to work
within the NEXT 12 weeks. But not holding my breath. I have 11
weeks until I'm done with chemo. HOPEFULLY the next 'kind' of
chemo (Taxanes) will be MUCH easier on me and I can start back
slowly. I am truly hoping it will be easier on me. I know, I know,
I'm getting ahead of myself. I have one more treatment of the
A/C chemo left to get, but I'm looking for that silver lining!!! I
repeatedly am whining about how sore my insides are. It's almost
like having constipation, gas, diarrhea, flu, and pregnancy pains all at
the same time. It's unbelievably hard to explain, but everything
hurts from my teeth (grinding more than usual) to my throat all the

213

way through. When I eat, my stomach does NOT enjoy digesting.
Then, after digesting, my intestines are NOT HAPPY doing their
business...and waking up every single night 8 times to run to the
bathroom to fold over in excruciating pain...just plain sucks.

I am super happy today that the snow seems to be holding
off. Ilyssa has her ENT appointment at 2:30 in Sheboygan and
after 5 or 6 ear infections this past year I'm hoping there is
something we can do. She had tubes put in her ears while in
kindergarten; she's now in 2nd grade. They are still in place but
possibly not working? She also had her adenoids taken out back
then. Now she has started SNORING again along with the ear thing.
Thinking sinus issues? Tonsils? Who knows? But it seems to be
her week for medical stuff. Tomorrow we are going to a new
dentist in Sheboygan. She had an abscessed tooth extracted in
2007? '08? Not sure. BUT since that tooth won't grow back in
until she's 12 or so, they had to put in a spacer; consisting of a
silver cover over the tooth in front, and a flat rectangle across
her gums, then a spike going down in front of the tooth behind the
removed one. Well, that spacer fell out sometime before Christmas.
Now tomorrow I am finally finding time to get her in to have it
replaced. I'm hoping I didn't wait too long or that her teeth haven't
shifted too much. She is very self-conscious of the 'silver tooth' and
I'm hoping they can put in a new spacer without the cap on that
tooth. The pictures I have found online all show it without that,
maybe she'll be lucky and not need it again? Who knows? TTFN ♥S

Monday, January 31, 2011 11:58 PM, CST
Quick update, then off to bed ☺ Ilyssa's ENT appointment ended up
with us scheduling surgery for new vents to go in on Feb 16th. Her
last ones have finally fallen out after 2 years and 1 month. HOPING

this will cure her ear infections!!! Her tonsils look nice and small. Whew! Happy snow blowing tomorrow everyone! ♥S

Guestbook Comment: Tuesday, February 1, 2011 7:18 AM, CST
Woo hoo, I am number 5000!!! I am so a number girl and I love it!!!! Your support amazes me every day. Your new picture is absolutely BEAUTIFUL! My kids have a 2 hour delay today and are already fighting. I am going to risk getting stuck in the driveway just to take them to school. I think we are doomed Shelly, every time we plan to see each other something comes up, sick kids, broken braces, and a BLIZZARD?!?! Hope today is a good day for you I will try calling you when I get the clowns to school. They are all going outside now to shovel for me....Love you and Miss you! Glad Lulu is getting tubes in. Love, Joey

Guestbook Comment: Tuesday, February 1, 2011 8:01 AM, CST
Hey beautiful...I wanted to be the 5,000th visitor! Oh well! LOL! Two hour delay here; debating if I should take them at all, but they are driving me a bit crazy already. I think I may chance it! It is supposed to get really bad around 3-ish right when we are picking up...GREAT! Probably will not see you tomorrow! Damn blizzard! Hope you have a great day! Love Ya Babe! Jenny

Tuesday, February 1, 2011 8:27 PM, CST
After sleeping for 5 hours, waking up and having a good cry, I am FINALLY feeling better. Thank goodness. ♥S

Tuesday, February 1, 2011 10:23 PM, CST
Ilyssa's dentist appointment went great....no need to reinsert the spacer-and no cavities! Yahooo! ♥S

Tuesday, February 1, 2011 10:24 PM, CST

Huge thanks to Crickett's Answer for Cancer; Cleaning for a Reason; Angel On My Shoulder, Wilderness Lodge, Angel Wishes Camp and France Luxe. Also anyone else I have missed. Please pass this post onto others struggling with breast cancer. ♥S

Tuesday, February 1, 2011 10:24 PM, CST

Hot flashes have become a daily occurrence for the past 2 weeks. 7 p.m. sharp nightly. ☹ Right now I would strip down to my birthday suit if I could! I have been soooo fortunate with menopause symptoms since my hysterectomy in December. It's been almost 2 months and I'm still doing pretty well. I'm not sure if the mood swings are related to that or if they are related to my severe increasing depression of sitting home all the time. And really? This effing weather does NOT help!!!!! I have not had any night sweats... to date. Just the HOT HOT HOT nightly. And to be fair, that could be because I spend most of the late afternoon covered up with 2-3 blankets; wearing 2 sweatshirts; a hat. My body may just be overheating! ♥S

Tuesday, February 1, 2011 10:34 PM, CST

Some amazing things have come to fruition this week....I have been researching online for sources of assistance for all the medical bills that keep rolling in, and other areas of assistance for people like me that are going through breast cancer treatment. I'd really like to share my knowledge with you, the readers here, and if I can pay it forward to ONE person in need of help through you, I'd love to be able to do so. After checking out the following, if someone you know pops into mind, PLEASE send them the information or links I'm sharing here. (All links listed were current as of printing)

http://www.franceluxe.com/i/goodwishesscarves/GoodWishesScar ves.html
This Company out of Washington State offers ONE free silk 'It's A Wrap' head wrap to any woman going through breast cancer treatment or has lost her hair. "Our Mission is simple: to provide, free of charge, one beautiful 'It's a Wrap' or 'Good Wishes' scarf to women or children experiencing the thinning or loss of hair as a result of illness or treatment, to in some small way, ease their journey. Our goal is to provide a small bit of comfort and to share the power of positive thinking and good wishes with these individuals on their path to healing and recovery."

You are able to choose from a few different styles and they pick one of those to send you. Along with mine came a heartfelt hand-signed card by the staff there, along with a personal email from Laurie. What a wonderful company and great way to "Pay It Forward". Thank You to them. It is a comfortable, soft wrap to cover my prickly head! Nice for days when I'm 'hot-flashing'!!! There is also a little Swarovski crystal 'fairy' on it!

http://angelonmyshoulder.org/
These people are UNBELIEVABLE!! Located in St. Germain, WI, they do so many things for cancer patients and their families/caregivers! First off, they fulfill wishes for cancer victims. Amazing, huh?! When you as someone living with cancer in some form, submit either a "wish" or request that will help ease what you are going through or make life easier, they evaluate and do what they can! Our family's wish was to take a weekend trip to WI Dells once my chemo treatments are over so that my children can enjoy being kids again and try to forget about all the medical 'jargon' we deal with day in and out. On the site they mention that they have sort of a 'partnership' with the Wilderness Lodge in the Dells, so we thought that would be a wonderful idea. Last week we received email and snail mail confirmation that we were approved for a trip there once I am done with chemo. They are also paying for our gas money!! What a blessing!
http://angelonmyshoulder.org/wp-content/uploads/2012/06/AngelWingsContract2012.pdf

Other things available through this site: Camp Angel-a weekend camp for children ages 8-12 affected by cancer through loved ones (parent, sibling or grandparent) or who have experienced the loss of a loved one through cancer-free of charge. They even provide transportation there on a Coach bus.
http://angelonmyshoulder.org/programs/angel-camps-2/camp-angel/

Another camp they offer is Camp Teen Angel, for ages 13-15, for young people affected by cancer through loved ones (parent, sibling or grandparent) or who have experienced the loss of a loved one through cancer.

http://angelonmyshoulder.org/programs/angel-camps-2/camp-teen-angel/

Angel Adventures-Camp for 16- to 18-year-olds affected by cancer through a parent, sibling or grandparent, or who have recently lost a loved one through cancer. http://angelonmyshoulder.org/event/angel-adventures/

The Angel Care Retreat is designed to offer those special individuals who sacrifice (or have sacrificed) their time and energies to care for those living with cancer an opportunity to come together and learn techniques that enable them to reduce fatigue associated with physical, mental and emotional stress. The overall objective of Angel Care is to learn how to take care of you while providing the best care and support for family, friends and other loved ones living with cancer. http://angelonmyshoulder.org/programs/angel-care/

Uplifting Angels: Angel On My Shoulder created Uplifting Angels in 1995 as its very first program. In the fall and spring of the year, very special "thinking of you" deliveries are thoughtfully planned, prepared and coordinated by Mary Long, our Uplifting Angels Director. These uplifting packages are delivered to 77 hospitals and oncology clinics throughout the state to approximately 4,900 adults and 230 children. These caring gifts are lovingly designed to brighten the cancer patients' day and let them know they are thought of in a very special way. http://angelonmyshoulder.org/programs/uplifting-angels/

Guardian Angels-Those truly "above and beyond" people that are a part of the caregiving community are gratefully recognized and honored through Angel On My Shoulder's "Guardian Angel" Program. These selfless individuals give of themselves from many dimensions to support, comfort, and console those living with cancer. Anyone can be a Guardian Angel: spouse, sibling, child, family member, nurse, doctor, hospice worker, health care professional or a longtime friend. Time is not a factor. A Guardian Angel could have helped with someone's struggle with cancer, perhaps for years, or is just now joining to make that difficult battle less painful.
http://angelonmyshoulder.org/programs/guardian-angels/

Healing Angels: Healing Angels is a unique retreat custom designed for cancer survivors. It is available to those now in the recovery time frame that have finished their oncology treatments, procedures and/or surgeries and are at the gateway of physical and emotional healing. http://angelonmyshoulder.org/programs/healing-angels/

http://www.crickettsanswerforcancer.org/
A non-profit organization in Pennsylvania that was formed in memory of

Crickett Julius, who passed away in October of 2006, only four months after being diagnosed with metastatic breast cancer at the age of 39. They provide wigs, mastectomy & lymphedema products, massage, facials and other pampering services as a way to help women feel feminine and beautiful despite losing their hair and/or breasts. We again were blessed with an acceptance letter from them, offering me some Mary Kay products for my "chemo skin" which really is awful! Also, I will be receiving some of the 'pampering' activities; a massage, facial, etc. from a local salon and spa of my choice. I only needed to provide a letter from my oncologist stating that I am 'allowed' to have these services done while on chemo.

www.cleaningforareason.org
They partner with professional residential maid service that is insured and bonded, to participate in their foundation. The companies have agreed to offer four free *general* house cleanings-one a month for four months as a way to give back to the cancer community. You apply online; send in a confirmation of diagnosis and need. We are still waiting for a response from them now that I have sent in the necessary confirmation paperwork. In Sheboygan, Gingham Girls cleaning service is the participating agency ☺

www.pinkribbonriders.com
The Pink Ribbon Riders "Patient Assistance Program provides direct financial assistance to men and women breast cancer patients. Program is open to patients in; MI, MN, ND, NY, **WI**, WY."

http://pinkdaisyproject.ning.com/
The Pink Daisy Project is a 501(c)3 organization dedicated to helping young women with breast cancer manage treatment a little easier. Our headquarters are located in the Seattle area but we help young survivors from all across the country and sometimes even beyond.

http://www.pinkparty1.com/
Pink Party is a not-for-profit 501(c)3 tax exempt foundation. "In addition to our annual benefit event held annually at Hollanders Pub and Grill, we host various events throughout the year, and we continue to provide grants to local organizations and individuals in need throughout our local communities."

http://www.scccf.org/
'The Sheboygan County Cancer Care Fund (SCCCF) is dedicated to improving the health, well-being, and quality of life for individuals and families of Sheboygan County who have been diagnosed with cancer or a disease of the blood.' They helped us pay our rent when we were going through really tough times.

http://tigerlilyfoundation.org/
http://tigerlilyfoundation.org/TigerlilyFoundationFUNDS4FamiliesForm.pdf
Funds for Families program: 'To educate, advocate for, empower and
provide hands-on services and support to young women (15-40),
before, during and after breast cancer.'

http://www.thesamfund.org/
'The SAM Fund is a unique non-profit organization created to assist
young adult survivors of cancer with a successful transition into their
post-treatment life, by providing financial support through the
distribution of grants and scholarships.'

http://www.bmcf.net/apply.htm
'The BMCF supports patients 18-40 currently undergoing cancer
treatment with services to meet daily needs. It provides home health
care services, co-payments required by many health plans for medical
care, temporary housing, and other expenses for those temporarily
unable to pay bills like rent, insurance, and food.'

http://www.ubcf.info/
'The United Breast Cancer Foundation is committed to making a
positive difference in the lives of those afflicted with breast cancer as
well as those families affected by breast cancer. The United Breast
Cancer Foundation financially supports a variety of programs dedicated
to breast cancer screening and prevention, treatment and patient health
and well-being.'

http://www.patientadvocate.org/
'Patient Advocate Foundation (PAF) is a national 501 (c)(3) non-profit
organization which provides professional case management services to
Americans with chronic, life threatening and debilitating illnesses. PAF
case managers serve as active liaisons between the patient and their
insurer, employer and/or creditors to resolve insurance, job retention
and/or debt crisis matters as they relate to their diagnosis also assisted
by doctors and healthcare attorneys. Patient Advocate Foundation
seeks to safeguard patients through effective mediation assuring access
to care, maintenance of employment and preservation of their financial
stability.'

www.rightactionforwomen.org
Right Action for Women (RAW) founded by actress and breast cancer
survivor Christina Applegate. She is funding a financial assistance
program to help young women who are at high risk for breast cancer
gain access to Magnetic Resonance Imaging (MRI) screening. Together
with the Cancer Support Community (CSC)
www.cancersupportcommunity.org and Patient Services, Inc. (PSI)
https://www.patientservicesinc.org/illnesses-and-

conditions/breastcancerscreeningprogram.aspx. Right Action for Women has created a partnership to bring financial support to young women who are facing the risk of early breast cancer as a result of a genetic predisposition.

http://www.cancercare.org/diagnosis/breast_cancer
Can help with costs such as:
Transportation to and from cancer treatment
Home care
Child care
Pain medication
Lymphedema supplies (breast cancer only)
If you need assistance with chemotherapy or targeted treatment co-payments, please visit the CancerCare Co-Payment Assistance Foundation

Anonymous Fund Program
US Bank at 1 South Pinckney, Madison WI 608-252-4000
Program description: ANONYMOUS FUND - An application is taken for people in need of emergency funds. NOT LIMITED TO MEDICAL CONDITIONS. Applicant will need a reference and should supply as much detail as possible. A board will review the application and decide if and how much will be given from the Trust Fund. Funds are dispersed on a quarterly basis. Maximum limit is $2000.00 per year. Applicants may re-apply annually, total maximum is $5000.00 per individual. Eligibility: Must be a Wisconsin Resident. Application process and reference required. Applicant must submit a fully completed application form and letter of recommendation from a professional who is familiar with your needs-such as a pastor, minister, social worker, doctor or dentist. Limit of distribution is $2,000 per year with a total of $5,000 for each individual. Moneys approved will be distributed to the creditor or retailer. Application reviewed quarterly in Jan, Apr, Jul, Oct. Completed applications must be received by: Mar 31 - for April funding, Jun 30 - for July funding, Sep 30 - for Oct funding, and Dec 31 - for Jan funding.

http://mrkf.org/
'The mission of the Margaret Rose Kennedy Foundation is to provide need based financial aid to those with cancer related medical expenses not covered by health insurance. Typically the lack of health insurance coverage involves a gap in coverage. For example, most medical plans cover hospitalization, chemo, oncologist costs, etc. However, quite often, medical insurance does not cover the cost of searching for a suitable donor in cases where stem cells or organs are required for a transplant.'

I hope you walk away from this blog with some info that will help
someone you know. ♥S

Guestbook Comment: Tuesday, February 1, 2011 11:01 PM, CST
Hey girl, I'm sure you got sick of watching the blizzard news on TV
all day! When Jen and I were walking back from the library, with
wind in our face we wanted to walk to your old house and sit by the
fire.   I hope Andy is going to stay home and help you with the
kiddos tomorrow, or hoping you have lots of melatonin for them lol!
Shawn is calling in tomorrow and I think it will be the first, possibly
2nd time ever that he called in because of the weather. We told the
kids he is staying home because the older 2 girls were physically
fighting even after DS and TV were taken away. For the first time
I couldn't wait to drive in the storm this morning just to get the
girls to school! It seems like it has been such a long winter and I
am sure the damn ground hog isn't going to see his damn shadow in
a blizzard tomorrow. Take care girl and I guess you won't be
coming to visit tomorrow. Well u better keep your butt home!!!! Talk
to you soon. Love ya lots and miss ya. Love, Joey

Wednesday, February 2, 2011 8:28 PM, CST
Moving onward and upward. Thank you God for another day of
feeling good and not being in much pain. Sleeping means I'm healing
my body-and I sure healed a LOT today!!! ♥S

Guestbook Comment: Thursday, February 3, 2011 5:12 AM, CST

222

Hey beautiful...I'm so glad that you felt good yesterday. It always makes my heart smile when you feel good...we all take feeling good for granted, but seeing you go thru all of this is making me take the time to enjoy the small things. Thank you for that! Thanks to our neighbor we got plowed out. We have great neighbors who jump in to help. Thank God! I think we may have enough snow now! Steph and I have been up since 4:45 this morning. She's getting a cold and her nose is stuffy and she doesn't want it to be stuffy. Let me know when you are headed this way again. Maybe just maybe I can catch a glimpse of you in passing since every time you come this way something comes up. I'll take just a glimpse...Love Ya Babe! Jenny

Guestbook Comment: Thursday, February 3, 2011 6:27 AM, CST
OMG, I got nervous for a few minutes! I thought you cleaned house and took me off your list. I entered my email wrong 3 times, yes 3 and it kept saying 'we do not recognize your email' so I'm glad it was my fat fingers on my little cell phone keys and the 2 kids over my shoulders with their hands touching everything! Hoping your day is awesome today and your appetite is back, because we all know food is our comfort! Stay warm today. Love ya. Joey

Thursday, February 3, 2011 2:19 PM, CST
AMAZING what a phone call from a friend can do to your mood! ♥S

Thursday, February 3, 2011 5:02 PM, CST
I just spent the best 8 hours EVER with my husband! He had a transformer blow at work, so he's home for the next 2 days. We cleaned, laughed, picked on each other, had fun with Alaina, got stuff done, worked on things we have let go for too long, and really had a nice day. I so enjoyed that time with him ☺ ♥S

<u>Guestbook Comment</u>: Thursday, February 3, 2011 7:26 AM, CST
So glad you had a good day. Your courage inspires me every day.
I hope Josh had fun on Sunday! Regina and her husband commented
on what a good kid he was...and he was so funny too. Love that little
man. I am glad that Jake and him get along so well. Think about
you and pray for your health every day. Gotta go wake Jake up he
crashed hard on the couch last night! Keep your chin up girlfriend....
Love ya lots!!!! Candice

<u>Guestbook Comment</u>: Thursday, February 3, 2011 6:22 PM, CST
Hi Shelly, I hope you are having a good day today! Love, Anne

Thursday, February 3, 2011 8:28 PM, CST
...made a wish & hoping like mad it is a doable dream & comes true. S

<u>Guestbook Comment</u>: Thursday, February 3, 2011 9:37 PM, CST
Hey Shell, glad you had an awesome day with Andy, you need that! I
am so glad you have been feeling a little better....you go girl and kick
butt!!!! Love ya, Joey

<u>Guestbook Comment</u>: Friday, February 4, 2011 8:09 AM, CST
Love ya! Mary

<u>Guestbook Comment</u>: Friday, February 4, 2011 2:14 PM, CST
Talk to you again soon! Love ya babe!!! Melissa

<u>Guestbook Comment</u>: Friday, February 4, 2011 10:16 PM, EST
What a great journal entry. I keep looking at the meal train thing
and for some reason I get intimidated. Gee....I barely scrape
together a decent meal for my kids, how could I do it for others?
That's my own problem, not yours! However, I do now have it

pointed out to me that it's not how much or how good, it's just that you (I) did something. Thanks Shelly! Ann

Saturday, February 5, 2011 8:53, CST
Had our first ever Wii Bowling League today...I came in THIRD! Wahoo! Beat Andy and Braunie's asses! Hahahaha! What a blast....loved having a house full of friends and kids and food and fun. Can't wait until next time!!!!!!! ♥S

<u>Guestbook Comment</u>: Sunday, February 6, 2011 6:35 AM, CST
Hey beautiful...it sounds like you had a really fun time yesterday! What a great idea. I'm glad that you were able to enjoy yourself, you deserve it! Yesterday Natalie had 2 bball games. One in Mayville at 8 a.m. which we lost and one in Campbellsport at 1 p.m. which we lost too. Oh well, they all played well and had fun doing it and that's all that matters. I can't believe how much Natalie enjoys it! They have all gotten so much better. Today is Sunday school, church, and the BIG GAME!!!!!   GO PACKERS!!!! I made sloppy joe's, bagel dip, and little wienies yesterday for the game today. I'm not cooking or making a damn thing today just plugging in my crocks. Here's to another day of you feeling GREAT! Love Ya Jenny

<u>Guestbook Comment</u>: Sunday, February 6, 2011 10:20 AM, CST
Today's riddle: What can you hold without ever using or touching your hands? Answer: your breath! Roberta

Sunday, February 6, 2011 11:47 AM, CST
What total bullshit. I feel like complete crap today. My head hurts, my stomach hurts, I'm tired, I feel nauseous, my *lack of* hormones are in full force...I have had tears streaming down my face for almost 40 minutes...for no real reason, just can't stop

225

crying. Which is NOT helping my headache and straight up....it's my hubby's birthday. I had plans, and now I feel awful.

I have brownies to make for his birthday treat and was going to go to the Pig and get some tenderloin this a.m. to cook out for lunch. His favorite. Then Dino's for supper....hopefully Ilyssa can make the brownies? Ugh. I guess that's what I get for feeling so good yesterday. I have to *pay* for having ONE good day. I swear, at this rate, I will never get back to having a normal life....where I can parent, and work, and go about my normal business. Sorry for being so whiny today...but you know what? I feel like shit. I'm allowed to whine. It's like having the flu without having the flu, and being hung over without having any margaritas, and having your ass kicked without getting a chance to fight back. ♥S

<u>Guestbook Comment</u>: Sunday, February 6, 2011 12:15 PM, CST
Sorry that you feel yucky today. Close your eyes, smile...come on just a little one for me, and give yourself a little squeeze. That's me giving you a hug. Love Ya Babe! Jenny

<u>Guestbook Comment</u>: Sunday, February 6, 2011 1:58 PM, CST
Don't ever apologize for keeping it real. Sending a big squeeze your way. Mary

<u>Guestbook Comment</u>: Sunday, February 6, 2011 6:29 PM, CST
Sorry to hear you feel like someone kicked your butt, it will get better. I know how you feel but think of something good & how you felt on Saturday. My prayers are with you and your family. Bette

<u>Guestbook Comment</u>: Sunday, February 6, 2011 8:05 PM, CST
I'm so sorry you are having such a rough day, Shelly! Praying you

226

get a wonderful nights' sleep & wake up feeling wonderful in the morning! This too shall pass...better days are ahead! Xoxo Charity

<u>Guestbook Comment:</u> Monday, February 7, 2011 9:22 AM, CST
Sorry you're having a shitty time. GUCK! We all have our ups and downs and feel sorry for ourselves but I think we are not patient enough with ourselves. I think there are times in life when you have to look at yourself as not you, Shelly, but as Josh or Ilyssa or Lainey's MOM. Would you tell her to cut herself some slack when she's having a bad day DURING CHEMO? Of course you would. Would you tell Andy's wife that it's ok that he didn't get his brownies for his birthday? Of course you would. Let in all the love and light that your heart can hold today & keep it there. Big hugs & smooches. Sheri

Monday, February 7, 2011 8:02 PM, CST
Thanks for the roses & chocolates...you're the best, Betsy & Miranda!

<u>Guestbook Comment:</u> Tuesday, February 8, 2011 9:14 AM, CST
Sorry you're not feeling well today. You weren't supposed to sit down and eat that WHOLE bag of noms last night!! I'm praying that as the day goes on you begin to feel much better. I have to take Bud in to the Dr. at 10 this morning. Larry decided to keep him home today. On a side note, I'm down one friend on FB. SO sad to have been deleted. Sigh. Can't wait till Wednesday! I know you certainly can. What are the rules of alcohol consumption when you're on chemo? Bets

Tuesday, February 8, 2011 9:22 AM, CST
Woken up to "MOMMY...my TUMMY hurts." AGAIN. For the second

time this week. AND now mine is upset, and so was Andy's this morning. Let's just hope for Josh to be well all day and week. I had a million things going on today-so I spent a good amount of time on the phone cancelling everything. Grr. But I guess it's good that they couldn't get me in for a root canal until tomorrow...I would hate to have to cancel that too. ♥S

Tuesday, February 8, 2011 8:55 PM, CST

Tomorrow is my fourth and final AC chemo...and I am SO dreading it. I have been home with the stomach flu-which is running rampant in my house-today. I have not thrown up, but feel like it may be in the cards.....ick. Wonder what that will do to my scheduled root canal in the morning and my chemo at 2 p.m.? Hoping for high counts and feeling amazing when I get up tomorrow.

As excited as I am to be having this fourth one out of the way and OVER....I just know how much pain the port access will cause me. (ALWAYS have had problems with that being excruciating-even with Lidocaine and the "spray") I also am NOT looking forward to how I will be feeling for the next 2 weeks. The diarrhea, the constipation that cripples, the nausea, headaches, fatigue.....did I mention I have 3 kids ages 9, 8, and 4?!?! This third one has been the HARDEST round of chemo YET. I had only one day that I felt good. Then I paid for it by feeling like dog doo doo for the next 4 days. I have so far been unable to work; barely having the strength to do ANYthing. It is a scary feeling-not knowing when you will be able to function again. Once done with the AC I will have 4 rounds of Taxanes-again every 2 weeks. Then I will start radiation. I have not met with the radiation oncologist yet...that's coming once the chemo gets closer to the end. Thanks for letting me gripe; I need my friends in pink to lift me up today.

<u>Guestbook Comment</u>: Tuesday, February 8, 2011 9:15 PM, CST
Praying you have a peaceful night & wake up feeling excellent. I
also hope tomorrow is a piece of cake all the way around for u. Kim

<u>Guestbook Comment</u>: Tuesday, February 8, 2011 11:58 PM, CST
Shelly you are definitely in my prayers tonight lady!! I am so sorry
for this hell you are in. Try to just decide the next 3 weeks are
going to suck and my life will completely be on hold, but then the sun
will start to shine. I remember thinking I would give anything to be
able to run to the end of the block. My girlfriend came and stayed
with me for a week at a time to take care of my 3 year old and 3
week old, and would take them to the park every day and it broke
my heart!! I would've given anything to have the strength to go to
that park with them. I feel so deeply the pain you are in, but I am
proof that this gets a lot better! There is light at the end of the
tunnel. In a year from now, this will start to feel like a complete
nightmare you have woken up from. Eventually life will get almost
completely back to normal. You will unfortunately never forget this
pain, as I have tears now just emailing you, but life will pick back up
where you left off in November. You will be a better person after
all of this, with an appreciation for life and your family that most
others will never fully comprehend. I remember my last day of
chemo, and it was horrific, but it was the start of a new day! Every
day since then has been better than that day! Stay strong, you can
make it one more day! Sounds like next round of drugs are much
kinder! I hate that you are having such port issues. I don't
understand that at all. What on earth are they doing to you? I am
a huge baby, and can tell that you are not even close, and I did not
have any port problems ever. Makes me think something is not
right with yours. Did they place it in the wrong place?? That should
just not be hurting you that way! I love that you are having a root

229

canal tomorrow as well. Mostly because I have not been to the dentist since my cancer dx. I tell myself, and others, I have been through enough shit, I don't need to sign myself up for any more pain for a while! I'm good. Then I realize if I have a cavity and it becomes a root canal (which I've had, and boy did that suck) I am going to be in a hell of a lot more pain! One of these days I will get to the dentist. Monday night is support group at Stillwaters, if you are up for it let me know... The guest speaker is from the new genesis (sp?) farm out near Delafield. It will be about how different foods are good for your body, organics, stuff like that. Should be a good one! Dying to meet this feisty lady I would call my friend! Amy

Guestbook Comment: Wednesday, February 9, 2011 4:50 AM, CST
Hey beautiful...praying that you had a night where no one else woke up and said mom my tummy hurts. Hoping you feel better when you wake up this morning. Everyone around here is still sleeping thank God! It is only 4:40, I couldn't sleep. I said prayers for you that your root canal is a piece of cake & when they even look at your port it doesn't hurt (much). Today one chapter ends with the last of your chemo which means you are getting closer to the end of all of this crap. In your journal entry at the end when you wrote everything you have gone thru it amazes me how far you have come. INSPIRATIONAL! Love Ya Babe! Jenny

Guestbook Comment: Wednesday, February 9, 2011 6:33 AM, CST
Hey Girl, my 4 kids are all laying up in their beds, too cold to get out this morning. It is 21 below zero with the wind chill and I was hoping for a late start so the kids could get some extra sleep, but NO!!! I pray that you feel better today, that all your kids are in good health, that Andy is feeling good, and that you can do your final chemo of this kind, so you can start anew. Prayers are sent your

way all day....why is it whenever we have plans to see one another, something always happens? Love ya lots....Joey

Guestbook Comment: Wednesday, February 9, 2011 7:16 AM, CST
I'm with Mary on that...don't ever apologize for keeping it real. You are human and you need to vent and let out all that pain and frustration...now more than ever. I hope everything goes ok for you today. So sorry you have to deal with all this shit right now...we pray for you every day. I know how you get the winter blahs so here's a little hope for warmer weather to come faster. Daylight savings time is in 4 weeks and SPRING is 5 weeks away!!! Almost done! You are an AMAZING STRONG lady and you have tons of people who love you so much! Candice

Wednesday, February 9, 2011 1:05 PM, CST
The first half of the root canal went well. No pain so far, but still kinda numb; the rest will be on the 14th. Now just waiting for Melissa to pick me up and take me to chemo. Great that it's my last AC; terrified about the needle. ♥S

Guestbook Comment: Wednesday, February 9, 2011 2:28 PM, CST
Glad the first part of the root canal was good! Now praying your chemo goes as well as it can. Praying for you girl... Love ya, Joey

Guestbook Comment: February 9, 2011 3:27 PM, CST
Eeeegads root canal on top of all this! It's not worth going through extra pain to try for sainthood! I know, I know. It's still cold here, in case you thought south might be better. Cheers, Roberta

Guestbook Comment: Wednesday, February 9, 2011 10:14 PM, EST
Hey girly! I was talking about ya today at work. Were your ears

ringing? Didn't share your name just what you are going thru. I'm a teacher so it's just a bunch of women (many the same age as us) sitting around having lunch. We were sharing.....several of my colleagues are BC veterans. Every story is just one more incentive for the rest of us girls to be preventive!! I also was thinking about you with your root canal and chemo today. Is the Taxane chemo more potent or is it easier on the system, I guess maybe you have to wait and see too. Take care and I hope you are not feeling too icky. Ann

<u>Guestbook Comment:</u> Thursday, February 10, 2011 8:06 AM, CST
Hi there, Tootsie Pie! Had a great time w/ you and Mel last night, even if all we did was gaze lovingly at each other. But we had CAK!! (← for those of you that do not speak Betsy Speak...that means cake ☺) Nom. Next time I'm bringing a bell for Andy and a naughty little maid outfit or maybe just the frilly little apron part of it! Hope you were able to sleep well last night. Don't forget I am bringing supper Friday night. Do you want it before 5 or after I get home? I'm sure we'll talk before then. Sweet dreams-Betsy

Thursday, February 10, 2011 7:02 PM, CST
Well. Mixed feelings/emotions/ health today. I had my FINAL (*lifetime* final) dose of Adriamycin/Cytoxan blend chemotherapy yesterday. YIPPEE FUCKIN' YAY!! Thank you LORD. Now, I get that chemo is chemo and as far as I know the next time will be meaner to me...but here's hoping NOT. From what I heard it's 'easier'...let's all say a little prayer. Taxotere is the next one up...it's a single medicine vs. the 2 together. Yesterday was a great experience...chemo (and ROOT CANAL) wise! They could only do the first half of my tooth procedure since they were an HOUR AND A HALF LATE getting me in (PISSED OFF) and I had chemo

scheduled. But it was pain free, and entertaining. Now I have to go back on the 21st-yuck-and it cost me over $1,145. Ugh.

Melissa took me to my chemo appointment at 1:45. New experience for her. First they numbed me. Twice. The pain was minimal....just a regular poke. THANK YOU GOD. (((And Sarah, R.N., you rock!))) Afterwards I went over for my visit with the oncologist and he discussed all the side effects that I'm experiencing...nothing out of the normal. He told me my blood work all looked good. I went back to the chemo room, and got into the "Big Chair". Premeds in order: Benadryl on board, Ativan in the veins to make me sleepy. They started up the chemo while Melissa kept me entertained for a while. I started heading off to lala land...so I politely told her I was tuning out! Before we knew it, it was time to head home. While we were there the social worker popped in to share some info with me, and promised to email me some additional info on some help with things like doctor bills, etc. Carol popped in too and said hi, got to meet Melissa then had to head out on her way. It's always nice to see her smiling face ☺ We came home and Ms. Ross from Parkview brought over a DELICIOUS meal for us....Josh's favorite-NACHOS! It worked out perfect, since Melissa was still here and Betsy came over too, there was plenty for all. We even had some to send home for Miss Kasie who wasn't feeling so great. I kept dozing off on my poor friends, and they headed home so I could rest. I spent the night snoozing, snoring and feeling nauseous. I even woke up 3-4 times reaching for the puke bucket. ☹ This is probably the worst I have EVER felt after chemo. Even right now I feel gross, (kinda how you feel when you have too much supper and you just KNOW that at bedtime when you lay down you'll be up hurling.) Well, that's where I am. And all I ate was half an apple, and 3 grapes. Over doing it, I tell ya...really shouldn't pig out like that should I????

Today I woke up feeling ok but sleepy. I spent the morning alone, working on paperwork, phone calls, emails and paying bills. Fun stuff, eh? Once Alaina got off the bus at noon we pretty much hit melt down mode-she was over tired and I was just plain old tired. So we had some lunch and hit the couches. WE WERE OUT LIKE A LIGHT. When I woke up at 4:15 I still had to go to Urgent care for my Neulasta shot (gotta bump up those white cells!) Hoping they are working overtime this week, I'd LOVE to feel human again. The shot was uneventful, just in my belly like always, and I got to leave. I totally cheated on the way home and stopped for McD's. This time the apple & walnut salad was NOT expired, nor were the apple dippers! Yahoo for McD's! And the whole order was correct! I also surprised the kids by picking them up from day care instead of Daddy, about 15 minutes early! They fought and bitched and moaned... so no big surprise for me lol haha. Once the kids finished all the yummy junk food, they continued their bickering and fighting. Then Daddy brought in the Valentine's Day bucket and everyone dug in to start on their Valentines' cards for Monday!!! I'm not sure if we need to make boxes or bags or whatever for school...so we just winged it and made some. Who knows if they need them or not, but they're done. Even Miss Alaina wrote her OWN name on all 21 of her Valentine's! In one sitting! Now we have to do the damage control clean up-once we're done watching Matilda-an old family favorite. ☺ Wish me luck for sleepypoo tonight. ♥S

Guestbook Comment: Thursday, February 10, 2011 8:59 PM, CST
Hope you can get a restful night Shelly, feel better! Tina

Guestbook Comment: February 11, 2011 10:08 AM, CST
Wishing you sweet dreams in lala land. Roberta

Saturday, February 12, 2011 3:40 AM, CST

...because there is NOTHING more that I like than being wide awake allllll night long until at least 3:40 a.m.

I can just NOT sleep, even with Valium on board. Any nurses reading this that can help me with any advice on that????? This is just killing me. I am so tired and feel so gross. When I lay down my stomach feels full and pukey, so I end up on my left side and then it feels better. (Remember all those months of pregnancy??) Then my tissue expanders (remember those evil-doers inside my chest??) start hurting my muscles/tissues because of gravity and the fact that they feel like shot puts inside my skin. Then I have a pillow crammed under my head/shoulder. A body pillow crammed under/between the foobs, between my knees, and more pillows under my back. THAT IS NOT EVEN COMFORTABLE. SO here it is almost 4 in the morning, I have stayed up past my hubby who is now snoring and because of EVERYTHING I can now not sleep. Grrr.

SO I thought I'd come on down and catch up on some DVR and blabber on here. I don't know if anyone else with these damn tissue expanders have such problems sleeping and getting comfortable OR if people like me that are having this shitty chemotherapy feel so disgustingly sick all the time either. But I'm one of the lucky ones, I guess. That's what everyone keeps telling me anyway. ♥S

Guestbook Comment: Saturday, February 12, 2011 5:08 AM, CST
Hey beautiful...It's 5:05 a.m. and I am up. Mike couldn't sleep so he turned on the TV so now I'm up & am downstairs. Rocky's in our bed so no room for me. Girls are still sleeping thank God because I have to wake them up early to be in Kewaskum by 7:30 for our 2nd game of the tournament. WE WON LAST NIGHT!! YIPPEEE!! Sad

face for the fact that you can't sleep and you are so uncomfortable. I hope and wish that soon you will be able to sleep on your tummy! Here's to a GREAT day! Love Ya Babe!!! Jenny

Saturday, February 12, 2011 5:13 AM, CST

Fuck fuck fuck fuck fuck fuck fuck fuck fuck fuck fuck fuck fuck fuck fuck fuck fuck fuck fuck fuck fuck fuck fuck fuck fuck fuck fuck fuck fuck fuck fuck fuck fuck fuck fuck fuck fuck fuck fuck fuck fuck fuck fuck fuck fuck fuck fuck fuck fuck fuck fuck fuck fuck fuck fuck fuck fuck fuck fuck fuck fuck fuck fuck fuck ♥S

Guestbook Comment: Saturday, February 12, 2011 5:57 AM, CST
Wow, I can't believe you can never sleep, especially with all those medicines....YUCK! I always thought it was unfair being awakened by a baby on their terms, but a mother of 3 children and having to be awake must SUCK, and especially in pain. I just made lunches for all the family to take to the tournament today. We are half way to your house, wishing you felt better so we could connect. Hope your day is filled with lots of zzzz's. Miss you like CRAZY! Love ya, Joey

Guestbook Comment: Saturday, February 12, 2011 4:24 PM, CST
You'll always be the princess w/ the golden locks to me! Mary

Saturday, February 12, 2011 4:40 PM, CST

Holy CRAP how can sitting in the car for an hour make me so tired? We went to Fond du Lac today to stock up on some gluten free food @ Festival Foods-I LOVE that store! I also popped into Wally World to drop off my paperwork and say hi to my cake buddies ☺ I'm a little nervous...I have exhausted my FMLA and am now on "non-job protected" personal leave. I don't know WHAT I would do if I couldn't go back to doing cakes....

I also have NO CLUE what I am going to do when I do have to go back.....loss of strength, loss of motion, and not to mention what the hell the radiation is going to do to my right arm/breast/pit area. HELLO?! GOD?! Did you forget I am RIGHT HANDED? AND I make cakes for a living??? Dammit. Evidently He has a plan, and all will work out in the end. Fingers crossed... ♥S

Guestbook Comment: Saturday, February 12, 2011 9:06 PM, CST
Sorry it's been a while, had no computer. I finally have my computer back. But I was always thinking of you and your family. Hugs and kisses. Pam

Sunday, February 13, 2011 4:48 PM, CST

Dear Shelly,

Sorry to hear you have been feeling so craptastic. I know it's tough, but you know what? YOU HAVE CANCER.....you are supposed to be feeling like shit so that you can KICK its ASS and feel better. Feeling sick means your BODY is working. Overtime. And no, you don't get paid more for working this kind of overtime. You get to live. You get to someday get 'the call' where you find out 'it's gone'. Or 'it's over'. Or 'you've done it, you've beaten it and kicked its ass, and now--for your grand prize you get to get NIPPLES!!!'

You don't get to spend a lot of time going about your normal day, doing whatever it is you want-whether it is laundry, or scrapbooking, or shopping.....you get to sleep. And lay around. And watch more TV than you have ever watched in your LIFE. You get your monies worth from Time Warner for once. You may have all kinds of things going on right now.....stomach aches, no appetite, nausea, tooth pain, bone pain, hair loss (or LOST!) no strength, muscle pain, depression, mood swings, lethargy, fatigue.....BUT. You have all these things going on TEMPORARILY. A few months, a year, 2 years...that is *such* a short amount of time out of your WHOLE life. You will get past this and move on. You will once again get up to your alarm clock and trudge to work and complain that you would rather sit home instead of going to work. You will once again shop til you drop. You will once again spend more than 20 minutes cleaning....and LOVE it. You need to realize that the reason you were 'picked' for this challenge....is that YOU ARE UP TO IT. There are many other people in this world that would lie down and let themselves succumb to it. They would let this take over their life and ruin them. NOT YOU. You are blowing everyone away with your strength, courage, hope and LOVE. You still GO ON. You drive to all your appointments, take care of all the things you need to take care of, and GO ON. You don't roll up into a ball and hole up in your bed day after day. You can do this. Just keep remembering that. ♥ YOU.

Love, Shelly {Hey-sometimes ya just gotta jack yourself up.}

Guestbook Comment: February 13, 2011 7:51 PM, CST
Hey Shell, love the letter to yourself...it was awesome. Still thinking if you publish your book, you won't have to go back to work! Then we can all just hang out and have a book club with your book (You can use Walmart to have your book signing and make cakes to celebrate!) Hope you have a little energy and feel good tomorrow, I will call you tomorrow and tell ya about my busy week! Love ya, Joey

Guestbook Comment: Monday, February 14, 2011 11:11 AM, CST
Hey beautiful...HAPPY VALENTINES DAY TO YOU!!!! I hope the sun is shining nice and bright in Plymouth because it sure is shining here in Horicon and it is beautiful! Spring will hopefully be on its way and then summer and just think you will be done with this and will have

238

kicked its ass outta your life for good! I can't wait for that day for you! It seems hard to imagine so I will imagine it for you and one day it will be here! Then we can sit back and watch the kids playing and swimming while we sip margaritas with umbrellas in them. OK...we both know we won't be sipping more like chugging, but the umbrellas sounds cute! Right? Hold your beautiful head up and smile like you always do and try to think of the day when you will say...I AM A CANCER SURVIVOR!!! Love Ya Babe!!! Jenny

Guestbook Comment: February 14, 2011 3:59 PM, CST
Valentine's Day is not just for romance, it is also a time to celebrate all forms of LOVE: friendship, relationships with family and workplace peers and the friendly interactions in church, community and neighborhoods.....all of which make life so much happier. Spread some joy today! Roberta

Monday, February 14, 2011 4:58 PM, CST
I just finished up my pity party for the day. Thanks, Carol, for kicking my ass outta my funk. I had to take Ilyssa in to her pre op appointment today. This was the third one...I had overslept or slept through the last two...and I actually made it there. EARLY even! She is in great health so surgery is GAME ON for Wednesday. I had to run her back to school; popped into McD's for a Hi-C orange drink (only because they are scrumptious) and head to Sheboygan for a fill-up on the ladies. It was not until 3:15, so I had about 40 minutes to kill. I headed down to BEAUTIFUL Lake Michigan... WOW. What beautiful sites...the waves crashing, the ice slushing, the glacier size ice chunks sticking up into the air...what a thing of beauty. Then Alaina and I headed to the doctors (I had to wait for him to get there, but he didn't even come in the room??? I think he's avoiding me! I make him laugh too much!) Kim gave

me a mini filler upper...just 25cc's each side. She had 50 in on the right and it just pulled and tightened up too darn much. I truly didn't want to be in the amount of pain I was in the last time, so she drew some back out, leaving in 25 cc's. Then we headed out in search of the 'perfect' Valentine's gift for Andy. Sears? Suck. Mall in general? Suck. Headed to Plymouth and found something he both needs and wants. Perfect. We popped into Wal-Mart and got a few things I needed, some things I wanted, and got the FLOCK outta there. Whew. What a long 4 HOURS! ♥S

Wednesday, February 16, 2011 11:22 AM, CST
ARGHHHHHHHHH!!!!!!!!!

There. Now I feel better.

So if you read FB, you already know my day started off for SHIT at about 12:40 this morning when I started barfing my brains out. I felt a MILLION times better after I puked but as with everything else cancer related......being sick is NOT GOOD. Neither is the 102 fever I had. Alaina (age 4) woke up this morning coughing and crying that her throat hurt. I called the clinic... ONLY because Ilyssa will be getting her ear tubes put in today, so I need to make sure all is well. SOooo...long story short she has STREP. Possibly influenza. The rapid strep was IMMEDIATELY positive. The influenza swab won't be back until Friday morning at the latest. It's not that she has strep that's the problem...it's that I HAVE NO IMMUNE SYSTEM that is the problem. Again, if she has the flu, no worries for her...but B-I-G worries for me and my few little tiny white blood cells ☹ I would have to go on antivirals then. She got penicillin; I got amoxicillin and a trip to the lab to check my counts. I also picked up Josh's new prescription and signed the papers I needed for my disability stuff; then went to have my blood draw. I ran Ilyssa home by Andy so he could take off her nail polish for surgery and get her to the hospital by 10:30. I had to go back to Walgreens to pick up NINE different prescriptions!!!!! Guess what.....all for only $9. LOVE insurance. Saved hundreds of dollars. Whew! They even caught that one hadn't gone thru the 2nd insurance and re-ran it...saving me $27! I ♥ Walgreens pharmacy! Alaina had in the meantime fallen asleep in the cart and I saw they had pillow pets...and the Mom in me got sucked in and I picked one up for each of the girls....not knowing they are on SALE for $9.99!!!! HALF OFF! Woot woot! I may even go back and get more! Shit, they have birthdays coming up, right?!! Once we got home, Alaina was in LOVE with her new FLUFFY UNICORN pillow pet! I drugged her up with Motrin and penicillin. She had a couple of popsicles and some ice water. I'm hoping that makes her throat feel better. I called Andy at the hospital to check in on Ilyssa, and low and behold....there's a problem. Are you folks shocked at this point?!?!? Of course you're not. Unless you've been skipping around this book...in which case you don't know 'exactly' how lucky I am. Hmpf. Apparently there was a box of crackers in his car, and without thinking, Ilyssa grabbed one and ate it.

Shit.

She is being put out for this surgery and can't eat. The anesthesiologist of course has to tell us of the risks...the cracker could aspirate into her lungs during surgery while her esophagus is all sleepy....causing BIG problems. He is checking with the surgeon to see if we can switch her surgery at noon with the following one (2-3 hour long one) so she has ample time to digest that darn cracker. Really? Does it ALWAYS have to be SOMETHING????? Oh, yeah, and BTW-the lab called, and my white blood count is 2400. That's a good thing. Let's hope the next 24 hours are healthy living for me. And Alaina. And Ilyssa. And Josh. And Andy. Lol. ♥S

Guestbook Comment: Wednesday, February 16, 2011 11:52 AM, CST
I love your letter to yourself! You CAN do it and that's why you were chosen. Boy, that sucks, huh? You continue to make me laugh & just remember, "I only wore it once." Amy

Guestbook Comment: February 16, 2011 12:43 PM, CST
AARRRGHHH!!! What else can go wrong??! I better not say that too loudly!! Is it Friday yet? Can't wait for this weekend to get here. Heard you had some helpers yesterday... I told D they should make it a point to schedule a day EVERY week at your house. Besides, Cody needs to come visit his vacuum from time to time. M misses you all. She's been moping around the house and asking why you don't need her anymore LOL. I told her she didn't have to wait to be asked! I honestly think she just likes having 2 moms nagging her. I could take a few lessons from you. I'm going to have to have Larry go pick up a penguin pillow for D. Her b*day is the 28th and the Littles would LOVE to get her one for a gift. See you soon! Love you to pieces! Betsy

Guestbook Comment: Wednesday, February 16, 2011 1:22 PM, CST
OMG I never thought a cracker would cause so many problems, gosh! So glad Andy is helping you today. I love pillow pets, all 4 of my kids have them, bought by Nana. The good thing about tomorrow is there is NO way it can be worse than today, unless you are a Jones....LOL. Love ya babe, Joey

Wednesday, February 16, 2011 2:13 PM, CST
Received my 2nd care package from my "chemo Angel" today-a

242

beautiful linen scarf. How nice! ☺ Alaina is resting on the floor...
poor baby. But she is surrounded by Pillow pets...lmao...she's good. I
have been busy bleaching and cloroxing and washing the girls'
bedding...hoping like MAD to kill all the germs living in the house! Hot
water...soap...and bleach SHOULD do it. A big thank you to my cleaning
elves yesterday---Davis, Miranda, and Codikins... thanks a ton.   Also
thanks to Brittany for my roses; they are blooming in the sunlight!
Thank you to the Rosenthal's for supper. YUMMMMMY! It really
helped our busy night run smoother! Thanks Kim @ Merge salon.....
you know what you did! Thanks to Sarah for helping me deal with
the craziness lol...and for the dilly bars! Thanks to Braunie for the
delish cookies and the card; thanks to Andy for being the bestest
husband ever-by cleaning up my puke and helping me when I am sick
EVERY DAY.

Prayers needed for my amazing friends A & M who are going thru
some stuff tomorrow & need everyone sending them love and light.

Ilyssa still hasn't had surgery....should be another hour or so. We'll
keep ya posted! ♥S

Guestbook Comment: Wednesday, February 16, 2011 2:23 PM, CST
Miss you tons! It was so GREAT talking to you today! It was
awesome laughing and laughing together. Hoping you get all the yucky
sick germs out...gotta love bleach! I wish I could take it and
sprinkle it in the air at my house. Love Ya Babe!!!! Jenny

Guestbook Comment: Wednesday, February 16, 2011 4:23 PM, CST
Popping in to say hello. Snow's melting. Spring's on the way. Hope
everyone's doing well today. Andy doesn't feel left out of all the
"attention" does he? Ah, something to talk about in old age..................

"Remember the winter of 2011 ...?" Roberta

Wednesday, February 16, 2011 7:05 PM, CST

At 5:30 tonight Ilyssa made it home safe and sound from the hospital after being there ALL STINKING DAY. I really feel for her and Andy-I know how taxing it all can be. THANK YOU HEIDI!! You not only treated my family to dinner and beers, but also gave me some VERY NEEDED support today.☺ It was wonderful finally meeting you and I can't wait for this summer when I feel tip top and we can do something fun! Another day down; closer to the end of this nightmare! ♥S

Guestbook Comment: Wednesday, February 16, 2011 8:50 PM, CST
Holy frickin crazy day. Hope Miss Ilyssa feels better fast, and Alaina and you of course. Ryan's cookies were pretty awesome huh...he is a better baker than me. Although Jake of course thinks they are gross, sometimes I could smack that kid upside the head and say just fl$#&% eat it!!! Sweet Dreams! Candice

Guestbook Comment: February 16, 2011 10:40 PM, EST
Holy Busy Week! If it wasn't so terribly bad timed, it would almost be funny how sick and tired you all are in your house! I sure hope you are sleeping more and so is everyone else in the house. Kind of ironic that even though your first round of chemo is finished you still found a "reason" to be at a hospital today. Sure hope the sweetie is feeling OK and sleeps tonight. Angels on you! Ann

Guestbook Comment: Wednesday, February 16, 2011 10:30 PM, CST
Hi girl, Hope Ilyssa is doing great after her surgery. Just wanted to let you know that I love you like a sister. hugs and kisses. Pam

Guestbook Comment: Friday, February 18, 2011 9:00 AM, CST
Feeling SMURFY today?? Bets

Guestbook Comment: Friday, February 18, 2011 10:44 AM, CST
Hey girl, I hope Ilyssa is doing well this morning. Thinking of you all,
Roberta

Sunday, February 20, 2011 5:39 AM, CST

It's *too* early Sunday morning, and I am wide awake. No fun at
all! The last few days (Thurs., Fri., Sat.) I have been feeling really
good. Finally getting back to my old-ish self! Three more days of
this (hopefully) until my next round of the new chemo med. Ugh. I
have been able to clean the playroom (no small task!!!!) I got to have
Betsy over for the evening Friday...LOTS of giggles and fun!
Saturday was date night for Andy & I. Miranda came to babysit
and we headed out for some yummy tenderloin! The service at the
restaurant was to be desired......for sure.....but the food was as good
as always! Then we did some shopping in Sheboygan ☺

Guestbook Comment: Sunday, February 20, 2011 7:27 AM, CST
Sounds like some well-deserved and much needed "you two" time.
mary

Guestbook Comment: Sunday, February 20, 2011 7:45 AM, CST
Hey beautiful...so happy that you have been feeling better! I'm glad
you and Andy got to get out alone and enjoy some time together.
That is always so important! Hope you continue to feel great and the
next round of chemo isn't as bad! Movie night went really well all of
the kids that came were very well behaved. The movie was cute.
Saturday we went to Portage for my friends' daughters' birthday
party. We bowled and I SUCKED!!!! Oh well we all had fun. Steph

245

wasn't feeling good and fell asleep at the bowling alley. No puking just fever. Was up throughout the night, but still no puking! THANK YOU GOD!!! This morning she is GREAT!! THANK YOU GOD!!! She has her first birthday party to go to at the Tag Center today at 1. We will see how she is doing. She is so excited to go. Well, I need to get ready for Sunday School. Have a great day! Talk to you tomorrow. Love Ya Babe! Jenny

Guestbook Comment: Monday, February 21, 2011 11:06 AM, CST
I'm in a crappy mood, it's a crappy day, the weather is crappy, and I'm at crappy work. BUT...I just sat down at my desk with a cup of tea & thought about you. BIG smile on my face! Betsy

Tuesday, February 22, 2011 10:27 AM, CST
Happy Tuesday! ☺ It's sunny and beautiful out through the window! I'm feeling extra cruddy-I woke up with sinus pain, pressure, my teeth hurt, my chest is congested, and a nasty cold. Ugh. I'm hoping for a better afternoon. I've been on antibiotics for what seems like ever...but still keep getting sick. Gotta love having no immune system! Tomorrow is a big day for me. I meet with the radiation Doc and see what's 'next'.

Guestbook Comment: Tuesday, February 22, 2011 10:40 AM, CST
Hey beautiful...the sun is shining so beautifully! I love it! Not so much the snow, but the sun I will take any day. It makes me smile! Miss you like crazy!!!! Love Ya Babe! Jenny

Guestbook Comment: Tuesday, February 22, 2011 1:23 PM, CST
Hi woman! Thinking of you again. It sucks feeling crummy on top of crummy! I hope that everything tomorrow is good; great news for you! I'll keep you in my prayers for this new treatment to not be

as "rough" as the last round!! Here's to hoping the cold sunshine warms you up!   I hope everything is going well with the kids too and starting to settle a little! I love you lots!!! Melissa

Guestbook Comment: Tuesday, February 22, 2011 6:59 PM, CST
Fingers & toes crossed! You'd better not laugh when you hear me fall! mary

Guestbook Comment: Wednesday, February 23, 2011 6:35 AM, CST
Hey girl, hoping you feel better soon, that has got to be hard going from feeling good to not feeling good at all. The sun is a wonderful thing, hoping it comes out again today. Madeline gets her 2 retainers today and yesterday she had her orthopedic appointment, costing me mucho bucks this girl....Can't wait to hear about your appointment today.....wishing you luck....Miss ya Joey

Guestbook Comment: February 23, 2011 8:23 AM, CST
Good Morning, my BEAUTIFUL friend! Hope you were able to sleep well last night. I didn't I had a dream about my pastor. His voice changed because he was sick and for the rest of his life he was doomed to talk like a 2 year old little girl on acid! I had to go over and take care of his kids because they no longer took him seriously and wouldn't listen to anything he said. I had to leave the church cuz there was NO WAY I could sit through a sermon listening to that voice! I'm wondering what the heck I ate before bed to set that off-too many nail polish fumes, maybe. Speaking of nail polish.... what's up for the weekend? Did you find someone to borrow your kids? I'll check with Larry, but I don't think we have plans. We'll talk. I'll give you a call today or tomorrow. How are you on supper plans this week? Even though the potatoes were yuck, I forgot to ask you how those brownies were. Worth buying again? The batter

was good anyway ☺ Well, Peach, I better get to my meeting. Take care ((((BIG HUGS)))) Betsy

Wednesday, February 23, 2011 9:04 AM, CST
Well it's CHEMO day. Ugh. The day I dread for 13 days straight....is here. Today brings the new drug....and my meeting with the radiation doctor. I still feel like absolute shit today. I woke up with a cold yesterday, and now it's moved into my lungs. I was up half the night coughing up yuck and trying to breathe. Ugh. My head and chest are all plugged up-BUT it kept me from thinking about them stabbing my port today. Andy is home with me today to go with; and we will have some time to grab lunch together between appts. Just have to decide where to go!   If the sun would be shining today, I would be feeling much better, but what other choice do I have other than to go?

Guestbook Comment: Wednesday, February 23, 2011 9:28 AM, CST
Hope all goes well today. ☺ Hopefully the sun will pop out a bit too. Always makes everything seem a little better, doesn't it? Kim

Guestbook Comment: Wednesday, February 23, 2011 10:37 AM, CST
Hey beautiful...lots of hugs coming your way for today! I'm glad that Andy is able to go with you and that you two will be able to grab lunch. Love Jenny

Guestbook Comment: Wednesday, February 23, 2011 1:24 PM, CST
Hey Shel Bell...I have the afternoon off and had to check your site out. I have to get on here more often! Praying that all goes well for you today. And if I could I would sing to you....you are my sunshine my only sunshine...you make me happy when skies are gray...you'll never know dear how much I love you...oh please don't

take my sunshine away... I responded on FB about this weekend and the kids. If you want, Alexis and I can preoccupy them. I work til noon but thought maybe I could take the kids to a matinee...have to see what is playing. Just let me know. Love you tons! Stacey

Guestbook Comment: Wednesday, February 23, 2011 5:12 PM, CST
With all the other things you do/go through, you write cheerful notes too!?! Thanks! You're sweet. My computer time has diminished to almost nothing this week; we've started the deep clean, trying to do one room a day....it's exhausting for me but Richard says I'm a focused driver to keep him going. It is getting done but it is going to take a while...we're doing the easy rooms first. I'm emailing you the asparagus cure I just got from a friend. Haven't a clue if it's really more than an old wives tale, but, I love asparagus so I think I'll do it. Cheers! Roberta

Wednesday, February 23, 2011 6:16 PM, CST

Finally home and settled from the day. It was so much shorter this time. The new doc is ONE HELL OF A CHARACTER!!! He examined me and let me know that I will be doing approximately 33 treatments of radiation once chemo is over. It will be daily for about 7 weeks. It will significantly bring down my chances of the cancer returning to invade my chest wall or further damage the lymph nodes. So that's a GOOD thing. Anything that will bring my chances from say 35% down to like 15% of reoccurrence....makes me happy. If I only have to ever do this ONCE in my life it's TOO MUCH. After that we ran to have lunch at Fountain Park Restaurant. It was pretty tasty. Then we even had time to stop at Hobby Lobby. Andy's worst nightmare! Once we got back to the cancer clinic, I got all checked in, and climbed up into my Big Chair. Lovely Nurse Sarah was all *mine* for the third week in a row. She knows how to spray the spray, and voila! I was numb enough to barely feel the stab of the port needle. My blood was sent off to check the counts and I had to be checked for fever/infection since I'm sick. I then went in to meet with the oncologist to discuss all my 'symptoms' and tell him how awful sick I have been for the last 2 weeks. He just shook his head...haha! Once back in my chair Sarah loaded me up with the premeds: simple saline and a minibag of Zofran, Compazine, Dexamethasone, anti-nausea meds and a steroid thrown in for good measure. Trying to keep them side effects at bay......then we added some Ativan (to make me sleeeeeeeppy). Once those were done we ran the Taxotere in very slowly for 15 minutes to make sure I had no adverse reactions...which THANK GOD I did NOT. Then she cranked it up to full speed and it took maybe an hour. No Mesna this time, but I did have to keep a BP cuff on the whole time, being checked every 15 minutes. It was ok, a bit low but that could have been from the Ativan slowing me down. It all went good...I feel ok tonight. SO far. Hoping the steroids don't keep me awake all night! Alaina is begging to snuggle...so I will wrap it up. Gotta love snuggle time......! ♥S

<u>Guestbook Comment:</u> Thursday, February 24, 2011 8:22 AM, CST
Hi Shelly, I hope you are feeling better. Stay strong!!!   Cory

Thursday, February 24, 2011 11:26 AM, CST
Knock on wood, today I am feeling okay! I got to go shopping at Wal-Mart for groceries and finally got to go visit Sandi since her hysterectomy on Monday. We brought her some tulips and dark chocolates--yummy! Once home I thought it'd be great to make some popcorn until I BROKE my 1/2 root canaled tooth on it. WTF!! Now I don't think it can be saved I don't want to be missing any

teeth! Here's hoping the whole week continues to be good health and feeling good... ♥S

<u>Guestbook Comment</u>: Thursday, February 24, 2011 4:05 PM, CST
I am so happy to hear that you are feeling that well!!!! But gosh that really sucks about your freaking tooth!!! That dentist owes you big time! Melissa

<u>Guestbook Comment</u>: Thursday, February 24, 2011 4:29 PM, CST
Hang in there; sounds like this week is better than some in the recent past. Do you think you have traveling in your future? Today's riddle: What goes round the world but stays in a corner? Stamps. Roberta

Thursday, February 24, 2011 5:56 PM, CST
Today has all around been good! ☺
I got to scrap a page or two.
My cleaning fairies showed up! ☺
I had a WONDERFUL parent teacher conference with Ilyssa's teacher.
DQ made supper.
Life is good. ♥S

<u>Guestbook Comment</u>: Thursday, February 24, 2011 7:26 PM, CST
Just reading your last few entries. Do you know when my mom had her port, they sprayed the numbing stuff the first time ONLY. After that, they just stuck her. And she never flinched! DeAnna

Friday, February 25, 2011 3:17 PM, CST
DeAnna-your Mom must've been waaaay tougher than me then! That f*ing needle HURTS! I flinch, cry and freak out!

251

Roberta-I don't know about travel plans...not til this chemo stuff is over ☹ We are going to the Dells sometime in the end of April/ beginning of May for a weekend getaway. Once my radiation and EVERYthing is done and I get to catch my breath...Andy & I are planning on going on a vacation together to get the HELL outta here! I've been under house arrest LONG ENOUGH! Thanks Jenny & Joey & Betsy-You know what you did ~wink~♥S

Friday, February 25, 2011 3:19 PM, CST

2 days post first Taxotere chemo...so far I've been feeling pretty good. Yesterday I felt guilty I felt so good. I'm not used to having good days! Today I feel good, have energy, made cake (inside of ice cream cones) for the FUN FAIR tonight at school...I *also* went to both the Dollar Tree AND Pick n Save, picking up boxes to carry the ice cream cone cakes in, frosting and sprinkles... all the goodies! Since I have gotten home and made lunch for me and the Munchkin....I have started with a headache.....and the weirdest side effect ever.....my nails HURT. All 10 of them digits are achy and hurt when I type (ugh) and when I bump them on anything like the remote...or Alaina....or the bag of frosting. WTF?? I know that there *can* be nail side effects like nail bed darkening...and some people have been known to lose a nail or two. Ew. With everything else...I don't wanna lose my NAILS!!!! I mean, I'm freaking BALD, even my nose hairs have fallen out, causing my nose to DRIP all the stinking' time. My eyelashes are just starting to fall out....leaving my eyebrows (for now). The skin on my ears has started freakin out-all of a sudden last week they started itching and swelling up and now they're red all the time and the skin is dry and cracking. WTF? MY POOR EARS??? Leave them alone, Chemo...they're almost all I have left on my poor head!! My body is achy, my insides ANGRY, and the skin on my hands is 60 grit. I have been trying to moisturize like

crazy, but it's like the Mojave...soaks that shit right up!

I've been getting headaches almost nonstop since the chemo all began....trying various meds and home remedies. Today I think it's just that my neck needs to CRACK once just really loud!! Mollie--I'm wishing I had your chiro right now!!!! I am hoping to go next week for a massage; my back muscles are all wrecked. Even my nightly back rubs from the Hubster aren't as helpful as they used to be. ☹ I think it's because I can't lie on my stomach at all right now during "the expansion". Maybe the massage at the chiropractor's office will be better--their tables are all adjustable and bendy....?

More on this broken freakin' tooth....So, the last time I had chemo (2 weeks ago) I had an emergency root canal that morning. It was a painful tooth that ended up having a crack in the filling, and a cavity formed inside that tooth, along the nerve, making it necessary to get a root canal. Now if you've never had one, it's NOT BAD. It's no different than going to the dentist for a cavity. They numb you up, stick the numbing needle in and start drilling out the old filling. Once that's done they go in and suck out all the nerves and juicy tooth stuff. They replace that goo with some sterile posts; covering it all with a temporary filling. Since we were on a limited time crunch...I had to head to chemo...they only did half of it. (NOT at all sure what they have left to finish???) But charged it up right away at $1000. Out of pocket=$300 on the spot. So do you think since this week HALF of my tooth fell out (BROKE OFF) and it's probably not fixable, I'll get half that money back? Fuck no. We all know how that will go...."oh, those charges are for the entire process, it pays for all the tools we had to use and films we took, and well, the next appointment would've been no charge ANY way....." But I would like my $$ back!! I'm sure when I go on MONDAY-they'll tell me sorry, can't help you, and send me to the regular dentist to have the remains pulled.

Nooooo0000000oooooooooooooooooooooooooo00000oooooooo!!!!!!!!!!!!!!!!

Just because I work at Wal-Mart, doesn't mean I want to LOOK like I work at Wal-Mart! I like having all my teeth! I received the phone call from Gingham Girls Cleaning service this week; they are partnered with Cleaning For A Reason (which I've mentioned in the past) and we are all set up for them to come to our home and clean (3 hours) each month for the next 4 months!!!! I've never been able to keep caught up on housework, since I've always worked full time. NOW I can't keep up on it because I don't always feel great. When I feel great I don't want to CLEAN! A vicious cycle, if you can see it my way! I also sent out a few more applications for some breast cancer "foundations" that our social worker at the clinic has sent us. She gave me multiple sites and places that help out with things such as rent, utilities, and gas money to get to your appointments. Some even help with co-pays on your Rx drugs. There are weeks I go to Sheboygan 7 times. There are days I go to Sheboygan 3 times. There are times I have to go to Walgreens for different prescriptions 5 days a week. Gas, drugs, ginger ale soda to feel better (doesn't work), aloe vera juice to drink to help my insides....then that tasted like ASS so I went back and got the aloe vera gel caps; trips to the endodontist for shitastic root canals; kids with strep-more copays, more meds; another kid with surgery on her ears to put new tubes in cause her ears are genetically built goofy; $160 week for my kid to see a specialist.... along with gas money to West Bend. See? All the stupid things that add up.
$$

OH! And did I mention that my effing disability company has cut me off as of 2/11??? Even though they told me over the phone that they have my doctors' orders keeping me off work until 5/8/11. WTF?? ARGH! Crap...I was on a roll, now I remembered I have to call them back yet. ♥S

<u>Guestbook Comment</u>: Friday, February 25, 2011 7:50 PM, CST
Hey Girl, don't you DARE feel guilty when you feel good, just look around you everyone else feels good, and if they think they don't....if they had cancer they wouldn't! I am so glad that you had a few days of feeling okay. I know it isn't "NORMAL" for you to feel good, so it is good that you have a "not normal" day for once. I am up in Wausau visiting my Grandma with my mom and my 4 children. We are here to help her look for apartments in Lomira. Her lease is up in September and she wants to move closer to her grandchildren and great grandchildren. In all my life, I have never lived in the same city as my grandparent and now that she is my only one left, I would love her to be 20 minutes away, versus 2 1/2 hours away. Well....better go make the kid's beds and hope they get the hint. Miss you lots, Love ya, Joey

<u>Guestbook Comment</u>: Friday, February 25, 2011 8:32 PM, CST
Hi Shelly!! Glad this round of chemo was not so rough. We need to plan a date night with the guys and go out for supper or something... have not seen u for so long...miss you. Let me know if Josh or the girls want to go to Cabela's with Jake and I on Sunday, I would be happy to take them. Candice

<u>Guestbook Comment</u>: Friday, February 25, 2011 8:40 PM, CST
I just wrote and the post timed out (I think). Soooo, as I was saying, I'm glad to hear the cleaning fairies will be coming 3 hrs. for

255

4 months. Any help is welcome in that department! There's a reason moneyed people have maids! Love, Roberta

Saturday, February 26, 2011 12:38 PM, CST
Woke up with "the brain pain" this morning.....a headache from HELL that NOTHING has touched. Fucking chemo. I took Tylenol, oxycodone, tried using moist heat, tried sleeping (couldn't do it), hot washcloth, and even broke out the peppermint extract in boiling water trick. Well, after SIX hours the only thing that worked was finding Mad Libs online to play with the kids. THANK YOU God for allowing us to have a laptop!!! The kids were giggling and giggling when Josh's tiger wanted to eat his turds! EW!!! I loved MadLibs as a kid and am so glad my children are at an age to enjoy (and understand) how to do them! I can remember buying the little notepads at Kmart with my own money when I was younger-I loved the silly cartoon characters on the covers!

Saturdays at my house are always hectic...the change in routine effs everyone up...too much free time...not enough to 'do'. Everyone wants to watch 'their' show. Everyone wants to go online. Everyone wants to aggravate each other!!!! LMFAO! Including me...gotta spice things up around here! I'm thinking about heading to the movies with the chicklets this afternoon to see Gnomeo & Juliet...let's hope I continue to feel well...It's only been 3 days since chemo. ♥S

Guestbook Comment: Saturday, February 26, 2011 3:20 PM, CST
Hey beautiful...enjoy your day today. Sorry I couldn't talk longer yesterday, but you know how it is with kids. Miss you like crazy! Love Ya Babe! Jenny

Saturday, February 26, 2011 3:44 PM, CST
Mondays are so nice when they go back to school! Tina

Saturday, February 26, 2011 7:01 PM, CST
Yes, Madlibs are great! The kids and I do them too, goofy silly fun!
I am glad that you found something to help!! I am relieved to hear
that you are still are doing better over-all with this new treatment!
I am finally home once!! This week has been busy. Monday the
weather was so bad I stayed home with the kids. Worked to keep
Kasie going with her room, I can see floor! I got laundry done and
hung out with the kids while making supper. We played some
sheepshead and then Poker. Tuesday was bowling, my first time in
almost a month. Tyler usually has games. I bowled my best in a long
time. Wed. was the meeting with the lawyer (interesting!!!) and parent
teacher conferences, which went well. Kasie is getting back to
where she should be. Thursday Kasie had Poms/Dance team and was
parent's night for them. Friday was Tyler's last reg. season game
for bball. Intense game to say the least, but Kiel came out on top!
I am trying to work on the piles of paperwork in front of me. It
is so hard to be motivated to complete it! I miss you, I hope things
slow down a little so that I can see you and share some laughs
again!!! There's always the replay of Andy's dance to play through
our head.   I love you sweetie, I love to hear you are having some
"normal" days! Melissa

Saturday, February 26, 2011 7:01 PM, CST
The cost to take a family of FIVE to the theater during MATINEE
is RIDICULOUS. Freakin' ridiculous. I think with popcorn and
drinks it was almost $70. JEEZ! But Gnomeo and Juliet was
AWESOME and we even ran into Stacey and Alexis! The kids were
fantastic and we really enjoyed the family time. So all in all=well

257

worth it. FYI....Kohl's has BREAST CANCER t-shirts and baubles in CLEARANCE in the customer service area...$4 tie dye t-shirts and other t-shirts as well. Money goes to Susan G. Komen! ♥S

Guestbook Comment: Saturday, February 26, 2011 8:19 PM, CST
Good to hear good things with your family; and days when you're doing better to enjoy them! We got another room power cleaned today. Wears me out-thank goodness for Richard. Snow dusted down all day, just didn't add up to much which is fine with me! Picked up a couple new books at B & N, and Richard found a replacement fuse to fix the GPS so we're back in business in that department. Now it's tax time ...Roberta

Monday, February 28, 2011 2:52 PM, CST
Whoa. Went to the endodontist thinking they were just going to 'check' my broken tooth......and ended up with the 2nd half of my root canal being done. They were able to save the tooth (hooray!!!!) BUT now I'm supposed to have it crowned ASAP. BUT my insurance doesn't start to cover crowns for two whole weeks yet. So it's a soft food diet for me for a few weeks! My mouth is a lot more sore this time...I think since they had to push around my gums a lot with the broken tooth. THANKFULLY Sandi was able to get Alaina off the bus for me! I didn't get home til 1:00. Now I'm practically BEGGING Lainey to nap and she's all full of energy....and I'm ready for SLEEP! STINKER! ♥S

Guestbook Comment: Tuesday, March 1, 2011 8:11 AM, CST
Soft food diet??? ICE CREAM!!! When should I pick you up tonight?!?! Just talked to my dad he had chemo yesterday (on his 35th wedding anniversary) but he is doing great today. The 2 week 'rest' really did him good. His platelet count was at 80,000!! He also

wants to sell us his boat if we're interested.... just needs to come up w/ a price. Hmmmm..... $5 seems fair to me! Let me know if you want to sneak out to DQ tonight just me & U! Betsy

Tuesday, March 1, 2011 8:00 PM, CST

Had a fantabulous day today!!!!!!!!!!!!
Felt great!
Did lots!
Made THREE fruit pizzas!
Spent WONDERFUL time with Joey, Roo and Jake...
Spent WONDERFUL time with Jenny, Natalie, Emilie, Stephanie and Rocky...
Stopped in at Mayville Middle School to visit our old favorites...what great teachers! We miss you ALL!
Josh got to see some old friends (hi Dylan!!!!!)
Had a nice quiet relaxing ride home from Horicon with the 2 kids!
Thank you God for another wonderful day. ♥S

Tuesday, March 1, 2011 8:04 PM, CST

AND!!!!!!!!!!! I came home to surprises galore! Thanks Paula and Secret Santa!!!!!!!!!!!! ♥S

Guestbook Comment: Tuesday, March 1, 2011 9:38 PM, CST
Hey beautiful...It was GREAT seeing you! Thanks for visiting and for bringing fruit pizza...it was delish! Love Ya Babe! Jenny

Guestbook Comment: Tuesday, March 1, 2011 10:53 PM, EST
Hey! I have been out of the loop for a while with you and your journal. A hellish 3 weeks @ work, birthday parties for Cole and Katie and just life stuff...you know! I was reading back thru your journal, and I gotta say, I hope you never, never feel like people

are wondering what happened to the benefit money. Number 1, it's not our business, we gave because we knew you and the family need it and we love you! Number 2...if someone does wonder, that's their problem, not yours! NO guilt. Your expenses are frickin' astronomical! Not including that life ($$$$) still happens even with cancer care bills! Even sick, you still out do me in your energy and "go to" attitude! You Rock! Ann

Wednesday, March 2, 2011 8:13 AM, CST
UGH. I was allllll in a great mood this morning...until I remembered that they'll be accessing my port today to take blood.

YUCK YUCK YUCK! It's my one-week-post-chemo-count-check to see how I'm reacting to the new chemo. My guess is that I'm feeling great, so I bet my counts are good as well. Wish me luck! Sandi is taking me craft shopping... should be fun! THEN Alaina has to go to the orthodontist at 2:30 for a consult to look into getting an anti-thumb sucking-appliance put in. Should be LOADS of fun....she's already pissed about it.....and to be honest I don't know how it'll go. I think I'll need more luck for that appointment than mine!!! ♥S

Guestbook Comment: Wednesday, March 2, 2011 10:01 AM, CST
It is so wonderful to hear how much better you are doing lately! I love it, as I am sure you and your family are as well! It has to be great to have a little "normal" back! Tyler's team won last night, so they play again Friday night in Manti. Ttys! Love you and miss you lots! Melissa

Guestbook Comment: Wednesday, March 2, 2011 11:32 AM, CST
Thanks for the wonderful visit and thank you sooooo much for helping me! The fruit pizza was awesome, I am so glad you can eat again,

that is my favorite past time with you! Love ya, Joey

Wednesday, March 2, 2011 12:48 PM, CST
So, today was wonderful! Got to the cancer clinic and I asked if
they could take blood from my ARM instead of my port.....YES THEY
CAN! Hot damn! Made my freakin' day!!!!! All my counts were
awesome! My white count, red count, and platelets were all within
'normal' and that, my friends, is AMAZING!!!!! Wahoooooooooo!!! A bit
close to anemic yet, but that for me is normal. I am pretty wiped
today. Yesterday was a long and energy draining day-Sandi and I
stopped at Joann Fabrics, Michaels, and the best part....CHILI'S for
lunch! YUMMM!!!! I am sooooo full I feel S-I-C-K!!! Which is kind
of a good thing! I haven't been able to eat full meals in SOOOooooo
long-I didn't think I still could. What a great day....and now off to
pick up Miss Crabby Pants! ♥S

Guestbook Comment: Wednesday, March 2, 2011 1:05 PM, CST
Hey beautiful...so HAPPY that they could poke your arm instead of
your port! WAHOOO!! Glad that you are feeling so sick because you
ate so much! WAHoOo!! Continue feeling good! Love Ya Babe!!!
Jenny

Guestbook Comment: Wednesday, March 2, 2011 2:29 PM, CST
I am so glad to hear you had a great day...CHILI'S is awesome! I
eat their appetizers as a meal, they are so good. Have a great
week! Jennifer

Guestbook Comment: Wednesday, March 2, 2011 2:38 PM, CST
SO happy for you...to read what a great day you are having and for
all of your counts to be normal!!! Celebrating with you! HUGS!
Charity

Wednesday, March 2, 2011 7:00 PM, CST
YAY!!! So happy you had such a great day!!!!!
Sending a great big hug your way!! Love ya!!! Jen

Wednesday, March 2, 2011 10:27 PM, EST
It was great to hear you talking so upbeat! I am glad that the
counts are all coming back good, let's keep it that way!
Good Luck on the orthodontist appointment! Ann

Thursday, March 3, 2011 9:07 AM, CST
No "thumbsucking appliance" yet for Lainey! They want to wait til
she's 7 and baby teeth start falling out b4 doing anything.
HOPEFULLY she will not suck her thumb THAT long ☹ ♥S

Friday, March 4, 2011 9:24 AM, CST
I think the DQ cure is best of all-it works for me! Roberta

Friday, March 4, 2011 11:32 PM, CST
If it makes you feel better (or maybe not)... Amber just stopped
sucking her thumb at night w/in the past year... when she was 11! At
least we THINK she has stopped... the problem was she would go to
sleep not sucking it but out of habit, she'd put it in her mouth while
sleeping and wake up w/ it in her mouth. She never wakes up with it
in her mouth anymore, so we are hoping she doesn't do it in her
sleep at all...LOL Charity

Friday, March 4, 2011 12:38 PM, CST
Whoever left the LEAD in my ass, kindly remove it. ☹ ♥S

Saturday, March 5, 2011 2:57 PM, CST

Sorry for not helping! Maybe my point should be... don't be too concerned with age... when she's 18 I guarantee she won't be sucking her thumb...LOL! Have fun at your parties today!! HUGS! Charity

Saturday, March 5, 2011 12:15 PM, CST

Do you know those Swiffer commercials? The ones where the women are wearing dresses made of poo or mud and get swept up by the Swiffer....finally?!?!?? Those are the DUMBEST most DISGUSTING commercials ever. Really.....people get paid to think of that? I have better ideas on the toilet. And NO ONE pays me for them. Swiffer could really use a new marketing team. Ew. Maybe that IS where they thought of those ideas...

Today I made it through Wal-Mart without seeing ANYONE I knew!!! Out the door I went ☺

I have some things going on today...our neighbor's b-day party; a card making party; and hanging out with friends! The weather outside is CRAP. This Wisconsin weather just sucks. Cold and WINDY...makes your ears freeze out there-especially when you have no hair! Hoping Spring is on its way NORTH. ♥S

Monday, March 7, 2011 1:04 PM, CST

Fun weekend spent with friends from all over!!! Sunday was nice and relaxing. This morning was run run run! Cleaning for a Reason came starting today, so our home is now sparkly and clean and smells good too!

Guestbook Comment: Monday, March 7, 2011 7:02 PM, CST
Hello Shelly, do u remember giving Anna your jelly shoes when you were kids? Anna still has them! She doesn't wear them now, but,

she said it was the nicest thing anyone had done! She'd been dying for some and I hadn't given in *you know being old and all and not understanding their importance ...I've learned so much in my old age! Love, Roberta

Guestbook Comment: Tuesday, March 8, 2011 7:09 AM, CST
Hey beautiful...sorry I haven't been a guest on here lately! Sorry I missed your call yesterday...I guess I'm just SORRY!!! LOL!!! I will try to call you today. Lots of sad news around this area with very sick children. Say some prayers for these children they really need them. I will call you later. Love Ya Babe!!! Jenny

Tuesday, March 8, 2011 3:41 PM, CST
THANK YOU to Thrivent Lutheran. THANK YOU to the anonymous donor that donated to the American Cancer Society in my name...doing so brought a bouquet of daffodils to my doorstep yesterday! Now please step forward so I can thank you properly! THANK YOU to Katie H!!

I have been neglecting the blog....not on purpose but with purpose. I have been afraid of bragging about how fantastic I have been feeling!!! This new chemo has *not* kicked my ass; I have felt great, had energy, and the side effects have been minimal! So I have kept busy running errands, going out and about, Andy & I have gone out to dinner, we've gone over to friends' houses....you name it. I worry that tomorrows chemo will take its toll on me and will add up with the last one and wipe me out. But you know what? No worries...I had two GREAT weeks...where I got to feel *normal* where I got to act *normal* where I got to be *normal*. I have been a fully functioning parent. THAT takes nothing short of a miracle to occur, trust me! ♥S

264

<u>Guestbook Comment</u>: Tuesday, March 8, 2011 5:23 PM, CST
Isn't it great when you can connect with someone that really touches a mutual chord! I'm glad you found the woman's blog; I'm looking forward to reading some of it. I'm so glad you've had a couple weeks of "normal life" whatever normal is! It gives strength to carry on. As for here, I'm reporting we finally have the main floor, the balcony and all stairwells deep cleaned. Left to do is the basement fireplace room, bath, and work basement (major work) plus the bedroom on the second floor (that includes some flooring to put down and bookshelves to add...eventually!) TV news time. Love, R

<u>Guestbook Comment</u>: Tuesday, March 8, 2011 7:16 PM, CST
Hey Girl, so glad you are starting to feel better. I pray that with this next round of chemo you will feel the same. Summer will be here soon and you need your energy to keep up with those little peanuts of yours. I would love to come see ya tomorrow if you are up to the company. We could do whatever you wanted whether it be shopping, watching TV or going out for breakfast...you name it we will do it. Text me in the a.m. and let me know what and if you want to get together. Have a great night...sweet dreams. Candice

<u>Guestbook Comment</u>: Tuesday, March 8, 2011 7:51 PM, CST
I'm so glad you have been feeling great!!! That is so awesome!! Hope it stays this way!!! So glad you can have 'fun'!! Miss you!! We need to get together soon! Jen

<u>Guestbook Comment</u>: Wednesday, March 9, 2011 8:46 AM, CST
Of course..... crap weather when you have an appointment. Kind of a norm, isn't it? Had a GREAT time last night (or as Tony The Tiger would say: GGGRRRREEAAAT!) I'm regretting not grabbing that cart last night lol! Picture it: Me pushing you down the middle of

South Milwaukee, your arms in the air, screamin' like you just don't care! HAHAHAHAHHAHAHA!!! (I'd make the ambulance noise!)
Love ya'! Betsy

Wednesday, March 9, 2011 6:58 PM, CST
Chemo went good again today! I am just really sleepy & my eyes are burning. Time for some sleepy poo. ♥S

Guestbook Comment: Wednesday, March 9, 2011 8:30 PM, CST
Hey girl, I am so glad you felt great after your last chemo!!!! I hope you feel great after this one, too. I am sending healthy vibes and prayers your way   Good things are finally coming your way....small but good. Love ya Babe.....Joey

Guestbook Comment: Wednesday, March 9, 2011 9:53 PM, CST
Another one down! Almost done!   You and I have to get together once we get done with this phase so we won't have to worry about getting sickly. My eyes water so much with this one......I'll just be standing there & start crying. It's like WTF!?   Lisa

Thursday, March 10, 2011 1:55 PM, CST
I've started to have a reaction to the chemo...my face started getting HOT and has now turned BRIGHT RED. We're talking albino-vacationing-in-Mexico RED. So, I called oncology and they told me to chug some Benadryl...so I did. Now I have to wait to see if any of this turns respiratory and get my butt to the ER if it does. UGH the joys of killing cancer...on the UP side, I was given the best massage of my LIFE today. Truly, Katie, you are in the RIGHT profession! ♥♥♥S

Guestbook Comment: Thursday, March 10, 2011 5:19 PM, CST

Hey beautiful...I'd rather be a lurker...it sounds so much more fun!!
Sorry you are having an allergic reaction.   I hope the Benadryl
helped. Miss you!!! Love Ya Babe!!! ♥...Jenny

Guestbook Comment: Thursday, March 10, 2011 6:38 PM, CST
I know I haven't seen you since the benefit but there are a few
things I need to remind you. You are an amazingly strong,
courageous, humble and caring person. You are a great role model
to cancer patients. Your children will grow up to be strong just like
their Mommy. I love catching up on your entries. Thanks for
putting a smile on my face & putting many people's lives into
perspective. Tina

Guestbook Comment: Thursday, March 10, 2011 11:05 PM, CST
I hope the reaction has cleared up tonight, Shelly! ((HUGS)) Charity

Guestbook Comment: Friday, March 11, 2011 12:17 AM, EST
Taking part in the Springfield, MO, Relay For Life for the 6th time
this year. Ours is held in late May, and every year I put the names
of my friends and family that has been affected by cancer. Proud
and very sorry to put your name on it this year. Also looking
forward to the day you can join us and wear a "Survivor" shirt. You
keep fighting, you're doing great!!!!! Riquie

Guestbook Comment: Friday, March 11, 2011 7:23 AM, CST
I'm glad this round hasn't kicked your ass too bad!! I say shout it
from the rooftops and tell EVERYONE how great you're feeling.
You deserve it!!!!!! Hope all continues to go well. Before I read your
post I looked at your picture and thought wow! She's getting some
color-I know that can't be from WI weather. Not so funny that

you are turning red, hopefully it will go away quickly. Continue to feel well! Kim

Friday, March 11, 2011 11:10 AM, CST
CRAP!!!!!!! I totally blanked and FORGOT that I was supposed to go see the lymphedema specialist today! SHIT SHIT SHIT. Effing Chemobrain.

On another note, my face has returned to normal albino color...but my tongue has become swollen. Now, no worries, it happens every time I have chemo...I have one day where my mouth goes all nuts, hurts to talk, and eat, and I get canker sores.....along with some tongue/taste bud swelling. Grr. SO I drug up, took Benadryl, and did the baking soda rinse already...........hoping it goes away so I can eat today.

Isn't that sad...I eat so little now that I just hope today is one of the days I *get* to eat. ♥S

Saturday, March 12, 2011 11:58 AM, CST
Here's an update on my tongue (God, did you ever think I'd write THAT in a sentence?!?!?!) Lol. Had to go into Urgent Care first thing this morning-I was there at 8:10, only one other person there and it took til 9:30 to be seen. Did I mention that that one other person was a ONE YEAR OLD??? Bullshit. SO I woke up this morning with THRUSH in my mouth.....oh the joys, eh?...for those of you that never nursed, thrush is a fungal infection that makes your tongue turn white and you get all kinds of white 'puffs' all over your tongue. (well, the nursing baby usually gets it.) Ew. As I was saying.....medical doctor that I am, I self-diagnose, tried calling the Clinic to hopefully do this all over the phone since I KNOW what I

have. There's no freakin' answer. Grrr. So since I have now been speech free and eating free for 24 hours, and it's gotten WORSE...I packed up the girls and went to the closer clinic. After waiting there in the little cramped room for an hour and a half with my RAMBUNCTIOUS girls...who were by the way SICK of being there when we walked in the door already....in walks the Dr....looked in my mouth..."yes, it's thrush" and LITERALLY walked right back out with a promise that she'd send the nurse in with a script. Nice. New Doctor there, not recommending her ANYtime soon. Now I wish my tongue would stop being SWOLLEN and HURTING...and just be a tongue. Like your nails, you just don't know how good ya got it when all is running smoothly......then your tongue turns WHITE and your nails fall off. Fucking cancer. ♥S

Guestbook Comment: Friday, March 11, 2011 12:38 PM, CST
(((((HUGS))))) Betsy

Guestbook Comment: Saturday, March 12, 2011 12:11 PM, CST
Sorry to hear your day didn't start off great. I hope your tongue feels better soon! We need to hang out and scrap sometime soon! Love ya lots! Sarah beara

Guestbook Comment: Saturday, March 12, 2011 1:51 PM, CST
I like the new picture; glad you didn't stick out your tongue. Gosh! How many nasty's are there to pick from?!? Well, the cancer is being killed. Hang in there, girl. And if it is as blustery there as it is here today, hang on to something so you don't blow away. The winds are really strong here and the cold is coming in. Roberta

Guestbook Comment: Saturday, March 12, 2011 2:16 PM, CST
Ugh! Sorry you had to take your butt to the doctor and wait just for

them to confirm what you already knew! Hopefully the medication will take it away QUICKLY and your old tongue will be back! ((HUGS)) Charity

Sunday, March 13, 2011 9:13 AM, CDT

OMG! Daylight savings time turns kids into BEASTS!!!!! Ilyssa was already up my butt-ok, not literally, but I was still in bed SLEEPING at 7:20 (ok, 8:20) because JOSH was still playing his Wii game that he rented-God forbid.....while she wanted to watch 'her' shows. UGH. REALLY??? We have like five other TV's in our house?!?!? But alas, no, she needs to watch something on DVR.....and the box is on the TV that Josh is playing Wii on......LOVE being woken up that way. So now all is well.....except Ilyssa is still missing her GUM that she bought yesterday, and is convinced that someone stole it, not that she misplaced it. Ugh. Andy's still in bed.....Alaina is playing with her dollies and just whacked Diego's head on the book case...bad Diego... LMAO!! Yesterday I spent the whole afternoon shopping with my favorite girls....Ilyssa Alaina and Brittany (Alex was missing only because it was her 'friend' birthday party day) and we headed to FDL and did some serious damage shopping! Brittany has her 8th grade recognition coming up, and her mom bought her a BEAUTIFUL black dress with red on it...so I spoiled her a bit and got her the shoes (heels!) a pretty sparkly necklace and earrings, and a new purse. ☺

My girls scored with clothes, shoes, swimsuits, a dress, headbands, lip gloss, crocs, you name it! We went to Fazoli's for dinner; stopped in at work to see everyone (barely knew anyone...) but did get to see Lisa! Sarah had left early not feeling good ☹ Stinker. So we hit up the mall, ShopKo, Dollar Tree, Wal-Mart, and Fazoli's before heading back home. I think I was asleep before 8 o'clock last night!! I don't have many good days like that where I can be out and about all day without dropping like a fly! So today, it's gonna be me lying' LOW!!! I can be the mean Mom and make the kids clean up the whole house....they LOVE that.

Health wise.....feeling a tiny bit better today. My mouth is REALLY sore!!!! But ice water numbs all, and I have had lots of it today!! I'm hoping Advil does its job and reduces the inflammation...so I can TALK again!

OH!!!! We are planning the kids' (Josh-10 and Alaina-5) Birthday party for April 3rd-open house style. I'll make snacks and stuff to munch on. Hope to see some of you there ☺ ♥S

Guestbook Comment: Sunday, March 13, 2011 11:29 AM, CDT
Shelly, you're simply amazing. You've been an inspiration to me. I am very proud to call you my friend. Paul

Sunday, March 13, 2011 8:14 PM, CDT
I'm quickly losing interest in this cancer shit. S.

Monday, March 14, 2011 6:55 PM, CDT
I have been felt up more in the last WEEK than in the last five MONTHS!!!! Lol. Last week my oncology doc and care coordinator got to 2nd base....and didn't even buy me dinner. This week, my plastic surgeon and his MA got to 2nd base....again, NO DINNER! And *I* have to pay THEM?!?!? WTF. I went to the Plastic Surgeon today, because of this pain I've been having in the 'cancer spot' where my right Foob is. It's been hurting me for say a month, and getting worse and worse. Felt kind of like a bruise, and then this past week starting turning into more of 'pressure'. So the

271

irrational freak in me right away thinks "the tumor is back, and it's bigger." Then the plain freak in me thinks "oh, shit, my TE has sprung a LEAK!" Then I, plain old Shelly, think awwww crap, I broke my Foob....

ah, well...I have another one......

So the PS tells me it's PROBABLY the muscle (pec) from where they had to cut it during my mastectomies and attach the Alloderm...and where it attaches to my sternum. That muscle is pissed, and stretching is no fun for it. So I argue that I haven't had a fill on 'the girls' since Valentine's Day! Doesn't matter he says. More movement, more pulling=more pain. I say "awesome." But, I *am* more active now. I *do* use my right arm more now than before during the killer chemo. And I do see his point...since he drew me a nifty drawing...Then we talked about the fears my radiation oncologist put in my head: that my Tissue Expander on my right (cancer) side may have to come out for me to have radiation or it may have to be emptied out. Either way... seriously...one step forward.....THREE steps back! Dammit! And once again PS doc assures me he won't have to take it out...the recovery time alone would be a nightmare. He will just suck back out all the saline we've been putting in over the last 4 months...THEN we'll do radiation...then put it back in to let things 'settle'.

And the grand prize after ALL that...the EXCHANGE surgery where they take out the DAMN tissue expanders and gave me real jiggly silicone boobies. CAN NOT WAIT! These hard as a rock hooters are NOT built for comfort, are NOT built for SPEED, are NOT built for ANYTHING!! So I left 50 cc's bigger...and am planning another 'fill' for Friday...

He'd like to see me get as many fills as possible before we drain them to do all the stretching of those pec muscles. Kickin' the girls into overdrive! ♥S

Guestbook Comment: Tuesday, March 15, 2011 7:50 AM, CDT
You are welcome Shelly I am so glad I can help you even if it's only to relax for an hour. I hope your mouth feels better soon. I would stock up on taking vitamin D3 about 2000 mg a day. Cole used to get cankers all the time and we found out he was deficient. The chemo may be zapping you of that. See ya in a few weeks. Stay strong. XOXOXOXOXO   Katie

Guestbook Comment: Tuesday, March 15, 2011 6:30 PM, CDT
Ah Shell you're a good auntie as well as a good mummie. It's rewarding to learn of the good hours, too. Love Roberta

Guestbook Comment: Tuesday, March 15, 2011 10:55 PM, EDT
Hey Shell, hope your tongue is feeling better. Yep, you're right, I also didn't think I'd ever write that in a sentence. These symptoms you are journaling about-are they new to this round of chemo, or just getting worse all around from all the chemo drugs? Either way, hoping for some relief soon. I also hope for pressure relief in your "foob" areas. Not that this is at ALL the same, but last spring I pulled a muscle that runs from arm pit to chest wall. It hurt so bad, I thought I was having a heart attack. I "sort of" understand how that pain scared your pants off, not that I get all of your stuff.   Good Luck next week with the kids home. Plymouth is on break too right? I have break, but my kids don't, totally sucky. So when Jack is home all week, I will be at work. I don't see why they didn't line that up, we share a bus company? Oh well! Enjoy your grape Kool-Aid!! Ann

Wednesday, March 16, 2011 6:26 AM, CDT

Yesterday was a good day! I went for a walk; got all the kids up and ready and to school; had my appointment with Sandy, the lymphedema specialist; ran to the store; cleaned the kitchen, scrubbed the place down, ran two loads of dishes in the dishwasher... did some laundry, and still had time to do some scrapbooking.

Once I got Alaina off the bus we went for a walk right away, her zooming on her scooter, me pluggin' along ☺ It was just soooo nice out!!! We had some lunch, and took another trip around the block. I was wiped out; she was NOT! She wanted to go around more and more...and more. BUT I won out, and we stayed in and napped. ☺ For supper I made baked ziti (easy enough...ziti noodles, hamburger, pepperoni, spaghetti sauce, and mozzarella) and it was delish! We tried the new GF noodles from Mrs. Schuh...and they were a HIT! Even Ilyssa liked them! When she hears the phrase 'GF' she instantly doesn't like something lol!

After dinner the 5 of us grabbed bikes and scooters and were 'trying' to make one last simple ride around the block. We were about 1/2 way around when I don't know what happened.....Josh looked away for one second AND BLAM!!!!! He hit Alaina on her scooter smacking it in a circle and hurting her ankle.....so had to carry her screaming and crying all the way home. UGH! It was all going sooooo well.........

Bedtime continues to be a struggle-I'm guessing it's still this daylight saving shit. The kids get 'full energy' at about 7:30 p.m. and are still nuts until about 9:30.....but when they drop, they drop!!!!

Seeing the OT/PT therapist yesterday went well. She is very nice!

She took some measurements of my range of motion in both my bad side and left side. She did an exam of my scars, looking for any areas that were not healing well...but she didn't find any! She said my skin is healing very well! She also did some measuring of my strength. While I know I have lost a lot of strength and muscle... she only found one large area where I'm lacking. So I'll be doing some exercises to stretch out where it's still tight... and when I go back Friday I'll start doing some strength training. She'll also educate me more on lymphedema signs and ways to avoid getting it!

At lunch time I was carefully chewing my pizza (root canal done, but crown not happening until next Monday) when

ccc---rrr----u---u-un-unu-nnnnnn---ch.

BROKE the rest of the effing tooth off. Well, not technically OFF, but split from the temporary filling so it's still connected to the root, but is split.....so it hurts, and I DEFINITELY can NOT eat anything on that side at ALL now. I called the dentist right away. She tells me they have NOTHING open before my appointment Monday. I tell her I'm not sure how messed up it is, if I can even still have the crown?? She puts me on hold, and talks to the dentist. He says as long as I am not in pain I don't need to come in. UGHHHH!!! So now I wait..... and hopefully SOMEONE cancels an appointment so I can get in early. ♥S

Guestbook Comment: Wednesday, March 16, 2011 8:54 AM, CDT
Glad you are getting some good weather and can get outside and enjoy it!!! Hope you have a wonderful day today too. Thinking of you always.... HUGS! Charity

Wednesday, March 16, 2011 9:24 AM, CDT
Hey beautiful...sorry I've been slacking on my guestbook signing! It
was great talking to you! You sound great. Glad that you are able
to get out and about and enjoy yourself. It will continue to get
better and better! Have a great day today with your dad and eat
lots and lots! Love Ya Babe! Miss you like crazy!!! Jenny

Thursday, March 17, 2011 10:20 AM, CDT
Getting disturbingly close to our $10,000 out of pocket max for the
year. *sigh* Just needed to VENT. ♥S

Friday, March 18, 2011 7:16 AM, CDT
Blah Blah Blah.
Up early today, due to my husband being a tool.....he insists on
setting his alarm clock EVERY DAY for 6 a.m. It has been 12
years since he's *actually* gotten up at 6 a.m. Or 7 a.m. So
of course it wakes me up. And then I realize all the aches and
pains I have everywhere, and outta bed I go. I don't know why
laying down gives me so much pain, or if that's even normal for
other women that have had bilateral mastectomies, but I have an
intense amount of pain under the foob; around the side under my
pit but down towards where your bra would go around; when I get
up EVERY DAY. I have even now been up for an hour and 20
minutes, and am still cringing with each 'shock' of pain. Ugh. When
will this fuckin' nightmare END???? I can no longer lie on my
stomach...due to the tissue expanders. Laying on my right side is out
of the question...due to the amount of pain that T.E. has been giving
me for the last few weeks. Also that side is just generally more
sensitive to manipulation-even though most of the skin there is
numb. So that leaves me lying on my left side with a body pillow
tucked here and there, and between my knees. Lying on my back

doesn't work, the TE's are HEAVY and the weight of my arms/ shoulders relaxing and pulling down hurts. So then I end up putting one pillow under each elbow to avoid that 'pull'. Sleeping should be relaxing, RIGHT?!?!?!?! Not here. I toss and turn and roll over a hundred times trying to alleviate one pain before the next pain starts. Then do it all over again! No rest here....

Another 'lovely' side effect that has started....I'm flaking away....Since last week Thursday when my face reacted not-so-kindly to the Taxotere....it is acting like sunburn. I started peeling/flaking/shedding my snake like skin. So I feel kinda gross AND IT ITCHES!!!! LIKE CRAZY!!!!!! From the top most point of my forehead, down under my chin, behind my ears...I'm all flaky. No comments from the peanut gallery, either! I'm 'NOT' always flaky! Yesterday I contacted Carol, my BCCC, and she talked to the oncology nurses about my 'issues'....got nothing new-take Benadryl for the itching, put unscented mild lotion on and hope for the best. Also since my tongue is still swollen and hurting-let's hope they can adjust the dosage next time and I won't react quite so strongly! Must be because it is cumulative-the first treatment I had NOTHING like this going on.

I heard the weather was really beautiful yesterday....I barely went outside after grocery shopping. I just felt BLAH and tired. I also had a headache from hell all day.

On a happy note, Alaina came home from school bubbling over with excitement about the 'Tricky little Leprechaun' that was all over their classroom messing it up and leaving them gold coins ☺ I tell ya....she is so flippin' adorable!!! She even had a little leprechaun hat that she came home with! So CUTE!!!!!

277

Today I meet with the lymphedema specialist again. Hoping I can remember that appointment! ♥S

Guestbook Comment: Friday, March 18, 2011 3:28 PM, CDT
I have a baseball bat laying in my yard that will remedy that F*@#ing alarm clock in no time! Great stress reliever, too! Betsy

Guestbook Comment: Friday, March 18, 2011 10:22 AM, CDT
Hey girlfriend, happy Friday!! I hope you are having a wonderful day!! We are thinking about you and your family constantly. If there is ever anything you need please let me know.
Love ya lots, Jen

Guestbook Comment: Friday, March 18, 2011 4:41 PM, CDT
Hi Shelly, thanks for stopping by my CB site. I'll take some time and catch up on your journal later on tonight so I don't "cheat" I do want to see the whole story. But just know, I am pulling for ya, and I'm glad you're fighting like a GIRL!!! Hope to meet you one day soon and I hope your aches and pains are fewer and fewer as the days go by. HUGS!! Beccie

Guestbook Comment: Friday, March 18, 2011 10:57 PM, CDT
Hey lady. Try using a lotion called Aquaphor. I bought the generic version 'cause the real thing is EXPENSIVE. It's got a Vaseline type texture but it's what they told me to use when my hands got 'burned'. Lisa

Guestbook Comment: Saturday, March 19, 2011 6:02 AM, CDT
OMG I am about halfway through your journal, girl! Eek. I just have to tell you that I am laughing and crying at the same time (you know how that is) about "Dear cancer.... Fuck off and DIE." That is

definitely how I feel already!! Go YOU. I'm a big big fan of yours already. I want your autograph! Beccie

Guestbook Comment: Saturday, March 19, 2011 3:00 PM, CDT
Hope you are having a good weekend. Thinking of you. R.

Sunday, March 20, 2011 7:59 AM, CDT
Yesterday and Friday: great friends....great food...great shopping...great time scrappin'! ♥S

Guestbook Comment: Sunday, March 20, 2011 8:42 AM, CDT
It's GREAT to see soooooooooo many GREATS!!! You deserve greatness! Love ya! Mary

Guestbook Comment: Sunday, March 20, 2011 4:32 PM, CDT
Great new photo! Roberta

Guestbook Comment: Sunday, March 20, 2011 8:01 PM, CDT
WOW!!! You have had some ups but more downs lately. Your picture is so adorable.....I love it!!!! It has been total crappy weather here all day..... rain.... thunder.....lightening and repeat over and over and over for oh about 13 hours   The driveway is a holy muddy mess!!!! My car washes are when it rains, it doesn't pay to pay for them and come home because I look like I went mudding in the van. So glad kids don't have school tomorrow, a crazy week once again, hoping Jake's x-rays are good so he can get the damn boot off his leg. He is so depressed and I can't do anything about it. It is too muddy to go outside with his boot on, he can't go in the hot tub with his boot on and when he sits on the couch he has to sit on a blanket so he doesn't rip holes in it. He also can't go up and down the stairs a lot because he always trips and then tumbles. Oh well, we

will see what the doctor says on Tuesday. Take care. Miss you.
Love ya, Joey

Monday, March 21, 2011 1:20 PM, CDT
...because God didn't feel we had enough going wrong in our
lives...Andy was laid off today. Looks to be permanent. ☹

<u>Guestbook Comment</u>: Monday, March 21, 2011 1:27 PM, CDT
Oh Shelly, I am sorry about the job layoff. Give him a big hug and
I'll pray that things turn around soon for you. Beccie

<u>Guestbook Comment</u>: Monday, March 21, 2011 2:55 PM, CDT
That's horrible timing with Andy's job. Hope he gets called back soon.
Abbie

<u>Guestbook Comment</u>: Monday, March 21, 2011 3:36 PM, CDT
Shelly, you talked about making this a book. I think we can help with
that. My husband is a printer and if you are really willing to do that
I think I can talk him into doing that for you. We have done things
similar to that so this would really be quite amazing to try to
accomplish. I think you are an amazing person and your mom would
be so proud of you and all that you have had to deal with. Let me
know if this is really something you would like to do. Also if you ever
need anything printed (we do shirts, cups, posters, and decals for
vehicles) just give us a call. All of our services will be there for you
to utilize whenever you need something and no matter how many you
need just let us know. Penny

<u>Guestbook Comment</u>: Monday, March 21, 2011 3:37 PM, CDT
Hey Shel, I am so sorry to hear about this. Do you know how long
or is it a "for good" kinda thing? I am thinking of you guys~ hang

in there! I know how hard it is to really believe that God has it all figured out for us, let me tell you I doubt a lot, given the hand we were dealt you wonder what he was/is thinking half the time! How are you handling the first day with kids off of school? I wish mine were back! Austin and Dylan just can't leave each other alone! Alex is ok right now for the most part! Dang kids! Sending you guys big hugs!!! I'm always hiring for help with Alex~ hope you guys get some answers! XO Tina

Tuesday, March 22, 2011 6:28 AM, CDT
I'm not whining or trying to gain sympathy from ANYone....please understand that. This blog here is for me to vent, and get everything out so that my head doesn't implode.

Andy's layoff was indefinite... they'll "call him back when the economy picks up." Yeah...that'll be like 25 years from now. So now, I have breast cancer....not working...and my husband, the 'bread winner' is now without a job after 18 years. Awesome.

He is in the printing biz...does graphic design, etc. And also heads up the mass mailings and promotional items. He also did some sales. If you hear of anything in the area...or beyond...PLEASE let us know.
He was working in Milwaukee at St. Camillus; a small printing biz that started out doing in-house work then branched out. The choice was purely economic, he was told, and he made the most, so he was the first to go.

I cannot believe the way our life is heading.....we have never had it 'easy'...there's always been trouble, or turmoil, or drama....but THIS?????? What the HELL? We were barely making it before...but now? I worry about paying rent, paying the car

281

payment, buying food for our kids...everything.   Never mind the
medical bills.   WHICH BTW we hit our $10,000 out of pocket max
yesterday---I don't know whether to be thankful that everything else
the rest of the year will be covered 100% or cry that we have to
pay $10,000 worth of medical bills......just for this year alone
already........maybe maniacal laughter?? Unemployment is there...but at
less than 50% of his previous pay? Wow. What the F. First, I find
out I have cancer on my Ilyssa's birthday...NOW this....and Josh's
birthday is tomorrow ☹ I'm afraid to see what Alaina's birthday
brings... Jeez. Thanks for all the encouraging words and kindness...
this is all just insane. Keep us in your prayers...again.

<u>Guestbook Comment</u>: Tuesday, March 22, 2011 8:06 AM, CDT
Hey beautiful...what can I say except that I love you and your family
and you will make it thru this! I know you and YOU can do this! I
wish there was a magic wand I could wave and you would be all done
with your treatments and cancer free and that Andy would have a
job, but I can't so in the meantime I am here for you when you
need me ALWAYS!!!! Keep your beautiful bald head up and smile your
smile that makes everyone around you smile! Love Ya Babe!! Jenny

<u>Guestbook Comment</u>: Tuesday, March 22, 2011 9:07 AM, CDT
Will do girl! Hang in there, I know it is hard, call if you need
anything ok! We should really meet for breakfast/early lunch next
week when kids are back in school and we can celebrate that! My
treat! Keep your chin up! Tina

<u>Guestbook Comment</u>: Tuesday, March 22, 2011 9:40 AM, CDT
First of all....SKIP Lainey's birthday and double celebrate it next year
when you are in remission and Andy has a much better job than he
ever did. I keep on thinking it can't get worse......but I don't want to

282

jinx anything. God has a plan and although we can't see it and understand it now...someday we will. Hang in there girl the best you can, you have so many people who are praying for you. Love and miss you babe. Joey

Guestbook Comment: Tuesday, March 22, 2011 5:11 PM, CDT
I'm so so so so sorry about Andy's job, Shelly!!!! These are definitely uncertain times. We were there almost 2 years ago when Chris was laid off. It's scary. But you WILL get through. Are you able to get food stamps? Not sure how all of that works up there. One day at a time honey. You can only live in the present and make the most of THAT moment. No one knows what the future will hold. I wish I could say something to magically make it all better for you! Just know I'm here and you guys will remain in my prayers! Love you! HUGS! Charity

Tuesday, March 22, 2011 5:17 PM, CDT
Therapy=GOOD. My range of motion has gone from 105 degrees last week to 165 today. That matches my left arm, and is straight up over my head. A little stretchy stretchy and it's getting better!!! Now I'm doing strength training with a rubber band....hoping that'll build back up my strength! Went in for a fill again too. I'm up to 525cc's. The TE's are 550's, but he told me he can take them up to 800cc's. God, that's a long way to go yet, isn't it?

Prayers for my friend 'K'...bad news isn't just at my house....and she could use some cyber hugs. Love ya babe... ♥S

Wednesday, March 23, 2011 10:45 AM, CDT
The plague has hit our house again...it started with the kids...the sore throats, the sniffling, the sneezes, the sinus pain....now it has hit me

full force. ☹ I hate being sick, and even more so hate when my sinuses are stuffed and HURT. Today is our sons TENTH birthday!!!! Time has gone by quickly, that's for sure. He begged for me to let him open his presents this morning right away-so I caved. He got a DS; Legos; and a game for his DS. Happy boy!!!! Chester's also opens today! For those of you not in our area....that is our old A&W drive-in with the yummiest artery clogging burgers you can imagine!!! (Andy is on his way there to pick up our food this VERY minute!) Today also marks my SEVENTH chemo. Sure didn't think I'd *ever* make it this far. After today I can shout from the rooftops that I only have ONE MORE CHEMO TO GO!!!! WOOOHOOOOO!!!!!!!!! After that last round-all the ill effects I had to go through-I am really dreading today ☹ they are possibly going to lower the dosage with today's treatment-I'm hoping that doesn't add another chemo to the end of this. I'm getting so close to the end of it! I will be asking today how long the gap will be between chemo and rads. 2 weeks? A month? We'll see.......... ♥S

Guestbook Comment: Wednesday, March 23, 2011 8:48 PM, CDT It is so trite for we who are not going through dark waters to say cheery things to those who are. But I haven't a clue how to make all this trouble not trouble you. And I surely would if I could. I do know when we've gone through the dark waters, eventually we came up for air and life went on and we survived, sometimes for the better. But in the meantime dark waters were one scary place. I am reminded of what your great grandmother Bertha Jaquette Phillips wrote in my autograph book:

They that wait upon the Lord shall renew their strength
They shall mount up with wings of eagles
They shall run and not be weary

They shall walk and not faint.
Teach me Lord to wait.
Roberta

Friday, March 25, 2011 7:52 AM, CDT

Chemo crap strikes again. It did take longer this time...my face
didn't start turning BRIGHT red until later in the evening....around
supper time. I took all my Claritin, dexamethasone and fluconazole
(to hopefully ward off thrush this week) and slathered aloe vera gel
all over my face, neck and ears. This morning I expected it to be
gone, but NOPE I still look sunburned. Maybe because it stared so
late yesterday compared to last time? It'll hopefully fade as the day
wears on.

Last day of spring break! YAY!!! Hoping to find something fun to
do...maybe go see Diary of a Wimpy Kid 2?? I have some free
movie passes left around here somewhere. Andy is off to 'work' at
his employer that laid him off...they have some work for him (probably
to show that asshat Jake how to do Andy's job.....grrrrrr) He's not
sure how long he'll be working today or what he'll be doing but his
boss called him in today. Money's money, right?? Pride vs. money??
Money has to outweigh this one...

He did finally finish his resume and now just needs to start sending it
out and dropping it places. Hoping next week without the kids and
without the chemo & all the doctor appointments he'll have more time.
Wish us luck. ♥S

<u>Guestbook Comment</u>: Friday, March 25, 2011 8:21 AM, CDT
I hope we'll get to meet sometime soon. Just a note to let you
know my husband is following your story and asks about you nearly

every day. He walked in last night and was ticked off to no end. He was thinking about some whiner he heard on the radio and was just livid as he recounted the "real" problems that are plaguing you & your family! Our hearts & prayers are with you as you fight to be well again. Beccie

Friday, March 25, 2011 11:50 AM, CDT

Geez, I didn't even update on my chemo treatment! My blood counts were well. I discussed all my crappy side effect/reactions with the oncologist. He upped the dexamethasone from 8 to 20... hoping that will prevent some of the itching/swelling. I also was told to take dex in the a.m. and one in the afternoon daily for 3 days. And to start the fluconazole (for thrush) on Saturday to treat/prevent it. Since I had it once, it's likely to come back ☹

The treatment itself went great. The port insertion was ok. That spray is magical!!! Had R.N. Ann again...she was my first chemo nurse. She's an angel. ☺ All went good...no reactions to the Taxotere this time; my BP was nice and even. No irregular heartbeat either!! The Doc did not alter my dosage of chemo at all....he left it the same.

That night I was kinda sleepy...and slept good all night long. Only one more to go! April 6th! Party at our house April 9th!!! ♥S

Saturday, March 26, 2011 9:53 AM, CDT

I had a looooooooooong night at the ER last night....now off to urgent care in Plymouth for Josh....thinking Strep. Eff. ♥S

Guestbook Comment: Saturday, March 26, 2011 1:26 PM, CDT
Sorry for your long night, Shell! Strep is going around here too.

Hope you are able to get a nap in today!!!!!! xoxo Charity

Saturday, March 26, 2011 9:08 PM, CDT
Last night at 6:30 I started to feel super shitty. Like not-myself-
shitty. So I went to bed...at 6:30. I was sick of the kids' BS, I
was sick of yelling at my hormonal 8-year old, and just didn't want to
deal with it anymore. The Oncology RN told me that the extra
dexamethasone I would be taking would make me lash out and be
irritable.....but Whoa.

Around 7/7:30 I was feeling yuckier. I had excruciating pain in my
legs....from the Neulasta shot I presume. I was having hot flash
after hot flash then chills and chills. I had Andy bring up the
thermometer and my temp was 96.9. WTH? SO I waited 5 minutes,
and took it again. 97.1. So low? By 9:30 I was so uncomfortable
and feeling flu-like that I had Andy call the ER and page the on-call
oncologist. I *never* initiate Doctor visits!!!!!! Dr. Bettag (from St.
Nick's) was on call, and called me back within 5 minutes. Once I told
him I was getting the chills, and my temp-he suggested it was time
for me to go into the ER in Sheboygan and get checked out. *Just
in case.* Heading to the ER on a Friday night at 10 p.m. with a car
full of kids is NOT my idea of a good time!!! But away we went. The
Dr. had called ahead and let them know I was coming. I checked in,

headed to triage where my temp had gone 'up' to 97.5. BP was ok and I was sent into a room to wait....little did I know it would be such a long night!!!

First, they wanted to see if my port was infected. By accessing it. We all know how much I enjoy THAT. I asked for 'the spray'. You know, the 'magic' spray that they have at chemo??? NO ONE HAD IT. Dammit. Lidocaine (emblacreme) creme does not help, which I told them straight away. Don't bother. Meanwhile they check with the oncology floor for the numbing spray. The nurse comes in with some banana smelling spray (that they use to spray the back of people's throats when they intubate them?!?!) to try to numb my port area. That DID NOT WORK EITHER. Did they REALLY think it would??? SO meanwhile, they tell me about a "saline wheel". It is where they insert a teeny needle at the port access site and inject a bit of saline (like a TB test bubble) under the skin and somehow it confuses the nerves and the poke 'doesn't hurt'. (That's the answer I got when I asked how it worked!!) My RN told me that she "gets all skeeved out from that little bubble" and will be having some other RN come in to do it. WTF? Who tells their patient that?!??!?! So 'D' does the saline wheel. 'S' STILL HAS TO ACCESS THE PORT THROUGH THE BUBBLE??? DUH!!! How is that any different??? To start out, oncology does NOT have the magic spray at the hospital. No one does. But 'S' has time to Google on Amazon...finds it and prints it and tells me I can buy my own for $6.10. Awesome. I am about to BREAK INTO THE CANCER CLINIC to steal theirs!!! My RN only had a 3/4" needle for my port...but I know from experience that we need to use a 1" needle. So she had to go hunt one down. Maybe she still used the 3/4" for all I know....she didn't get any blood outta my port. Instead of feeling my port, and finding the sweet spot, they went through where the scab was from chemo on

288

Wednesday. Didn't work. OH MY FUCKING GOD. It was like I was the donkey, and they were trying to pin the tail on me...

The saline wheel actually helped....the poke was uncomfortable, but not painful. They had wanted to go thru my port ONLY to see if I had an infection there. Since I was not red there, or sore in that area...they thought maybe they could just start an IV, instead of stabbing my port again-that way they could draw blood AND if needed give me antibiotics. My RN comes back in. Tries to stick the back of my hand to start the IV. No blood return. She then decides-maybe this isn't necessary. Let's just call the lab guy.

ARGH!!!!!!!!!!!!!!!!!!!!

ALL of that was for NOTHING! Lab guy hits the jackpot, first try, in the crook of my elbow. He takes 4 vials of blood, and the Dr. ordered cultures too. Then he tapes me up and tells me that when they order cultures they always take double the blood. Awesome. So ANOTHER poke. Port-missed. Hand-missed. Elbow pit-hit gold TWICE! Lol. That man is a GOOD vampire. I'm bruised from here to there and look like a junkie, but he got what he needed! In the meantime, the doctor wanted me to go get a chest X-ray to make sure I don't have pneumonia. Still having chills and sweats. Hanging out in there alone, hubby was in the waiting room with all three kids. It is actually next to impossible to find ANYONE to babysit your kids at 10 pm on a Friday night!!! On the way back from X-ray, I had to pee in a cup. They also gave me Tylenol AND Motrin....hoping for the best for that fever, I guess.

Once back in the room, the Doc peeked his head in to see how I look and feel, and I tell him 'the same'. I think this was midnight-ish? He then tells me my white count is 'through the roof' which in

289

chemo land can be bad. Or good. I had just had my Neulasta shot a day before, and he didn't know if it 'kicked in' that fast? Or if I was fighting an infection? There was no way to tell. It was supposed to be between 8 and 11. Mine was 55. (Go white cells!!) Like I said, good or bad? He then tells me he wants to admit me to the hospital, unless I am STRONGLY against that. Yes, I tell him, I am STRONGLY against that. I do not feel as though I need to stay overnight in the hospital ($$$$$$), and I leave on a promise that I will call in 5 hours, at 6 a.m. to report how I am feeling before he leaves for the day.

I gimp out to the waiting room where my whole family is passed out sleeping. I tap Andy on the shoulder first, telling him what I all know in my vast knowledge of 3 hours in the ER for a freakin' blood test. Josh sits up INSTANTLY when he hears my voice, and squeaks out---my throat is KILLING ME. Ugh. Then Ilyssa pipes in that HER throat hurts too. I look at Alaina and she had a pee accident in her sleep. And she's sick too-as in yucky cough and feeling cruddy. Awesome.

TIME TO GET THE FUCK OUTTA THERE.

I did NOT call on time, and they called me at 6:30 to check in. I was actually up, but too lazy (i.e. TIRED) to get up and get the phone number for the ER...which I had left across the upstairs. I told her I slept ok, and was feeling more even with my body temperature. She said NOT to hesitate to call or come back in if it continued. I took my temp and it was still only 97.7. I usually run hot (99) so still kinda weird. I slept until NINE O'CLOCK!! When I got downstairs, Josh hadn't improved. In fact he was SO MUCH WORSE. I made the quick decision to take him in to urgent care. We were there by 9:30 a.m. and were told of the hour long wait. Ok, I decide. Not sooooo bad. There were LOTS AND LOTS of people there!!!! Everyone was sooooo sick...NOT the place for chemo girl!!!! I called Andy and asked him to relieve me of my 'mom' duty and within half an hour he was there, my Knight In Shining Armor ☺ I got the HELL outta there! 3 1/2 hours later, Josh's rapid strep test was POSITIVE, and Andy got to finally come home.

In the meantime, I get all uber freaked, because I of COURSE cannot afford to get sick, much less STREP. So I page the Oncology Doctor again. He called me right back, and I told him the circumstances of last night and this morning. He felt that my high numbers were definitely from the Neulasta shot (YAY!!!!!!!) And that I should not worry about infection in my port. He was on the fence about putting me back on an antibiotic to ward off strep, til I told him about the other 2 kids being sick...and then he realized I'd be around them all weekend yet...so he did call in a script. Peace of mind for me and my immune system. I'm supposed to follow up Monday with my Doctor to make sure I'm still alive lol.

Whew. I'm tired just reliving that all.

Josh is going through bouts of feeling better and then his throat hurting. Alaina slept most of the afternoon away....coughing like an old smoker the whole time...Ilyssa has said NOTHING of her throat all day...hoping that was just a fluke. And I missed the scrapbooking crop I was so looking forward to for weeks ☹

Oh, well, maybe I can scrapbook tomorrow. If I feel better. It's been a menopausal day...hot flashes, and mood swings, crying every time the clock ticks. WTF. This is NOT me. My legs are also

KILLING me (I know I've explained before, but for those of you just joining my blog...) I get a shot of Neulasta the day after chemo to force my body to produce white blood cells to counteract what the chemo does...which is kill off those important infection fighting cells. So while my body is mass producing these WBC....I get pain in my larger bones....legs, hips, shoulder. Mostly this time in my lower legs. This is the worst it's hurt. Ever. Mantra...one more chemo to go....one more chemo to go....I hope I can live through it. ♥S

Saturday, March 26, 2011 10:21 PM, CDT
My last blog sounded like I was kinda down on my health care facility...On the contrary...I am VERY happy with my quality of care there and love the choice that I made to stay in the area for my cancer journey. I am sarcastic by NATURE.....and can turn anything into bitching. Sorry if I came off that way! I just re-read it and thought MAN!!! But I'm tired and hopped up on pain meds....you get what you get!!! Spending the night in the ER anywhere is sucky, especially when it's a circus, they don't have what you need them to have, and you leave knowing nothing. ♥S

Guestbook Comment: Saturday, March 26, 2011 11:00 PM, CDT
Cool, sounds like Andy is going to try to get a job. Man, poor little Josh has strep ☹ When my kids had it they were burning up and miserable....but on the upside after antibiotics for 24 hours they are back to normal, which may or may not be good for you! What a long night for you, hope you are feeling better today.....how ridiculous, like everyone tells me maybe rent a room at the urgent care, ER or hospital? Save you more gas. Prayers sent your way....miss you babe...love ya. Joey

Guestbook Comment: Saturday, March 26, 2011 11:20 PM, CDT

Hey Beautiful....HOLY CRAP!!!!!!! I'm exhausted just reading everything you have been thru in the last day. I am praying that everything starts getting better for all of you and you all start feeling better. Can it get any worse? Who knows and let's not ask that question EVER again! Let's just thank GOD that the last 24 hours are over with. I love you!!!! Jenny

<u>Guestbook Comment</u>: Sunday, March 27, 2011 8:52 AM, CDT
OMG what a terrible weekend, and all I had was the flu... I better suck it up; I'm a total wimp compared to you! Tie a BIG knot... sounds like you're at the end of your rope. I'll visit as soon as I am better, promise. Need anything? Just give me a call. Maybe we can sneak out to DQ. Love you a TON! This will all be over soon. Betsy

Sunday, March 27, 2011 12:53 PM, CDT
Life just keeps throwing punches. I cannot believe all that God is throwing at us. It is hard to not get 'down' and be depressed while life just goes on around us. It's easier to just go online, or get lost in a book. Andy & I are dancing around each other, trying not to upset the delicate balance between us. We are also trying to entertain the kids after NINE LONG DAYS of Spring Break. They can go back RIGHT NOW. The DS and the movies and board games only get us so far. Hoping someone who loves us won the mega millions last night and will soon be knocking on our door with a ridiculously oversized check to share ☹ ♥S

<u>Guestbook Comment</u>: Sunday, March 27, 2011 7:57 PM, CDT
Sorry for your loooooooong too eventful weekend! Praying you can have a QUIET, relaxing Monday! oxox Charity

Monday, March 28, 2011 2:18 PM, CDT

Last night sure was a night. WHY do things always get WORSE at night! I spent yesterday with EXCRUCIATING pain in my bones: my legs, hips, and knees. After dinner, I started having pain under the TE's...where my big 10" incisions are. Ugh. You don't KNOW pain until you have it *inside* where you can do nothing about it. Hoping it's just scar tissue pulling apart, and doing its stretching thing...like 'Dr. Andy' said. I truly did not sleep all night last night. It was 12. Then 1. Then 2. Then 3. Then 4. Then 5. Then 6. Then the alarm was going off........at 7. I struggled to pull my buttooski outta bed, ONLY because I had to take Alaina to the Dr. at 8:15....Surprise! She has bronchitis! We're hoping she heals up fast & that Ilyssa does not get the strep/bronchitis floating around here!

I also had an amazing massage (AGAIN!!!) today, at Plymouth Professional Massage. Katie truly is an artist at her work, and I feel amazing. There's nothing like being pampered when you're feeling your cruddiest-it's a true mood lifter.

Once home I got the 'spring cleaning' bug....pulled out all the appliances, swept, dusted, mopped, scrubbed.....and Lysol-ed the **SHIT** out of everything! Hoping to KILL THESE GERMS!!!

Andy has been hammering out his resume to appropriate channels and applying online to jobs that are in his profession. Thank you to all our friends who have passed on leads and tips, and offered up their opinions and advice. We will get through this too...right?!?!?

I received some great news today from Carol, my *BCCC* Angel. Once again, girl, perfect timing. Xoxo ♥S

Guestbook Comment: Monday, March 28, 2011 7:39 PM, CDT
Hang in there, chickadee! I'm thinking I'll call you tomorrow afternoon... after I've had a chance to see what my doc says about the pain management plan. Eek. Beccie

Guestbook Comment: Monday, March 28, 2011 8:56 PM, CDT
Geez you could open up a lemonade stand with all those lemons being handed out to you lately. I hope things start to get better. Here's to hoping that the sickies get the hell outta your house soon! Let me know if you are in need of anything at all. I feel like I haven't seen you in a while. Love, Kim

Tuesday, March 29, 2011 1:14 PM, CDT

My mind is sharp--but the body could use some help! I did my last therapy this morning! Graduating outta there! I have full range of motion back in my arms and chest. Now I just have the 'homework' of strength training! Build up those kid lifting muscles again! I also ran to Sheboygan for my latest fill up of 'the girls'. We're at 550cc's now. I believe I was in the 600's to begin with? I don't think we need to go THAT big again....but the Doc said we'd have to definitely go bigger...to do what magic he needs to do with the skin.

Tuesday, March 29, 2011 3:20 PM, CDT

...by this time tomorrow my eyebrows will probably be all gone. ☹ They have RAPIDLY starting coming out-just to the touch. In fact I already have a bald spot up there...Vanilla Ice style... lmao. Rock On. ♥S

Guestbook Comment: Tuesday, March 29, 2011 3:26 PM, CDT
Holy sickness in the FAMILY!!!!! Your picture is beautiful, but it is almost weird, seeing you with hair again....how can that be? This day

looks so nice outside and for the most part it is....but I am ready for summer!!!!! Joey

Guestbook Comment: Tuesday, March 29, 2011 4:11 PM, CDT
I was inclined to make some smartass comment about the new photo but thought better of it. Besides, you do look good. Grab the brass ring-this ride isn't over, but it will make a great story. Love u Roberta

Guestbook Comment: Wednesday, March 30, 2011 8:51 AM, CDT
Eyebrows, schmybrows! Nothing a sharpie marker won't fix!
DeAnna

Guestbook Comment: Wednesday, March 30, 2011 9:40 AM, CDT
Hey Beautiful...love you and miss you like crazy!!! Who the hell needs eyebrows anyways...I'm plucking the shit outta mine!!! Love Ya Babe!!! Jenny

Guestbook Comment: Friday, April 1, 2011 6:20 PM, CDT
Hi Shelly...thinking good thoughts for you. I graduated last Thursday, too! Got a certificate, confetti and warm wishes from the nurses. Now a three week wait to the next step. Hang in there...as long as we have our sense of humor we're still winning! Saw a t-shirt the other day. Printed right across the chest was "Yes, they're fake. My real ones tried to kill me!" Love to everyone! Uncle Rick

Guestbook Comment: Saturday, April 2, 2011 10:22 AM, CDT
Hi Shell! And congratulations Rick on your graduation! That's good news. A spot of good news is always welcome. ♥ ♥Roberta

Saturday, April 2, 2011 8:33 PM, CDT

Whew! I haven't been to a doctor all week!!! Lol! I won't lie; it has been a rough week. My mouth is still recovering from chemo. That blasted tongue! I spent a lot of the week hurting from the Neulasta shot-this time in my legs mostly. It's already the weekend and another day closer to my last chemo ☺ Wednesday is THE DAY. (Also the day we get our taxes done.....yuck!) We have a busy week ahead-quite a few appointments scheduled, and by then all the birthday parties will be a thing of the past again!

It was hard enough accepting that Josh turned 10 a few weeks ago-but my itty bitty babe Alaina is now (officially) FIVE. Wow. Even worse was the fact that we had to take Josh to his middle school lock-in (so they could get used to their new school.) Ugh. Middle School! I feel old!!!!!!!!!! ♥S

Guestbook Comment: Sunday, April 3, 2011 1:42 AM, CDT
I am thinking about you every day. Thank you for your support. Give a call when you feel up to it, it must suck to have mouth issues to deal with among all else. I am excited you will be graduating your chemo treatments!! Good work kicking that cancer to the curb! Beccie

Sunday, April 3, 2011 9:16 AM, CDT
Today's the day! Open house at our place for the kids' birthdays! Noon....taco dip & chips; summer sausage & cheese & crackers; chicken tacos......cake(s) and ice cream......YAY!!!! ♥S

Guestbook Comment: Sunday, April 3, 2011 9:42 AM, CDT
Enjoy your day today! Charity

297

Sunday, April 3, 2011 10:06 AM, CDT
Have a great day Shelly~ have fun! You rocked those cakes! Tina

Sunday, April 3, 2011 7:51 PM, CDT

Ugh. The blisters on my tongue are BACK. No idea if it was too much talking, too much eating salty foods, or just luck of the chemo draw....but having blisters on your tongue HURTS LIKE A BITCH....and makes ya talk funny. They are white and swollen and hang off my tongue. This is a pain like no other. ♥S

Sunday, April 3, 2011 4:04 PM, CDT
Happy Birthday Open House Day to all the kids. Sounds like a grand day to me. I love to have people over (which we did today, too). There's nothing like having a professional baker in the house. Photos of cake(s) soon??? And feeling good enough to do this, Shelly, is a milestone. Happy day! Roberta

Tuesday, April 5, 2011 12:26 PM, CDT
I am sorry we did not make it on Sunday for their birthdays! I would've been great to see all of you!!! I miss ya! Kasie and I had gotten back late afternoon from being at the Women's Retreat with our church. Then she had poms try-outs from 3 to 6. Tyler had to work from 2 to 6. Then all the fun stuff-getting caught up with laundry and the house cleaning from Tyler being home alone with the dog all weekend! Then other "issues" to deal with! I hope the party went well!! Middle school, wow, I can't believe it! And the "baby" being 5. It does go quick, insanely quick! Enjoy every insane crazy moment, along with all the sweet and loving moments! I love you, miss you like crazy, and think about you all the time! Love you, again! Melissa

Tuesday, April 5, 2011 12:30 PM, CDT
Almost forgot, Tyler came home from work on Sunday with a 100
degree temp, so he was off school yesterday too cause it was still
99. Then this a.m. it was 96.4-that's a change! He had his basketball
banquet last night, which none of us went to with him being ill. Kasie
had the second part of her tryouts, and me I just sat around... (JK,
I wish). I wouldn't have wanted to spread his germs, I know how
you love them and all but I decided to be selfish this time! ☺ I do
pray that you are feeling better from the leg pains and the other
discomforts! Melissa

Tuesday, April 5, 2011 3:41 PM, CDT
Day-before-last-day-of-chemo. ☺ ♥

Wednesday, April 6, 2011 2:52 PM, CDT
Sitting in the 'big chair' for the LAST time here! Hopefully for the
rest of my *LIFE!* Met with the Doctor: he said I can have my port
out in 3 weeks!!!!!!!!!!!! KICKASS!!! He also said that I am to meet
with the radiation Doc in a month to start rads. The first
appointment is in 2 weeks....where I'll go through a simulation CT
scan...get all lined up and positioned for it, then they'll tattoo the
spots that have to be radiated, so they do it in the SAME spot each
one of the 33 times I have to go. After radiation is coming to a
close, I will see the oncologist again for a checkup. He tells me I
will not need a CT or BONE scan at the end of this unless my lab
work comes back wonky. WHAT???? Seriously? No final 'scan' to
let us all know that the cancer is gone, or that it is under control??
I do not in any way shape or form understand that. I will have
blood work every 3 months for 2 years. He tells me it is to
monitor the tumor markers in my blood. I will also then start the
Tamoxifin-the chemo pill that I will take for five years. Whew. ♥S

Guestbook Comment: Wednesday, April 6, 2011 4:58 AM, CDT
Happy last chemo day!! Hope everything goes smoothly today and all
those nasty side effects decide to leave you alone this time. Way to
go kicking this cancer's butt!! Talk soon and love ya chica! Sarah

Guestbook Comment: Wednesday, April 6, 2011 7:15 AM, CDT
Thinking of you today as you go in for your LAST Chemo! The cake
looks so yummy, great job! Hope the celebration goes well
afterwards. Beccie

Guestbook Comment: Wednesday, April 6, 2011 8:07 AM, CDT
YAY, HOORAY for the last chemo day!!!! Good luck today! Karen

Guestbook Comment: Wednesday, April 6, 2011 8:52 AM, CDT
Yay!!!! Thinking of you today as you go in for your last treatment
☺ Kim

Guestbook Comment: Wednesday, April 6, 2011 10:46 AM, CDT
This is the first day of the rest of your life. Here's to long &
beautiful. Roberta

Guestbook Comment: Wednesday, April 6, 2011 3:16 PM, CDT
YAAAAAAAAY! No more 'big chair'!!! So happy for you. Xoxo
Charity

Guestbook Comment: Wednesday, April 6, 2011 6:54 PM, CDT
Simulation CT? Mary

Guestbook Comment: Thursday, April 7, 2011 8:34 AM, CDT
Another chapter closed and a new one open!!! So glad you are done
with chemo. Your cake looked soooo yummy and pretty. I'm going

to be ordering-just need an occasion! ☺ Kim

Thursday, April 7, 2011 12:58 PM, CDT
Kim H: who needs an occasion for cake?!?!?!? Enjoy! ♥

<u>Guestbook Comment</u>: Thursday, April 7, 2011 3:35 PM, CDT
Way to go girl! Roberta

Friday, April 8, 2011 6:42 AM, CDT
Things are moving/changing quickly around here. The kids are loving being able to have the whole neighborhood over to play again (outside only!) But it's so fun to walk outside and see 10 kids hanging out here! I love being 'THAT' house! It also seems the sickness has finally left the house! WOO HOO! Andy has had some possible good news. Let's leave it at that.

I have been a "baking whore" as Kim says....baking cakes like crazy and enjoying decorating again. (Pictures on my Facebook page) The extra income is great while Andy isn't working (for the third week now--UGH!) and I have orders coming in every day! VERY exciting!!!! It's also good to know I "still got it" after being off of work since the end of October! On that note I have been released to go back to work on May 2-my choice-and I gotta say I'm EXCITED!!!! It will be nice to get back to 'normal' and get back to functioning in an environment other than the HOUSE!!! I'm to the point where I'm bored silly being here, and Andy and I are just tripping over each other. It's time. I'm done with PT, my scars are healed nice, & other than getting my port out that first week back, there should be no hitch.

A week or two later I'll be starting radiation. That will mean driving

301

from Plymouth to Fond du Lac for work, then from FOND DU LAC to SHEBOYGAN every day for treatment; and back to Plymouth home. I'm hoping I can have radiation late in the afternoon so that I can at least work mornings when I **do** work. I dunno. We'll see. I don't even know if I'll be able to keep my full time status when I go back--since I used up my FMLA at the end of January... they hired someone else full time to replace me. Now all they have open in the bakery is one part time cake decorator spot...so I said I wanted it, since I really like doing it AND it's nice and light duty while I reintroduce myself to working. I also talked to Leigh to see if I could be secondary elsewhere in the store to keep my full time....the hours would be nice while my hubby is unemployed....because part time I'm only guaranteed 16 hours a week...and by experience you don't always get that. My Manager has been WONDERFUL ...she is checking into all that this week. It will be nice to know what's going on! I'm not sure when I'll be back on the schedule-it takes a while to get back in the computer system. But they are good at just filling you in on paper. So like I said, GOOD CHANGES!!!! The weather is changing, the flowers are blooming (I saw purple crocus' BLOOMING outside at the VLCC!!!!!) and summer has to show up eventually!!!!! ♥S

Guestbook Comment: Friday, April 8, 2011 7:11 AM, CDT
I cannot tell you how great you looked yesterday!! It was as though a weight has been lifted off your shoulders! Again the cake was so awesome! In looks and taste. I don't know how you do it, but you continue to amaze me! Have a great day, Kim.

Guestbook Comment: Friday, April 8, 2011 7:13 AM, CDT
Hey beautiful...What an accomplishment! Never doubted that you could or WOULD do it! You are amazing! You have been so busy and

that is GREAT! Of course you still have it...talent like that does not come and go it just IS!! You are an inspiration to all of us!!! Thank you for that. Keep on going...love ya and miss ya! Jenny

Guestbook Comment: Friday, April 8, 2011 6:34 PM, CDT
☺ Jen

Saturday, April 9, 2011 5:43 AM, CDT
Today's "whine" list....

Neuropathy (see definition in next paragraph) in my hands and legs from the knees down; excruciating bone pain in both legs, so far only from the knees down...usually today, day 2, it goes up to my hips and upper leg bones. Awesome. Bloody noses around the clock; my face is still BRIGHT red 2 days later than usual AND I woke up this morning with the tongue 'issues' again. Anything I forgot? Ugh. Thank God this is the LAST LAST LAST time of this.

** Chemo Induced Peripheral Neuropathy
Disorders of peripheral nerves are frequent complications of chemotherapy and certain other drug therapies. As more and more effective therapies for cancer are found and patients are living longer, peripheral neuropathy complications of chemotherapy is increasing in prevalence. Chemotherapy can cause degeneration of peripheral sensory and motor nerves and cause patients to present with sensory disturbances, balance problems or weakness.

Symptoms
The symptoms of chemotherapy induced peripheral neuropathy depend on the type of chemotherapy and which nerve fibers are affected. In chemotherapies that affect mainly the sensory nerve fibers, the

303

patients experience unusual sensations (paresthesias), numbness, balance problems or pain. In cases where the motor nerves are affected, the patients may experience weakness of the muscles in the feet and hands.

<u>Guestbook Comment</u>: Saturday, April 9, 2011 7:04 AM, CDT
Hang in there girl! Hope you feel better~this is the last time!!!!! Have a great day! Tina

Saturday, April 9, 2011 7:07 AM, CDT
My PEACH FUZZ is growing back on my dome!!! ♥S

<u>Guestbook Comment</u>: Saturday, April 9, 2011 8:15 AM
Way to go!!!!! You are simply amazing, you inspire me. Love ya, Joey

<u>Guestbook Comment</u>: Saturday, April 9, 2011 6:45 PM
Hi Shelly...talk to your docs and nurses about taking extra B12 and Selenium to maintain healthy nervous systems. I had "drop foot" in my left foot coming out of the hospital last year, and started myself on B12 tablets twice daily. That and simple at home physical therapy helped. Later I started taking Selenium. Drop foot gone in about 3 to 4 months. Still taking the B12 and Selenium. Take care...Uncle Rick. P.S. Luv the "fuzzy" photo!

Sunday, April 10, 2011 3:24 AM, CDT
Well, of COURSE it is the middle of the night. Miss 'I'm 5 Now and Don't Need To Sleep' slept from 7:30 pm til 1 am. That's it, that's all I get. Of COURSE once she was up playing and turning on all the lights upstairs, I was up. Now it's 3:30 in the morning, and she's eating a yogurt....and I'm waiting for the Ambien to kick in!

We had a pretty good day yesterday! The girls were outside ALL day-like from 12 til 7!!! Josh was in the house with me for a few hours upstairs watching a movie (Transformers 2) since he wasn't feeling quite right... headache; throat hurt (STILL WTF!!!); tired; lethargic......he was locked up with me......until the neighbor came over to play...and he BEGGED and BEGGED and BEGGGGGGGED to go out and play. So since I was half asleep already (trying to keep my mind off my leg pain) I said GO!!!!! Andy had to give him some Motrin, and that helped him I guess. He was okay until it was time to come in-then he still wasn't feeling great. After a hot shower-straight to bed he went...so we thought! 1 1/2 hours later....sneaky Pete snuck downstairs to 'hang' with us and watch the THREE cops swirling their lights parked in front of our house. Three? Really? Slow night in Plymouth or WHAT?!?!?! But at 10 I went upstairs with him, snuggled him up (doesn't happen often at 10 years old anymore!!!!) and he was snoring lightly within a minute! Just crazy! They are so tired....but just won't give in! The girls also both took a hot bath......and I think there was about a POUND of dirt in the bottom of that tub! I LOVE WARM WEATHER!!!!!! Today we have a special BIRTHDAY PARTY to go to! Happy 14th Birthday Alexis!!!! I'm not sure how long we can stay; but it will be fun! And nice to see everyone too. I get the honor of making her birthday cake and will post pictures of it later today on FB when I frost it. ☺

After that we will be heading to Fond du Lac-the kids do not have school tomorrow-so we're taking them for some fun and good times! Crossing my fingers that everyone is feeling awesome when they get up!

My hubby had a great meeting yesterday with a potential employer-keep your fingers/legs/eyes/you-name-it crossed! This is our THIRD week at home BONDING together....and it's getting OLD!!! I love my hubster to PIECES....but not 24/7/365!!!! We have watched all the new movies....watched all our DVR'd shows...now we're just feeling guilty lying around all the time! We've cleaned the garage; cleaned the office; gone through the play room and purged 'stuff'; we are caught up on laundry-almost; now we have started some light yard work. Pretty soon we're going to be desperate enough to start painting! Lol. ((((oh, SARRAAAAH ......whatcha doin' today?!?!??)))

Craziness. Boredom. Guilt. I could never sit home every day (ok, for longer than I have been...) THANK GOD I'm going back to work soon!!!!! ...and let's all say a silent prayer that Andy will be too. ♥S

Guestbook Comment: Sunday, April 10, 2011 4:25 PM, CDT
Just a note to say Hi. You and Andy are in my prayers. Loved seeing all the awesome cakes. Hope you are feeling better and stronger every day. Toni

Monday, April 11, 2011 7:31 PM, CDT
...some days it's so easy to get down...but there are days like today that you really need to stop and appreciate what you have; the good times you've been shown; the things you've been given.

A few weeks ago we were VERY fortunate to be given a Gift Certificate for an overnight stay at the Holiday Inn in FDL-now to most people, that doesn't seem like a lot-BUT it is to US!!!! It is VERY rare for us to spend money on us and go do a 'getaway'. And that's under 'usual' circumstances! Now that we've been under the whole stressful situation that we are in-and add to that Andy's lay off....UGH! The best I can hope for is an overnight inpatient stay in the hospital LOL! With some luck they'll let me back out...

So on a SPUR OF THE MOMENT last minute decision....I made reservations to head outta town last night.   There was no school today for the kiddos... and with the both of us off of work it was easy timing. We got there after supper; and within 5 minutes the kids were in the pool!   We spent quite some time there swimming (the pool was sooooooo warm!!!!) And jumping and splashing, and sitting in the hot tub!!! Ahhhhhhhhhhhh.   Around 8:30 we headed to Duffy's Steakhouse--the restaurant there and immediately were ushered out to the lobby for a tornado warning. The kids were fine with that....but were nearing the end of their day, getting tired and HUNGRY. Luckily the isolation only lasted 5-8 minutes and they stayed open longer to accommodate us....the kids were so happy to finally eat! Part of the "deal" in booking our room included all kids' meals FREE-supper and breakfast the next morning. We also received free cocktails w/ supper and 10% off our meals.

After dinner we all headed back to our room (VERY nice rooms as well!) and Alaina and I fell dead asleep. Andy took the kids to the arcade to use up the last of their energy....I barely heard them come back in!

This morning we got up early again...and headed in to the restaurant (our whole meal and all drinks were FREE again!) before heading out to the pool. We got lucky and got about an hour and a half of swimming time before we had to check out. The kids were so good...had so much fun, and were smiling nonstop the whole time in the pool. Life is good. ♥S

Guestbook Comment: Monday, April 11, 2011 7:55 PM, CDT
Sounds like a lot of fun was had! How awesome!! Happy you guys

were able to get away! Didn't hear ya beep when you went past tho??? Tina

Guestbook Comment: Tuesday, April 12, 2011 7:47 AM, CDT
How AWESOME (aside from the tornado evac.) You so deserved it (especially the good behavior-from Andy. Lol.) Mary

Wednesday, April 13, 2011 9:20 PM, CDT
The days keep ticking by...today was my appointment for another fill. Getting close to the end...for God's sake. Talked to the plastic surgeon today about what we'll have to do next week at my simulation CT scan. If you will remember, there was talk of emptying out my tissue expander to do the radiation. The PS told me that it would be a 'day of' decision. Since the clinic is right next door, they can just run over and stick me to draw out what they need. Sometimes it's the opposite boob that needs to be emptied because of the angle they need to go at the cancerous area from.

Andy has continued to have a great week-the 2nd meeting with his potential employer yesterday went amazingly well. There are some details to work out yet and hopefully he can start on Monday. I'm still trying to not get excited-you just never know what will happen! He also received a call last night for ANOTHER interview elsewhere-he's keeping his options open, knowing that we need to put our family FIRST.....and not think about who what or where he's working. Life has been tough-you have to be selfish. It all boils down to money! ♥S

Guestbook Comment: Thursday, April 14, 2011 11:28 AM, CDT
Hey beautiful...just got caught up on your posts. Sounds like a lot of fun and positive things happening the last couple days! Hope you are

feeling good. Great news about the job offers for Andy. Praying that one of them fits your family just the way you need it to! Dreary day here today...YUCK!!! Makes me crabby!! Kids stuck in the house all day especially after the last couple days being outside all day. Oh well... Continue to be your amazing self! Miss ya & Love ya!!! Jenny

<u>Guestbook Comment</u>: Thursday, April 14, 2011 1:06 PM, CDT
Glad to hear I made you smile, but I think double D's could be a little dangerous! ☺ Mary

<u>Guestbook Comment</u>: Thursday, April 14, 2011 10:32 PM, EDT
Hey Girl, it's good to see you writing that things are looking up in your house, hope it continues. I have had your hubby in my thoughts and prayers that he finds a job SOON. I can't even imagine his stress level, not to mention your own. I am so glad that all 5 of you were able to have a tiny, mini vaca! For kids a couple hours in a warm pool is the total best! Back to work, that will be fun? Not so fun: your commute for Dr. appt.'s, but you will deal with it in typical Shelly style, I know it!! LOL! Love the pic of your fuzz! Ann

April 15, 2011 7:04 PM, CDT
Such a HECTIC day! I got up at 6 am and headed to FDL to pick up my frosting that Sarah had gotten @ Sam's Club. Came home, did a cake for my cousins son...Happy Birthday Bryce!!! Andy & I went to a few rummage sales in Plymouth; headed to Chilton; came home; got Alaina off the bus. After lunch I had a horrible headache and slept for a few hours. Something with this last chemo.....I feel sick. I have about 4-7 severe nosebleeds a day (where out of nowhere it starts running out of my face!) The nosebleeds are

309

from chemo-wrecked my soft tissue. And I have been getting SUCH bad headaches every day. Ugh.

May have something to do with burning the candle at both ends lately...spent the night out with Bets & Mel last night! We went to Texas Roadhouse (my first time there!!!) and had some laughs and chit chat. Great food too! Now we're having a family night watching Bedtime Stories ☺ ♥S

Guestbook Comment: Friday, April 15, 2011 8:45 PM, CDT
TGIF......haven't been on here for a while, so fun to catch up. We have had so much sickness in the month of March, I was hoping for a wonderful APRIL but NO!!!! Any who, I am keeping your family in our prayers for Andy to find a job that he loves or pays bucko bucks...it sounds like you and Andy are having lots of quality time together just loving each other lol. Jake and Shawn left tonight for turkey hunting and I had some special things planned for the 3 girls and myself until Roo puked all over me, then the plans went down the drain. The joys of being a mother Now the 3 girls and I are going to have a lazy weekend locked up in the house together because of the weather-actually doesn't sound too bad for me. I just started Castaways today, so at least I have a book! Well, sickie is moving so I better get the bucket! Love and miss ya. Joey

Sunday, April 17, 2011 10:39 AM, CDT
Thrush is back ☹ Nosebleeds, headaches, and crankiness...blech. S

Guestbook Comment: Sunday, April 17, 2011 2:08 PM, CDT
ohhh that sucks. Just remember hon it'll only get better from here! We're almost to the top of the mountain and after rads it's all downhill and smooth sailing. Lisa

Tuesday, April 19, 2011 4:19 PM, CDT

If it isn't one thing...it's another. Last summer I had some serious stomach issues....I ended up in the hospital; had an endoscopy; found out I have GERD; Barrett's esophagus. There were 5 healing ulcers and my stomach was herniating 'UP' into my esophagus. ☹ During the endo, they had to push it back down....I've been taking Prilosec for the past 10 months: no problem. Saturday night I woke up with the most crippling stomach pain....deja vu of last June. It feels like your stomach builds up pressure and could explode. Add that to the horrific acid reflux....UGH. And I'm not one to overreact and make it 'worse' than it really is. But that is a LOT of pain. When your stomach is all acid, with nothing to neutralize it.....yuck.

So I made a doctor appointment right away for this morning. I have to double my omeprazole and also start taking Zantac in addition to. It's possible the chemo meds ate a hole in my stomach tissue and gave me another ulcer. Awesome. If in the next two weeks this doesn't help...then I have to have another endoscopy to investigate. That was my EARLY morning. Then my Dad popped in to visit; the bus missed our house when bringing Alaina home; had a shitty drive to Sheboygan in all this SLUSH-but had a great lunch with Ann and Ashley ☺ Came home to snooze...and the darn phone kept ringing. Silly hubby. BTW his new job is going well so far. Thanks for the prayers....they're being answered.

Woke up 5 minutes too late to go get the kids (yikes!) and flew outta the house to go get them. Josh had the BRILLIANT idea to start walking home, since I wasn't there. (It was 3:50....they were let out at 3:45) I was sooo ticked at him. And of course Ilyssa went along with it. So they both got CHEWED OUT in the van all the way home. I am so dang tired lately....hoping for some energy soon. ♥S

Guestbook Comment: Tuesday, April 19, 2011 10:08 PM, CDT
For my gastritis they gave me 40mg of Nexium and 1gm of sucralfate (which helped the most). I can identify with some of your pain, and it's not fun when it's just that. Mary

Guestbook Comment: Wednesday, April 20, 2011 9:30 AM, CDT
Way to go Andy! Way to go Shelly! Not that there aren't bumps in the road (always) but you make a good team and live life. Blessings, Roberta

Guestbook Comment: Wednesday, April 20, 2011 11:03 AM, CDT
I'm so thankful for you and Andy. Way to go, Hubby!! An unexpected blessing to have him get a job nice and close to home. I know what you mean, my Mister works an hour away and it sucks having them out on the roads so much especially in this "craptastic" weather (craptastic, how funny!). Hope all your tummy problems get worked out very soon. And, Shelly, thanks so much for your support on my CB, too. I'm thinking I might get back to work soon but I still have next week off for sure and then only I'll only be working three times a week so let me know if I can buy you coffee or ice cream soon! Beccie

Friday, April 22, 2011 6:10 PM, CDT
This week I had my 'simulation' CT scan. That whole appointment consisted of the doctor examining the cancer site, my scars, and tissue expanders. He also talked about the whole experience, AND the good news......I only need 28 days of radiation, not 33 because I had clean margins within 5 cm (I believe that was the # he said....he was kind of talking to himself, and I was eavesdropping) So that is GOOD! 25 at the 2 'preventative' sites, and 28 in the 'cancer spot' and lymph node area. Wahooo! 5 days closer to the END!!! Originally

I was told 33 days of it. Then he told me that my TE's were probably going to be OK and not in the way. That they like them to be taut, and MINE ARE! LOL! Hoping that remains true...not that either one has to be deflated. Then I was taken into the CT simulation room with Nurse Carrie...she was VERY nice, and helpful, and informative. Yes, I know it is her job, and it's what she does every day, but she definitely made it personal and that made me feel better. I have in the past had some NOT SO GREAT experiences with Nurses that are PMS'ing.....and that, my friends=disaster! She verbally went through what was all going to go down, and then we got to it. I had to lie on the table, and put my right arm up (like raising your hand half-heartedly in school-elbow bent) and there was a peg to hold on to. There was also a 'rest' for my elbow that was fully adjustable. Once I was 'in place' she fired up the lasers (Jeez that sounds like it's straight out of an Austin Powers movie!) And they mapped out the area that I was to get the radiation. Dr. P came back in, drew all over me with a Sharpie, and when he left, the nurse did some more definitive drawing, measuring and marking by millimeters. Then they put on some tape that has some wires running through it (the tape itself looked like a clear twist tie, but it was more like that packing tape that has the strings in it that you can NOT rip through...) The CT scan would pick up the wire.....since sharpie doesn't show up on there. One thing that she stressed repeatedly.....is that you can NOT MOVE. NO talking. NO heavy breathing. NO adjusting to get comfy. Once she had it all on and positioned, she put me into the CT scan... only to find out the table was 'to the left' too far, and my left arm was gonna bump into the scanner.....therefore throwing off all the measuring.....and we had to redo the measuring. No biggie I guess. Once we redid everything, I went in and out of the machine about 6-8 times. I had to have my head turned all the way to the left; looking away from 'the side';

right arm over my head, left arm under my body and ass; knees up on a pillow....for about 20 minutes. Now I'm sure to all of you that seems like no big deal...but MAN!!! Am I stiff today from holding that position...trying not to flinch, or twitch, or take a deep breath! My legs are so sore!! The pillow under my knees was a bit too high...and I *should* have said something right away...but I never do. So I dealt with it. SHOULD NOT HAVE DONE THAT. They did all their scans, and then she applied India Ink to 4 spots (above my cleavage line, in The Valley, one under my chest line and one under my pit-down my side) and stuck me with a needle to tattoo the places that they will use as guidelines to do the daily radiation. They're about the size of big-ish freckles, and look like blackheads. A little painful but NOTHING compared to what I've been through.   Finally I could get up (like a 90 year old grandma!!!) and she showed me the building ....the treatment room, the waiting room, changing room and entrance. It will take the Dr. about 5 business days to come up with a treatment plan, and then they will call me. It will probably be at least the 2nd week of May when I start...I also go back to work May 2 and removal of my port is on May 5th YA-FREAKIN-HOOO!!!! Having the port in is just one more sick reminder of chemo ☹ one more discomfort every time I move my head, and swivel my neck; one more pain by my tissue expander which now pushes against each other (port and TE) so when I lay down there's more discomfort. The scar is ugly enough....get the damn thing OUT!

I talked to Carol and found out it's an in-office procedure....they numb you up with lidocaine (Since it doesn't work on me...she will be bringing the magic spray. ☺) You go into the office, they numb you up, and pull that nasty sucker right out. YUCKY!! I think I may pass out....just imagine that long, slick nasty bloody thing slurping out of your chest.....UGH.....total willies. (Sorry Sarah--I <u>know</u>.) So I am kinda panicking about that...I've gotten the heebie jeebies over smaller things...and that wasn't even ME. Not the pain; that I can take. That nasty pulling feeling.....blech. And Carol, if you're reading this...I am DEAD serious...you better bring a pillow and smelling salts. Ok. That is coming up quick....going back to work is coming up....our trip to the Dells is coming up.....all kinds of great things in the future. Keep up the prayers.....they're working!!! ♥S

Guestbook Comment: Friday, April 22, 2011 11:59 PM, CDT
hey lady...well ur officially ahead of me in the 'game' now. I was supposed to meet with my Rads Doc on Wednesday and do my simulation but on Monday I had blood drawn for a different genetic test-some abnormality found in only like 2% of all breast cancer patients. However it causes MANY different cancers and if you have rads it WILL cause more cancer so my doc wanted to wait till I got the results which obviously I have no problem with. So now my appointment isn't until May 9th. Was hoping to be DONE with rads by early June...looks like that ain't happening. Lisa

Guestbook Comment: Saturday, April 23, 2011 4:56 PM, EDT
Again, I love to read positive things here! It's gotta feel good to write them when things are starting to look up. 'Cuz it's about time you see the end to this tunnel. I hope you have a great time on your vacation & going back to work goes smoothly! Ann

Guestbook Comment: Sunday, April 24, 2011 8:43 AM, CDT
Happy Easter!! Got caught up on your good news! Port out and 5 less days of rads! Yay! So glad you're done with the crappy chemo, you're getting so much closer to being cancer free!! Beccie

Monday, April 25, 2011 9:28 PM, CDT

What a beautiful day!!! Lots of outside time...did some bummin' around...went to see the doc about my port incision...which has some itty bitty infection-nothing to worry about though. Squeezed in a nap, laundry, baked 6 cakes and made dinner. Why am I not in bed? ♥S

Tuesday, April 26, 2011 8:40 PM, CDT

Awesome time with Sarah tonight ☺ ♥S

Tuesday, April 26, 2011 8:45 PM, CDT

Well, today I got 'the call'. I am to start radiation next week already ☹ This Thurs I have to go for some scans (thought I did that already?!?!?!) Then I'll start my 'rads' next week. Ugh, daily trips to Sheboygan AND back to work in Fond du Lac all in the same week!?? WISH ME LUCK. I'm concerned about my stamina during rads; I'm still so tired from chemo/being sick/doing nothing for 6 months. Here's to hoping work is very accommodating, and as flexible as they say! ♥S

Guestbook Comment: Tuesday, April 26, 2011 6:53 AM, CDT
Glad I didn't come and bug you or I would be exhausted!! Mary

Guestbook Comment: Tuesday, April 26, 2011 8:46 PM, CDT
We need to do that again soon! I'll keep looking for cake ideas. Sarah

Guestbook Comment: Tuesday, April 26, 2011 9:44 PM, CDT
So glad things are looking up for you girl! Prayers are still being sent. Miss you girl, Love ya... Joey

316

Wednesday, April 27, 2011 8:09 AM, CDT
Hey beautiful...it's been awhile since I've been on here. Naughty
naughty me!!! It sounds like things are finally coming to an end if
not moving along nicely. I can't believe you will be going back to
work next week. You will do amazing like you do everything, but
remember not to push yourself and if it is too much it's too much!
Remember to take care of yourself and not push it because you
have come so far you don't want to go back, but if you do you will
again move forward like you always do! You have gone through so
much and have overcome so much you simply AMAZE me and that
makes me feel honored to call you my friend! I love and miss you
so much. Know that even when I don't sign your guestbook or talk
to you for a while you are ALWAYS on my mind! Love Ya Babe!!
Jenny

Thursday, April 28, 2011 7:47 PM, CDT
I went today to VLCC and had my scans done. I'm all clear for
radiation! Today was just get naked (in a gown) get on the table,
and don't MOVE!!!! Then they took X-rays to make sure everything
lined up right; my tissue expanders were NOT in the way at all
THANK YOU GOD; and then they drew all over me again with
marker. It took about 30 minutes, and I was dressed and back out
the door!!! ♥S

Thursday, April 28, 2011 9:35 PM, CDT
Have a super duper time this weekend!! Love ya! Mary

Friday, April 29, 2011 7:58 AM, CDT
Hi Shelly, sorry it's been awhile. I have been working two jobs (no,
it's not to stay out of trouble) but I am always thinking about you.
Yes May 11 I will be going to get my mammogram (they come to

317

work). When my doctor talked to me he wanted to make sure I get this done because of my age. I told him, of course I am going, I know someone who would "Kick my Ass" if I didn't. I won't be so long next time to write. Pam

Monday, May 2, 2011 7:49 AM, CDT

Wish me luck today; my first radiation treatment is this morning-I'm nervous about it!!! Just another 'new' thing. Then my kids are all starting their daycares today (they're nervous too) because I am going back to work today for the first time in 6 months and 2 days.

WHOA.

I'm torn--I'm really excited to go back to work; but at the same time it's not like I've been on vacation this whole time....I feel jipped!!! So I'm going back SLOWLY.....4 hour shifts.
I'm also having my port removed this week!!

Big things big doings.... ♥S

Guestbook Comment: Monday, May 2, 2011 10:51 AM, CDT
Wishing you well today along with stamina and patience, and humor. A whole new chapter begins. Still love that picture! Roberta

Tuesday, May 3, 2011 4:26 PM, CDT

Radiation yesterday morning was a piece of cake. Returning to work also involved cake...but more frosting than anything! ☺ When I decorate, I am usually a palette of all colors of frosting! Thank God for aprons!

For radiation, I go to the VLCC. Once there, I go into a changing room, put on a fancy schmancy gown-you know the ones-the ones that give you a *draft*! And either a robe (fancy hotel-quality terry cloth, or crapola gown material....which would YOU choose!!!) I personally just throw on my sweatshirt over the gown. Warmer and more comfortable......and it has POCKETS! Love pockets!!!! Then I go over to the waiting room and have a seat. There are tons of magazines there that need to be rotated more often!! ***in my four visits there I have read all of them ☹ A basket of snacks and some water. It is a very nice and comfortable area. From there, you are called back to the magic microwave room....where they radiate you. You lay on a hard table with a round pad for your head. I get a soft round pillow under my knees; my right arm goes up above my head on an elbow pad/support and my hand holds a handle to keep it still. Once I'm all comfy cozy, they start to line me up and put my body where it needs to be. My arm is up, my head has to be turned to the left to keep my throat safe from the radiation, and the table gets turned. Literally. I'm turned counter clockwise to go under the machine that zaps me. They line me up & down to the millimeter to make sure that the radiation goes *exactly* where it should. I have to NOT MOVE while they do all this. Once in a while I even fall asleep! There are four areas that are treated, and between numbers 2 and 3 (I think...Zzzzzz) they come back in the room, draw all over my side and chest and armpit with a marker (which REALLY TICKLES!) for whatever reason they need. (I know it's for the lining up and making sure nothing is over lapping kind of thing, but who needs specifics?!?! I hate asking questions.) Then the machine turns and whirls and does its thing and I am treated in 2 more areas. Then my lovely ladies from Rad. Onc. come back in and help me sit up (you get VERY stiff being still for 20 minutes!) Then I am free to change back into my street clothes and I'm out the door until the next day.

Like I said, yesterday was no problem. Today though...I sure am
sore. I have some tender spots where the rads were; I am
unsure if this tenderness is from that or from my physical therapy
that I had right before that. Technically I am all done with PT, but
after our super busy weekend in the Dells, I had some pain going
from my elbow up my arm & through my pit down to my ribs. So I
thought it best to get checked out. Turns out it's more than likely
muscle related; no cording yet. I could have strained that area
raising up my arm for radiation....I could've strained it working
around the house, opening the garage door, reaching up into the
closet.....you name it. My WONDERFUL PT did some measurements, and
then some soft tissue manipulation (an armpit massage....Ahhhhhhhh....)
and it felt WONDERFUL! After she did that she measured my
mobility again, and of course it increased! ☺ Good things. Tomorrow
brings Day 3 of radiation.....and Thursday 'port removal'
WAAAAAAAAHHHHOooOoOOoO!!!!!

Going back to work went great....I got there and they had made a
cute sign that said Welcome Back Shelly!!!! It was really touching. I
spent the first hour getting accustomed to the area that used to be
so familiar, and CLEANING. I'm sorry, but I am OCD with my work
area being clean. And organized. I quickly got into the swing of
things, making some cupcake cakes and some Mother's Day cakes.....
and before I knew it, it was time to head out!

Today went a LOT faster....I mostly spent the morning cleaning,
again, cleaning out the sales floor case til it **sparkled** and filling it
and relabeling it. THAT took most of the morning. But after how
sore I was last night...I knew today I had to take it easy. My

feet/back/neck and wrist were WRECKED last night!!!!!!!!!!!!!

Today not as bad......YET.

Friday, May 6, 2011 9:04 AM, CDT
Update on the port removal coming soon...too sore to type. VERY SORE from it yet ☹...but it's out. It fucking sucked, but it's out. S.

Guestbook Comment: Tuesday, May 3, 2011 9:23 PM, CDT
Glad things went pretty well at work and at radiation. I can't believe you go all balls to the wall right away. Stay strong and keep up your great spirit! Love and miss ya lots. Joey

Guestbook Comment: Thursday, May 5, 2011 7:56 AM, CDT
Am thinking of you on this very momentous occasion! Cinco de Mayo de Porto Outo Day!!!! Wahoo! Beccie

Guestbook Comment: Friday, May 6, 2011 11:19 AM, CDT
Let them eat cake, I say! Yours! It's nice to hear you are back to work. Can't say enough for stability and routine. Have a great weekend. Roberta

Sunday, May 8, 2011 6:41 PM, CDT
One just has to laugh...or go cRaZy. SO. If you're reading this blog on ANY sort of regular basis...you know how life here at the Jones' household rolls. If anything bad *can* happen...it will. This brings us to the morning of May 5th, 2011. Cinco de FREAKIN' Mayo.....

I woke up early...as in super early. 4:30 a.m. to be precise-I spent all night tossing and turning worrying about the procedure to remove my port at 8 a.m. Finally 6:30 rolls around, and I *try*

321

repeatedly to wake up the family. NO ONE wants to get up; the kids need to be AT daycare at 7:30. I *need* to be at the clinic at 8 a.m. At 7 they finally were conscious enough to come downstairs but everyone was PUTZING around driving me FREAKIN' CRAZY!!! If you know me, you know when I'm nervous or worried about something-I'm OCD and need to be there ON TIME. Well, 7:36 rolls around, and Josh is still eating cereal! OHMIGAWD. LET'S FUCKING ROLL! I throw my cake that I was baking in the oven for 5 more minutes and set the timer for Andy.

Well, I get pissed that NO ONE is moving. And I mean PISSED. Andy and I were going to have to drive separate anyway, so I figure he can take the kids to daycare and meet me there. Tension is high; my temper is OUT OF CONTROL. I hop in my van, check my mirrors, and gun it.

OF-FUCKING-COURSE I run something over.

Something relatively big. I SLAM on the brakes....whip it in park, and go to check out the damage....there, lying in pieces under my van is what used to be our Weber grill. GODAMMIT. Andy had grilled out the night before and it had been too hot to put away. So he didn't put it away. I start WHIPPING shit in the lawn...the wheels; the cover; the racks; a leg here and a leg there; the grill bottom............ARGHHHHH!!!!!!!!! After a few 'steam relieving' SCREAMS at the top of my lungs, I continue down the alley and head to Sheboygan.

Of all the damn luck, eh?

....this brings us to the Doctors office. I should have known by now to turn around and go RIGHT the fuck back to bed.

I was scheduled to *simply* have my port removed at 8 a.m. This is to be easy peasy....numb the skin, make an incision, cut the suture holding the port in place, tug it a bit and out it will pop. SURE. Fucking liars.

Carol brought the magic spray; yay!! I get the gown on; lay down; the doc started covering me up with all the drapes to keep his area tidy.....Carol did her *thing* and numbed me up. Then he stuck me 6-8 times with a syringe to numb up the insides. Next he took his scalpel and made the incision. YES I felt the whole thing. Not God awful pain and torture, but I wasn't 100% numb. From then on my eyes were sealed SHUT. I hate blood, I hate needles, I hate DOCTORS and I hate PAIN. Here were all my favorite things wrapped up in one place. ☹ So as far as the 'popping out' part goes....the damn thing broke (or came apart) inside me. It came out in three (as far as Andy can tell me) parts. Eventually. From where the incision was, the port was approximately 2 inches lower than that. While PULLING --something let loose and blood splattered my face. Ugh. My stomach was already ROLLING. I'm sure it wasn't much but blech!!! Then he had to go digging to get the rest of it out, and pull the tube out that was in my vena cava. Port was on left, vena cava is on right....so I could feel him tugging it *under* my right tissue expander---PAINFUL. And just gross feeling. Finally he got all the pieces out, and sewed me up (internal stiches) by this time I was no longer numb. Felt them all, and super gross when he had to tug to tighten them and tie off.

LOTS of tears, lots of pain, and LOTS of stress. NEVER again. Forget it.

Then I drove across the parking lot to get radiation. Sucky day all around.

Fucking grill. ♥S

Guestbook Comment: Sunday, May 8, 2011 8:03 PM, CDT
So happy it's out but so sad to hear the pain associated with it-like you haven't been through enough! I can feel my face cringing as I read your description. Eewwwww! Thank goodness that part is over! Molly

Guestbook Comment: Monday, May 9, 2011 4:51 AM, CDT
At least you weren't attacked by space aliens! Hang in there! Richard

Monday, May 9, 2011 11:21 AM, CDT
Uncle Rick-not YET anyway.....At this point it wouldn't surprise me. ♥S

Monday, May 9, 2011 11:24 AM, CDT
Oh YEAH!!!! The cake I left in the oven for 5...more...minutes.....

Same shitty day, just forgot to finish up the story. So I had put my 1/2 sheet and 1/4 sheet in the oven for 5 more minutes, then set the timer. Took off, ran over the grill, had shitty luck getting the port out, went to radiation (thankfully no drama there) and headed home.

When I got home I drove past that God forsaken grill....wanting to just go over and KICK it. Or put the van in reverse and run that bitch over again. But I didn't. {Note my self-restraint.}

324

I park, go into the house, and the W-H-O-L-E place is NUTSO. All of the smoke alarms are screaming; the house is filled with smoke...SHIT. No one took my cakes out.

ARRRRRRRGggGGgGGGGHHhhhhhhhhhhh!!!!!!! Fuckin' A.

Burned the piss outta them. Let's just say the 9"x13" cake was about a 5"x7" by the time I got it out. And that half sheet? About 1/2 the size it was when I put it in ☹ Thank God I don't waste money on the lottery....we all know I wouldn't win!! ♥S

Guestbook Comment: Monday, May 9, 2011 7:27 AM, CDT
Oh Shelly...I am so sorry, for the grill. LOL Good thing it wasn't the one my parent's spent 2 1/2 hours putting together for Ryan that sucker would have totaled your van. At least that sucking thing is finally out! Love ya! Mary

Guestbook Comment: Monday, May 9, 2011 3:06 PM, CDT
I'm sorry. I had to laugh! But what a god-awful day! I think I woulda died on the table. And as much as I hate smoke alarms...well, you survived and the house didn't burn down. I hope you were well treated for Mother's Day. Roberta

Guestbook Comment: Monday, May 9, 2011 4:28 PM, CDT
I'm SOOOO sorry, but I'm in TEARS laughing here at work after reading your last couple entries. I am exactly the same when I am stressed and need to be somewhere (twins separated at birth???) Ask Larry about the gallon of milk I cursed and kicked across our yard sometime. I could make a fortune as a place kicker for the NFL! So glad all this shit is on its way to becoming a distant memory. It's been a long hard road and I think you've taught us

all a little something about strength, perseverance, and appreciation for what we have (and DON'T have). I pray God continues to heal you. Keep that kick ass attitude and sense of humor for which we all love you. Your mama would be SOOO proud of you for the way you've fought this battle. I am proud to be your friend & remember I'm just a block away! Betsy

Guestbook Comment: Monday, May 9, 2011 10:36 PM, EDT
Hey Girl....so glad to hear that nasty lookin' thing is out of you- for good! I sure hope you are feeling less pain now! I loved your story of backing over the grill; if that doesn't show frustration....I once got really mad and was taking it out on my van and was backing out of our driveway all fast and pissy like and BAM right into our mail box, the one concreted into the ground. Humbling....It was good to hear you're losing yourself at work, it's a good day when it goes fast. Keep the good posts coming!! Ann

Guestbook Comment: Tuesday, May 10, 2011 10:23 AM, CDT
I am sooo glad to hear that your nasty port is out! I am sorry to hear that is took so much drama and pain to do so; never again though!   I hope this doesn't sound bad, but I love reading your updates! It is humbling to say the least! It is a great reminder that I have nothing to complain about because I could have more to tackle. Your strength and perseverance through all that you have gone through and continue shows me how much God has blessed you. Now hopefully HE will continue to bring more and better blessings your way! You are an amazing example of how to handle and conquer life and things that come our way. You're an example for me & it helps A LOT!!! I love you babe, you're in my thoughts and prayers always! Melissa

Guestbook Comment: Wednesday, May 11, 2011 8:03 AM, CDT
Hang in there, Shelly and I hope your week gets better! Beccie

Wednesday, May 11, 2011 11:16 AM, CDT
Frustration. This is BS. The post cancer diagnosis weight gain pisses
me off. None of this helps either:
Stress.
No more ovaries.
Stress.
Post-chemo.
Stress.
Progesterone balance wanky...no estrogen to balance, too much
stress/cortisol.
Lack of activity.
Poor nutrition while sick....lack of appetite; food cravings; etc.

I feel that if I have to be going through this hell, I should at
least lose 50 pounds. NOT gain. And gain. And gain.

Us cancer patients are on SOOOO many meds....I can't imagine that
helps the body, either.

Just venting....I don't miss periods, but would like to wear something
other than a tent. ♥S

Guestbook Comment: Wednesday, May 11, 2011 12:16 PM, CDT
Hi Shelly, Well I am on my way down to my Mammogram today. St.
Mary's brought the mammo-van here, so everyone can go and not
even leave work. I hear some women complaining that they have
to do this and it's such a pain. I'm thinking "this is nothing."

PLEASE EVERYONE WHO IS READING THIS, GET YOUR
MAMMOGRAM DONE ITS EASY. LOL PAM

Thursday, May 12, 2011 5:45 AM, CDT

Last week I requested complete copy of my medical records; I
picked them up earlier this week. It's an interesting read....and
intriguing. As well as an emotional roller coaster reliving everything
I have been through since November 1st.

I am often asked if I go back and read through my CaringBridge
journal entries. The answer? Nope, not really. Unless I see a
spelling error and NEED to fix it. It is hard enough just getting
caught up in everything during treatment, and going through bills
with a fine tooth comb. You sort of disassociate yourself with the
person on the paper. Then something sneaks in...creeps up...and the
brain starts working overtime. Next thing you know, you're lying on
the table in the radiotherapy room having an anxiety attack and
tears are leaking out of your eyes. But you still can't move. The
most interesting part of my med records is the pathology report
from my tumor. For those of you without a medical background, I'm
just using the *big* words for this. Feel free to Google.

Mammo, U/S, Biopsy appointment:
BIRADS: Category 5 Highly suggestive of malignancy
Final Path report on biopsy of mass:
Invasive, poorly differentiated carcinoma, compatible with Invasive
Ductal Carcinoma, at least 1.2cm
Angiolymphatic invasion is present.
ER/PR to follow
Intraductal carcinoma, solid type, high nuclear grade without
comedonecrosis, representing approximately 5-10% of tumor volume.

Friday, May 13, 2011 1:35 PM, CDT

$298,737.16 is my billed total so far. Ugh. ♥S

Thursday, May 19, 2011 6:00 AM, CDT

Not feeling the best today...pretty tired and UGH. I really wish I
didn't have to work the next 4 days. Sometimes I push myself too
hard...and I think this week is one of those weeks!!! ♥S

Guestbook Comment: Thursday, May 19, 2011 12:48 PM, CDT
Yes, my dear sweet friend, you do need to remember YOU too! I
know how amazingly strong you are but you still need to rest, it is
ok to do it! I pray that God brings you some good rest and the
strength to continue through! Always thinking of you! I love you
babe!! Melissa

Guestbook Comment: Friday, May 20, 2011 12:43 PM, CDT
Is it weird that I am anxiously awaiting a field trip to rads with
you?? Lol Beccie

Saturday, May 21, 2011 7:51 AM, CDT

I know, I know... I've been slacking on the updates! Besides being
too busy to breathe.....my hands are also bothering me BIG TIME
from going back to work! They have been falling asleep around the
clock. I've been doing stretches and wearing braces to bed at
night. If anyone out there has any other wonderful suggestions...I'm
game! My great friend Arlene in Beaver Dam used to give me the
most WONDERFUL hand & wrist massages. So great that I could
literally FEEL the good blood flow back in my hands instantly. *sigh*
...sure miss that!!! On the 'busy' front...I have been back to work
for 19 days now. I am still doing 4 hours daily during the week, so
I can leave work, drive to Plymouth; pick up Alaina; go home and

329

make lunch; get back in the car; drive Alaina to Kelly's; drive to Sheboygan for radiation; drive back; pick up Alaina; go to the big kids' school to get them; head home; try to make supper; and crap out on the couch. In between all that there's shopping, and bill paying, and doctor appointments for everyone else, and errands to run. It seems like the last 6 months were the only 'down time' I'm going to get!!!! Right back to my old life. On a happier note, I've been doing cakes left and right from home! It is very satisfying to make something beautiful and tasty for people I know! Don't get me wrong...work is satisfying too....but in a different way. I have been in contact with the state, trying to get set up to be licensed...but it looks like I am unable to with how our house is set up. We do have a separate kitchen upstairs-which I use, and where all my 'stuff' is set up.....but our bedrooms are also up there, which is why I am unable to get licensed. *Sigh* our old house in Horicon would have been PERFECT....I could have used our shed/garage in back. But then I wouldn't have the orders that I do here...reason #597,937,895 that I am ecstatic to have moved back here!!!

Radiation is going well. I am OVER half way done!!! I have had 15 rads, out of 28. I cannot WAIT for them to be over.....just because gas is as expensive as gold!!!! The driving is KILLING me!!!! And mentally I know that will be the END of all my treatment!!! From November first when I was diagnosed, to June ninth when I will have my last radiation treatment is a loooong frickin' road. I will still need to see the onco doc in June for a blood test to see if the cancer is gone.....talk about a nerve wracking appointment! Those results can't be back FAST enough! And I will also have to take a pill called Tamoxifin every day for FIVE years...to try to prevent that nasty cancer from coming back. Hopefully EVER. So continue to pray for my family and myself....we're not at the end of this road yet......and don't even get me started on the reconstruction process!!!! Boobs out...boobs in....it'll be a few months before I go through all that hell...... ♥S

Saturday, May 21, 2011 8:24 AM, CDT
More medical record updates:
Histologic Grade:
tubule formation: 3/3
nuclear grade: 3/3
mitotic count: 2-3/3
Total Nottingham score: 8-9/9
Greatest extent of invasive carcinoma: 1.2 cm
Venous/Lymphatic invasion: present.
Micro calcifications: present.
Prognostic marker: ER, PR to follow.
Ductal Carcinoma in situ
Histologic grade 3/3 Van Nuy Classification
Nuclear grade 3/3
Comedonecrosis: not identified.
Architectural patterns: solid
Extent: 5-10%
Marker:
Estrogen receptor: POSITIVE. Allred score 8 (5+3) 95% of tumor nuclei, strong
Progesterone Receptor: POSITIVE.   Allred score 8 (5+3) 80% of tumor nuclei, strong

Interesting. I did not receive any records of anything that happened out of the clinic...i.e. the Hospital-even though the same Doctors were involved. I'm going to have to look into that, and request copies of those as well. I do have a summary of the pathology that the oncologist went over with me after the mastectomy. But as we all know the Docs don't always get everything right in their dictation. In one report they mentioned I had cancer in my left Breast. I did not. It was in the right. Those little errors are heart stopping!!!

In his summary:
....bilateral mastectomy performed on 11/8/2010 showed invasive duct carcinoma grade 2/3 in the right breast with a maximum dimension of 3.2 cm, margins of resection were negative. There was associated DCIS. The closest margin was 0.7 cm. One of the 2 sentinel lymph nodes was positive for cancer. Extra capsular extension was identified in the sentinel lymph node. Three out of 15 axillary lymph nodes were also positive for metastatic carcinoma. Her HER2/neu is 2+ by immunohistochemistry and FISH studies pending. The left breast mastectomy showed a fibrocystic change including apocrine metaplasia and cyst formation. T2 N2 MX breast cancer.

WITHOUT further treatment after the bilateral mastectomy, my chance of reoccurrence is 84% and a 63% chance of dying within 10 years. WITH endocrine therapy and chemo...there is an absolute improvement by 48% in terms of tumor recurrence. That is down to a 36% chance of the tumor reoccurring. ♥S

Guestbook Comment: Saturday, May 21, 2011 8:37 AM, CDT
Here's to the end of one week (Saturday) and on to better things in the new week ahead. Wishing you good humor and patience and strength. AND more practically- cheaper gas prices and the next lottery win to be yours! Roberta

Saturday, May 21, 2011 8:46 PM, CDT

WHEW. After a loooong 5 hour work day, I am sooo ready for bed! I feel crappy; work was hectic, and I don't want to go back tomorrow. ♥S

Guestbook Comment: Sunday, May 22, 2011 10:20 PM, EDT
Catching up on your journaling tonight. I love your new FB site with the cakes. I actually found myself wondering if I have any occasions coming up that I could order from you, LOL! However we are a winter birthday family, sigh! Mine's in August, but I can hardly get a cake for myself=boring! Keep up the beautiful work, talk about edible art, holy wow! I was telling my mom about your cakes, and Jack interrupted me to ask if you were the one who made his Phineas and Ferb cake. Out of all the cakes he has had, that one is the best. Reading your medical reports, I can hardly understand any of it, it's simply mind boggling. Take it easy you busy momma! Ann

Monday, May 23, 2011 9:31 PM, CDT

WHEW. What a day. You know, I know the side effects that *can* happen from this whole disaster....cancer, chemo, going back to work... but some days it's just hard to remember that. I just have been going along feeling 'normal'.....and the last few days happen to be an exception. I am exhausted. Like can't pull my dead ass outta bed exhausted. I am also experiencing muscle issues.....when I get up...or walk, or go up and down the stairs....my legs feel like they weigh a million pounds. I literally have pain when I do <u>anything</u>...it makes me feel like I'm a little old lady...gimping around....

LOVE my life........grrrrrrrrrrrrrrrrrr. ♥S

Wednesday, May 25, 2011 1:46 PM, CDT

Do you think if I *accidentally* slept through radiation today that I'd get in trouble?? It's cold and raining and I don't wanna leave the couch ♥S

Thursday, May 26, 2011 8:51 AM, CDT

Well, last night could have been better. I spent a good portion of the night in pain and crying. I'm not sure if it's just my body still reeling from the mastectomy...or if the radiation is burning my scars first. My guess is the radiation. The larger of the scars under my right breast is burning and tingling and hurts like HELL. Anywhere the skin touches other skin or rubs against skin (where my side touches the inside of my arm) or sweats...hurts like crazy. I'm gonna need to talk to the peeps at the radiation oncologists.....maybe there's something I can put on besides lotion to help the burn that is slowly creeping over my right upper torso. ♥S

Thursday, May 26, 2011 12:42 PM, CDT

Today, let's all pray REALLY loudly that my ticker is in tip top shape! I had an X-ray taken to check it out. I have been having increasingly swollen legs, feet, ankles and arms since I went back to work. We all are pretty sure it's only because of going back to work and being on my feet so much. But. Just in case. The reason they have to check the heart/chest is because chemo kicks your hearts ass...and can send you into congestive heart failure. Awesome, eh? All the labs are also to get to the bottom of this swelling...& let's hope my kidney function is good, as well as my thyroid, etc. ♥S

Guestbook Comment: Thursday, May 26, 2011 1:32 PM, CDT
Oh girl, I wish there was something I could do to ease or take away

some of your pain!! I will continue to keep you in my prayers for great test results and to ease the pain that you're going through! I love you dearly!!!! Melissa

Thursday, May 26, 2011 7:12 PM, CDT
Hearts good.
Kidneys are good.
Blood's good.
Electrolytes are good.
Waiting on thyroid result til tomorrow. ♥S

Guestbook Comment: Friday, May 27, 2011 9:02 AM, EDT
How you describe the pain from radiation, ouch! When does the pain get to go away for you, permanently!!! I hope you are able to enjoy some of the long weekend, maybe a day or two that you aren't working? Pain, Pain, go away.....Ann

Guestbook Comment: Friday, May 27, 2011 11:44 AM, CDT
Thank God for all the "good" news!!! I love to hear it! I miss you tons! I am going shopping this weekend for Tyler's graduation, I still need a dress! So busy with other stuff, I forgot how close that's getting! I love you babe! Melissa

Guestbook Comment: Friday, May 27, 2011 3:20 PM, CDT
Hurrah for the good reports. Prayers are still continuing for you all! Kathy

Tuesday, May 31, 2011 6:00 AM, CDT
Thyroid was good too!
T minus 8 more treatments!

T minus 15 days til my 'big' blood test that will tell me if the cancer is gone or not.
GULP. ♥S

Tuesday, May 31, 2011 8:20 PM, CDT

Radiation number 21 done. Starting to have some skin breakdown.... it's where your skin is raw and FUCKING HURTS. Google for more info...and pics. It sucks. My pit and under my right Foob is the worst.... ♥S

Wednesday, June 1, 2011 4:23 PM, CDT

6 More radiation treatments to go! Next Thursday is my last one and I couldn't be any more excited! Not that it's going great...but it will be the END of very Looooooooooooooonnnnngg 7 months. I mean, really, look at all the shit I've been through in just half of a year!!!! It seems like it was the longest winter in the world! I can still remember trick or treating like it was yesterday...that was the last "normal" day I had. I think that will be engraved in my head forever as 'the last good day'. It was a beautiful sunny day...we were together and surrounded by our amazing friends...and the kids had a BLAST! It was such a change from trick or treating in Horicon! I mean, the sidewalks were literally PACKED to where you had to squeeze through! What a great time. Today I got there early for my radiation...since I always go at 2:30 and there's no one before me...they told me I could come earlier. So I was there at 2:05. I got to stop and chat with Carol the BCCC wonder woman, about an email I had sent her earlier in the day. More on that below. While in the waiting room, the nurse came out and told me

their machine had lost power this morning at 10 am and was 'down'. They didn't call me since they thought it would be fixed in time. About 10 minutes passed, and the nurse told me that they had the serviceman there all day and that it was now fixed...but they were having the physicist double check the whole thing. Two sets of eyes are better than one!!! While walking into the room with the "all fixed" radiation machine...I told them "oh, sure I get to be the guinea pig with the machine! If I burst into flames or something, you better put me out!" Lol! Needless to say, I'm still here, blogging, and no more burned than when I went in. Back to Carol. I had emailed her asking how exactly this blood test I'm supposed to have on June 15th can tell for sure if the cancer is gone or not. I mean, I thought they would scan the whole body or something like that. But nope. Every three months they check my blood for a tumor marker. Everyone has a tumor marker, but they are looking for it to stay semi-steady. When it rises up after being repeatedly checked, then I suppose its B-A-D news. So it will be quite a while of waiting on egg shells to make sure that number is staying put. I also found out that plastic surgeon doc may make me wait 4-6 months at least before doing more with my chest. ARGGHGH!!!!!!!! That sucks BIG TIME. I just want to rip these fucking tissue expanders right out of my skin!! I also can't believe it'll take as long as it took to get to this point to wait for the radiation stuff to stop messing with my skin and be able to get my new boobs. WOW. Here's some general info I found online about tumor markers (from webMD...)

Tumor Marker-Description: Tumor markers are substances that show up in your blood, urine, or tumor. These are hormones, proteins, or parts of proteins that are made by the tumor or by your body, in response to the tumor, or particular benign conditions. Some tumor markers are specific to one type of cancer, and some are for general oncology use.

Use of Tumor Marker Tests:
Oncologists use tumor marker tests to detect, diagnose, and monitor cancer. These test results are used together with other data, such as biopsy results, to get a clear picture of the stage of your cancer, what type of treatment will be most effective, and to measure your progress during treatment. You may have a tumor marker test before starting treatment, to get a baseline level. This score will be used to compare with later tumor marker tests. Ask for a copy of your tumor marker tests and keep these with your health records.

Uses for Tumor Marker Test Results: Your test levels will show how well your treatment is working. If your tumor marker levels decrease, that is a good sign that the cancer is responding to the therapy. An increased level indicates that the cancer is resisting the treatment, and a change may be required. After you have finished treatment, another tumor marker test may be done to check for any return of the cancer. During your follow-up visits after initial treatment, tumor marker tests may be done to monitor for recurrence.

Tumor Marker Tests Do Not Screen for Breast Cancer:
Mammograms, ultrasound, and breast MRIs are imaging tools that can screen for breast cancer. These tests are highly sensitive and specific enough to detect breast cancer before there are symptoms. A tumor marker test alone does not provide enough information to screen for breast cancer.

Help! My Tumor Marker Levels Went Up!:

Rising levels on your test results can be, but are not always worrisome. Although changes in tumor marker levels may give you cause for alarm, other non-cancerous diseases can cause test results to vary. Conditions in the lab that processes your test may also throw off the results. Always talk to your oncologist about your test results and keep asking questions until you understand how these results will impact your prognosis and treatment plan.

Breast Cancer Tumor Marker Tests:
• Urokinase Plasminogen Activator (uPA)
• Plasminogen Activator Inhibitor (PAI-1)
These are measured with one test, called the uPA + PAI-1 Tumor Marker Test.

You Won't Need Every Tumor Marker Test:
These tumor marker tests are useful for only a small fraction of patients. Your doctor will recommend these only if you need them.
• Cancer Antigen 15-3 (CA 15-3)
• Cancer Antigen 27.29 (CA 27.29)
• Ki-67 Labeling Index
• Carcinoembryonic Antigen (CEA)

Confused yet? Yeah, me too.

Guestbook Comment: Wednesday, June 1, 2011 6:33 PM, EDT
Wow. The medical lingo is still amazing to read, or at least I try to read and understand it. Good luck on the count down, can't wait to read your post on your last day of radiation!! Ann

Sunday, June 5, 2011 8:32 PM, CDT

This week marks the beginning of the end ☺ I have been through so much HELL I don't even want to think about any of it anymore... but I truly don't have a choice. When I look in the mirror....there's no hair. When I shower there are so many scars. When I lay down to sleep....there is pain. When I work...there is limited movement; pain; low stamina. When I shop...there are stares. When I drive...it's a big chore to turn the steering wheel; look beside and behind me. When I work in my flower garden...I can't bend over and do just anything. BUT. I am alive. I am stronger than this. I have been through the worst anyone can go through. I am kicking its ass. It will not break me. It will someday become a distant memory. It will someday be "that shitty year." It will SOMEday be 'that thing' that happened. It will someday no longer be 'it.' There will be more. More memories. More time with my babies. More trips to the Zoo. More 'Family Nights' at school. More birthdays. More Christmas'. More fights with my husband (lol). This week I will wrap up radiation. It will take 4-6 months minimum for my skin to return to 'normal'. My arm pit darkens and darkens... turning shades of black I never thought could happen to a Caucasian girl from Wisconsin! I hope that within a few weeks my stamina will improve. I want to be back to normal and be myself again. I want to go for a long walk. I want to have energy to live my life. I want to ditch the bandanas & wear cute scarves & barrettes again. I just want to fast forward to The End. ♥S

Guestbook Comment: Monday, June 6, 2011 7:06 AM, CDT
AMEN! Mary

Guestbook Comment: Monday, June 6, 2011 7:37 AM, CDT
So happy for you that you are almost done! Loved your past journal description, makes me proud that I have such a strong beautiful

friend. YOU CAN DO THIS!   Candice

Monday, June 6, 2011 5:49 PM, CDT
Three!

Today I met with Dr. Pao-he looked at my underarm and said "it's not good." He is going to talk to the PA tomorrow when she's in to see if she can order some special dressings for 3rd degree burns. We're not going to stop treatment since we're almost done...we're just going to push through and get it done. Hopefully it will start getting better towards the end of the week... ♥S

Guestbook Comment: Monday, June 6, 2011 6:49 PM, CDT
Oh man, that sounds awful. Praying for strength for you to get through the rest of the week & on to recovery! Beccie

Guestbook Comment: Monday, June 6, 2011 9:26 PM, CDT
Oh man!!! I hope you heal quickly so you can put this whole thing behind you. You are one strong amazing lady and I admire you more than you could ever know. Kim

Monday, June 6, 2011 9:31 PM, CDT
Took some pics of my radiation burn to show all you fine folks... ♥S
*that's the picture of my armpit in the photo pages...

Tuesday, June 7, 2011 6:27 AM, CDT
Two!

Couldn't sleep for CRAP last night ☹ I tossed and turned...but it all boiled down to how painful my underarm is. Couldn't those nerve endings have waited a while longer to come back!!! Skin touching skin is BAD. Skin touching skin that is sweaty is WORSE-complete hell. And yes, it is in the 90's here in WI with 99% humidity. F-N-A.

341

Today I am going to stay home; stay cool; and take care of myself.
♥S

Guestbook Comment: Tuesday, June 7, 2011 12:48 PM, CDT
I pray they get you something TODAY that will take care of and
help ease the pain and discomfort of the burn!! I am surprised they
wouldn't have done something for that sooner! I am very glad to
hear you're going to stay cool and comfy today and take of
yourself!! Love it! Talk to you soon! I miss you and love you tons!
Melissa

Wednesday, June 8, 2011 6:32 AM, CDT
ONE!

Thursday, June 9, 2011 11:34 AM, CDT
My last day of radiation!!!!!!!!!!!
THANK YOU GOD for getting me through this!
It has been a week from hell. Major burns up by my throat and
chest and armpit. I have been unable to even go to work. Ugh.
Here's hoping I continue to heal quickly and move past this! ♥S

Thursday, June 9, 2011 3:38 PM, CDT
GOOD BYE Vince Lombardi Cancer Center!!!!!! (Yes, I know I will
still have to go there for follow ups BUT!) No more cancer
treatments!!! Four months of chemo-CHECK. 6 weeks of radiation-
CHECK! Thank You to every single one of my nurses, doctors, PA's;
MA's; Care Coordinator, and AMAZING friends!!!!!!I just can't get
over the amazing support system I am surrounded by. I have THE
BEST and most loving husband on the planet. Eat your heart out,
ladies! Betsy-my most amazing, funny, supportive friend in the
UNIVERSE: you have repeatedly pulled me out of the black hole I am

342

in. Without your kindness, thoughtfulness, and love, I would NEVER have gotten through this. And that's not just some Hallmark statement! It is a fact. You took charge of my family, and took over where we needed it the most. God knew I needed you back in my life, and He seems to always be right. Melissa--we both have been going through the wringer for TOO LONG!! What a roller coaster! Thank you for being there for me to lean on; your perfectly timed phone calls, texts, and margaritas lol!! I hope looking at my life makes yours seem not so bad haha! Carol--you are so amazing. Without you I would be LOST. I would still be in SHOCK not knowing what to do next. Your compassion for others going through Cancer is a Gift. You have most definitely found your calling-and EXCEL at it. You are always in our thoughts and prayers. We repeatedly thank God for YOU. Mary-Mary, Mary, Mary. You have sent me a card every week for as long as I can remember....long after all the other cards stopped rolling in your HILARIOUS cards make me laugh when pretty much nothing else does! Your support and friendship mean the world to me. When we're old and grey(er) I hope that you will pull up a rocker next to mine on the porch and we can grow old together! Dave & Kelly... where in the HELL would I be without you guys?!?! You also moved right back into lives and helped us out tremendously. Having you as an addition to our crazy family is WONDERFUL! Sandi, Brittany, Alex, Adrian and Dad...you have been so supportive and helpful with the kids and our whole family. Having you to lean on has been great-so many last minute appointments to go to, chauffeuring my ass around when I couldn't drive, or just Brittany doing 'Just Dance' to entertain me lol!!!!! Alex-you have made me so many great cards and pictures, I will keep them FOREVER. Jenny & Joey-- thanks for the visits and phone calls. Sometimes NOT talking about cancer and listening to someone else's life takes some of the burden

343

off!! I miss you guys EVERY day ☹ I know that's not everybody, but it would take me YEARS to say thanks to everyone!!!! I'm not at "the end" yet, but the light at the end of the tunnel is getting brighter!!!! The worst HAS to be over! ♥S

Guestbook Comment: Thursday, June 9, 2011 4:17 PM, CDT
I'm soooo happy for you!!! It's time to go out and celebrate that this thing is finally over! Love ya babe!! Sarah

Guestbook Comment: Thursday, June 9, 2011 7:58 PM, CDT
I'm already old and gray so you let me know when you're ready to rock and my chair will be there! Love ya, Mary

Friday, June 10, 2011 7:33 AM, CDT
It's not fun when you go to bed at night and realize that you have burn blisters along your whole (mastectomy) scar...under the FOOB. Grateful that my employer is understanding and letting me take off when I need..... cause this week has been hell. Hoping my kids take it easy on me today~I need to make sure not to pop those blisters ☹

Guestbook Comment: Friday, June 10, 2011 9:23 AM, CDT
Thank God for giving me you as a friend!!!! Your strength and being here for me has helped me in more ways than you will ever know!!! I would have loved to have been there more for you through this! Thank you, thank you, THANK YOU for being here for me while you had so much of your own going on and to deal with!!! I am so glad to hear that you are through so much of your treatments! I am praying the worst is over for you and that while you still have to have checkups and get your foobs eventually made to boobs and more that your life will continue to regain some "normalcy" again! I believe it will be even better than a normal life!!! I love you tons

and you are always in my thoughts and prayers! Melissa

Guestbook Comment: Saturday, June 11, 2011 11:30 AM, CDT
Hi Shelly, I knew you could do it! You're one the the strongest and bravest people I know. You don't know the words CAN'T or GIVE UP. Thinking of you all the time, especially when I went for my check-up. All good. LOL Pam

Guestbook Comment: Thursday, June 16, 2011 2:54 PM, CDT
Hi Shelly, how are u doing? People have been asking me if I've heard anything from ya. How's the arm doing? I've started to burn but we'll see how bad it gets. I don't really have any pain though, just a few twinges here and there which I guess is good for me. I only got 11 left to go! Can you believe it's almost over!? Just a little more surgery and we're free of this horror! Well you take it easy...drop me a line sometime. Lisa

Monday, June 20, 2011 1:03 PM, CDT
Seriously. If I were to write a book about my breast cancer journey, would you buy it? About my journey and craZy life...? ♥S

Guestbook Comment: Monday, June 20, 2011 2:33 PM, CDT
Yes, I would! I also think it could be hugely beneficial to others that may be beginning, going through or have gone through a similar experience facing, dealing, and living with cancer and LIFE! For them and their families, friends, any one that's affected. It could also help you! Miss you like crazy!!! I love you and am sending you big hugs!! Cuz I know how much you love them! Smurfy hugs! Melissa

Tuesday, June 21, 2011 6:10 AM, CDT
Wish me luck today! I'm finally able to head back to work! YIPEEE!!!

It's been a long 2 weeks...... ♥S

Guestbook Comment: Tuesday, June 21, 2011 9:20 AM, CDT
Still thinking of you, even when I don't show up on this. Going back
to work is a milestone on the road to everyday. Have a wonderful
first day of summer! Love, Roberta

Wednesday, June 22, 2011 2:50 PM, CDT

Today is the day I have my 'after' blood test. The one I talked
about the other day-where they monitor the tumor markers. It was
a very nerve wracking morning, thinking about it all day. WORRYING
about it all day is more like it! I even had nightmares about the
results last night. I could just imagine the oncologist telling me that
the blood test results were not what we hoping for, that they were
higher than ever, and the cancer has not responded to the
treatments we have done. I dreamt that the cancer had
metastasized to my lungs, bones, brain. I dreamt that this was the
end. I ended up going a bit early, thank God, because the Heavens
OPENED UP 2 minutes after I got there and MAN did it pour!!!
While I waited uberanxiously, all I could think was "Sure. TODAY
they're running behind. For the FIRST time!!!" I was called into the
lab, and after 2 sticks, she struck gold. I mean blood. Back to
the waiting room I went. Julie was there with her fantastic smile to
call me back, and she gave me one of the warmest hugs ever! It
was such a relief once I got over myself, and just realized the
worst is OVER. Once again, she checked my weight; vitals. We
chatted about the sunflower cupcake bouquets I had brought in; how
I was doing; how radiation went; and living through cancer. I
remembered that this young woman had to go through this hell as
well. I cannot EVER imagine having to go through chemo as a

teenager. The oncologist came in and immediately made my day-he told me my blood test looks good!!! Awesome!

Cancer Antigen 27-29 (CA 27-29), also called breast carcinoma-associated antigen, is used as a marker for breast cancer. Eighty percent of women with breast cancer have an increased CA 27-29 level. This marker may be used with other procedures and tumor marker levels such as CA 15-3 to check for recurrences of cancer in previously treated women. Serial measurements monitor treatment response and identify recurrence. Levels of CA 27-29 may also be increased in cancers of the colon, stomach, kidney, lung, ovary, pancreas, uterus, and liver. Noncancerous conditions associated with elevated CA 27-29 include first trimester pregnancy, endometriosis, ovarian cysts, non-cancerous breast disease, kidney disease, and liver disease. Read more at: http://www.answers.com/topic/tumor-marker#ixzzljZ7HiZtH

I still will have to repeat blood tests every three months, but yahoo! the cancer treatments have done what they should. I also was given a prescription for Aromasin (chemical name: exemestane) that I will have to take daily for FIVE years. That medicine will stop the production of estrogen that is still being released from my adrenal glands. This means that less estrogen is available to stimulate the growth of hormone-receptor-positive breast cancer cells. That's a good thing! He also ordered a bone density test for tomorrow here in Plymouth. This medication can affect the density of your bones, and we'll need to know what we're dealing with before we start so we can treat or prevent. You all know me though, I'm too nervous to celebrate. I probably won't celebrate in three months either. Or in 5 years when I'm done with these meds....the thought of this cancer coming back will always be in the back of my head. My whole adult life I have always been waiting for the other "shoe" to drop.....I can definitely celebrate the fact that I finished and made it through all my cancer treatments. But to say I'm in remission.....or that the cancer is all gone...makes me feel like I'm jinxing myself. ♥S

<u>Guestbook Comment</u>: Wednesday, June 22, 2011 3:37 PM
Congratulations!!!!! I am soooo happy for you. You have been an inspiration, and continue to be... Continued prayers, Jennifer

<u>Guestbook Comment</u>: Wednesday, June 22, 2011 5: 41 PM
Shelly, I am just like you, afraid that celebration is jinxing, but I am sitting here crying for you because I am soooooooooo happy! I don't think I would be strong enough to deal with ALL you have gone through but you are an inspiration to do better every day! Love Mary

<u>Guestbook Comment</u>: Wednesday, June 22, 2011 6:50 PM
Sooo happy for you!! You are such a strong woman!!!! You will always be in my prayers that you will never have to endure all this again!! I love you!!! And you are such a great inspiration for so many! Jen

<u>Guestbook Comment</u>: Wednesday, June 22, 2011 10:06 PM
Shelly, to answer your question about buying and reading a book your journey, yes I would. You are a STRONG AND BRAVE WOMAN. LOL PAM

<u>Guestbook Comment</u>: Wednesday, June 22, 2011 10:08 PM
So happy for you and waiting for your book to become a best seller & an award winning movie. Love & hugs to your whole family. Riquie

Thursday, June 23, 2011 5:18 PM, CDT

Today I had my bone density scan. It was just as harmless as they told me it would be! They were late getting me in (no biggie!) because they couldn't 'find' me. Evidently the tech thought I was a GUY since I had my back to him while in the waiting room. (bald head...) Instead of calling my name, he walked out to check with the receptionist! Nice! Once I was in the room, it only took a few short minutes. There was absolutely no pain, and nothing from the machine even touched me! That's a switch for me lol! What you do is lay on a table, they line up your spine on a line, and an arm attached to the machine passes over you. They checked the bone density in my spine and hips. The radiologist will read the images and send the summary to my doctor. Once again, let's hope all is well! On my way home, we stopped and picked up my new medicine- the stuff I'll take for the next 5 years. The information sheet tells you what your insurance saved you in cost.....My insurance saved me $1133.89. On this ONE prescription! THANK GOD FOR YOU, BLUE CROSS!!!!! Now I understand why so many elderly people cannot afford their prescriptions if I had to pay out of pocket for this stuff I couldn't do it. It would literally be a decision between food or meds. ♥S

Friday, June 24, 2011 1:31 PM, CDT

I have so much I want to do....literally, there are LISTS. Unfortunately I am so damn exhausted I can barely keep my eyes open. I want to do an update here on CB. I want to do some editing. I want to play with the girls outside. I want to walk downtown to see the Walldogs murals'. I want to scrapbook. I want to clean. I want to get on the PC and go through some paper work. But I reaaaaaaallly want to nap. Guess what takes priority???? Night night. ♥S

349

Friday, June 24, 2011 2:41 PM
Your entries just leave me speechless. I don't even know what to
write. Just know that I am so proud of you...your strength,
determination, bravery, sense of humor...the world needs more people
like you! Jenny B.

Sunday, June 26, 2011 8:54 PM, CDT

238 Days ago I was diagnosed with breast cancer. I started down
this road of crazy; this road of doctor appointments; this road of
hell. 231 days ago I had a bilateral mastectomy that changed my
life. Not just the physical aspect of it, but the emotional too. We
found out how far the cancer had advanced. We found out that we
had not caught it early. We found out that breast cancer doesn't
discriminate. 35 year olds can be diagnosed with it too. Last night,
while we were out walking through town looking at the murals being
painted by the WallDogs, I ran into a fellow breast cancer patient.
While she was still going through chemo (only two more for her!!) I
can happily say I'm DONE with that! Hers is every 3 weeks; mine
was every two. She did not have node involvement; I did. She had
a lumpectomy; I had both breasts removed. While her hair was wispy
and barely still there, I can finally go without a bandana! There are
so many different stories. So many different experiences. It's
hard to read books from the library about others' experiences-each
experience is so different. Every single person, regardless of age,
race, or religion, has a different story to tell to others. But I still
"need" to gobble up those stories. To know that everyone has so
many different things happen to them. To know I'm one of them.
I'm 'normal'. To know that I'm not alone. As a patient you hold
back and customize the tale based on who you're talking to-you tell a
different story to neighbors; to family; to coworkers. You put on a
brave front and when asked "How are you doing?" you say "Good."

You hold back some details that may hurt people-parents, siblings, your children. You tell about 80% of the story to most everyone, keeping the really bad stuff to yourself. Talking to your husband late into the night about the nightmares, the fears and the pain. I like being able to tell it all-the same-to each and every one of you. People I know well. People I used to know well. People I barely know. People I have never met. The reason I like spilling it all (besides it being cathartic) is to spread awareness. To let every one of you know that this COULD happen to you. Let's hope and pray that it DOESN'T ...but if it could happen to me...well, you know. I used to go through the store and barely notice all the breast cancer paraphernalia. I've participated in the Relay for Life numerous times, supporting but not really thinking about it all. I've picked up breast cancer awareness T-shirts at Wal-Mart. I've bought pink measuring spoons and cups at ShopKo because I liked the color more than for the fact that the Susan G. Komen foundation was making money off the proceeds. I bought a pink ribbon thermal mug at a rummage sale last summer. I've donated to others' fundraising efforts. Prayed for my family and friends; Moms and Aunts and Grandmothers going through breast cancer. Breast Cancer pink seems to be everywhere, but for that I am very, very thankful! It's true; there are many many many different cancers out there with a color signifying each one. It just so happens that pink is the cancer that picked me. Their fundraising supplies money to research a cure for this shitty disease. Breast cancer is not curable. So yes, run for the cure. Donate to the cause. Buy the breast cancer awareness stamps at the post office. Participate in Relay for life. DO MONTHLY BREAST EXAMS! I did not. I never did. Once in a while I would remember to do one...but haven't done one in years. Just look where THAT got me. I have met many amazing people on this journey. I have met survivors and patients.

I have met women going through it ahead of me, and women going through it behind me. I have read stories of women that beat the cancer, moved forward with their lives, and barely even think about it anymore. That in itself is inconceivable to me! I have met people that have found religion in their cancer experience, leaning on God for all. I have met people that have taken on the "crusade". They are spreading awareness; organizing walks and fundraisers. They are booking speaking engagements, getting tattoos, wearing their ribbons proudly. I have also met women that are taking this opportunity to do great things in life: they go on adventures, vacations, travel; make the most out of opportunities and just go-for-it. I'm not any of those. I have a very lax view on religion. I am not an up-on-the-soapbox kind of chick. I haven't (yet) seen this as some sort of 2nd chance in life, to do everything I have yet to do. And how in the hell can anyone AFFORD to go on vacation after breast cancer!!!! I can barely fathom it. I am barely making it through each day attempting to get back into my old life. I would love to be back to work full time; coming home and renting movies; running errands on my days off; being a taxi for the kids. But I am struggling. REALLY struggling to be normal again. It's tough being mentally healthy, but physically at only 80%-but still needing to function at 100%. Life with three kids is hectic in itself...then throw in all this medical stuff, and hectic changes to CRAZY!!! Along with struggling to return to my former self, there is incredible GUILT. I feel that I *should* seize the day. I *should* make life changes. I *should* enjoy every small moment...because before I know it, they may be all gone. The kids will grow up and apart, becoming more self-sufficient. Not relying on me for their basic needs. Every heartbreaking moment; every sweet smile; every infectious laugh should be reason for celebration. But I just am not there yet. I'm not at that point in my healing where I can focus on everything else. Right now I need to be selfish and focus on me. And that brings guilt too! ♥S

Guestbook Comment: Sunday, June 26, 2011 9:26 PM
Your Sunday 6/26 is well said and honest. Thanks for sharing. R

Guestbook Comment: Monday, June 27, 2011 7:03 PM
Shelly, I have been reading your entries and I am amazed at your story. I think the last one was most heart wrenching. I can only imagine what you have all gone through and in all honesty hope to never experience it. But you need to hold your head high girl! I'm sure that there is guilt there but there is no shame in what you have been through and accomplished over the last 238 days. That is more than most people will go through in a lifetime. So maybe you aren't booking speeches or organizing walks but you ARE accomplishing tons! Through your amazing strength you have been able to log all these entries and tell your story. With great honesty which is not easy to do. With this amazing ability you have empowered so many people and enlightened the rest of us. You have been able to reach mothers, daughters, husbands, friends and loved ones who can read your entries and get a glimpse of what their loved one is going through. You have been able to bring your knowledge and wisdom to make women more aware of breast cancer. Try not to feel guilty because you don't feel that you've accomplished much because you have! You need to learn to rejoice in the little accomplishments right now-the big ones will come later on. Take care & stay strong! I am honored to be able to read your entries. Tammy

Guestbook Comment: Tuesday, June 28, 2011 2:56 PM
It's OK to be selfish at a time like this. You have to remember that

after all the pain and agony (i.e. "treatment") you still have a "self"!
Celebrate what needs to be celebrated. Yourself, your family, and
your friends. Uncle Rick

Wednesday, June 29, 2011 8:51 AM, CDT

Yesterday I got a bug up my ass to paint my living room. So I
gathered the troops...drove to the store for paint...and stared it
yesterday afternoon! When Andy came home he said "this is how I
know you're finally feeling better...you're painting!" LOL. I guess I
am finally getting back to my old self!! I have been staring at the
boring white walls in here for SEVEN months wanting to paint them!
I guess I am about 3/4 of the way done. I need to wait for Andy
to come home tonight to move the TV and stuff. I'm doing a light
brown/mocha color. It looks great with the white trim around the
windows ☺ Now I need to find a new couch that I like! Ours is
falling to PIECES! ♥S

Guestbook Comment: Friday, July 1, 2011 7:55 PM
Shelly, regarding your post about not seizing the day: You really are
when you share with all of us who have not gone thru this other
than as a bystander, supporter, friend, etc.... When you share, you
are doing something beyond breast cancer-you are becoming an
advocate of the first rate! Until recently breast cancer didn't touch
me as close, but in the last year, there are three great women (you
included) who are raising little children and trying to get thru chemo,
radiation and life beyond the treatments, hoping like hell it never
revisits. You have seized the day, and you shake it every day!
Thanks!! Ann

Thursday, July 7, 2011 10:14 PM, CDT

Amy you are a ROCK STAR! Now I don't want you to move back to

Colorado! I was able to finally meet up face to face with an internet friend tonight! We were introduced through a mutual friend (thank, MONICA!!!) This unbelievable soul has endured SO MUCH. She found out just after having her 2nd child at age 33 that she had OVARIAN cancer. The scariest cancer in the WORLD. Soon after she found pre-cancer in her breast, followed by surgery, and chemo. I mean REALLY??? 33 and ovarian cancer. PLUS the boob thing, AND a 3 week old baby. She may think my road has been rough, but I think hands down hers was worse. How awful to have the happiest time in your life (childbirth) turn into the most unimaginable news ever (O cancer). WTF. We had good conversation, told many stories, compared notes and horrors, and laughed out loud! What a great night! Thanks Amy, for trekkin' up here!!!! ♥S

Guestbook Comment: Friday, July 8, 2011 12:28 AM
OH Shelly, I love you, and had such a great time hanging with you! And that is the fastest I have ever whipped my boobie out for anyone! Your cake smelled wonderful all the way home! Stay in touch, can't wait to get together again! Amy

Friday, July 8, 2011 7:40 AM, CDT
I'll admit, I have been slackin' on updating everyone here. But I really am at a (wonderfully) boring part of my treatment! I have been having a lot of problems with both my computer-typing on it bogs it down somehow and then I end up with letters missing/run-ons, and things that don't make sense at all! Then I have to go back through and fix it all...what a pain in the ASS! Now I switched to google chrome, and it's going better. Another 'excuse' I have is my hands are getting HORRIBLE now that I'm back to work. Carpal tunnel is setting in, and I just don't know what to do! The pain in

355

my hands/forearms wakes me up at night, and they fall asleep even while sitting and watching TV. I had my chiro check them out last week, but it was only once, and I don't really know if it helped. ♥S

Guestbook Comment: Friday, July 8, 2011 7:50 PM
Shelly...Can't read anymore right now....burst into tears and can't stop crying....And I ran out of puffs......Later......Helen

Guestbook Comment: Friday, July 8, 2011 9:29 PM
Green Tea is awesome for joint and or arthritis pain. I've had Chronic Inflammatory Arthritis (diagnosed for 7 years, but probably since HS). I hope you find something that helps, but I've been successful with diet stuff, berries (all kinds), no processed food (sausages, dips, etc...) and lots of Advil. Did painting your LR start it? I feel your couch problems, we have had our LR set since I was just out of college and it is starting to look like it! However, not a good time financially to replace...so we just cover up the worn spots with pillows and blankets. Hope your hands and wrists get some relief soon! Ann

Saturday, July 9, 2011 12:10 PM, CDT
Alaina fell at daycare yesterday on the playground-she fell off the monkey bars & broke her wrist. A 'torus fracture of the distal radius.' Ugh. ♥S

Guestbook Comment: Saturday, July 9, 2011 6:16 PM
Shelly, just read your Tuesday, November 23, 2010 entry. LOVE IT...LOVE IT..LOVE IT!!!!! I feel like that A LOT! Sometimes just to keep my sanity...I have to tell myself, WHO wants to be normal (average) anyway!? When things seem to go wrong sometimes you just have to say oops...or Oh Well...and leave it go at that. (My

therapist told me that once because I was always being so hard on myself... and SOMETIMES it even works!) And we need to remember that we're not in control anyhow. God has everything in His Wonderful Hands. Even the little things, like dirty dishes! Helen

<u>Guestbook Comment:</u> Sunday, July 10, 2011 6:30 AM
I feel REALLY bad bout Lainey ☹ But it's a plus because of it being on the thumb sucking hand. Brittany

<u>Guestbook Comment:</u> Sunday, July 10, 2011 9:03 PM
Thinkin' about you tonight, we need to get our families together soon. It has been waaaayyy to long. I hope Alaina is doing ok, I am sure she will be. She may be small but I think she is a tough little cookie. My brother Bruce is coming up this weekend but maybe if you guys don't have any plans the weekend after that we could get together and grill out. Saturday or Sunday. Let me know what your work schedule looks like. Miss you, hope you are feeling well oohh and Jake misses Josh, they need to play!!! Love ya sweetie!!! Hope to talk to you soon. Candice

Tuesday, July 12, 2011 5:52 AM, CDT

Well, Alaina met with the orthopedic Doctor yesterday. They ended up casting her; she chose bright pink! The x-rays showed that the fracture wasn't so bad, a mild break. It's on the bone in her arm that goes from elbow to thumb, about 1/2 an inch before the end of it. A torus fracture is more of a crinkling of the bone, not a big crack, since she's so young and her bones are still bendy. Thankfully the growth plate is intact. No surgery needed! Thank God!!! She did well all day yesterday, but last night after 7 she was crying that her wrist hurt pretty bad. ☹ I gave her some Motrin, hoping that would ease the pain so she could sleep, and it appears to have worked. In one week she goes back for more x-rays and a new cast (she's still very swollen now). Then she'll wear that for another 2 weeks, and that will come off. Let's hope she heals fast!! ♥S

Guestbook Comment: Tuesday, July 12, 2011 1:44 PM
Thank God that is wasn't that bad! Has to be uncomfortable with it being so hot and muggy outside though! If she's anything like her mom, she'll make it through just fine!! I am so thankful that you have made it through, that God has given you everything to get to this point and continue!! I love you, thank you for being a great friend and always being here for me even during the hard days!!! Many great adventures to come! I mean we gotta see how rich the three Amiga's will be with our "dangler cup" coming out! Melissa

Guestbook Comment: Wednesday, July 13, 2011 12:00 PM
You certainly have a full life! Of course-it's called kids! Ya gotta love them. I love the pic of you! And crazy me would like to rub your head. You are doing great! I'm so glad that Andy works close to home it must be a sense of relief to you both. Have a great day. Luv ya Kathryn

Guestbook Comment: Wednesday, July 13, 2011 3:25 PM
Hope Alaina heals fast! If she is anything like her mom she will heal amazingly! Penny

Wednesday, July 13, 2011 7:36 PM, CDT
Life has taken a pleasant turn from running my ass from doctor to doctor...to taking the kids to all their appointments! It's still annoying to run all the time, but considering where I was 5 months ago--I'm ok with that! Today was orthodontist for Josh in West Bend, after driving to FDL and back for work. Also chiropractor for me-this is

my third week of going 3x per week...and I'm not seeming to get much better. My neck is SCREWED UP!!!! It will be nice tomorrow to not have to work. Looking down at my cake table wrenches my neck and causes my muscles to tighten up even more ☹ But tomorrow also brings a ROOT CANAL for me bright and early at 7:50 a.m. Josh has an eye exam in the afternoon (his headaches have increased, and his vision was pretty crappy at his physical 3 weeks ago) then we have a visitor coming over from the Plymouth Gift of Life. I continue to be overwhelmed by the great things that happen in our lives...how lucky we are and how blessed we are. There are more challenges than you can imagine in our lives...but at the same time I am humbled by this. There are so many other families out there that could benefit from this. I have a hard time accepting help, and my pride keeps me from being super excited. We have been dealt a raw deal and it is great to continue receiving love, support, and prayers 8 months from the beginning of this.
Thank You. ♥S

Guestbook Comment: Wednesday, July 13, 2011 8:20 PM
Shelly, you deserve to be one of the recipients from the gift of life tournament! You are a strong, beautiful woman.....who deserves a break.....who deserves a little "extra". So.....don't feel weird or like you shouldn't be getting the help.....we live in a wonderful, caring community with people who are eager to help families. And even though you are feeling better...any little extra help is a wonderful gift. You are very loved! Paula

Guestbook Comment: Wednesday, July 13, 2011 8:28 PM
Normal? You were expecting a normal life (with kids)? Well you gotta love them! If I'd had any idea ahead of time what it was like raising kids, I'd never had the nerve. So I'm glad I didn't know; I've

loved them so much. There's a lot of joy mixed in with the frustration. And as for receiving the blessing of help from others: just be grateful, always, and look for ways to pass on the gift of generosity to someone else in need as the years go by. Then the world becomes a better place. Looking forward to seeing you later this month! Roberta

Guestbook Comment: Wednesday, July 13, 2011 10:52 PM
You keep on keeping on and keep rolling with the punches! You've come so far with the support of sooo many. I hope your chiro helps you manage to get along better, too! Bet you can't wait until 2011 is just a distant vision of mostly only the good memories. Beccie

Thursday, July 14, 2011 6:59 AM, CDT
In my canoe, floating along....
I've become pretty good at rolling with the punches...even before the big 'C'. I think kids truly change your life for the better. You get used to getting up every 2 hours to feed them; you get used to loud (and I mean LOUD) noise; you get used to clutter (and I'm pretty OCD!!); you get used to crying, and sometimes don't even hear it; you get used to giving up your one day off all week to run them here and there, and back again. You also get used to running to the store at 9 p.m. for milk and lunch meat! They've taught me patience (ha!) and really how to just go with it. All that they have taught me has really helped me with what I've gone through since November. I can 'let go' easier; I can be 'ok' with the house being wrecked; I can pick up/pack up and be outta the house in record time. I can come up with last minute meals in a flash. I can organize my life better. I pick my battles....they're not always worth it. ♥S

Thursday, July 14, 2011 5:36 PM, CDT

When I sit back and think about my diagnosis, my surgeries, my treatments, I remember how truly lucky I am. I have an amazing team of medical professionals helping me out. I have a huge circle of friends and family behind me rooting me on and lending helping hands when needed. I thought I was truly blessed on January 8th, at 5 p.m. when I came home from the benefit that was held for our family. It overtook me and I sat and just let the tears run out of my eyes. Of course I was smiling, but my heart was just FULL. Now we found out we have been chosen to receive another unbelievable gift-the Plymouth Gift of Life (www.plymouthgiftoflife.com). We are among 4 families that were nominated and later chosen by a board to receive this. It is a softball fundraising event the weekend of August 26-28 here in Plymouth, out at Quit Qui Oc fields. We just had our meeting with Ranae-the woman who contacted us originally to see if we would accept this-who told us all about the event! She needed a photo for the web site (and we all know how much I LOVE my picture taken) so we gathered the kids, and took some photos. For the 1,000,000th time, I am reminded why we chose to move back to Plymouth last year. What an amazing, loving community we live in. I have **so** missed running into people I know at the grocery store; going on walks through town and seeing people I know drive by. I've missed last minute visits by friends, and having my kids go to school with kids with whom I know their parents. I don't think I will ever again make the mistake of leaving Plymouth-it's our home. ♥

Guestbook Comment: Friday, July 15, 2011 6:33 AM
We are all so excited, happy and blessed to have you back!! Mary

Guestbook Comment: Saturday, July 16, 2011 3:11 PM
So glad to hear that you guys were chosen as one of the gift of life

recipients! And also that you are all back in Plymouth where you belong. We had fun with the kids last night but missed you. Tell Ilyssa thanks for making me all the videos on my phone! I don't even know how to do that yet, she is one smart cookie. Hope you have a great weekend. Candice

Guestbook Comment: Saturday, July 16, 2011 9:28 PM
Way to go Shelly, I too am very happy you were chosen for the gift of life recipients. You and your family deserve it. LOL PAM

Sunday, July 17, 2011 7:57 PM, CDT
Holy sunburn batman!!! I even used sunblock like a good girl. It is just so FREAKIN' HOT OUT!!! YUCKIE. I like warm...but this melting shit weather blows. ♥S

Guestbook Comment: Monday, July 18, 2011 1:57 PM
Hi Shelly, I'm still trying to play 'catch-up' on your journal. I'm on page 32 (Dec. 22, 2010)...And I gotta say....If anyone has the right to stand on a SELF-WALLOWING PITY SOAPBOX, you do! How can you possibly act like the world is all roses and ice cream when you were going through ALL THAT CANCER BULLSHIT? Tell it like it is Lady! The world is not all 'UPS', there's plenty of 'DOWNS'. It's how we get through them that is important and I think you're doing JUST FINE! Hugs, Helen...

Wednesday, July 20, 2011 12:32 PM, CDT
Another super busy day 'off'. Yesterday I felt so sick that I left work....I NEVER go home sick. ☹ It was only an hour or so, so I don't feel too guilty. I think I was going too "gung ho" and got overheated. Hard to imagine when it's 105 outside, right? All of a sudden I started feeling faint and thought I was gonna throw

up. I went on break, had some water and sat in front of the fan...but after 20 minutes just felt worse. So, knowing my health isn't the best, and that I had a 45 minute ride home, I went home. Today I'm still feeling ick, but not sure if its heat related or health related. Could be my aromatase inhibitor pill-lots of awesome side effects from those.....I went to the radiation oncologist today for my 5 week checkup-Dr. P examined all my radiated skin, and said it all looks good! ☺ Just one more check-up in 6 months with the radiation oncologist and I should be all good! The kids are finished with summer school this week-uh oh! That means a lot of 'bonding' time with them haha! Wish me luck!

Guestbook Comment: Saturday, July 23, 2011 8:16 PM
So glad to see a wonderful, deserving, family has been chosen for the Gift of Life! Yay for the Jones'! Ann

Monday, July 25, 2011 10:05 PM, CDT

I am so SHOCKED that it is almost my birthday. 9 months ago I was convinced I wouldn't be around for this. AMAZING what can happen in less than a year. Let's see...what is there to update on.....well, work has been frustrating. I'm really struggling being "normal" and balancing life, and kids, and work. I'm trying to keep the kids busy and have a fun summer-we've been hitting the beach a lot! LOVE Long Lake. The kids have had a busy social life lately-they've been to Bay Beach, Deerfest, gone for Pedicures, had sleepovers, finished summer school; we had a great family day @ summer school--Ilyssa performed in her first play: 'Skippy Jon Jones goes to Mars', had her piano recital (she played 2 songs) and we enjoyed a family swim. Love being able to be there to watch my kids!! We have celebrated birthdays, graduations, anniversaries...and had some girls nights out ☺ Strength wise I'm faltering....I am

363

feeling weaker and having a lot of aches and pains. My hands continue to get worse.....they wake me up at least 7 times a night now. ☹ I have been seeing the chiropractor; been in for massages; had Katie work on my hand/arms/back to try to work out some kinks...to no avail. Always a short term fix.....they always fallback asleep and hurt and tingle and then I get these weird low voltage shocks going up my ring finger....so I went to the doctor for it finally. I go see the neurologist in a few weeks for the carpal tunnel test where they put needles in your muscles and measure the nerve damage from the neck down your arms to your fingertips. Good times. Life just keeps flinging monkey shit at me. Along with my wrists/hands...I have a lot of joint pain. Some days I think I should go out back where they can shoot me! My ankles, knees, and hips HURT. Add to that some good news...I have a group of nerve endings 'awakening' on the right side...near my scars. Yay that it's returning, but BOO because it feels like a knife stabbing into me! We affectionately call them ZINGERS. Let's hope someday I'll even have feeling in my arm above the elbow. Alaina broke her arm on July 8th. We had cast number 2 put on last week, now she will have it removed a week from Friday. That time sure flew! It does not slow her down in the LEAST!! She used that neon yellow cast as a weapon! Ilyssa lost a tooth a few weeks ago.....we're waiting for the other one to come loose and fall out. Josh just got his new glasses this week....he is now amongst the 24/7 glasses crew. Poor guy! He's also been busy going to the orthodontist each week for the process of getting a space maintainer put in and cemented. This Wednesday is the big day-it will stay in until his 12 year molars come in. Andy is busy working; he went to Chicago last week for the big ASI trade show. 7 years ago that was the show we went to Las Vegas for. That is the life! I could get used to those kinds of business trips! ♥S

Tuesday, August 9, 2011 6:58 AM, CDT

What a crazy few weeks. I know I haven't been on here much, my hands are still bothering me, falling asleep all the time, and hurting. I had the EMG test done for carpal tunnel, and it showed moderate CT. BUT I would rather NOT have surgery. I am going the route of massage and chiro. I will be starting a new chiro this Friday..... and hoping like hell he can get the kink out of my back that is causing all the problems. I have been going to the chiro for a month-3 times a week for my neck/shoulder. Somewhere in there something is pinched. Which messes up my neck, shoulder, arm, and makes my hands fall instantly asleep when I type. ☹ Today I have a quick stop @ the lab for some non-cancer related blood work, then to the plastic surgeon for the first time in MONTHS. I may be getting a fill...who knows. But at least I can discuss when to expect my next surgery. Keep you all posted... ♥S

Tuesday, August 9, 2011 2:27 PM, CDT

TEN MONTHS!! It is so crazy to think it has been 10 months since my bilateral mastectomy! Can you believe it?!?!? Let me tell ya-it seems like a LOT longer than that! Even every day seems like a lifetime! This morning I went in for some labs-I needed to have my cholesterol and glucose levels checked; I had never had that done. And since I'm 36......I also had an appointment with my plastic surgeon. It is the first time I had gone to see him since April? May? Something like that. After he did a visual exam of my scars and radiated area he asked if I was happy with the size I was. I said "sure". I haven't really even thought about it! The last time I saw him, he had said he was going to fill me more, so that it would stretch my pectoral muscles out a bit more and have more "sway" when I got my implants. I guess now that it's been awhile, he's happy with the results. I will go back again in 6 weeks with the

hope of scheduling SURGERY!!!!! I can't wait to have real boobs
again! LOL! He also checked out the skin irritation I have going on
under my right arm pit-the radiated side. Yesterday I had seen my
general practitioner about it, and she told me it looked like eczema to
her. BUT with the radiation and the skin breakdown I've had-the PS
wanted me to see the dermatologist. He told me he had never seen
anything like that happen after radiation. He also wanted to make
sure it wasn't an infection so that the tissue expander wouldn't get
infected. Well, that turned into seeing the dermatologist NOW. We
trekked across the whole clinic to derm. He checked out my pit, my
back, and my hands... took some scrapings... and yep-it's eczema. I
have NEVER in my life had eczema. My guess is with everything
I've had done since November, my immune system is off kilter.
That's why I have skin issues, this whole tired thing going on, GI
issues, joint pain...you name it. I know, whine whine whine. I got an
RX from the Derm doc along with an appointment for 10 days out;
then back to the PS office to schedule an appointment for 6 weeks
out....I'm so high maintenance! We (yes, I had all three kids with me
all morning!) then stopped for some 'stuff at Hobby Lobby, and Kohl's
for gym shoes for Josh. Ilyssa got hers yesterday along with her
back pack. I think I'm FINALLY done school shopping!!! Yahoo! ♥S

Tuesday, August 9, 2011 9:40 PM, CDT
88 more visitors until 10,000!!!!!!!! Holy cow! ♥S

Guestbook Comment: Wednesday, August 10, 2011 9:31 AM
That was a tricky way to get to 10,000. Can't wait until tonight Mary

Thursday, August 11, 2011 7:44 AM, CDT
Job interview this morning....not really nervous! Just happy to look
at new opportunities. ♥S

Thursday, August 11, 2011 8:40 AM
Good luck on your interview today, be yourself, you are wonderful!!!!!
Hope your baby settles down sometime soon, she is for sure keeping
you on your toes and keeping the doctor bills a coming. Just caught
up on your journal entries and it just reminds me of how blessed we
are to have you so strong. Love ya and miss ya, looking forward to
the 2nd day of school......Joey

Thursday, August 11, 2011 9:55 AM, CDT

BUSY 24 hours! 24 hours ago was calm, boring, and laid
back. THEN Andy calls me at work to tell me that Alaina had taken
a fall. (Yes, she's the one who just got her cast off! That was my
first thought........) He told me she had hit her face, and he was at
the ER having her looked at. OF COURSE panic set in! He told me
the ER doc was going to stitch her up. WWWwwwait a minute....I
said. NO WAY. I told him to have them call the plastic surgeon.
Now. I left work and traveled back to Plymouth....by this point he
was at home with her. We couldn't see the PS until 3:45 or so, so
we had a few hours of waiting. She was steri-stripped up and had a
band-aid over the bloody ick on her face. (BTW-I can NOT handle
blood.) So Andy headed back to work and I hung out with my poor
baby. The afternoon ended with the PS nurse telling me he is not
available at all today; he has a surgery in Two Rivers that started
late, and he would not be back to Plymouth. REALLY?? WTF. So
she told me the ENT Doc could stitch her up, but when she checked
with them, his schedule was booked solid. Ugh. I in the meantime
am calling my insurance to look for a PS. They tell me there is
another one in Sheboygan, so I call. He tells me that the process to
see him is to go to the ER at the different hospital; they will evaluate
her, and stitch her up if they feel comfortable doing so. "If they
feel she should need a PS consult, they will page him, and he will

evaluate her. BUT he tells me, he's in a meeting for another hour. So, the meeting takes precedence over an urgent patient? Well, I call my PS's office back; she reassures me that the Doc in the ER is good. And that yes, she would take her kid there to get stitches on their face. By this time it's 3:30, we dredge back to the ER, and have the doc she saw earlier stitch her up. And why ask if we would like her to see a PS if that isn't possible???? She received 12 stitches and is looking pretty rough today. She is banged up and bruised and bandaged up...and her face is still swollen; the inside of her mouth all contusions and swelling. POOR BABY. ☹ She also was put on antibiotics (3x day for 10 days) since the wound was open for over 4 hours. I just hope it heals nice and quick and that her pigmented part of her lip still matches up. NOW we have to go the the doctor today again. This time for Ilyssa-she has bloody gross drainage coming out of her ear. Yes, she DID have vents put in back in February. Grrrrrrr. Thank God my employer is understanding....I'm going to be late again today. Fuck. ♥S

Guestbook Comment: Friday, August 12, 2011 8:23 PM
Shelly! Man you are a busy momma! With all the injuries in your house, you should start getting a punch card for trips to the ER (not that I hope you need it anymore), but ya know if you have several trips, you should get one for free, or something like that ☺ I sure hope the skin issues and boobie issues get tolerable for you soon, as for those Zingers, I wonder what those feel like, especially in that area. Take Care!! Love ya! Ann

Tuesday, August 16, 2011 12:55 PM, CDT
....if one of those bottles would happen to fall....
I write on CB to enlighten most of you with what I go through on my cancer journey. I don't write on here much about all the day to

day stuff for some privacy reasons, some lack of time, and usually-because I forget. I know the CB journal has a negative tone, for the majority of it, because it is my CANCER journey. I do try to make light, joke, or poke fun of myself....usually it doesn't work all that well. So let me tell ya that this isn't a happily ever after kinda story ...more of a "...and then...and THEN ...AND THEN???" story. My shit heap is very tall, and well, why not keep piling it on! I just want to say that my life is GOOD. My kids are good. I have an outstanding husband. I am able to work, I have insurance, LIFE IS GOOD. But. This is my cancer part of the story, and truthfully....there isn't a lot of "YAY!!!! I get to go see the doctor again today!" I wanna thank Barb from work, who is a faithful reader of my blog, and who supports me more than anyone else I work with. I appreciate more than you know-the well wishes, and the prayers. I may not be Ms. Talkative at work, but know that I include you in all my thanks and prayers too! It's nice to have someone at work that knows what I'm going through, and understands the magnitude of my disease. Your medical background helps, I'm sure! Yesterday I took Alaina in to have her stitches removed. She ended up getting 12 stitches from her run-in with her big sisters' scooter. She was somehow riding it, then all of a sudden wasn't. We repeatedly told her it wouldn't hurt. We were wrong. It did. There were some scabs formed over her stitches (2-3 of them) so the tugging was painful, and pulling off the scabs wasn't much fun either. She was whimpering and crying...but really was a trooper. She must get her bravery from me! The PA we saw said she was healing fantastic for only being 5 days out. The inside was healing slow, but healing. After her appointment, I went to see my PT/OT/lymphedema guru. I have been having increased problems with my hands falling asleep; neck, shoulder, back/shoulder blade/armpit area. I know, "just that" huh? Since July I have been seeing the chiropractor for my neck issue-my neck was messed up, giving me blinding headaches. 12 trips there and the headaches were better, but the neck is still messed up. Because of all this messed up muscle stuff, I had gone to see my friend who is a massage therapist. She told me she thought that something was pinching in my back/shoulder causing my hands and arms to fall asleep. I agreed. I also in the meantime had seen my PA...she sent me for an EMG. That's the nerve study where they put needles in your arm to check for carpal tunnel. It showed I do have some mild carpal tunnel in my right hand, but nothing horrible. They didn't do my left. After there, I went to a new chiro in Sheboygan, an amazingly nice man, and had a thorough examination going through all my health history, and issues, treatments...the whole shit. He felt that possibly all my pain was connected; muscle spasms, everything not gliding how it should after my surgery, some issues from radiation that made everything angry.....just a combination of everything. Ok. Narrows it all down, doesn't it?!??! So, I'll be heading back to the massage therapist this week. Ok, back to my visit yesterday with the PT, OT, lymphedema guru. She did her own evaluation...checking my range of motion, my neck and spine, and muscles. She evaluated for carpal tunnel, and has it all narrowed down to one thing. I'm a mess! My current doctors' orders are from my oncologist et al for post mastectomy and lymphedema treatment. Now I need new orders to address all the muscle tightness and weakness; the numbness and tingling. When I lay flat on my back and my shoulders relax down... my arms fall asleep right away. PINCH POINT for my nerves! HELLO!!! Guessing that is where things are messed up, but we'll see. I'm waiting for the orders to be ordered. While I was there, she had asked me about the red area under my right foob. I had noticed it on Saturday-just a red area underneath, by my intersection of scars. Sunday I showed it to Andy, since my boobs don't move, I couldn't just 'pick it

370

up' and look under it. I'm sooo not a contortionist! He said it just looks red, like maybe my bra had rubbed it. Monday morning it was bigger and more swollen...and felt like a blister to the touch. Luckily I have no feeling under there. I emailed Awesome Nurse Kim over at the plastic surgeons office with the details and a picture of my boob-LOL-I know what you're all thinking-but it is just easier that way, instead of rushing to Sheboygan over a red spot of skin. Well, THIS morning, it was HUGE. The size of a teaspoon and them some; and along with the increase in size, it was puffier...and felt 'funny'. 8 a.m. I rushed to call the PS office, and they said to COME IN. So I left then, taking my girls with me. Once in there, my BCCC showed up--and let me tell you that is NOT a good feeling. When your cancer care coordinator shows up "unexpectedly" you think the worst. Tumor, cancer, infection, mad cow disease................I'm in on the table and Doc shows up, looks at it and tells me it appears to be a skin infection. The dangerous part is that it is centimeters away from my tissue expander...which we can NOT let get infected. If the TE gets infected, they need to come out, heal up and we start over from the beginning. Noooooooo!!!!! I had to ask him to explain a few things, like how the TE could get infected... I thought he meant the inside of it, but he meant the outside of it, and the surrounding tissue. He goes forward and cuts it open (no numbing needed, I have no feeling under there!) and it gushes. If you're reading this, you know I hold NOTHING back, so be prepared ......I warned you. I felt some 'wet' leaking under the site, on my ribs, and yep-you guessed it, it was all full of pus and bloody nastiness. I almost passed out. Couldn't see it or feel it, but that wet feeling made me think of blood and the thought of blood makes me want to pass out. I kept looking up at the ceiling, praying to God I didn't pass out in front of my girls......or anyone else! THEN the Doctor feels the need (for no good fucking reason) to SHOW ME what was coming

371

out. He holds up a goo-covered, chunky, bloody, nasty gauze square and I just about PUKED on him. Just because **you** chose the medical profession....does not mean I am ok with bodily fluids or nastiness. In fact I am MORE sensitive to all that crap since my diagnosis. BLECH. So he does his thing, drains it, takes a culture, cleans it out with sterile saline, and then mentions we have good tissue/muscle coverage over the TE and it 'appears' to only be in the skin. But he's concerned. I can see it all over all three of their faces. Which makes me concerned. THEN to make everything awesom-er....he tells me we need to pack the wound twice a day. 'We' as in Andy or myself. Hahahhaaaaa.....that's a good one. I can barely watch my kids pull out a tooth! And you want me to stick what where?!?!?! Kim produces a mirror so that I can see the open cut that I need to pack, and WATCH him pack it so that I can do it at home. There was that hot/lightheaded/puke feeling again.....so I looked away...but had to look back to see how much of this strip of stuff was still sticking out to do @ home. Bleeeeeeccccch. Total willies. We're supposed to use the end of a sterile Q-tip at home and cram that strip into the hole in my skin twice a day. I'll tell ya right now, that I will be driving to Sheboygan later this afternoon for Kim to do it for me. And tomorrow morning. Andy isn't so comfortable doing it....and I'm not so sure I am comfortable with him doing it either. I'm on some heavy duty antibiotics, to keep this from getting any worse-God forbid we get the TE's infected. ☹ I go back in on Thursday to see the PS, and he'll check this infection again. Prayers needed. AGAIN. Ugghh. ♥S

Guestbook Comment: Tuesday, August 16, 2011 2:24 pm
Shelly if you ever need someone to go with you or drive you it would be my honor to do so. I don't write to you much but please know you all are in my prayers daily. I do read all your postings. I'm

not much of a writer but you are so loved. You certainly have had a summer plus!!!! Love, Kathy

<u>Guestbook Comment</u>: Tuesday, August 16, 2011 2:34 pm
You are always in my thoughts and prayers...but I am sending extra ones your way!! Sending ((((hugs))))) also!! Jen

<u>Guestbook Comment</u>: Tuesday, August 16, 2011 2:59 PM
You are in my thoughts and prayers as you embark on yet another part of your very long, long journey. Try to hold your head up. You have so many people that care about you and admire you for being you! Take care! Tammy

<u>Guestbook Comment</u>: Tuesday, August 16, 2011 3:02 PM
OMG I got the willies myself just thinking about it and can't imagine how you musta felt being that it is on YOU and all that??? Oh ick. I can only say EWW. I know exactly why the question: The med professionals are in the biz of dealing with the goo, why the hell must they "show and tell" sometimes?? Sorry you have yet another yuck to deal with and I hope your numbness subsides with more massage and the physical terrorism. ☺ Honestly praying that you feel better soon without further complications!! Holy crud monkeys. ☺ Beccie

Tuesday, August 16, 2011 9:51 PM, CDT
Andy just got done doing his husbandly duty-packing the wound under my boob. Thankfully I feel nothing under there, and he has a strong stomach. The slurpy, drippy noise of him pulling the old one out-ICK. I had to hum the whole time, I couldn't stand it. It took us about 10 minutes, but he wanted to make sure he did it right, and didn't hurt me. In the morning I'll be heading to the PS office to have them repack it. Blech. ♥S

Wednesday, August 17, 2011 10:48 AM, CDT

I went in this morning and Kim and the doc repacked my owie, and
he said at least three times that it looked really good! Andy did a
great job last night, even Doc said so. I go back again tomorrow.

THURSDAY, AUGUST 18, 2011 4:04 PM, CDT

I went in again this morning to see Kim at the PS office and she
repacked and dressed my owie. It's looking real good still! Good
news! Bad news-I'm feeling crappy today. I just slept for FOUR
hours, letting my kids run wild like heathens lol. The house is
TRASHED....stuff and drinks and toys everywhere. But I just feel
drugged, like I can't stay awake, I feel like I have medicine
head. But didn't take any medicine. I checked for fever-98.1. No
fever. This stupid infection is kicking my butt. I'm hoping it's just
my body using all its power to heal fast. They're outta the office
tomorrow so we all know that is when something will go wrong! I'm
hoping to wake up from this nightmare soon........ ♥S

FRIDAY, AUGUST 19, 2011 6:57 AM, CDT

http://www.youtube.com/watch?v=6iyU4S7yHFo   I hope everyone reading this has someone like this in their lives-to be there, loving and supporting them. I sure do. ♥ you Andy... ♥S

Guestbook Comment: Friday, August 19, 2011 12:37 PM
Hey girlie, I am so glad Andy was able to help you! I am also thankful to hear that it's healing so well!!!! I pray you get your energy back and finish healing so you can continue on with trying to regain a "normal" life! Not that we really know what that's like any more, especially you!   But you know what I mean! Talk to you again soon! Love you sweetie! Melissa

Guestbook Comment: Friday, August 19, 2011 6:50 PM
Hope you're feeling better today, I'm just glad there weren't any more kid incidents for you. Looking forward to September 2nd, or next Tuesday.....we could meet u in West Bend at a park, there is an awesome one there! Joey

Monday, August 22, 2011 8:38 PM, CDT

Great day! Only a few more days until the Gift of Life Softball Tournament!!! I do have to work Friday but I'll definitely be coming out after! I won't be able to make it on Saturday-I work all day-but Sunday I took vacation to go! It is still so unreal that this is my life. That this is happening.....and that we are so loved in our community that we were chosen for this!   I'm sure I will be overwhelmed once we're out there......but I hope to see each one of you and hug you!! I received GREAT news from the plastic surgeon today! The cultures are all in on my boob infection...it came back basically as acne-type infection! Still gross and all-but pores can get infected, causing an infection under the skin. THANK YOU GOD it is

375

not a staph infection!!!! Or anything bad. Woot! I'm going in tomorrow or Wednesday to be seen again, and have them look it over. It was another busy day 'off'...had physical therapy up in Kiel- since that's where they had an opening sooner. I didn't even know Kiel had an Aurora! He is using ultrasound to work on my carpal tunnel-they put the cortisone 'goop' on, then rub the wand all over my wrists for 5 minutes each. I was also given more exercises and some therapy putty to strengthen the muscles & tendons. Let's hope it gets better soon! Then I went to visit Melissa for a while; headed to Plymouth to get Alaina while Andy signed Josh up for football. Next stop was the library and DQ....yum! It was another night with all the neighborhood kids here playing! LOVE our neighborhood! They were all playing football.....until the girls joined in and became witches...trying to put a spell on the boys lol! My friend S has some family issues going on right now...and her family could use some extra prayers. Especially her Mom. Thanks everyone! ♥S

Thursday, August 25, 2011

Is it bad that I am already looking forward to retirement so that I can relax for once?!?!? Yes, I know I'm only 36...This week brings MANY appointments again. As a mom of 3 and a woman dealing with breast cancer I just don't know how I can minimize all the running! If I do it all in one day I get wiped out. If I stretch it out and do one a day...I feel like I'm never home! This week was PT for me (Kiel) plastic surgeon for me (Sheboygan) ENT for Ilyssa (Sheboygan) football practice (Plymouth) doctor appointment for Josh (West Bend). I'm pretty sure I put on 185 miles Tuesday, since my day started out going to Fond du Lac for work. Go go go is NOT my style! I like to sit outside, under our gazebo, reading, or listening to all the kids play. I like to watch TV or putz around on

FB. One more appointment today then I'm free for a few days lol!
I have to go to physical therapy one more time this week to work
on my hands/wrists, and whatever is messed up in my back.
Thankfully I know people that do massage therapy for a living, and
got to enjoy another wonderful massage today. I like it better when
the massages are for relaxation....but working out all my knots is
good too! ☺ Josh has been signed up (by his Dad!) to participate in
the Plymouth Junior Football league. He does not really feel a desire
to join anything-could be some of the social issues that come along
with Asperger's. So Andy and I felt it was important to start him
in a sport that he has shown some interest in. It's also a sport
with positive enforcement, where he can learn to be a 'team' and
build camaraderie. When we left, he was pretty upset and crying.
When I pried it out of him; he didn't like being 'guided' what to do. I
think it will, over time, be a good experience for him. He needs to
be corrected or pushed in the right direction by others. It is
something that he doesn't have a lot of experience with...I like that it
unsettled him-he's used to us correcting things, but that doesn't
mean he likes it! ♥S

Friday, August 26, 2011 9:44 PM, CDT
I love my friends. xoxo♥S

<u>Guestbook Comment</u>: Friday, August 26, 2011 10:56 PM
Will be thinking about you all weekend as this is an honor for you and
your family. Love ya lots and miss ya.....count down is on for school
to start-5 more full days of summer vaca! Joey

Saturday, August 27, 2011 7:55 AM, CDT
I also went to Riverview Middle School this week to sign Josh up for
MIDDLE SCHOOL! O.M.G! I don't think I'm ready for that! I

HATED middle school soooooo much. Very glad that my son is the first one going there, not one of my daughters! Boys seem-for the time being- to be less drama. Walking the halls there brought back such a flood of memories! The old lunch room where Crystal introduced me to those Hostess 'chocolate' pies...I never even knew they made them. And I remember swooning over the Monkee's with her lol! I walked through the library-which was pretty new when we were there-and remembered buying those black and white folders with designs all over that you could color in (I bought my kids some of those this year from Target! I was so excited they still made those!! I know, simple minds....) I walked up to Josh's homeroom. I believe that room was Mr. H's room. He was a young, new teacher. I cannot remember his actual name, but I think I was in there for 7th grade homeroom? Mr. NOVAK'S room......what haunted memories there! The lab tables are all gone, replaced by desks. I remember he had all 4 of us Michelle's sitting in the same area. I also remember dissecting frogs.......BLECH. But until a few years ago I still had that little frog's brain and spinal cord in my tube of formaldehyde! The old office...the band/chorus rooms...the art room....I still could remember where all my lockers were every year. So crazy! I can't remember what I did 10 minutes ago, but I can find my locker from 1986!! I was unable to go to the school sneak peek coming up so I decided to go ahead to Josh's new middle school and drop off his stuff. I had most of it already in his locker from the week before when I stopped in alone. So, the four of us headed up to his floor so he could check things out. We climb the six flights of stairs to Josh's locker. AND his stuff is gone. Someone else's stuff is in there. So we go into the classroom-no desk for him either. UGH. Of all the damn kids-they have to move HIM??? HELLO???? The kid has Asperger's...he does not do well with transitions! OR CHANGE!! Back down to the office we go...and she doesn't know a thing about it! So she gets on the computer, finds he's been switched to a different classroom across the school. So, again, back UP the six flights of stairs we go (did I mention it is 96 degrees and HUMID??) Well, we got to meet his new teacher and I feel really confident it will be a good match. The teacher is a younger man-and a former soldier and cop. All of Josh's favorite things! We met the support teacher, filled up his desk and locker. He was happy then, once we got it all figured out-and he knows he has a good buddy in class with him. ♥S

Guestbook Comment: Saturday, August 27, 2011 8:19 AM
Was great to see you last night! Hugs, Beccie

Guestbook Comment: Monday, August 29, 2011 9:52 PM
Shell, you still amaze me each time I read your journal! The stuff you and the family go thru on a weekly basis! Your foobie stories actually made me squirm and made mine feel ouchie! Considering the hormone rushes I have right now they are sensitive enough anyway, I think hormones are worse the older you are cuz I cry at stupid pampers commercials now too! Weird huh? Your running around is amazing, I wish I could say something magical to lessen those miles you put on that van, but unfortunately you know it doesn't work that way, darn it! At least the kids are going back in a few days to school. Hopefully, that will help you and Andy out! Reading your narratives on CB helps to remind us that you are STILL going thru this; that it's not all over yet. It also helps to keep us women and the men who love us, ever vigilant of our Boobies! I was so bummed that I did not make it to Gift of Life, I was going to wear my t-shirt that I got at your fundraiser, cuz I thought that would be so neat at the softball games to wear the 'Save 2nd base' T-shirt. Life happened! I sure hope that the turnout was great and

that all recipients had a nice time and see a great gift from it. I was able to see some pics on FB from it. Love ya! Ann

Any day of the year:
Andy makes me laugh. Daily.
Andy loves me and my bi-polar-ness (:
Andy is ok that he's my lobster ♥
Andy likes most of the same TV shows I do.
Andy will bring me a glass of milk at bedtime when my stomach is acidy.
Andy will go to the gas station day or night just to get something that I'm craving ☺
Andy sometimes wears my bra to make me laugh!
>>Yes, I have pictures!!<<
Andy is an amazing hands-on Dad.
Andy cleans the whole house top to bottom every weekend while I work.
Andy drives 'Fat Albert' so that I can take 'Steve' to work & back.
Andy rubs my back every night before I go to sleep.
Andy likes hugs. I do not. He's OK with that.
Andy will let me have the last Mountain Dew!
Andy encourages me to scrapbook ($$$).
Andy and I like the same foods.
Andy loves to spend time with us, his family.
Andy will try new things at my request.
Andy shares the remote with me!
Andy is OK that I have no boobs. For now. (LOL!)
Andy is the love of my life.
Thank you, Andy.

WEDNESDAY, AUGUST 31, 2011 9:10 PM, CDT

Gift of Life weekend!! Attending the Gift of Life tournament really opened my eyes and gave me a better perspective on life and people.

It was absolutely awe inspiring, the amount of people that were in attendance!! It lifts you up-puts a smile on your face! I know not everyone is there because they personally know us or the other three families honored. They are there because they like being a part of something so GREAT!!! They may have had a family member or loved one go through trying times-or they themselves had been through it. All I know is that when I left there Saturday morning-once my 'Class of '93' had played (and WON!!) I was in such a great mood as I drove to work; music blaring, windows open, singing, feeling great having witnessed these people gather and sweat and laugh for such a great cause. Left me SPEECHLESS. I'll be the first to admit, the players on our team were not all part of my normal social circle-some I had not even SEEN since graduation! I was so pleasantly surprised with the crew of people there! I will hang our group photo on our wall along with the group photo from the Better Boobie Benefit! When I'm feeling sick, tired, discouraged, or just alone, I will definitely go to that photo and remember all the people that are behind me holding me up. There were quite a few people that I didn't get to talk to or hug-just know my thanks are HUGE-I know you are supporting me. I also came away from this weekend feeling a bit sorry for myself. I'm struggling with my lack of energy-my chronic pain-my lack of interest in anything. I've *really* been struggling lately with being 'Mommy'. Ilyssa is the most vocal about it. Her drawings of being sad because I never play with her; her crying because she doesn't get any 'special' time with me -all breaks my heart. Not so much because she feels left out-I think that's normal for a middle child in any family with HIGH MAINTENANCE siblings... more so because I literally have NO INTEREST in playing with them, or doing projects, or snuggling. I just want to be left alone. To disconnect. Now don't you dare judge me-you have no idea what I go through in my head. What this journey has done to my 'whole' self. You know the things I share with you-and if this were you-there is just a whole other mental struggle that is IMPOSSIBLE to put into words. Most likely cause-depression. I also have pain 24 hours a day-that makes it hard to have kids climbing all over your body 24/7. I have very little time to myself between work, doctors, errands, etc. The hour before bedtime I'd like to just be left alone to read or relax or nap. I have an extremely hard time relaxing. I feel tense like I gotta GO GO GO or clean clean clean all the time. The kids are tornados!!! The worst part-I feel NO desire to be a Mommy right now. It's easier for me to plant my ass on the recliner and space out on the TV or on the internet to quiet the constant barrage in my head. I also feel I'm detaching myself from the kids and Andy as part of a coping mechanism. There is still a chance I'll have to leave them. I think distancing myself from them will make it easier for them. And Me. I have detached myself from Andy as well, and I catch myself doing it with the friends I have left. I start crying instantly when I think about him; I love him so much. I feel guilt and sadness when I think of what I've had to put him through. The stress I've added to our family. The sacrifices we've made for ME. He's left to be this 'single parent' while I've been depressed, sad, sick, bald, tired, in the hospital and just NOT ABLE. Our relationship has suffered-we have grown accustomed to just being roommates-just being contained in the same house, not making a 'home'. I'm sitting here, on my lunch hour in the middle of Subway crying my eyeballs out and twenty to one, I'm BRIGHT RED. I wish a million times a day I could be normal. Have a normal family. Have a 'normal' life. I feel so ashamed to admit that being a mom to my three kids isn't even fun. I don't get to enjoy my kids-they're so out of control all the time. Maybe it's what has occurred due to my being so ill for so long-there was an obvious lack of discipline and structure for a good

382

10 months. What do I do about that???? I still am only about 70% of what I was "before." I am mentally and physically slower, I can't just "hop up" and chase them around, or immediately be on top of situations that have gotten out of control. I am and have been overwhelmed for years. Having a kid (or two!) with Asperger's is a LOT of work! I can honestly say God has given me Waaaaaaaaaay more than I can handle. I feel so absolutely lost.

What an insane week. Today is nice and relaxing so far, but let's just say today is the FIRST day like that! Tuesday I worked the late shift and while I was on my way home from FDL, my sister called. She was calling to tell me that my Uncle Rick was going back into the hospital Thursday morning for 5 days. They will be administering aggressive chemo. Two weeks ago, he had a follow up PET scan, and his cancer (Hodgkin's Lymphoma) has spread and grown, he now has tumors up in his chest and near his collarbone. (All 2nd hand info at this point.) I don't know why I took that information so hard, but I sure did. It could be because he and I have been going through our treatments together so we have a new bond. It could be because it makes me face my own mortality. Could my cancer come back? Definitely. Could ANY one of my blood tests change my life? Definitely. Could I die from this shitty disease? Most definitely.   It could hurt so much because it dredges up all my memories of my Mom-he is still one of my strong ties to her. He has always been one of my favorite Uncles... growing up we rarely saw him...he was in the Military, and usually lived far away. He would tickle me til I cried (because I was pissed off!!! LOL!) He would be funny, tell jokes, and just was younger and 'cooler'.   I am so very sad that we have lost touch over the years. I truly don't know why. We both have busy lives and I have since married, started a family, gone back to work....But thank God for

Facebook. I am so lucky to have had a chance to reconnect with him!!!! That same day that she had called me, I had received a FB message from him telling me how nice it was to hear from me, and that he's been thinking about me too. I'm not a fan of vaguebooking, so I had that gut feeling something was up. Usually there's some back -n forth about his disease, etc. But, I had already heard from Sandi at the time I got his message. Maybe that's why I had a bad feeling. By the time I got home I was a blubbering mess. Emotions just took over me, and I could not shake it. I reflected on his and my treatments, our highs, lows, advice we swapped, memories, thoughts of my upcoming blood test..........I walked into the house, put down my purse and bag by the doorway, and went straight upstairs to bed. Andy knew something was up...I never do that, but he never came up to check on me. He sent Josh up to ask if I was ok. The girls wandered up eventually to snuggle and sleep with me. I'm pretty sure I cried myself to sleep that night. After talking to my sister, I just felt I needed to go down and see him. I had looked up flights on my phone, and did some investigating. Do I or don't I? I have a hard time with these BIG decisions. And I hate spending money! The next morning, I woke up at 3 a.m. with more of EVERYthing on my mind. ♥S

Monday, September 5, 2011
Labor Day. Andy was changing my packing in the boob wound and some weird white skin flap looking thing came out of the hole. He thinks it's all weird, and wants me to check it out. Well, I looked in the mirror, couldn't see it well, so I gave it a tug. Well next thing I know it's bleeding ALL over. EW. I HATE BLOOD! So, hubby doesn't want to mess with it anymore after that so we head up to the urgent care to have it checked out. I don't have any feeling at all under that area so it didn't hurt and most definitely I could have

384

ripped the wound more without even feeling a thing. The walk-in doc left me dumber than when I came in. He was NO HELP at all. Then the nurse came in after to re-pack the wound and asked us what that white thing was? UUGGGGHHHHH. So we explained...THAT'S WHY WE'RE HERE!!!! Off to the plastic surgeons office tomorrow I guess.

Tuesday, September 6, 2011
The PS explained it all to me, but I can't remember what he said exactly. Basically, that white flap thing was part of the tissue healing...all good.

Wednesday, September 7, 2011
My sister's 41st Birthday!! Happy Birthday Sandi!
And lucky her-she got to start her day off by getting up at 3 a.m. and give me a ride to Uncle David's!

She volunteered to take me over there to catch our airport shuttle to Milwaukee. I am headed to San Antonio, TX with my Uncle to see and visit and cheer up my other Uncle, Rick. These two men are two of my late mom's three brothers, the oldest and the youngest. Unfortunately, Rick-the youngest-is battling cancer, like me. He has either N/H lymphoma or Hodgkin's lymphoma-I can't remember which it is. So. Here I am. Getting ready for bed in a Motel 6 in San Antonio, TX. He had been declared in remission a few months ago. Unfortunately his newest PET scan showed new, larger cancer up and into his chest, so it's obviously spread. He is at the point of stage 4-he was admitted to the hospital for the past 5 days-to administer a nightly regime of chemo. Days 1-5 he will have chemo, then 16 days off. In between, near his nadir, they'll check counts. Then on day 21-five nights of chemo again. He is realistic in the way he is facing this-he knows it's advanced, yet what else is there to do than stay positive?!?! I know how it goes-fake it until ya make it! I get all my frustrations and negativity out on paper or CB so that I can burn it off & move on. So. In hopes of a miracle I will ask God to carry us both through this & lead us to whatever is next for the both of us.

Gone for vacation......

Thursday, September 15, 2011 10:21 PM, CDT

I know, I know. I'm slacking. So shoot me. I've been busy...jet setting around the continent lol! Updates are all in my paper journal....just need to type them on here! Back to work tomorrow after 2 weeks off. Wish me luck. Hopefully I'll get there and have been fired...wish me luck lol ♥S

Friday, September 16, 2011 8:55 AM, CDT

Back to work. Boo. I had taken vacation for a week, enjoying the Sheboygan County Fair, and getting the kids back to school. Then I flew to Texas and did not want to come back! .....hello?!?!? Mother Nature?!?!?....it's only SEPTEMBER! 40 degrees is just NOT NICE! Yesterday I had to go in for a few procedures...an upper endoscopy then the dreaded colonoscopy. My lower results were fine. No polyps, no cancer. They did some biopsies though. My upper was consistent with last year's findings when I was SO SICK in June. GERD (Gastro esophageal Reflux Disease-who doesn't have that these days, huh??) Hiatal hernia and Barrett's Esophagus. I was given a script for new meds, so out with the omeprazole and in with the new. The procedure itself was quick, but I definitely remember most of it. I even remember them giving me more meds to knock me out further. I woke up in my room & there were yummy fresh chocolate chip cookies waiting for me-a small prize for them shoving a garden hose up my wazoo! ♥S

Guestbook Comment: Friday, September 16, 2011 7:03 PM
GERD...say that out loud and it just isn't a good acronym! Maybe it's good considering what it is? Sounds like you at least enjoyed some of you time in Texas, hope your uncle's feeling better/stronger?? Back to the real world!! Ann

Sunday, September 18, 2011 5:54 AM, CDT
My first two days back to work went nice and quick! ☺ One more to go then a day off. Ahhh. Last night I found a rack at Wal-Mart with breast cancer t-shirts and sweatshirts...pinks, white, black and purple. Head there quick! They won't last long! I did find a cute sweatshirt in Texas for BCA month...with a fuzzy hood and so warm! Then at Target in the $1 section they have a bunch of Breast Cancer Awareness stuff...pens, paper pads, bracelets, shoelaces, window clings, socks, hair stuff, gift bags and reusable grocery bags. Get there fast too! Fun stuff! It's not about the donations to the research that they boast on their tags...those are always sketchy....but it's about awareness, all that pink...people notice, and think about it, and remember to do their self-exams and mammograms. Being back at work again reminds me how much I am starting to HATE the lack of routine in my schedule. I work early some days, late some days, in the middle other days, then I close one day and open the next-like today. ☹ I have 3 days in a row, with three different shifts, and absolutely no time to see my family...or do anything but quick grab a meal and sleep. Then back into the car. I am trying to focus on that big picture...the money, the insurance, the time out of the house. Even the fact that not that long ago I was unable to do anything, even work. I had been

387

so excited to go back......but now that I'm there, it's a big disappointment. I have been waiting for 4+ months to get transferred, but it just isn't happening. It's disheartening. But the work I do from home is reallllly taking off! It all takes time, I guess. This week brings my 2nd 3-month appointment with my oncologist... the dreaded blood test. I am so unbelievably nervous about this one. I just have this dark cloud over my head just waiting for them to tell me that the cancer is back, hasn't left, etc. I really want to be happy with what I've made it through and move forward, but I just can't. It's a total head game.

<u>Guestbook Comment</u>: Sunday, September 18, 2011 9:59 PM
Hey Shell! Are you planning to do any Breast Cancer walks this October? Sheboygan is having the pink brigade walk on the 15th of October (I think that date's right?) A team from my school is walking....just wondering if I would see you there? Not sure I will make the whole walk.....my arthritis acts up in damp weather...and with it being fall...well enough said. I'm gonna give it my best. Ann

Tuesday, September 20, 2011 6:37 AM, CDT
As EVERYONE should already know, October is Breast Cancer Awareness Month. Wal-Mart is full of BC clothing: hats, socks, packaging on foods (save your Yoplait tops!!!!) even Mike's Hard Lemonade has the pink ribbon on their box this month. Target has BC goodies in their $1 section.... shoelaces, gift bags, window gel clings, headbands, bracelets, pens, paper, you name it. That pink ribbon did not have any meaning to me last year. I would not purposely buy the bag of Sun Chips because they had the pink ribbon/Susan G. Komen stuff on there...I bought the bag we wanted. Same with the yogurts ....I'd buy what we wanted, not which one was donating part of their sales to the Susan G. Komen

foundation. Not anymore. I still am not that screaming-from-the-
rooftop-crazy-overboard lady that INSISTS that everyone buy
NOTHING but breast cancer supportive products. I am not (yet!)
into the 'eat organic, natural, no artificial hormones, DON'T EAT ANY
SUGAR' person that claims that food causes breast cancer. I know
it's all connected somehow....but there are so many other things (i.e.
genetics, environmental, bad luck) that can cause cancer. Now I do
my part to raise awareness and any funds I can to breast cancer
research. I know most of you reading this aren't my close
friends....you probably don't even know what kind of car I drive, but
you know who I am and either through me or a friend of a friend
found this journal....and you have been reading about the Hell I have
been through for the last 11 months. And it just keeps going...I am
unable to (yet) walk in any of the breast cancer walking
fundraisers. My body is still unhappy with all it's been through...I am
in pain for a good majority of the day. The 5-year-pill that I take
seems to have some pretty crappy side effects. First on my list of
concerns...the weight gain. UGH. Like I was 'too skinny' to begin
with?!??! We all know THAT'S not true!!! 20# and counting........The
swelling in my legs and feet-I wake up in the morning and literally
can barely walk; my feet are so sore and so swollen. My toes look
like little pork sausages that are going to explode! I have major
joint pain.....seemingly everywhere. It starts in my toes, ankles,
knees, hips, shoulders, wrists, and hands. I get around like a little
old lady most days (not that there's anything wrong with little old
ladies!!!) but I limp and gimp.....ugh. I leave work and can barely get
from the car to the house-I can't imagine walking more than a few
minutes. I suppose I should not let this get me down; I am alive.
I should be happy with how far I've come compared to what I've
been through...& happy that there is medicine available to help keep
the cancer away. Right? ♥S

Guestbook Comment: Tuesday, September 20, 2011 9:50 AM
Read your post this morning. I've been supporting SGK walks for
years. Starting last year it took on a whole different meaning. If
you don't have the strength to walk, don't worry. Just know that
I'll be there to walk for you. We're family...blood is thicker than
chemo. Richard

Wednesday, September 21, 2011 4:01 PM, CDT

Another weight lifted! WHEWWWWWWWWWWWWW. My blood test
was all good! Today was my three month check with the oncologist.
I was so damn nervous I think I gave myself the shits for the
next MONTH! Hopefully the insomnia and nightmares will now be
over. Until December. I spoke with the doc about the intense body
(joint) pain I've been having; a side effect of the Aromasin. He
asked if I would be interested in switching to a different medicine,
and I declined, letting him know I'll tough it out. He continued to tell
me that the other medicine was equally effective. Some people just
seem to have more of the joint pain side effects than others. I-like
always-am one of the "lucky" ones. So I said ok, I would try it. I
also met with the plastic surgeon today. ☺ He took one look, said it
looked fantastic, and to come back in 6 weeks! Hopefully at that time
we will be able to schedule my surgery!!! ♥S

Guestbook Comment: Wednesday, September 21, 2011 9:14 PM
You are definitely one of my "peoples" that I will walk for....that damn
list is getting longer each year. Not a list that I want to grow. I
liked your comment about pink yogurt. My daughter thinks that that
yogurt, when it's in our fridge, is just for us girls. You know, cuz
its pink! Take care girlie....I've got nothing to give you when it
comes to the foot/leg pains and aches. I have the same darn thing,
my only relief was pregnancy. Increased blood volume seemed to

help, and that isn't helping me any more (I mean that in an OK way, really). Can you use painkillers or anti-inflammatory meds to help with symptoms? Ann

Guestbook Comment: Thursday, September 22, 2011 12:29 PM
It is wonderful to read that so many wonderful things are happening, despite the reasons why! Good news is good news! I love it and am happy for you! I pray the new medicine will bring you comfort and less/no joint pain AND no other side effects! You are always in my thoughts and prayers!! I love you dearly! Looking forward to the night! Love ya babe! Melissa

Saturday, September 24, 2011 8:16 PM, CDT
Autumn is here in Wisconsin! When I was young, I was a total Summer girl. LOVED the hot, LOVED the sunshine. I loved the lack of routine, and would sit in the pool for hours. I would hang out in the garage and talk on the phone to Julie or Amy for hours. I would listen to my boombox that had to be plugged in out on the deck, slathering on the baby oil to get that awesome summer tan! Now that I hate to sweat, fall is my favorite season. I have slowly fallen in love with this time of year over the last ten years. Today was a grey blustery day-both before I headed to work and again (or still??) after. It was very pretty. No sunshine, but dark grey clouds-low and fluffy. Tomorrow I only work a half a shift, so I'm hoping to have some time outside to start getting the house ready for winter. We have been starting the process of searching for a home to buy, with no luck. It seems that if it isn't overpriced, it's a place that's been let go beyond what we can personally do with it, and I don't want to buy and still have to stick $20,000 into it! We enjoy where we live now, but continue to outgrow it every day! Darn kids have so much STUFF! Hopefully

this winter is as UNEVENTFUL as we're accustomed to, and there will NOT be a repeat of the Winter of 2010. I'd like to have a boring, mellow, traditional holiday season this year!!! Our kids really enjoy living where we do-there are a lot of kids in the neighborhood to play with. It's cool now that Josh is in middle school, all the kids in the neighborhood that had been going to different elementary schools have all come together. Josh has a great variety of friends and knowing kids from each school helped make those first few weeks of Middle School go more smoothly. We have on average 6 kids here on a regular basis...all playing outside or upstairs. Army, school, dress up, or video games! They all play ok together. MOST of the time. There always has to be some drama with the girls. Grr. And no, my kids are not innocent of this either! This past week was Homecoming here in Plymouth, and we added some additional kids over here besides who we're used to! It's interesting to see the dynamics between boys and girls at this age. Their idea of 'dating' is so innocent ☺ FOR NOW. Ugh. I received some good news from my Uncle in Texas this week. His counts are still looking good THANK YOU GOD. Low counts just add more complications and inconvenience. He will soon be having another round of chemo...a very high dose. God willing he handles it well again, and continues to stay strong and maintain his sense of humor! I still can't believe it has only been a week and four days since I was in Texas! I don't travel all that much, so I have to reminisce as much as possible!!!!!

My Uncle David and I went down to San Antonio to visit my Uncle Rick. He is my Mom's youngest brother, and is also battling with cancer. When my Uncle David decided to go visit him, I decided I wanted to go too. It had been 15 years since I had last saw him, and long overdue. I'm not really sure why we had no contact all these years. Busy lives, I guess. I am kinda scatterbrained too when it comes to correspondence! It was really nice hearing all their stories from their childhood; from their military years. This vacation was a once in a lifetime opportunity...I had quality time that is irreplaceable with 2 of my Uncles. I will never forget it! Family is so important. I have a very small family to begin with; we've had many losses over the years. I have lost all 7 of my Grandparents; my Mom, my Aunt. All I have left are 4 Uncles, their families, including my 5 cousins. That's it for immediate family. It's unfortunate that we live far apart but that made it that much more special when we were down there. In a perfect world, I would go back monthly to visit.....but I of all people know that there is no perfection in life. I also got the chance to "meet" my cousin Jordan! The last I saw him, he was a little guy of 3!!! Now he is 24, and already an adult. It truly is unreal. It was kind of neat to learn that he shares a birthday with my daughter Alaina!!! 19 years apart, but......still cool! We did a lot of eating out (lol!) and sightseeing. David and I kept busy being tourists since I had never been to Texas before! It also allowed Rick to rest up, and also to take care of some things since he had just finished up his round of chemo. We did so many things it's hard to remember it all!! We went to the Alamo, Sea World, saw a historic Mission, went to the Riverwalk, went spelunking, drove through a safari, and experienced a SteamPunk movie event at the theater. We did a lot of driving, quite a bit of sweating, and a lot of talking. I could tell Rick and David really enjoyed each other's company. I have to admit that I felt like a kid again; there with no responsibilities, no kids, no time line...I have not spent a lot of time with either of these men as an adult. Growing up, Uncle David lived the closest of all my Moms brothers, and we spent a lot of time with him and his wife Elaine, and their kids...my cousins. So, again, I felt like the kid in the candy shop....since I had never been, we did a lot of things that I wanted. It was really nice since I have spent the last 11 years of my life being Mommy. You kind of give yourself away when you have children, and spend the rest of your life trying to find yourself again. I feel like the last decade is just a blur....babies, and diapers, and colic and sleepless nights, and toys, and Doctors visits, and pregnancy, and running....to school, to playgroups, to the store....all requiring a 2 hour notice to pack all the shit kids need! After being pregnant for what seemed like 3 straight years we moved an hour away to Horicon. It was a good choice at the time, but I really could have benefitted from living closer to our families. While Josh was young, we went through so so SO many trying times, trying to figure out what was going on with him. We dealt with misdiagnoses, both behaviorally and physically. He struggled a lot when he was real young with social skills and controlling himself. After many years of going from doctor to doctor, at a time when NO ONE knew crap about autism....we finally heard about a place in Milwaukee that knew their stuff, and would do a screening/ diagnosis/ observation for free. Back then, our insurance wouldn't even TOUCH any sort of "autism" testing. Not so sure they do now, either. I spent so much time driving from Horicon to Madison for help. Horicon to Beaver Dam for occupational therapy, speech therapy, physical therapy. Consults with his pediatrician. Finally through WEAP and the Waisman Center we had an "expert opinion" that he falls below the "normal" placement on their CARS test...but well above "autistic". He *could* have an autism spectrum disorder called Asperger's...but there was no official test to determine that. He was removed from his preschool, he was *kicked out* of his day care (at age 4) for issues he had. It just seemed to be never ending.... he just really had a tough time finding his natural self. After we just started accepting that we would have a lot of work ahead of us in every aspect of his life (social, emotional, behavioral....) he started getting sick. He would

394

have headaches repeatedly. His belly looked like he had swallowed a beach ball. Never mind his small stature, his slow growth. His stomach always hurt...he never wanted to eat. At his pediatrician appointment one day, after trying the umpteenth acid reflux medication...I asked her about testing for Celiac disease. With all the reading and all the research I had done about autism, and Asperger's...I knew that there was often a link between the autism spectrum and Celiac disease. I knew enough to know it was an autoimmune disorder and that you couldn't have gluten if you had it. He had some symptoms, but NONE of the classic signs. So on a whim, the Ped checked his blood IgA levels. They came back high, so she referred us down to Children's hospital in Madison. After about 2 years of biopsies, gluten free diet, back to regular diet, more biopsies, upper and lower scopes, another 6 months of GF diet, the gastrointestinal (GI) doctor found evidence of damage in his duodenum, consistent with Celiac disease. WHEW. FINALLY something concrete! Unfortunately, we received that information on his 7th birthday, so that was his last hoorah with birthday cake. After going back and forth for so long, he was so confused, and always happy when the GI doc told us to go back to a regular diet. It was heartbreaking to tell him that this would be for good. For LIFE. Even though it was a relief to have a diagnosis to explain some of the things going on....it still sucks. We have no family history of this on either side. There's a reason for everything I guess! I think I spent more time crying and angry with God back then than at any other time in my life; other than when my Mom died. And don't think that I don't wish EVERY DAY that she was still alive to help me with my babies and support me when I was the only one advocating for my son. My kids definitely are missing out. Now that we are back living in Plymouth, it is SUCH a relief to have my Sister and Dad to support us. Even before all this cancer crap started! Just knowing that they are minutes away is great. I can spend time with my nieces, go to some of their concerts, or games, or just hang out. I also love that my kids have a closer relationship with their cousins too! It used to be that we only saw each other 4-5 times a year. All I have to say is it is such an amazing thing that we moved back when we did. Definitely goes to show that there is a bigger picture & there is a God. Ok, serious carpal tunnel going on here....time to wrap it up! ♥S

Monday, September 26, 2011 10:07 AM, CDT
Cancer update: there is no cancer update. YAY! Right now I'm in the blissful middle stage where you've forgotten the horrors of it all (like childbirth) and are feeling better and everything is sailing smoothly. It's a rainy crappy day here in WI. I already ran the kids to the dentist in Sheboygan and dropped them off at school. Now I can enjoy my day off by myself with some chai tea....and one (ok, probably TWO!) of my Chai Tea Spice cupcakes with cinnamon cream cheese frosting.........Mmmmm. ♥S

Guestbook Comment: Monday, September 26, 2011 11:28 AM
Ok, I so would love to be joining you right now!!!! Enjoy your day off and the bliss of your chai! Along with your middle stage, it's been a long road to get to where you are now! Thank God! Love you! Melissa

Guestbook Comment: Monday, September 26, 2011 4:58 PM
Ah...refreshing rain here too. Rain is a good thing! So good to read your perspectives on life. One day at a time and every day is precious. I'm so glad you had time with David and Rick. Good memories. The ties that bind. Roberta

Monday, September 26, 2011 6:54 PM
Yay for you! Mary

Wednesday, September 28, 2011 9:33 PM
Thanks for sharing more of your life with all of us Shelly. Your
writing about Josh is enlightening for me...my nephew is on the
Autism spectrum, and has always had diet issues. I often wonder if
he has celiac or something else close to it, or if it's just the Autism
and that's it. I just know your kids are going to someday, if not
already, realize what an awesome mom they have and be ever so
thankful!! If they're like mine, they don't "get it" yet. I look forward
to the time, these kids realize how much work they are and all the
heartaches and personal pain you shove on the "backburner" of your
life, so that you can deal with their stuff. It's just a good thing that
we both have great husbands to help us out too. Enjoy the
wonderful fall weather. It's definitely been a classic Fall week!
Warm days, cool nights.   Ann

Thursday, September 29, 2011 8:41 PM, CDT
I need to appreciate my good health. I spoke with my Uncle Rick
this afternoon...he is in the hospital for another session of
chemo. Let's all say a prayer that it continues to help, and he
continues to feel good. One of my best friends' mom found out
today that she has breast cancer. I say a prayer every day for
her...now I need to add her Mom to that prayer list. Unfortunately,
Another good friend has been through some rough shit this past
month. I pray for you every day. You are always lifting me up.....I
wish there was anything I could say to you to help. Just know I
am here if you need......

I had a cortisone shot in my right hand carpal tunnel today ☺ My

397

fingers are still tingling-I would think the Novocain would have burned off HOURS ago. Grrr. With my luck it's a 1 in 1,000,000 side effect, and I get it. My dad has his other carpal tunnel surgery done today. It didn't go as quick and painless as the first one. There was a big callus on there, so tougher to cut through. He had quite a bit of pain by 2 p.m. Another great friend of mine is going through a heartbreak....it's so sad, she is an amazing person and deserves the best. I told her to just convert to a lesbian! I continue to struggle with my job.....I just don't have the love for it that I used to. Hopefully something will come up or give. It needs to. This is another super busy cake weekend at home! So many events this time of year! Prayers too for my good friends that are traveling-be safe and make sure your butts come back! Also thanks Val for the goodies! ♥S

Guestbook Comment: Thursday, September 29, 2011 10:21 P
Isn't it amazing when the crap that happens in your own life makes you even more sensitive to other peoples' misfortune? God has an odd way of teaching us lessons. The question is did I really need to learn this one or that one? I hope that you, your Dad and Uncle are feeling better as quick as possible!!! Ann

Sunday, October 2, 2011 4:31 PM, CDT
Today has been a very emotional one. This afternoon I started hauling out our Fall/Halloween decorations-the very ones that were crammed into boxes last year during the worst time of my life. I relive that week every time I look at these damn 'things'.....pumpkins and witches and costumes, candles and jars and wall decos. In my head, it all goes hand in hand with crying and horror and pain-surgery, and CANCER and being SICK. I think I may have to box

it all up and haul it to Goodwill in another city. Seriously. This is my favorite time of year, & I don't know if I can take seeing it all. ♥S

Monday, October 3, 2011 4:26 PM, CDT
Last Thursday, the 29th, I saw a Doc at the hand clinic in Sheboygan, and got a cortisone shot in my carpal tunnel on my right (worse) hand. It was all numb and tingly for the first few hours.....now the numb and tingly isn't going away. ☹ My ring and middle finger are *asleep*. Let me explain (again, because I have the memory of a gnat....not because you all need to know every flippin' detail.....) The fingertips of those 2 fingers have been tingly since the shot. Tingly feeling as though they were asleep, now they're 'waking up' pins-and-needles-type tingly. That's just the tips, the top knuckle to the end of my fingers. My ring finger is numb-like I rub my other fingers along it and can't so much feel it inside, but can on that other finger. ALSO since having this cortisone shot, my 'numb and sleepy hands now have the pleasure of getting a ZOLT! Every time I bend at the wrist. The same 'ZOLT!' you get when you hit your funny bone. Feels crazy, as though the tendons are twisting or something....just in those 2 fingers. ♥S

Guestbook Comment: Monday, October 3, 2011 10:19 PM
Been a while since I visited CB to catch up (even for my own Eek) but I've been thinking of you and heard you even traveled a bit. Awesome that you're comfortable jetsetting! LOL. Hope you get some relief from your carpal tunnel and joint pain soon. Beccie

Guestbook Comment: Tuesday, October 4, 2011 10:07 AM
Honey, lots & lots of prayers are going up for you. You are so brave through all this. I send you my best & please call if I can do anything. Kathy

Wednesday, October 5, 2011 7:46 AM, CDT

It's bill paying day. ☹ How depressing! Thank God the weather
outside is beautiful, that'll pull me outta that funk! This year started
out with me being off of work 5 months (seven all together including
the last 2 months of 2010) While I was off, I received short term
disability pay.....which 72% of that went right back to work, for my
insurance premiums. So of the 50% of my pay that short term
disability paid me, I received only 14% of my regular pay before
TAXES for SEVEN MONTHS. During that time, Andy, my husband,
lost his job. He was laid off. He was out of work for a month,
collecting only unemployment. Any savings that we did have was
already gone, spent on bills, and gas, and co-pays, and childcare, and
over the counter medicines and over the counter medical supplies.
Once I was able to return to work, I went 2 months without
getting a paycheck...my hours were not enough to offset my
insurance premiums. So I was paying for gas for my 90 minute
round trip commute.....daycare for all three kids before and after
school, and not getting paid. In fact.....there were a few weeks that
I had to pay in *more* out of pocket because my checks weren't
even enough to pay the premiums. Those 2 months were spent
driving to FDL; working 4 hours; driving from FDL to Plymouth,
picking up Alaina from school, taking her home, feeding her lunch,
taking her to a babysitter, driving to Sheboygan for radiation, having
treatment, driving back to Plymouth, picking up Alaina, going to the
school, picking up the other 2 kids, and going home, making supper,
and crawl up to bed, since radiation kicked my ass. I was spending
$100 a week on gas. During those 7 months I went to the Doctor
on average 2 times a week. For at least 6 of those weeks, I went
daily. I think I personally supported the gas supply coming into Kwik
Trip. During my illness there were months I had to have all three
kids in daycare just because I could not care for them. Couldn't

400

even make them a sandwich-I was SICK. Exhausted. Miserable. Once summer rolled around, and I finished up my radiation, I was so burned from the treatment that I needed to be home for 2 additional weeks. I had burns and blisters you could never imagine. That was 2 more weeks of no pay. No short term disability pay. No income period. It again took me until the end of summer to work back up to regular hours. In fact, this past week was my first week that I worked full time hours. Slowly I am trying to get back my strength and stamina and wages back to where we can live comfortably. Yeah it's been months (yay!!!!!!!) since my treatment finished up. I "look" normal again. I am "healthy" again. I can go to the store alone and have energy to shop til I drop-but doesn't take long! But there are so many agonies I still deal with. I have chronic pain from both lingering chemo effects and from the meds I take every day to keep the cancer away. I still have these DAMN tissue expanders in-making my life miserable every day. Imagine someone sewing a shotput under your pec muscles. I have issues in my right armpit/shoulder/pec major and minor from radiation. I have to do stretches 2-3 times a day for half an hour each time just so that I can have normal range of motion. Radiation changed my tissue so that it no longer stretches and acts like normal tissue. That's something that will never go away. I have pain just lifting up my arm to wash my hair. I find myself doing more things left handed. In December (cross your fingers) I will have my next big surgery to swap out my tissue expanders for silicone implants. The left side will take approximately 2-3 weeks to heal. The right side...up to 6 weeks. So once again, no money at the WORST time of year-Christmas. Cancer has pushed and pulled and taken from every aspect of our life in the last year. And unfortunately it will continue through next year...but I'm pushing back. We will get through it ♥S

Wednesday, October 5, 2011 9:21 PM
It's simply amazing the driving you have had to do while you were so ill. I don't know how you did it, and even if you put the kids in daycare while you were FIGHTING for your life, they still came home to you each day. I know your hubby was amazing and helpful, but moms still feel like they have "to be there" for the kids. When I lost Owen, the last thing I wanted to do that night was read Katie a bed time story, but I still knew in my heart that she and the boys needed normalcy of some sort, they were hurting too. After all, kids take their cues from mom and dad, and we always try to put on the bravest front we can. I know you never wanted your kids to learn this lesson this way, but can you imagine 15 to 20 years from now the empathy and humility they will have for others (whether ill or healthy). I see them being amazingly strong, caring, and independent adults who can really put themselves in others shoes. I think of you every day (REALLY) and I pray that you stay healthy FOREVER and can enjoy life again, the way you should. Love U!
Ann

Friday, October 7, 2011 7:47 AM, CDT

The day I have had nightmares about is here. This morning I found a hard BB size lump under my "good" fake boob. Trying to figure out who needs to see me and how soon they can. I'm not freaked out....just deep in thought. Today I get to enjoy my kids. A field trip with the youngest; the oldest has his own field trip to Maywood; then lunch with Ilyssa at school. THEN Mommy time-lunch together with a good friend! Hope it's even half as beautiful out as it was yesterday! ♥S

Friday, October 7, 2011 2:06 PM, CDT

Just back from my doctor. She doesn't feel that the hard lump is anything to worry about. I am still going in on Monday to the Oncologist (no offense!!!) to have him check it out. Sandi came over today to show me her new tattoo ☺ It's in memory of our Mom, and in HONOR of me! So sweet...♥S

Monday, October 10, 2011

We put an offer in on a house today! Whoa! How did that happen so fast?!?!? We crunched the numbers, and it will be $200 cheaper than renting. WISH US LUCK!

Guestbook Comment: Tuesday, October 11, 2011 6:06 PM
So if the GP doesn't think it's anything to worry about, does he/she have any idea what it is? Will it go away, will more happen? I imagine these are all things you think of when anything appears in that general area??? At the same time...one can't overreact, since then you live your life just waiting for the other boot to drop! I hope the field trip was lots of fun! Being the teacher who has to organize several each year, I always worry about what the parent is thinking and did you think it was worth the time? However, no matter what happened, I'm sure it was great to just spend time with your babe! Ann

Guestbook Comment: Tuesday, October 11, 2011 6:18 PM
Shelly! You are a great person, you made me cry and smile today when I opened the mail!! So sweet of you to think of me like that. Love ya!! Ann

Monday, October 17, 2011 5:51 AM, CDT

I did indeed see the oncologist last Monday-he agreed, that the lump was nothing to worry about. Keep checking it every 2 weeks to see if it has changed or grown in size at all; if it gets bigger-then come back in to see him.   Otherwise I have my next blood test on the 21 of December. This week has been so flippin' hectic! I received a phone call at work offering me a transfer! It is a different position, but it is sooooo much closer!!!! After this week no more 50 minute drives to work!!!! In fact, Thursday is my last day in FDL! woo hoo!!! *Just* in time....cause the snow is gonna be flying soon enough ☺That also frees up me to be able to pick up the kids from school every day, and not put them in daycare daily for 2 hours!!   Geez, just THINK of all that money I'll be saving!! LOL. Today I woke up with a sinus infection and sore throat. I did have a tiny sore throat yesterday at work, but last night I couldn't even SLEEP it hurt to swallow so bad, and my sinuses are pounding. I definitely didn't miss this last year! I don't think I was sick AT ALL last winter. (duh-the cancer doesn't count...we're talking colds flu and sinus crap.) I bet it has something to do with all the crud blowing around these last few days... probably got a corn stalk up my nose or something...! This week is back to the orthopedic surgeon guy about my hands...that cortisone shot super helped my carpal tunnel stuff-my hands don't hurt anymore and they don't fall asleep at night, waking me up. BUT my two fingers (middle and ring) are still without feeling all the time. I know. WTF. ♥S

Tuesday, October 18, 2011 9:30 PM, CDT

Another hectic week. I toured my new store today. A lot different setup than I am used to! Waaaaaaaaay smaller. I'm hoping to learn all kinds of new things, pass on some knowledge and experience, and add some ideas to their crew. I have been with the company long enough to be able to spot some things that are or are not working; things that could be done differently. It will be a new experience, that's for sure! Andy and I have been very busy working on some stuff in our lives (yes, it's still a secret, no I'm not vaguebooking!)

404

so we've truly been busy. No time to spend with friends or family. But we did manage to get an overnight trip to Appleton in last weekend. Just the 2 of us...it was very nice to have some time together. Thanks too to Sandi for taking the kids overnight for us, and taking them to the Pumpkin farm! They loved it! That's it for tonight....the countdown is here, only 2 more days of working in FDL!!!

Guestbook Comment: Tuesday, October 18, 2011 10:02 PM
ohh....a night away! Sounds nice! We are taking the family to Appleton ourselves next weekend. Trying to do a getaway, we will be doing the family thing. NEW zoo, museum for kids, some toy store shopping. Good luck on the starting in the new store. Bye, bye FDL!!! I can't remember are you on the north or south side? If it's the north side, you can make Wal-Mart by taking 'J' in less than 15 minutes. Something I have found out since I was moved to an elementary school that's on 'J'. Ann

Wednesday, October 19, 2011 7:41 PM, CDT
Ann, you are so amazing. You consistently are supporting me and are one of my biggest cheerleaders! ♥S

Guestbook Comment: Monday, October 24, 2011 10:41 AM
I am so happy to hear you two got away alone! Everyone, especially married couples need to have some time with and for each other!!! I am excited for your move to a closer store. I know how much that will help you and your family! The driving, the time the money on day care and so much more! I hope God continues to bless you and your family, no matter what it is or isn't in your life! As always you are in my thoughts and prayers! I love you all, Take care! I miss you tons! Love you! Melissa

Wednesday, October 26, 2011 11:45 AM, CDT

'Not having you in my life when I needed you most really hurt. It hurt more than the cancer'. And you SHOULD feel bad. ♥S

Guestbook Comment: Wednesday, October 26, 2011 1:22 PM
Hi Shelly, Just poppin' in to say you're on my mind. Love, R

Guestbook Comment: Wednesday, October 26, 2011 9:29 PM
Just got your last journal entry...what's up? Not that I don't understand your statement! It's amazing when something really sucky happens in your life, some people can disappear or not even try to make an effort to reach out. Your entries are poignant and heartfelt. You really make your readers feel what you are going thru. I sure hope all those secret things you and Andy have been working on are panning out and that you have continued good Karma and achieve your goals! Sorry, if not secrets anymore....I have been super busy at school and at home and not really reading much of my FB stuff. Have a happy week! Ann

Saturday, October 29, 2011 6:24 AM, CDT

If you haven't yet watched the Lifetime movie 'Five' about 5 women, intertwined with breast cancer diagnoses, you DEFINITELY should check your On Demand channels. They are all affected differently. They are all at different stages of their lives. All walks of life... including a stripper....and it really gets across some messages from our point of view. I hope you'll look it up and watch it. Well, today brings me one year and one day PAST the day Andy found my 'lump'. Thank God for hubbies needing to grab a feelski! I don't know how long it had been growing there, or how long it would have been before I found it. It is so unreal what has all transpired in the last year. Physically I am a completely different person.......

Emotionally I am still a wreck!!! But Mentally.....mentally I think I'm getting there. I have my bad days and my REALLY bad days, but I am finally moving a teensy tiny bit closer to having less really really bad days. I've started seeing a counselor. I don't really know if that is helping? It's only been 2 times. I'm hoping she can just zap me back to 2010 and I can just fix this sooner! Wow. It's really been a whole year...and I'm not dead yet. ♥S

Guestbook Comment: Monday, October 31, 2011 10:55 AM
Shelly, just know we love you more each day! Kathryn

Guestbook Comment: Monday, October 31, 2011 9:34 PM
Gotta love that husband! The fact that you are seeing someone outside of the situation and not related to you, your husband or the kids is a great decision. Hopefully, then you can just be totally, freakishly honest! Not that you haven't been honest will all of us on CB!! And we love it! I'm glad you make the decision you have. You continue to amaze me in that you can make all these real life decisions as if all this past year you weren't fighting for your life! That you could still make those stupid, mundane little decisions. I like to take forever to think about things before I decide to do anything ...drives my husband absolutely nuts! Your events of this past year, definitely put more things in perspective and that's got to help narrow the field of what's important and what can just go away. Hoping for good news about that house!!! Ann

Monday, October 31, 2011 10:40 PM, CDT
In an hour and twenty minutes my beautiful Ilyssa will turn NINE!!!! HAPPY BIRTHDAY ILYSSA!!!! We love you sooooooo much! She was so damn cute when she was born, all 7lbs. 8 oz of her ☺ A lot of

black hair and she had the most shrill cry. Some things never change!

In roughly ten and a half hours it will be finally be one year from my 9 a.m. mammogram appointment where I found out I had breast cancer. That was the worst day of my life. I really feel like I've been dreading this day for 364 days....I think mentally once I've gotten past tomorrow, I'll be able to exhale....

Not to mention tomorrow should be the day we find out if we get a definite yes or no on the HOUSE we put an offer in on!! C'MON mortgage underwriters! Hurry up already!!! ♥S

Wednesday, November 2, 2011 6:40 AM, CDT
Ilyssa's birthday was GREAT! She brought and shared her treats at school, and everyone enjoyed. She was beaming!! She also chose DQ for our family supper, and yum yum yummmmmmmm was it delish!!! We then headed home and opened presents ☺ It kept my mind off of what yesterday also was. One year......and WHEW. That day is over! ♥S

Wednesday, November 2, 2011 6:48 AM, CDT
...and oh yeah, the house crud. THIS IS SO DAMN STRESSFUL. We are supposed to close in 13 days. We still have gotten nothing from the underwriters. Yesterday we were told by our mortgage broker.....it *might* be Thursday, might be longer. She doesn't know, and doesn't want to keep asking, since then they'll just get crabby and say no or take longer. I don't know if I should start packing? Give the landlord official notice? Cry? Ugh. This is going on TWO weeks since our mortgage application. So disgusted right now. ♥S

408

Wednesday, November 2, 2011 9:30 PM
Sounds like you are definitely balancing your highs and lows this week.
Hoping for a great big HIGH by the end of the week at the latest!!!
Wishing you all the speedy luck! Ann

Tuesday, November 8, 2011 10:23 PM, CST

Crazy few weeks! The new job is going well, just working with
young(er) chicks=DRAMA. Yes, already. O.M.G. Oh, well, I'll just let
it roll off my shoulders. We celebrated Ilyssa's 9th birthday. We
threw our First Annual Family Friendly Costume party this past
weekend! What a fun time! It was nice to have all the kids
corralled in one spot and we were able to relax and enjoy! I'm
hoping to be around for 40 more!

We **********finally********** got loan approval on our house!!!!!!

It has been a ?????????????STRESSFUL??????????????
month, trying to purchase a home for our family. Mostly because
the crap income I had for the first 5 months of the year. But,
God has blessed us with this opportunity and we are so happy to be
able to provide this for our family. It will be great to start anew in
this new house! Hopefully soon (December) I can have my final step
checked off my list-my reconstruction!!!!! I will be one happy, busty
Mama when I can close this chapter of the book and move
beyond........ ♥S

Guestbook Comment: Wednesday, November 9, 2011 7:26 AM
So happy for your family! Always love when God answers prayer! Jen

Guestbook Comment: Wednesday, November 9, 2011 8:40 PM
All I can say is "it's about frickin' time!!!" I am so happy and excited

for you guys! What an exciting time. It's so nice to see some good positive things coming your way, keep 'em rolling in! Ann

Monday, November 14, 2011 6:06 PM
Shelly: loved your amazing story & truly not the fact that you had to have one, but it was fun to read. Made FB friends with you recently. Thought I did that a month ago!? Might be the chemo memory garg I encounter at times. I know you'll like this message 'cause getting a guest message makes "wonderful feelings." I myself love it. We didn't know each other well when I worked at Wal-Mart. But, I do remember good memories. I remembered when u hugged me when I was just going thru the cancer diagnosis period. Thanks for the memory! I'm also on CaringBridge & just have "My Story". Did enter the background story recently & deleted it somehow!? I'll blame it on this cell killing drug. My mind was better prior to chemo ~ Now is in a lull at times. I don't get frustrated & mind that my memory is half-staff too much. Thanks to the great meds for that! Will update soon with facts. I had great lab results recently & am elated with the results. The chemo must be doing its job 'cause it shows my liver is functioning well. Thank God! Cause they would of changed the chemo to one that could cause many issues I didn't want to deal with. Your story is wonderful & I hope for the best in the future. ~Wendy

Monday, November 14, 2011 8:19 PM, CST

Frustrated. I am getting so frustrated. Now it looks like we won't be closing on our house until next week. GRRRRRRRRRRRRRRRRR. The seller has had everything done (roof, electrical, etc.) that they were required to, but the lender has not received verification of those services. And the appraisor needs to come out again to verify that they were done. That could take a few days.....Let's just mention that

Thanksgiving is next week, and we know how this is gonna go....."oh, it's a short week and we're soooooooooooooo busy....and I won't be in the office....and and and well, since I only work one hour a week anyway....the closing will have to be in December....and only on a leap year when there's a harvest moon and the wind is blowing straight south..... ♥S

***the following is a journal entry I found on a stack of loose papers in my office-no date on it, and I know it repeats a lot of what I've discussed in the past. But I still need to include it, so I figured here is as good a place as ANY! Here goes...

OMIGAWD. I'm running on like 5 hours of sleep in the last MONTH! Not for lack of trying either! But this whole house buying thing is STRESSFUL!!! We looked at it twice before thinking long and hard for a few days; then we put in our offer. Tick Tock Tick Tock. Our offer was accepted! It was a week and a half after that yet that we had to wait for our appointment with the mortgage broker. On a stinkin Saturday even! THEN it didn't even get sent IN until Tuesday. We were told 48 hours...tick tock...then 72 hours...tick tock. Came and went. THEN another week went by. THREE WEEKS AND TWO DAYS after our approved offer, we received a "conditional" loan approval. YAY! We bought a house!!! All that sleep OUT the window! Stress about money; stress about NO money; stress about utilities, cable, rent, insurance, FLOOD insurance, inspections costs, mildew in the basement, replace the roof, electrical upgrade, carpet or no carpet, island or no island? Assessment, new job...ARGH?!?!!? My head may explode! And...I felt the need to throw a costume party in the middle of it all! Once we are all moved into our new home life WILL be stress free. Really. I swear! This blog HAS to end somewhere!!!

Wednesday, November 16, 2011 7:33 PM, CST
heel pain= Plantar Fasciitis=fucking OW!
Closing on the house next Wednesday. So far.
tomorrow I meet with the plastic surgeon----HOPING to schedule my surgery!!!!! ♥S

Guestbook Comment: Wednesday, November 16, 2011 9:15 PM
Good Luck on the closing, hope all goes quick and smooth! It will feel like you are signing your firstborn away. Sign here, sign here, sign here, sign here, initial this, initial this, initial that, etc...Plantar Fasciitis, so yucky! This time of year, always makes it bad. I invest in good slippers after work. SECRET....sometimes I wear my slippers at work on bad days. I realize that this poses more problems in your work. Good luck!!! Ann

Guestbook Comment: Thursday, November 17, 2011 12:28 PM
Sitting here at Bemis eating Ramen at my desk and thinking about you. Hope your week is going well. Let's try to see each other this weekend and that doesn't mean me driving past your house creeping on you! LOL Betsy

Thursday, November 17, 2011 6:50 PM, CST
The appointment went great. Doc said my skin looked great; we'll be scheduling the reconstruction surgery very soon. They will call me in the next few days to set it up. He will be revising my scar from my port insertion/removal-for whatever reason it healed up big and puffy and angry....he wondered out loud why the heck it did that, since my mastectomy scars were nice and healed and flat. I told him it was because he didn't do it lol! He also will be tightening up and removing some of the extra skin under my pits (tactfully

412

nicknamed 'dogears'). I have folds of skin that increased and had turned into 'flaps' of skin/tissue/fat once my breasts were removed. Nowhere else to go I guess. That part is normally pulled taught when you have breasts....I will be there just as an outpatient, surgery will only be about 3 hours! I will be feeling better after about 2 weeks, off of work for 3 weeks, and it will take 4-6 weeks for the incisions to fully heal and be at 100% strength again. We have to tread very carefully on the radiated skin. Hoping it all comes together (house and surgery scheduled) by Turkey day!!!! ♥S

Guestbook Comment: Thursday, November 17, 2011 8:32 PM
...just to forewarn you he may revise your scar but it may go back to the way it is now. Mine looked so nice after my PS did it but it slowly expanded out again-must just be something with that area. Lisa

Guestbook Comment: Thursday, November 17, 2011 10:56 PM
LOOK at you with all that hair! I haven't seen you like that before! The last time I saw you, your hair was green LOL! So are you excited, scared, nervous or just all 3 about the upcoming booby day! Yes, you need to name it something better, you are very good at labeling your events! It's weird to say, but I'm very happy for your upcoming "next step". Good luck, can't wait to see more updates on the surgery and the house!! Ann

Friday, November 18, 2011 9:43 PM, CST
Nothing too exciting today! Just working on my book; catching up on emails; packing some more; watching Twilight ☺ ♥S

Saturday, November 19, 2011 6:53 PM, CST
Every month (regardless of your age) you need to do a self-exam.

413

Taking a few minutes to do a breast self-exam a minimum of once a month can make the difference of a lifetime, literally. Nearly 70% of all breast cancers are found through self-exams. Write it down on your calendar. If you find a lump, schedule an appointment with your doctor, but don't panic-8 out of 10 lumps are not cancerous. Once a year you should have a clinical breast exam by a qualified nurse or doctor to check for lumps or other physical changes. Get a mammogram once a year. A mammogram is an X-ray photograph of the breast and the primary tool in diagnosing breast cancer. Early detection is essential ladies. If you forget to change the oil in your car...your car may have engine problems...if you skip your self-exams, you just might lose your life for it. Take the time. ♥S

Saturday, November 19, 2011 6:57 PM, CST
IF I HAD MY LIFE TO LIVE OVER - by Erma Bombeck

(Written after she found out she was dying from cancer)
I would have gone to bed when I was sick instead of pretending the earth would go into a holding pattern if I weren't there for the day. I would have burned the pink candle sculpted like a rose before it melted in storage. I would have talked less and listened more. I would have invited friends over to dinner even if the carpet was stained, or the sofa faded. I would have eaten the popcorn in the 'good' living room and worried much less about the dirt when someone wanted to light a fire in the fireplace. I would have taken the time to listen to my grandfather ramble about his youth. I would have shared more of the responsibility carried by my husband. I would never have insisted the car windows be rolled up on a summer day because my hair had just been teased and sprayed. I would have sat on the lawn with my grass stains. I would have cried and laughed less while watching television and more while watching life. I

414

would never have bought anything just because it was practical, wouldn't show soil, or was guaranteed to last a lifetime. Instead of wishing away nine months of pregnancy, I'd have cherished every moment and realized that the wonderment growing inside me was the only chance in life to assist God in a miracle. When my kids kissed me impetuously, I would never have said, 'Later. Now go get washed up for dinner.' There would have been more 'I love you's' and more 'I'm sorry's.' But mostly, given another shot at life, I would seize every minute. Look at it and really see it. Live it and never give it back. STOP SWEATING THE SMALL STUFF! Don't worry about who doesn't like you, who has more, or who's doing what. Instead, let's cherish the relationships we have with those who do love us. Well said, ma'am.   ♥S

Guestbook Comment: Sunday, November 20, 2011 9:28 PM
We should all print that and tape it to the mirror, so we have to be reminded of what's important each and every day! Thanks for reminding me & sharing! Ann

Monday, November 21, 2011 3:19 PM, CST
UNACCEPTABLE.
Called the PS office this afternoon on my way home from a particularly frustrating day. I was told that the Doc is continuing his education/training in Alabama. He is only available for surgery in December on the first, second, and third. The 1st and 2nd are booked up...and there are eleven people on the waiting list to be scheduled for the 3rd. I have been told MANY times over that there would be no problem having this done by the end of the year.....now? Problem. I completely find this unacceptable and have already started researching other PS's within 180 miles. I will have this surgery done this year regardless of who does it. Since my

415

deductible is met, I can NOT afford to wait until the next calendar year to have this done. It would cost me $10,000. ♥S

MONDAY, NOVEMBER 21, 2011 5:30 PM, CST
Why oh Whyyyyyyy has my guestbook been so quiet lately???? Come on people! ♥S

Guestbook Comment: Monday, November 21, 2011 6:50 PM
Wow! Do you have a good supply of other options, other Docs to go to for the surgery? Yes, I think well over 13 months is long enough to wait for this culminating event! I wish you luck finding a surgeon that you are comfortable with and that has an open schedule!! Ann

Guestbook Comment: Monday, November 21, 2011 7:51 PM
HI...just dropping in to say hello. Hope you and your family have a wonderful Turkey day. I remember last year we did it at your house and you were feelin' crummy. This year will be better for you. When are you guys planning on moving? I will hopefully have the day off so I can help do whatever you need help with. Thinkin' of you always and hoping you get your surgery before the END OF THE YEAR!!! Candice

Guestbook Comment: Monday, November 21, 2011 7:54 PM
So happy to hear about your new house! You have to let me know where it is! Sorry we missed the party, looks like it was a blast. ~Ang~

Tuesday, November 22, 2011 2:14 PM, CST
I have had the BEST DAY EVER with Jenni!! Had a yummy lunch, and an awesome few hours of RELAXING!!! I even got her

laughing so hard she was crying....lol- I love you Jen!!! ♥S

Guestbook Comment: Tuesday, November 22, 2011 2:35 PM
Sooo need more days like today!!!! Love you too Babe!!! Jen

Guestbook Comment: Tuesday, November 22, 2011 3:10 PM
I misplaced your phone#. Call me this evening if you can. Glad to
hear you had a great day. Keep laughing it beats frown lines!!
Kathryn

Guestbook Comment: Tuesday, November 22, 2011 7:12 PM
Yay for good friends and making them cry! Mary

Guestbook Comment: Wednesday, November 23, 2011 8:30 AM
I can understand the frustration with PS delay!! Wth?? You need
to get this done by the end of the year, seriously. I sent you my
PS's name and location he's an Aurora doc. Hugs to you and best
of luck scheduling this for DECEMBER 2011! Love the hair!! Beccie

Wednesday, November 23, 2011 5:39 PM, CST
We're having Ilyssa's birthday party tonight! Holy moly! It is LOUD
here!!! I have scheduled a consult with a different PS, and am
hoping they are able to get my surgery DONE this year yet. It's a
waiting game, like everything, but I am hoping for the best. Josh
met with the orthodontist today, we're going forward with braces in
2 weeks....not a whole set, but partial-top only. We received
notification tonight from our mortgage broker that the assessor
acknowledged and APPROVED the situation we have been waiting for.
☺ Since it's a HOLIDAY tomorrow....we don't know if the underwriter
is in on Friday....so of COURSE it may be even longer to get to the
closing table. I'm tired. Stick a fork in me, I'm done. We have a

417

busy few weeks ahead of us now! I have started packing up our house-but it's really tough! We really do live within our means, so we don't have a lot of "extra" lying around. I can't pack up what we still use, right?! Thankfully I think we can all agree that summer is over (first snowfall yesterday) so the summer stuff was the first to be packed. Then miscellaneous toys and books and crap from the playroom. Before I knew it I had about 10 boxes packed! So, it's slow going, but it's also enough to keep me busy! We ordered the new flooring for the kitchen/dining room from Home Depot this week! The super OOGLY carpet HAS to go! Ick! We chose vinyl planking (thanks for the recommendation Sarah and Mary!) We can install it ourselves and it will survive the kids! It will hopefully be in early next week so that once we finally close we can get to it!! That is one of our BIG projects! One of the other big projects is to remove the paneling from the one wall in the living room and all down the hallway-which should be a piece of cake! Painting will be up next, and again, piece of cake! I have had all kinds of volunteers to help with that already. And don't think for a MINUTE that I won't take you up on it!!! We want to get all the painting done before we move much in. Less hassle, y'know?? For the living room, I want to keep the brown that we have now, same in our room. The girls want lime green walls! Let's just say that is NOT gonna happen! We'll come up with something cute! Josh is undecided. He picked out a bright blue color that would be pretty dark-we're working on that. The bathrooms will be a wait and see. The kitchen/dining room-some shade of orange to go with the floors and still mesh with the cabinets til I paint them white. Oh! I forgot! The other big project is to take out the built in stove top, cut out the cupboards beneath, and remove the wall with the built in oven to be able to put in our range. Nothings ever easy, eh? I'd like to tear out some other cabinets too-much to Andy's surprise-since I haven't told him yet!

418

I would love to move the fridge to where the oven is so we can widen the kitchen wall opening someday! We lose a small amount of cabinets, but we can put some in under the windows if need be. I'd love to put the island in but that's a wait and see how it fits, how the flow is around it. That's where I'd like to put all my baking stuff! Then I can have a GF area away from the other stuff. Josh can have his own area, and I can use it for all his baking along with my decorating stuff. I am still going forward with my goal to get licensed-I received a GREAT quote for the insurance so I just need to find a kitchen that will rent to me! Ok, back to the reasons I can't sleep...

New job
New house
New life!

I can't believe what these last few years of our life have been like! Andy and I literally have been tested on everything from here to FRIDAY!!! Enough already, God!!

I am FINALLY at a turning point in my life. I have been waiting for this! Waiting for those "good" things that come to those who wait. Finally it feels like it's our turn! I have finally stopped praying out of selfishness i.e. "please don't let that cop catch me SPEEDING!!" "Please let there be CHOCOLATE somewhere in this house!!!" I have matured enough to know that there is a bigger picture everywhere! Throughout my cancer treatments and surgeries I have prayed as needed-from "please God let me wake up from this surgery" to "please just let me die. I do NOT want to do this ANYmore." I find myself moving past these. I am praying to "do the right things." Praying to thank God for all I have already; all I have been blessed with. I let Him know how much I need His help during very difficult situations. Praying for guidance, strength and understanding. This is all a VERY big step for me. ♥S

Guestbook Comment: Wednesday, November 23, 2011 8:11 PM
You have so much going on! I just want you to be able to be more comfortable for Christmas, that is my wish for you ☺ Beccie

THURSDAY, NOVEMBER 24, 2011 7:15 AM, CST
Happy Thanksgiving Everyone!!!
I know that my faithful friends and family know how grateful I am for this past year; how grateful I am for EVERY one of you-even you lurkers that barely know me. I am grateful for all the support I have received. I am grateful for every person that has taken me to doctor appointments; every person that has sat with me in my house taking care of me. I am grateful for all the cards I have received throughout this (and will keep everyone of them until the day I die!) I am grateful for the flowers, the bracelets, the blankets, the scarves, the hats, the books, the movies, the food, the cookies, the Christmas caroling, the babysitting, the shopping trips, the DVD's borrowed; the time and friendship given to me. I am grateful for the technology, skill and knowledge that God has given the medical community to treat my cancer in the aggressive and successful manner they have. I am grateful for everyone in the medical community that I have encountered-both face to face and behind the scenes-that has worked together like a well-oiled machine to treat the volume of people they do. From CNA's to RN's to LPN's to med students to Doctors, to specialists, surgeons, care coordinators, volunteers, and everyone else that I see your bills but never meet! (pathologists, etc.) I am grateful to the staff and parents and volunteers at my children's elementary school. They

420

have donated their time and hearts to watch over my kids when I was super sick. They have donated meals and movie tickets; a Thanksgiving dinner and gift cards. We ♥LOVE♥ this school and feel like a part of their family. I am grateful to my employer for all they have done to support me while I have gone through this. They have bent some rules and helped me out when we were in a crisis. Please, everyone enjoy the holiday today, and have a happy Thanksgiving. Enjoy the day with your loved ones and family, even if they're not your favorite people-be grateful for what they have done for you, what they have brought you (your spouse!) and take a look at what their lives have contained (loss, sickness, hard times) and realize that everyone has their own story....that has made them who they are today. Even if they grate on your nerves....just let it roll off your shoulders....just for today ☺ Enjoy your turkey dinner today everyone! Happy Thanksgiving, Andy, I am most grateful for YOU. I love you so much. ♥S

Guestbook Comment: Thursday, November 24, 2011 8:55 AM
Happy Thanksgiving to you. I am thankful to have you as my friend....you are strong, amazingly talented (I don't have half that talent in my little finger) witty, caring and beautiful. Your strength throughout this last year inspires me to be a better person. Have a great Thanksgiving to you and your family...we love you. The Braun's

Guestbook Comment: Thursday, November 24, 2011 11:58 AM
What a wonderful tribute to all. We are thankful for your road to recovery & you sharing your heart with us, when it had to be difficult. Here's praying you and family have a wonderful day. Love....Kathryn

<u>Guestbook Comment</u>: Saturday, November 26, 2011 9:49 PM
Hi Shelly! I think of you often, even if I'm not telling you so here! This has been a long year with many changes and challenges. Patience, my dear, on the house. It's really going through quickly as real estate goes. Sounds like you're avoiding the horror stories that some experience. How many days until Christmas?? Love, R

Monday, November 28, 2011 9:29 AM, CST
In my dreams last night I got my new boobs, and my plastic surgeon moved in with us. Not like creepy-I-like-your-new-boobs-moved-in. But like, hey...I'm moving in. What's for breakfast? Can you tell what's been on MY MIND?? ♥S

Monday, November 28, 2011 10:21 PM, CST
Struggling with the immaturity at work. I have been through a lifetime of "grown up" experiences this past year....it's SO TOUGH for me to function with others on their level ☹ How do you put up with the mindless drivel they find "important"? How do I tell them kindly that I do NOT want to partake in their gossip groups?! I find myself beyond my peers, having done the time that I have in the Big Chair-decades before normal people even have to face that? I find myself without things to converse about; without any manners in the way I discuss my cancer journey. I don't hold back! (surprise, right???) But during my day to day encounters, I have to bite my tongue; repeatedly. We continue to sit and wait for the house to be ours...now the underwriter is going BEYOND ridiculousness. She is arguing the wording in the roofing confirmation. Finally, our mortgage broker had to speak up and go to bat for us. She called her on how UNBELIEVABLY trivial this is...and even had her boss involved. We're all still naive in hoping that we'll close this Wednesday ☹ ♥S

<u>Guestbook Comment</u>: Monday, November 28, 2011 7:56 PM
Does it feel weird to look forward to a surgery this much?
Considering what your last procedures have been, it's definitely a
little more positive! "All Shelly wants for Christmas are her two
front boobies!" Gotta imagine/sing that with the right tune! Ann

<u>Guestbook Comment</u>: Tuesday, November 29, 2011 9:51 PM
I found myself removing myself from a situation this past week
where I was supposed to attend an event where immaturity runs
wild and not among the children present. My decision will inevitably
cause bad feelings and someone will try to engage me or my
husband in an argument about it. The decisions we make when we
realize that we cannot put ourselves through more stress and
heartache then life already hands us on a daily basis. I REALLY do
hope that whatever it is that you are facing or listening to or are
involuntarily involved with, I hope that it resolves itself with as little
pain to you or your family! I think you may need a caring bridge
site for buying a house.....what an experience! This house better not
give you any problems after you are in, but then again, you plan to
do some remodeling.....! I hope to read good news tomorrow! Ann

Wednesday, November 30, 2011 8:14 AM, CST
It is now 8 a.m. and we STILL don't know if we will be closing on
our house today at 1:30. WTF doesn't even BEGIN to touch it. ♥S

<u>Guestbook Comment</u>: Wednesday, November 30, 2011 8:25 AM
I am so sorry you guys! I will keep everything crossed all day for
you. Mary

Wednesday, November 30, 2011 11:27 AM, CST
YOWCH. This morning I had to go in and get a cortisone shot in

MY HEEL. Can I just tell ya.....it FUCKING HURT!!!!!!! I do NOT recommend it. EVER! Even though I'm sure the pros will outweigh the cons....in 24 hours...holy shit did that hurt. I'm falling to PIECES! Planter fasciitis in my feet. The crown that I had done during chemo is loose, so when I chew it hurts my gums. Not sure if I posted this, but the tissue around the crown is not healing well at all. The DDS thought maybe since it was during chemo that my body just wasn't working the way it should to heal it. Who knew? So now, that not-healing tissue is aggravated. I go tomorrow to have a 48 hour heart harness put on. My heart has been doing some funky things. Since it seems to be happening more often, I wanted to get it checked out before the end of the year. (deductible starts over) Since chemo is so hard on your heart, we're being proactive to get it checked. Next week is my consult with the different plastic surgeon...thanks Beccie for the recommendation. Let's hope he can squeeze me in if my current doc can't. ♥S

Guestbook Comment: Wednesday, November 30, 2011 12:33 PM
I cannot imagine how painful that shot had to be!!! Hopefully it will give you some relief! With no crappy side effects! I can't believe that lady is being that difficult, does she know how she's messing with your life and the things you could be doing! It is good that things are moving along for you, no matter how slow at times! You are always in my thoughts and prayers, LOVE YOU!!!! Melissa

Wednesday, November 30, 2011 12:44 PM, CST
ARE YOU FUCKING KIDDING ME???????????????????????????
Just had the mortgage broker call. The roof paperwork has all been cleared and is good to go. While going through whatever they found 2 dates that needed to be changed. It could take up to THREE HOURS to get that stuff changed and back to who it needs

424

to be. We could still close as late as 5 tonight. Or it would need to be tomorrow. Or maybe Groundhogs Day. Or the summer solstice. Or when the south pole melts. I am officially NO LONGER EXCITED about buying this home. WHAT THE FUCK!!!!!!! WHO ELSE DOES THIS SHIT EVEN HAPPEN TO?????????????????? ♥S

Guestbook Comment: Wednesday, November 30, 2011 2:05 PM
Well I wish your surgeon was more available for you considering what you've been through this year, but I bet you will like Dr. Andy and I hope you get those damned tissue expanders O.U.T. and have your new rack all set in time for Christmas!! And the house..... how much more patience must you muster???? wth. Beccie

Wednesday, November 30, 2011 7:50 PM, CST
We got the call at 3:45 p.m. that we could close on our house at 5. At 4 we had to go through it one more time before the deal happened.

But.

As you can imagine, it wasn't smooth sailing, and there was a big ole BUT. We can definitely close tonight, but since it is after 5 p.m. the money can NOT be wired tonight, and we will not be turned over the property nor will we be allowed in (get the keys) until tomorrow when the mortgage company wires the money to the seller's lawyer and it's "official". This literally almost gave me a frickin' heart attack. I was ready to EXPLODE at this news. We signed all the paperwork, did a "dry" closing, meaning they didn't get their money, but you bet your ass we had to pay our closing costs, down payment, etc. We have an insurance policy that went into effect WHEN we signed the papers. There is NOTHING we could do to the house that would hurt anyone but us. But the seller didn't feel comfortable letting us in before she was wired the money. WHICH you can't do until the closing documents are all done. When we got to the lawyers office, they had not even gotten the HUD approval. So we literally just sat there in the conference room for 40 minutes doing nothing, waiting for the attorney to receive the email. She finally called down to Texas to speak with the bank herself and got the document she needed. It took almost three hours, but it's all good. Maybe we'll get the key to get in tomorrow. Unfortunately I have to work the next 2 days all day, home late...maybe I can enjoy the new place Saturday?! My foot that I had the cortisone shot in is K-I-L-L-I-N-G me. Quite possibly I won't be able to stand on it tomorrow-today I haven't been able to. ♥S

Dear Andy ♥

What can I say? I love you. I can't imagine my life without you. Not now, not a year ago, not one, two or three kids ago, not 12 years ago, not 17 years ago. You make me laugh, you support me in all my hare-brained endeavors, you are there for me every night, rubbing my back until I fall asleep. You give 100% of yourself to me and the kids. When times were ghetto tough-you made the sacrifices...without hesitation. You take charge and get things done that need to be. You. Are. Just. The. Bomb Diggity. You are strong for me. You take care of me. You make the four of us priorities in your life. You work hard, you provide, you love. That's all I need.....XOXO ♥Shell

Thursday, December 1, 2011 9:32 AM, CST
Crazy pain today. The heel that the shot was in? HOLY CRAP. I literally cannot bear weight on it. I had to call in to work today ☹ I NEVER MISS WORK. I also went this morning to have my Holter

Monitor placed so we can monitor my ticker for the next 48 hours. That went ok, but like everything else, the tissue expanders may pose a problem. The initial reading while we were there looked good and strong tho. Not a lot of interference. Now if I could only stand up....do some driving, get the DAMN house key for our new place and get STARTED ALREADY! But of course.....I can't. Need to stay here on the couch, foot elevated, and get it better asap. ♥S

Monday, December 5, 2011 9:06 PM, CST
4 straight days of balls to the wall working! House/Sleep/work/errands/shop/house/paint/demo/fight with Andy/ugh. Rock on. ♥S

<u>Guestbook Comment</u>: Tuesday, December 6, 2011 9:34 PM
the girls' room looks great! Mary

Thursday, December 8, 2011 4:30 AM, CST
You. Will. Not. Believe. This. My surgery is SCHEDULED!!! With 2 days to spare, even! AND even with my great PS...not the new one! Wish me luck!!!!! ♥S

<u>Guestbook Comment</u>: Thursday, December 8, 2011 7:46 AM
Your long awaited squishy foobs!! Time to celebrate a new year!! Beccie

<u>Guestbook Comment</u>: Thursday, December 8, 2011 7:56 AM
Woo Hoo! It's about time! Glad it finally all came together! Jen

<u>Guestbook Comment</u>: Sunday, December 11, 2011 10:45 PM
Yay for you! Guess things are looking like they are finally turning your way! I hope the move went well this past weekend. I thought of you, wish I could have helped. I didn't even know it was

happening so soon. We had last minute visitors anyway. Mat's brother from IL came up on Friday night with our two nephews. What chaos all day Saturday! 5 kids running all over the house, with 2 men completely oblivious! Merry Christmas! Ann

Friday, December 16, 2011 6:04 AM, CST
I cannot believe all our friends that came out and busted their frozen butts to help us move last weekend!!!!!!! THANK YOU!!!! It is so nice to be here in the new place! At the same time it is hectic, chaotic, and overwhelming! There is SO MUCH to do! Then at the same time to function as Mom and go to work. I needed to get the Christmas tree up too-the kids were begging! I have the bedrooms all set up for the most part. A few things we need to unbury from the garage & basement yet. We finally have cable/internet set up. Josh got braces on most of his upper teeth, and they are already moving and looking great! Ilyssa had her Christmas concert. ☺ Alaina is enjoying her *big girl* bed (a full-her part of the bunk beds!) Busy busy busy! ♥S

Guestbook Comment: Saturday, December 17, 2011 11:57 PM
I for one did miss your daily updates on here and FB! I thought of you guys all week. I wanted to help, but what a CRAZY week, as you know! Our Anniversary, Jack's birthday, special day at school for Katie, helping with Jack's Christmas program at school, and oh yeah being the Art teacher in an elementary school at Christmas time is a fun, but chaotic time of year. Anyway.....I am so glad you guys are in the house and getting settled! You are just so amazingly busy.....how did Cancer ever catch you? I can't believe in the middle of all this chaos, you are also having surgery. WOW! I am experimenting with Cake Pops for the holidays! I bought a book and got hooked! I kept thinking....."How would Shelly do this?" Finding

stuff is the hardest part. It's so much prep.....I certainly have another new respect for your talents! Ann

Monday, December 19, 2011 8:59 AM, CST

Well, it's almost that time again.....Wednesday will be my 2nd 3-month blood test check to see where my tumor markers are at. I just get all in a knot when this creeps up on me. It could change my life in just minutes...I don't know when this feeling of doom will stop hanging over my head. I don't know if it ever will? I constantly live with this, and always feel that it will be a *when* it comes back/spreads, not an *if*. 10 days from today I will again go under the knife and have reconstruction surgery done. It will be about a 3 hour surgery...wish us luck. ♥S

Guestbook Comment: Monday, December 19, 2011 10:43 AM
It's good to know your surgery is set before the end of the year! I'll keep you in my prayers for your blood test and to ease your mind. I hope you are slowly settling in, let me know if you need more help! Love you! Melissa

Guestbook Comment: Monday, December 19, 2011 9:15 PM
I would think that this test will always be a little unnerving to go thru. Not that I have personal experience, only others. It has the ability, which you well know, to change your life in an instant, again. However, don't give a small amount of blood the ability to define you. You are winning! Is it weird that I think about you and your boobies every day? I think about your surgery often, and hope it goes smoothly and your pain is little. Yay, the expanders will be gone! Ann

Wednesday, December 21, 2011 9:01 PM, CST
After a few very anxious hours, I did indeed pass this latest blood test with flying colors! Doc said all my blood work was good! We spent most of the time talking about the issues I am having with my heart. I received a call yesterday from my other doctor telling me that the Holter monitor showed that nothing was happening when I had pressed the button, but that my heart is beating too fast-an extra beat every 4 beats. So they want to put me on some meds to even out my heartbeat. I would like to wait until after my surgery to start it. I don't know why, just do. My blood pressure is still a pain in the butt-I don't know that I've mentioned this before, but no one can read my BP. They always have to get the BP machine to read it. Also my BP is usually low. Anyhow, I left with the peace of mind for another 3 months! ♥S

Guestbook Comment: Thursday, December 22, 2011 7:39 AM
Prayers have been answered again my dear friend. Have a Merry Christmas around the table! Luv all of you! Kathryn

Guestbook Comment: Thursday, December 22, 2011 10:18 AM
Thank God for another clear result! How wonderful! Now surgery and after that hopefully the heart "things" will balance out and improve!! Thinking of you and praying for you! I love you, have a Merry Christmas!! Melissa

Saturday, December 24, 2011 9:52 PM, CST
Merry Christmas Eve 2011!
Time to get all nostalgic, and reflect on this past year...The negative: a year ago I had just gone through three horrific surgeries. We all know what they were; no need to go over it all. Christmas has always been a hard time for me since my Mom died. Well, let's just

throw CANCER into the mix, and start chemo. Another challenge-
Andy's being laid off. As unfortunate as the timing was, it most
definitely turned itself around and he is no longer driving an hour
and a half each way to work! He has been able to be around for
more things, he is home *much* sooner, and enjoys what he is doing.
The positive: I completed all my chemo without any big hitches, and
without getting too sick. I made it through radiation. I am right
now, today, at a great spot in my life. I feel okay, am regaining
strength, and can for the most part resume my normal daily
routine. I was able to keep my full time status at work through a
few different stores and transfers! That's a BIG DEAL!!! I got a
transfer to Sheboygan for work, and my drive is 20 minutes.
Tops. That definitely helps out when I over sleep and wake up 15
minutes before I am supposed to start work! Josh, Ilyssa and
Alaina had a great year! Great report cards, new things learned in
summer school, new adventures, fun trips, lots of beach time,
fireworks, shopping, road trips, playing, teeth lost, braces put in, new
school; new teachers. Everyone is thriving, healthy, and the best
news of the year? All my blood tests have been great! I am still
in remission....right now this second, I am smiling, and happy about
that! Normally, I am depressed about that-I don't know why....not in
a sick weird I want to still have cancer kind of way, but more in a
when it's coming back, not an *if* it comes back kind of way...so
I'm afraid of saying I am in remission. I actually don't think I've
even said it out loud? We just stay thankful daily that God answered
our prayers, and I have gotten through this nightmare. A few
weeks ago we bought a new home-not a small feat for us. It was a
big struggle, financially and emotionally. We weren't sure it was good
timing, or if this was something we wanted to do while I was still in
the *iffy* stage of cancer. But everything went through, and I
guess what was meant to be was! We have very slowly been getting

431

settled. The kitchen is the WORST room in the house!!!!! There is SO MUCH to unpack and organize and figure out!!!!! ARGH!!!! We did a lot of getting ready-painting, and remodeling. Slowly I am making the house ours by personalizing it with our stuff! Tomorrow we will be hosting our first Christmas dinner here! ☺ There have been so many upswings and downswings this year....but I have to believe that the ups are prevailing and outweigh the downs!!! Where we are now versus where we were year ago----it's just amazing! ♥S

Guestbook Comment: Sunday, December 25, 2011 1:55 PM
You guys are amazing!! Mary

Monday, December 26, 2011 7:00 PM, CST
I started out the day heading to the plastic surgeons office to do a quick once over with Doc's nurse regarding the skin prep I have to do to prepare for Thursday's surgery. It's this new thing they're doing, to try to prevent me from carrying germs from our home on my skin/clothing to the hospital; therefore upping my risk of post-surgery infection. The night before I am to use these special 'wipes' and cleanse my skin head to waist, put on clean clothes, clean sheets and head to bed. They will also do that again in the hospital the morning of. I dropped off all my LOA paperwork today for work. I also received my call from the hospital going over my health history, meds, allergies, etc. So I am all set to go, I just need to wait for the phone call from them to give me my time of surgery ♥S

Guestbook Comment: Tuesday, December 27, 2011 9:23 AM
Foobs here you come!! What a blessing to be getting back to "normal"! So, did you decide to go with the deluxe model, get all the bells and whistles??? J/K!!! Glad you are getting settled, moving can be very trying and a lot of work! Pray that your health continues to

improve and your blood work keeps coming back good, and you can say you are in remission! Love you!! Melissa

<u>Guestbook Comment</u>: Tuesday, December 27, 2011 12:03 PM
Thinking of you and wishing and praying for a smooth, painless surgery! I have off until next Tuesday, if you need a runner for something let me know. Again, all my love and prayers. Ann

Tuesday, December 27, 2011 10:18 PM, CST
T-minus two days til my new FOOBIES!!!!!
I had my pre-op physical today.....ready to go!!!!!! ♥S

<u>Guestbook Comment</u>: Tuesday, December 27, 2011 11:09 PM
Decided I could not stop reading even though it is after nine. Had a great visit tonight! Definitely need more of those and there definitely will be. I will be thinking of you all day Thursday. Can't imagine you to be any more beautiful than you are...but I imagine after a couple weeks of recovery you will feel like a sexy goddess. You will need to get one of those hands on a stick so you can slap Andy's hand(s) away ;) Lots of love to you! Stacey

Wednesday, December 28, 2011 3:57 PM, CST
I received the call this morning...I need to be at the hospital at 8:15; my surgery is going to be at 9:45. Breathing in......breathing out... ♥S

Wednesday, December 28, 2011 4:03 PM, CST
"I have heard there are troubles of more than one kind. Some come from ahead and some come from behind. But I've bought a big bat. I'm already you see. Now my troubles are going to have troubles with me!" -Dr. Seuss

Thursday, December 29, 2011 6:12 AM, CST
Three and half hours until surgery. I woke up super nervous and afraid. I'm not a fan of IV's, doctors, blood, or pain. Today brings them all. ☹ Wish me luck. ♥S

Guestbook Comment: Thursday, December 29, 2011 6:36 AM
Praying for a quick recovery for you Shelly!! Will be thinking of you all day. Feel the prayers and love that surround you today XX OO Stacey

Guestbook Comment: Thursday, December 29, 2011 7:06 AM
I'm so excited for you to get to return to some level of comfort by getting those TE's o.u.t.! Happy Swap Day to you!!! Hugs, Beccie

Guestbook Comment: Thursday, December 29, 2011 10:16 AM
I am excited and nervous for you!!! You will be in my thoughts and prayers all day!!! That all goes the best it can, that you feel comfort before, during, and after surgery. That your pain will not be too bad and recovery will be swift! Love you and good luck! Melissa

Guestbook Comment: Thursday, December 29, 2011 10:24 AM
As I read your message I'm sure u are in surgery. Prayers are for u & the docs. You have done some great things this year and many more to come. Sending prayers & love to u & your family. Kathryn

Guestbook Comment: THURSDAY, DECEMBER 29, 2011 4:05 PM
Thinking of you! RPD

Thursday, December 29, 2011 4:59 PM, CST
Surgery Update

(Andy for Shelly typing here) It's 5 pm. Shelly is doing good. We are still at the hospital. Her surgery was from 10a.m. to 12:30p.m. She got back from recovery about 2p.m. and has been sleeping most of this time. Some pain so she had 2 pain pills and seems much more comfortable now! She is awake and more "herself" now. The PS is happy with the outcome of the surgery. The scar revision will have to wait till a future date as he did not want to pull too hard on the tissue he had just stretched. I'm sure Shelly will post more later! Andy.

Guestbook Comment: Thursday, December 29, 2011 7:45 PM
I hope everything turned out well. Thinking of you! Angie

Guestbook Comment: Thursday, December 29, 2011 8:18 PM
Thanks for the update Andy. Sounds like everything went o.k. Still saying prayers Love you all. Kathryn

Friday, December 30, 2011 3:54 AM, CST
424 days later, and I finally have new boobs!

Yesterday morning I had to report to the hospital in Sheboygan at 8:15 a.m. My amazing friend MaryAnn came over at 7:30a.m. to take care of the kids for the day. I think she had the harder job yesterday! Andy and I left our new house in the sleet and snow, and drove to Wal-Mart so I could get some sweat pants to live in for the next few days. From there we went to the hospital. I have to say-I wasn't nervous; I wasn't stressed; I was just ready. Ready to have this chapter of my life hurry up and close. *I have had to wait over a year to get these expanders out and God knows it has been a VERY long road. I have gone through many expansions being stabbed with syringes; pain, infection, uncomfortable*

435

exams and painful heart tests due to these damn things and now they are OUT! I checked in at the front desk; was called in to register; walked up to the fifth floor. The lovely woman volunteer that took us up kept our minds off of things by telling us about her holidays involving her Norwegian guests. She told me she had 5 or 6 Lutefisk dinners for her different friends/ family. What a lovely lady and great tradition. We got up to the outpatient surgery floor and were greeted by the whole crew! The nurses took us to my room, and the fun started. I had my vitals taken, and was given a gown. Before I could dress in the gown though, I needed to wipe down my whole body with some special wipes. They help kill any bacteria that may have traveled in on my clothing from home. I also had to do this the night before; putting on clean clothing and climbing into our bed with freshly washed sheets. Let me just say that the hospital room was small. Maybe 9' by 13'? So the chair was right next to the bed. Poor Andy got to watch me do the WORST striptease ever, and the LEAST sexy process of wiping myself down with these wipes. And unfortunately he had a front row seat lol.....and the worst view! Let's just say that I had to bend some pretty weird ways to reach all the places I needed to!!!! Tissue expanders do NOT allow for any bending at the chest. Some days it's all I can do just to put my shoes on! The wipes are a great idea-anything to cut down the risk of infection is awesome! When you're done, they leave you cold and your skin tacky. And ITCHY! Thankfully that only lasts a few minutes. Next we got down to business going through my medication and history, etc. The nurse informed me that I would need some premeds mostly for my stomach. I drank some seriously nasty stuff to neutralize the acid in my stomach, then I was given something in my IV-which I can't remember what it was-oh yeah, it was Pepcid. Then I got a shot in my upper thigh (OWWWCCH) that was to dry up the acid. With my already delicate stomach, I thought that this was a GREAT idea. My pain meds are kicking in, and I'm getting seriously sleepy...to be continued...

.....Once I had the IV in, taken all my premeds, and had gone over the last of my health history, the nurse asked if I would like a massage......um, YES!!!!!!!!!!! So their massage therapist came in and I kicked everyone else out-but Andy-he could always learn some new techniques lol! She had worked on my back, my shoulders, and was stretching out my neck when the Doc came in-I put my hand up and told him he had to STOP right there, she wasn't done yet, and this was the ONLY JOY in my day!!! He was amused, waiting patiently, and then it was his turn. He took a seat, asked me what kind of implants I preferred-there are many. Saline vs. silicone gel. High profile vs. elongated. I told him whatever he felt would work best for me, and whichever he was happiest with the results. He told us that he had ordered both, saline and silicone, and had them in the OR. He wanted to originally go with silicone, but is concerned they would sit up too high on my chest, and straight up-I don't want to be able to motorboat MYSELF!!!! He told us also that while I am under they slip in and out some sizers, and different profiles, and sit me up, to see how they look, then fiddle with them some more. The he whipped out his purple marker, deja vu of 424 days ago! He marked my baseline chest top to bottom. He marked around my port scar, but discussed with me that if I ever wanted to do nipples-we should leave the port scar alone til then, not that he tightens it up too much today, and then my nipple doesn't sit right. I was disappointed, but completely understood. My port scar bothers me more than anything at this point. Guess I need more turtlenecks! He then had me lift each arm up separately, so he could mark what he was all cutting off as far as the dog ears. If you have been able to access my pictures on here, you have seen what I mean. I felt like a piece of art work when he was done, he just needs to sign his name on my hip next time!! Once he was done the RN came in with some squares of adhesive remover to get the sticky off of me from the Holter monitor a month ago! She got it right off, but then I had to re sanitize those areas with the wonder wipes again. The anesthesiologist came in, perky as all hell! She asked all her questions, etc. I let her know she was my new favorite person, and that anesthetic is not my friend-therefore she needs to JACK UP THE DRUGS!!! She had me sign her paperwork, even mentioning the risks of chipped teeth and pinched lips. Well, here it is 2 days later and I have one HELL of a fat lip still! I'm guessing I was accosted by the trachea tube! My designated driver showed up to wheel me to the surgery room, and I was able to say goodbye to everyone-I think I was the only one not crying. I know Dad was-which makes it IMPOSSIBLE for me not to cry! Sandi sure was, but I think Andy was still dry eyed. I shivered all the way to the surgery room. Familiar territory again, seeing all the ugly yellow tiles and green walls/lights in the hallway on the way to the surgical room... I got my sexy hairnet put on, covered with more warm blankies....and while in the surgery room, I had to scoot over from my wheely bed to the surgery bed, the woozy meds already kicking in. And that by God is the L-A-S-T thing I remember. This was at about 9:50 a.m. The next thing I knew it was after 4 p.m. and I was in the room with Andy. Sandi was there too, but I was so out of it! I remember massive amounts of pain. I remember my mouth being totally dry and my throat hurting like hell. I remember eating a popsicle, but not how I got it! I remember opening my eyes and everyone was standing around me staring at me like a wake of buzzards! There was lots of falling asleep mid conversation. I remember Sandi having to leave, and then more sleeping. More

pain. Asking Andy 10 times what the Doc said......He told me that the
doctor was in about 12:30 p.m. But I was in recovery for a few
more hours. The Doc said the surgery was a success. He felt that
it went very well, and was pleased with the results. He ended up
putting saline implants in versus the silicone ones. He just liked them
better. He was very cautious on the radiated side, making sure not
to stress the skin out too much. He had explained that radiated skin
will not heal the same as "normal" skin-it will heal slower, react
differently; possibly not heal at all. When I started waking up more,
I was able to discuss with Andy things that had happened during the
procedure, and why.   I had another set of pain pills, and more
popsicles to help my sore throat, and to try to bring down the
swelling on my lip! When the nurse came in to undo my "bandaging"
and take a look, we realized that the only bandaging was the Velcro
bra like last time; NO DRAINS!!!!! NO DRAINS!!!!! NO DRAINS!!!!! NO
DRAINS!!!!! But that's also when I found out the devastating news...
.my incisions were NOT 3-4" long. They were 9-10" long on each
side. When the doc had to remove the 'dogears', he also tightened
up the skin, did some liposuction, and sewed it back up. That incision
ended up going back further than my original mastectomy scars did,
further towards my back. But they didn't go all the way to the
front of where my original scars were. So bigger, but not. Once I
sat up to go to the bathroom and got to take a look at my new
chest I was really surprised. They were not as big as I thought
they'd be....don't take that for disappointment-just what I had pictured
vs. what I received. The dog ears looked FANTASTIC. He did
SUCH a great job getting rid of those!! I didn't really notice how
bad they were until the 'before' shot on the camera!! The shape and
placement of my new boobs were great. Lots of narcotics later, I
was still at about a 5 on the pain scale-they asked me how I felt
spending the night and getting some morphine. I said no thank

you...I would rather go home, see my kids, and sleep there. That would definitely make me feel better. Around 7 p.m. I was discharged with a script for oxycodone and we left! It took about an hour at the pharmacy-the absolute WORST SERVICE I have ever received. EVER. Even worse than the Horicon pharmacy! Then we headed home finally to relieve Mary Ann from her babysitting duties (THANK YOU MARY ANN!!!) and then I crawled into the recliner, and fell fast asleep. What a crazy long day. ♥S

Guestbook Comment: Friday, December 30, 2011 7:18 AM
You are truly an amazing, strong woman, not that you have too much of a choice, but you are!!!! So glad your surgery went so well, wowzers, big incisions, I felt the pain just looking at it. You are beautiful. I love your curly hair, too cute! Take care, love and miss ya.....Joey

Guestbook Comment: Friday, December 30, 2011 2:04 PM
Not going to lie, I was a little nervous about looking at the pictures! What a difference, they look great!!! The before and after are wonderful! It stinks they had to make such large incisions and had to cut through your pecs again. Good for you for making it to this point and thank God for getting you here and now with new boobs!! You are an amazing woman! Melissa

Guestbook Comment: FRIDAY, DECEMBER 30, 2011 10:12 PM
I agree with Melissa, I too was a little unsure to look. I'm not sure why exactly, this is the part where you get to share the good parts of this story. Thank you for sharing! I think that those of us who have not personally gone thru what you have still need the visuals to stay vigilant and what beautiful badges you have to remind us all, and especially those two beautiful daughters. I know you may

440

hear things like this all the time, but I want you to know that I think about you and your family constantly. Hopefully, that doesn't weird you out! I have had lots to pray about this past year, and with all of those prayers, I have developed a new and stronger connection to God and my own inner strength. I think for the coming New Year, we all deserve only great things to happen for us, and the strength and peace to make those great things happen. I hope your pain is being managed well, and those long, hellish incisions are not giving you ANY problems! Love you! Ann

Guestbook Comment: Saturday, December 31, 2011 10:03 AM
Oh Shelly...I cry and laugh when I read your entries. How amazing you are! The new boobs look great!! I too was hesitant to look with me and my medical phobias, but I am amazed at the outcome! I hope the pain goes away quickly for you. And I know Andy can't wait for that first motorboat of the year...even if it is months from now. I love you dear friend...what an inspiration you are! I can't wait to read your book! I will need a box of kleenex for sure! Happy New Year!!!!! Stacey

Saturday, December 31, 2011 6:35 PM, CST
48 hours later...
...I was discharged about 48 hours ago. I am still in excruciating pain. I cannot get comfortable. I find no relief with the pain meds-they just put me to sleep, not take away the pain. I went in today to see the plastic surgeon for my follow up. He still feels that the surgery was a success! My breasts look good and the incisions look good too. No stitches this time either, just glue-DermaBond. I have the ok to lift up my arms on a normal basis, just no quick reflex movements, like if you're falling on the ice or something, to put your arm out to catch yourself-that would cause some serious

damage. I have an area on my right 'girl' out front that is reddish/tan. I was worried about infection right away. Doc feels it's just the beginning of bruising-which I will have a lot of eventually. The incisions are starting to bruise. He talked about the shape and skin condition of my new girls. He also said that we could continue to shape and fix the implants as needed. Eventually he will do more lipo under my arms to suck out more fat from the dog ears. I told him to feel free to do my whole body-haha. I'm trying to rest, but am hurting too much. I can't concentrate to read, or watch a movie. I'm just trying to pass time until I can sleep the whole night in the recliner again. ♥S

Guestbook Comment: Saturday, December 31, 2011 7:00 PM
Oh no, all that pain, I wish I could take it away and give it to someone else (just not me-I'm not good with it.....had 4 kids and didn't have one epidural!) Hopefully when you awake in the morning, since it is a New Year, you will feel like a new woman!! I have heard some people say that it feels like an elephant sitting on your chest (with implants) but I'm sure yours is much worse, especially because it wasn't an elective surgery. Any who...hope you can sleep soon, even though I am sure it will only be for a few hours, if I know you! Love ya, and after the kids Christmas Vacation ends, mine starts, so I will come and see the new house and boobies in person...
love ya....Joey

Sunday, January 1, 2012 2:16 AM, CST
Happy 2012!
Here's my toast to all of you:
May you all find happiness this year; in life, at work, in love, and with your health. May all your loved ones be safe, staying on top of all health issues before they can turn into something serious. May your

friends and family surround you often and support you in all you do....new ventures, dieting, going back to school, you name it. May you be lucky enough to have your home be "the place" to gather....with children, their friends, your family, your friends, coworkers.....you name it. May God continue to work miracles in your day to day life-guiding Doctors, spouses, and yourself. May you each find happiness in every day. Life is too short to stress over things that don't matter. May you learn to appreciate your spouse-for who s/he is-your love, your support system, your best friend. Treat them with respect-they love you with their whole heart. Speak as you would like to be spoken to. Do loving, kind things for them as they do for you. Appreciate that he isn't a drug addict, alcoholic, wife beater or worse-he may have faults but those are your faults, not his. May you appreciate what you have-and not wish beyond what you do have. Be satisfied with your life; don't waste it wanting more. Realize that whatever your situation is-there are people out there with it WORSE. Do not pity yourself or others, God is there to guide. Be grateful every morning, think first of what you are blessed with...not what your struggles are. I will be the first to try all of the above! 2011 sure was a challenge from day one, but I have fought and struggled tooth and nail to get through it. It's finally over! With this new year brings many new things for me....I need to focus on one at a time!! I will get licensed this year for my cakes. I will lose at least 10% of my body weight by joining weight watchers so I can enjoy the success that Molly is! I will stop drinking soda, and exercise more. I will get out of my dead end job and move forward. I will spend time with the friends that ARE my friends, not people that call themselves my friends. I will make time each week to spend with my family. Best of all I will publish my journey as a book! Baby steps, but doing some each day will get me through! Happy New Year!!!!! ♥S

Sunday, January 1, 2012 4:20 PM
Happy New Year Shelly and to your family as well! It's going to be a
better year for all us! We have to believe that only good things are
going to happen. Your plan for the year is good inspiration for the
rest of us. After an argument with my mother earlier this
afternoon, I need to work on not being annoyed by others'
insensitivity and thoughtlessness. I need to keep things in
perspective and remember what really matters. Your words always
kick my butt into remembering that whatever is making me stress, it
could always be much worse. Love your new picture of you and
Betsy! Ann

Monday, January 2, 2012 5:26 PM, CST

...another day closer to feeling better, right? I am nauseous, sore
and feel wanky. I have no appetite, and do not want to do much of
anything. I did forget to mention that I started my heart medicine
the night of my surgery. I do feel that is making me feel
'off'...can't wait to see one of my friends tonight, and hoping I can
stay awake while she's here! ♥S

Monday, January 2, 2012 7:22 PM
Shelly, I've read your journal and must say that I could only hope to
be as blessed as you are with the wisdom that you have. To read
your New Year's entry was tear jerking. I don't exactly know how
to say this without sounding awful but I'll try... I think God "chose"
you to have cancer because He could see how strong and amazing
you are. He knew that you would have the ability to change MANY
lives through your ordeal. He knew your strength and strong spirit
would speak volumes to so many. He knew that you would give
courage and hope to so many people. He knew that you and Andy
would be people that others would look up to. I'm not trying to

444

sound all religious or stupid about you having cancer. But I really believe that God does not give us more than we can handle even though we would beg to differ and what doesn't kill us makes us stronger. I applaud you for everything you have done. I wish nothing but the best for you and your family in this coming year. I hope you do publish your book because I would surely buy a copy or more. Thank you for sharing your most intimate thoughts with us. Tammy

Tuesday, January 3, 2012 8:28 AM, CST
@Tammy K- so strange! I said that to my Dad at the hospital. I don't think he appreciated my way of thinking, but I also don't think he could argue!! I told him that God chose me to go through this because I'm such a toughie...like him!

Guestbook Comment: Tuesday, January 3, 2012 10:16 AM
I pray each day you feel better and better!! You are right about appreciating everything one has, because life could be very different and we/I am blessed with so much! Thinking of you and praying for your swift recovery, I pray your pain gets better and your meds will have a positive effect instead of negative. Your strength is remarkable! Love you babe! Love the picture of you and Bets btw! Very cute! Melissa

Guestbook Comment: Tuesday, January 3, 2012 3:10 PM
Shelly, you have no idea how good that makes me feel to hear that you understand what I meant to say. Ever since I put it on there I was worried that it didn't come across the way I wanted it to and thought about how I could get it off here because the last thing I would want to do is hurt your feelings or offend you or sound like an idiot. I just want to try to convey to you how amazing I think

you are and what an inspiration you are to so many. Please continue healing and inspiring so many with your words. You have an amazing gift for telling the truth. Take care and may you have a blessed New Year! Tammy

Guestbook Comment: Tuesday, January 3, 2012 9:40 PM
After your last post about Tammy's post, I went and read it. I think what she said makes so much sense too. You have helped me understand this disease in a way that other women that are also fighting just haven't. You represent yourself, your family, and the obstacles you're up against in such a way that many of us feel that we are right there with you. I have become so much more aware of my own body and am being more vigilant; I hope that never "pays" off. So many people have told me in the last few months that God has a plan, he has a reason......and "oh boy" is that hard to hear when you're in pain. However, I think.- no I believe-that your story alone is proof enough of how strong of a woman you already were, but now you are doing amazing things with that strength. Love you! Ann

Wednesday, January 4, 2012 10:27 PM, CST
What a horrendous day. I overslept, so that made the morning all rush rush rush. Which made Josh cranky. I couldn't get outta bed-I think it was 8:15 before Ilyssa finally guilted me out. I ran the girls to school, then crawled back on the couch and slept off and on until after lunch. Dad did come over to visit, but I spent the whole time yawning...I think I chased him away. I feel bad that I slept the whole time Andy was home for lunch-waking up only in time to say goodbye. I then slept til I had to go get Josh and managed to stay awake the hour until I had to get the girls from school. I had a small burst of energy, so we headed to Sheboygan and shopped at Home Depot. They didn't have anything I was really interested

in. We checked out the Goodwill store there, and headed back home. The shopping trip went great...then we came HOME. I all of a sudden was in an unbelievable amount of pain, and just couldn't take it. I spent over 2 hours crying, and wondering what the heck was going wrong. My left 'breast' HURT. Not the incisions, but the front part where the nipple would be. I took some pain medicine for the first time today, and it took quite a while to kick in. I don't cry often, and usually NEVER in front of the kids, but I couldn't help myself. Ilyssa curled up on the couch next to me, and was rubbing my arm, telling me it will be all right. It was so touching it made me cry MORE. I had a ton of anxiety and stress over some things we have going on tomorrow-along with house stuff, school stuff, kid stuff, you name it. Add to that everyone being pissy-I would have given a kidney to switch places with anyone else tonight. Now I'm overtired, have a cry-headache, & refuse to give in to go to bed ♥S

Thursday, January 5, 2012 10:51 PM, CST

The bare truth, right?? I am seeing Dr. Gavin tomorrow (I have a total crush on her. I wish she was my Mom!! AND Holy shit, she had ONE opening tomorrow! God must know how bad I need this) because I think something is seriously going wrong with me. I have to have some sort of imbalance going on, or my meds are malfunctioning or something. About half an hour ago, I started LOSING IT. I was in bed, all warm and cozy and sleepy. I turned off the light and just had a breakdown. I cannot stop crying, anxiety is overtaking me, I am having TOTALLY irrational thoughts about stuff-like that I am going to die in my sleep. Tonight. That my heart is beating wrong, I am uber listening to it, and it sounds 'wrong'. Finally, after the 25th Kleenex, I get up and go into the living room to try and wake Andy up from the couch to try to talk this out and calm down. He is falling asleep as I'm SOBBING next to him, pouring my heart out, and he has woken up and repeated the same sentence 7 times, and is just pissing me off. I don't care how fucking tired you are, YOU WAKE THE FUCK UP WHEN YOUR WIFE IS HAVING A NERVOUS BREAKDOWN. I'm so mad at him, I could smother him. I went online and checked Dr. Gavin's schedule, and somehow a miracle has occurred and I can get in tomorrow. Not in July- tomorrow. Thank you God. Now stop fucking with me. Or let me go completely off the deep end without being conscious of it. Peace out. ♥S

Guestbook Comment: Friday, January 6, 2012 8:23 AM
Don't smother him yet wait until you have all your strength back so you can make sure it works. Lol!! Mary

Friday, January 6, 2012 11:31 AM, CST
...doing ok as of right now. WTH is with all this bipolar shit going on with me?????? Ok. I challenge you to tell me a funny/embarrassing holiday story. My story? Hm. Need to think on this one. Ok, got one. When Andy and I were dating, yeeeeeeeeears ago....Greg S. used to throw a costume party. So we went to the costume party- Andy was a hillbilly farmer, and I was a prisoner. A male prisoner, where I painted a beard on with makeup. It was our first time going to Greg's costume party, and truthfully we knew maybe 75% of the people, but not everyone. We were there about 2 hours, and Andy was mingling, but no one was talking to me. I was all paranoid, like "what's going on? Is everyone mad at me for something? Is there something they know that I don't-like Andy's gonna break up with me or something???!" I got super drunk, and think I gave myself an ulcer worrying.....Well, FINALLY Candice says something to me, and when I respond, she says SHELLY?? Oh my God, no one recognized you! We didn't know who you were! Well, that's why no

one would talk to me. ☹ Come to think of it, that was a pretty
damn good costume, then, if no one knew who I was!!!!!! I should've
won a prize! I'll try to wrangle up some pictures... ♥S

<u>Guestbook Comment</u>: Friday, January 6, 2012 3:29 PM
Shelly, I just read your last couple posts and I'm pretty sure that it
is just stress catching up with you. I'm no doctor by any means so
please don't take it that way. I'm pretty sure the average person
would have lost it HUNDREDS of times by now considering what
you've all been through. Try not to dwell on the fact that you're
having a rough couple of days but try to remember how amazingly
strong you have been through all this. You're allowed to lose it a
few times. No one will think any less of you for doing it. And don't
smother Andy 'cause I'm pretty sure there aren't too many guys
out there like him! You may not find a replacement. LOL! Try to
hold your head high and hang on cause I'm sure things will get
better soon. Take care of yourself and allow yourself to lose it. It
will be ok after you do. Tammy

Friday, January 6, 2012 5:00 PM, CST
Back from the Doc. Fortunately she doesn't think I'm psychotic.
Maybe UNfortunately? We talked a lot about what's been going on
with me, and how I've been having a mental breakdown when bedtime
comes. We talked about what is all involved in my life on a regular
basis, and what is NOW on my plate the last week, month, year. She
talked about depression, and how sometimes your body plateau's on
your meds. How your body needs a 'boost' now and then, and how,
when your body and mind are freaking out, you need to listen to
them. Of course I listen to them-they're the loudest voices in my
head. She asked if I was seeing things that aren't there, like
animals in the house, or boy scouts in my living room. I said OF

COURSE I see boy scouts in my living room, they live there! So in the most professional tone she could muster, she asked me how many there were? And I answered 5 or 6 depending on the day of the week. Then I finally broke into a smile. I MADE A JOKE! Holy crap....it's been like a month since I haven't been an emotionless zombie. She laughed, and said as long as there aren't 7. I'm going to be getting a booster for my antidepressant. A second medicine to help kick the first one into helping. She feels I am totally justified in LOSING IT lately, trying to simultaneously be a Mom, Wife, full time employee and cancer fighter. I don't feel the same. I do not allow myself to lose it, so until I can get my mental health under control, I'm going to continue to bitch about it. ♥S

Guestbook Comment: Friday, January 6, 2012 7:09 PM
Whenever I start wanting a pity party, I have to think of other things like.....YOU!!!! Omg, the Halloween party story is so hilarious....I can't believe no one would talk to you! Post a pic asap!!!!!! Hopefully your meds will kick in soon and you can start to feel semi- normal even if it's just for a few hours. It is nice to hear sometimes that you aren't the super mom, wife and worker.....you need to have someone take care of you every once in a while.
Love & miss you! Joey

Guestbook Comment: Friday, January 6, 2012 9:53 PM
I think many of us on here feel you are amazing. If you need to go out in the backyard and scream or throw things, you would be justified. YES, being 'it all' to everyone in your life and working too, does qualify you for some sort of shortcut application to the World's Most Amazing Woman award! I was just sitting on my couch vegging online, and thought I really should go scrap or do something

worth-while. Hmmmm......I wonder what Shelly would do with extra
time? Probably more than I'm doing right now! Ann

Saturday, January 7, 2012 8:44 PM, CST
Thank you Annie-you're a source of support and strength, and just a
great friend. Thank you from the bottom of my heart. ♥S

Sunday, January 8, 2012 6:20 PM, CST
Hmmm. Just found a stack of cards (NOT CHRISTMAS) that I
never mailed out. ☹ Wonder where they've been hiding............ ♥S

Thursday, January 12, 2012 10:05 PM, CST
I went to see the plastic surgeon today. He is happy with the
healing I am doing. It is still a struggle every day to keep myself
from overdoing it! He said he is happier with the shape of my left
one (again, non-cancer side). I agreed. My left foob is nice, and
protrudes well, and has a nice round mound. My right one-well, it's
sad. It's tired. It's not pretty! Oh, now I don't really mean
that. It is filled more than the left, but it is hangin' lower, and does
not protrude well at all. He said that if I am still unhappy with it in a
few months, we can revise it. There are 2 other kinds of implants
he can use. But he also said that the radiated side will *tighten up*-
meaning the skin. It takes a while after treatment ends, and after
a surgery like mine, but at some point it will tighten up, and in fact
pull that implant up a bit. Ok, I'll give him that. I'll wait it out (lol....as
if I would want another surgery...........) I told him where I was still
having a lot of pain (the ends of the incisions-towards my back) and
he said that is totally normal, that's where he had done a lot of

451

work. I also had a darkish brown/red area on my right one last time, so he upped my antibiotics by adding a 2nd one. ***just in case*** Thankfully it was nothing but some bruising. He said your body will capsulate scar tissue around the tissue expander; he had to break up the scar tissue so it would soften up and just be nicer. He described it as dicing up the tissue. Awesome, right?! That's what he thinks that bruising was caused from, because he had done a lot of manipulation in there too. Since I still have pain, and also am not allowed to do any lifting, I will be off of work until the 1st of February. For now. Let's all pray that I get better fast!!! When I return I will not be allowed to do any lifting.....but Wal-Mart has a policy that if you're not 100%, then stay home until you are. I know the other WM's have really worked with me, but I'm not sure how this one is.

The fridge guy came back today for the THIRD time. And will be back again tomorrow-last time, I hope. It's driving me insane! We had stored it in our garage while we rented...running.....BUT. The tubing froze and sprung a leak. Once that was fixed, he found the defrost drain frozen shut/plugged. That night, we found MORE water under the fridge. He came back & found that the OTHER tube was also leaking. He didn't have the parts to fix that, so had to order them. Oh, AND he found another leak in the back-the water valve had frozen and cracked. Had to order that too. Today he came to install/fix both things....forgetting that he had separated the caulk seal inside the fridge the other day.....which he did not have the caulking with him. Now he's coming back tomorrow. AGAIN. Frustrating to have to make time in my schedule EVERY FEW DAYS for this to happen. The kids were all NAUGHTY tonight. I tried getting everyone to bed early, but they all fought it and well, right now Alaina is LITERALLY sleeping in the hallway. Josh is still up and kickin' the wall to let me know he is NOT HAPPY about being in bed, and Ilyssa is OUT. Me next! ♥S

Friday, January 13, 2012 7:38 AM
Morning Shelly!!! I was just catching up on your journal and remembering when you dressed up as a prisoner. That was so funny! Honestly, no one knew who you were!!! Are we still on for tomorrow? If so what time should we go? Hopefully you will be feeling good. It will be good for you to get out of the house and away from the kids for a couple hours, sometimes that the best medicine. Looking forward to seeing you tomorrow!!! Have a good day hon. Candice

Friday, January 13, 2012 3:22 PM, CST
It is not that I am happy that Heather Locklear was taken to the hospital, reasons unclear, but *depression* has leaked out. People of all ages, stages, classes, and lifestyles struggle with this disease. It is NOT only people that have a sucky life (helllllloooo??? cancer!!!!) The rich and famous can have it. The woman next door with 2.5 kids, a dream house and a Lexus can have it. The single mom you only see at school in the hallway that is always smiling and talking to friends can have it. It is way more common that you think. Awareness of this disease is nice too–cut everyone some slack.....you never know what they're going through. ♥S

FRIDAY, JANUARY 13, 2012 8:33 PM, CST
Thanks Roberta for the pic. I would like to get this tattooed on my palm. YOWCH!!!!! No way! Almost as much as I'd like a tattoo on my woo hoo. ♥S

453

Guestbook Comment: Saturday, January 14, 2012 3:48 PM
Shelly, I've got two tattoos. One larger one on my back and one on my forearm. They were not that painful. I've never been through what you've been through but something tells me cancer is WAY more painful. If it's something you want then by all means do it- You've earned that right! Tammy

Guestbook Comment: Sunday, January 15, 2012 7:54 AM
You can totally get a tat, it isn't painful and for everything you have gone through, it would be like a walk in the park for you. Love catching up on your journal entries.....hang in there girl....love and hugs...joey

Guestbook Comment: Sunday, January 15, 2012 9:31 PM
What a surprise to get your Christmas card in the mail last week!! Thanks, but I sure hope you didn't overdo it to get those out! I am really getting to the point where I think next year I won't even do them myself. However, I will probably cave and end up doing them. Can you private message me your address? I realized that I wanted to keep it after I threw the envelope away, and nope I wasn't up to digging in the trash for it. It's nice to hear that things are looking up for you, well at least the left one is?!?! How do you feel about the right one coming along in time? Would you consider having it adjusted, meaning another surgery? Considering your pain and stress load, I am praying all works out in a few months! I'm sure the house is keeping you busy in these weeks off, but at the same time, not being able to lift, or probably push the vacuum or such things would start to annoy. Hang in there, before you know it, you'll be back to being expected to be Martha Stewart in the cleaning and working department. Rest....try not to notice the chaos....I know, I know, that's impossible!!! Ann

454

Saturday, January 21, 2012 6:17 PM, CST
Boobs are doing good.
Over. ♥S

Guestbook Comment: Sunday, January 22, 2012 7:31 PM
Hey Shelly! Sorry it's been a while since I've checked in. Alot of
crazy in my life too. Glad to hear all your good news: good
checkups, the house, you finally getting your surgery. I was tickled
to see your shout out about the hostess cakes and the Monkee's!
That brought back such good memories! I wish life wasn't so crazy
so that I would get back there to visit more often. By the way,
Mr. H was Mr. Hopfensperger, and is Mr. Novak's room still a lab or
did that change all together? It's strange to think that most of
those people are probably all retired now. As for some of your less
happy news, I hope you'll take comfort in knowing that I can relate
to your pain. I had my first cortisone shot in the foot for plantar
fasciitis about a month ago. IT REALLY SUCKED!!!!! It's a bitch
getting old, ain't it? I also refinanced my house recently; applied the
first week of October and didn't close until 2 weeks ago.
Underwriters are a pain in the ass! They demanded the appraisal be
redone twice; more pics taken and different comparisons which
resulted in my losing more value in it. Then there were the holidays
as you also experienced. Well, gotta go. If you get a chance send
me an email sometime. I have a couple of things I want to ask/tell
you, but not here. Looking forward to more updates! Take care!
XXOO Crystal

Thursday, January 26, 2012 10:07 AM, CST
I had an appointment with the Radiation Oncologist yesterday. She
just did a skin check (visual) and breast exam. Asked me if I had
any concerns....told me my skin is healing FANTASTICALLY (!) and

455

sent me on my merry way! I also had lunch with a great friend, and headed home just in time to pick up the kids from school. Last night was a big milestone for me too–I attended my first weight watchers meeting!!! I have fought tooth and nail for my life the past fourteen months....and it's time I get off my ass and realize that I cannot continue to go down this path of self-destruction. I eat when I'm stressed, I eat when I am bored, I eat when I am depressed, I eat just because I can. I have been shoveling any crap I can into my mouth-because when you think you're going to die, why not die happy? Why NOT eat as much of anything you want? Why practice self-control and willpower?

Because I'm worth it. My kids are worth it. My husband is worth it. And I don't want to become diabetic; have heart health issues; die. So, wish me luck, and cheer me on! ♥S

Guestbook Comment: Friday, January 27, 2012 6:47 PM
You continue to be my hero in every way! Mary

Friday, January 27, 2012 9:54 PM, CST
GREAT day! Thanks, Betsy, for kidnapping me!!! ♥S

Guestbook Comment: Friday, January 27, 2012 11:06 PM
So proud of you for doing WW, keep it up!!!! You can eat anything you want, no food is forbidden....just have to watch how much. I would always allow myself one bad meal a week. Great job girl!!!! Love ya Joey

Guestbook Comment: Saturday, January 28, 2012 10:28 PM
Hey Shelly! Thinking of you! Leigh

Sunday, January 29, 2012 9:46 PM, CST
You are not going to believe this! I took the kids sledding TWO
days in a ROW! If you know me AT ALL, you know that I
hibernate all winter. I HATE WINTER and being COLD. I do NOT
do the fun outdoorsy parent thing! And, I even took a few rides
down the hill! ☺ I went to a scrapbooking crop on Saturday and
got quite a bit done! I have been doing WW for 4 days now and am
doing FANTASTIC. I have been following the program, and really
feel good about it. Fingers crossed that my will power keeps up! I
had some pretty strong cravings this weekend for something
crunchy and salty!!! But I powered through it, ate my fruit and
veggies, and got past it. I have pushed completely out of my
comfort zone and have been putting lettuce on EVERYTHING.
Again, if you know me at ALL, you know I HATE lettuce on anything
but a salad. Not on tacos, burgers, subs, NOTHING. But, I have
been eating it on all of the above and then some! I am not on
here, blabbing about this for any other reason than to hold myself
accountable for this new lifestyle, and have you all here for
support! I want to get comfortable with the changes in my diet
(and get through my soda addiction withdrawal!) and then move on to
working out. Today while sledding, my heel started hurting again (OF
COURSE) so the planter fasciitis in my left heel is coming back. Just
in time to go back to work and stand for 9+ hours a day. ☹ I just
emailed the podiatrist to try to get an appointment soon. I do NOT
NOT NOT want to get a cortisone shot in THAT heel. I could cry
just thinking about that pain! ♥S

Guestbook Comment: Monday, January 30, 2012 9:20 AM
Thank you for the tip of the fruits and veggies to get through the
salt and chocolate craving, because yesterday I couldn't get over it
until I had eaten probably 200 extra calories. Mary

457

Guestbook Comment: Wednesday, February 1, 2012 3:28 PM
Just read some catch up on your journal. Sounds like you're in the middle of life as we know it with hubby and children. We're at Anna's and suddenly dealing with plumbing/ sewer problems (second plumber coming this afternoon) and leaking roof (roofer coming tomorrow). These problems were too much for the "daddy do" list! Had to call in experts! Saturday and Sunday call for some fun! Keep up the good spirits. Thinking of you. Love, Roberta

Wednesday, February 1, 2012 7:30 PM, CST
2 big milestones today! I went back to work and today is my 1 week anniversary on WW. Weigh in tonight-I lost SIX POUNDS in the first week! ♥S

Guestbook Comment: Wednesday, February 1, 2012 8:05 PM
Congrats on both milestones today! So proud of you! Happy that you had NO drama and LOVE that you lost 6 pounds! Keep it up! Jenny

Guestbook Comment: Wednesday, February 1, 2012 9:47 PM
Me too, me too! I am doing the Biggest Loser program with a bunch of other teachers at school. Doing the work outs and the diet. I lost 7 pounds last week. The party for Katie was hell! I wanted to eat everything! I too have a serious Coke addiction and eating before bed. I have not eaten before bed in 2 weeks and have had only a few soda's in 2 weeks. It is amazing how soda does affect how you metabolize food. I have gotten a few compliments already, so that's good inspiration to keep going, right? Once those clothes get a tiny bit looser, you'll know that it's working! Good Luck!!! We can keep each other going. Ann

Sunday, February 12, 2012 7:06 PM, CST

Week 2 of WW was great as well!!!! Down three more! I found a
friend (sucker!!!) to go along with me and join so we have each other
to hold accountable! What a relief!! This week I go back to the PS
for hopefully my last check up for quite a while! I know it's just a
quick appointment, but I am finally at the point where I'd like to
distance myself from all the medical CRAP. I'd like to just move
forward! I also go see the podiatrist the same day. Being back to
work brings out the worst in my feet-the whole plantar fasciitis thing
is back in full force-I've bought 2 new pairs of shoes this past
week...trying to find something, anything to relieve the pain. Fallen
arches, pain in my heels, and just plain suckiness. ☹ I know I have
to cut this whole blog thing off somewhere, at some point. I know I
have to draw the line and move on; move past....but it is so difficult-I
know no one can understand that. I also want to get this whole
book thing rolling............but it is not very easy to go back to the
beginning, read everything about my life the past year, and actually
have it sink in that it is ME this has happened to.......there is so much
I've forgotten, & don't want to remember. My goal is to have it
done by Mother's Day. Hold me to that! ♥S

Guestbook Comment: Sunday, February 12, 2012 8:17 PM
Whooooo hoooo ☺ so proud of you for the ww program! ☺ You are
doing fantastic! I had to reread that you ate lettuce?? What????
All the times Jenny and I wanted lettuce and you wouldn't eat it??
Love ya girl....stay strong ☺ joey

Guestbook Comment: Wednesday, February 15, 2012 10:00 PM
I know that this might be a silly question, but do you rub anything on
your feet? Icy hot, Dr. Scholl's peppermint rub, etc....I found that it
helps, also slippers and socks and never, never bare feet anywhere.
PF totally sucks, I hope that it leads to no other feet, leg issues.
The limping can weaken other joints in your body. I hope relief is
yours ASAP!!! Ann

Guestbook Comment: Wednesday, February 15, 2012 10:03 PM
Sorry I forgot to mention CONGRATULATIONS on the weight loss.
It's amazing that you are continuing to lose even with your pain in
the feet. Ann

Guestbook Comment: Sunday, February 19, 2012 9:38 PM
Hi Shelly ice your feet at the end of the day and first thing in the
morning too if they still hurt. Rogans had arch supports also for
$30 and they seem to help some. Mention they're for plantar
fasciitis and they'll point you in the right direction. If that doesn't
help after a month, they told me you may need special made
orthotics for your feet. Also a friend told me her doc said to
never run around the house without her shoes on which sucks, but
may help. Good job on the WW-I wish you continued success! Crystal

Guestbook Comment: Tuesday, February 21, 2012 10:01 AM
It was a good thing I was sitting down when I read you were

eating lettuce!!! Good to hear you are sticking with it! 6 lbs, that is awesome! I can occasionally check in to see how you are doing and your progress with the book. Could they possibly use an insert in your shoe to help with your feet and give you some comfort? I hope they figure something out and soon! Keep kickin' butt and taking names! Love you and miss you! Melissa

Monday, March 5, 2012 9:53 AM, CST

Today I have a lot weighing on my mind. It's not much to anyone else, but to me, knowing what I know, and having done all the reading I have-it's concerning me. Here's the weird pieces of me- I've been not feeling well for about a month. The last week I have been nauseous and throwing up daily. When I eat I get sick. Both ends. (awesome, eh?) Could be the flu....who knows. I'm exhausted. I have crazy bruises showing up all over-my legs, thighs, feet, hands, wrists, forearms, and back. I don't think I'm *that* klutzy. But don't know what in the world is causing this. I also have much pain in my back between my shoulder blades and along my spine. I brought it up with the oncologist last appointment, and he and the PA said it was probably caused by the tissue expanders. My surgery was 2 months ago, and it's still hurting. I had been doing chiro, PT and massage therapy since last summer. You know how freaked out I get......and add to that losing weight....which of course makes sense, since I am not eating, or keeping anything in. Now don't get me wrong, I LOVE that I'm losing weight....but for whatever reason it's happening too easy. I have my 3 month blood test on the 21st. I get all whacked out when that comes up.........♥S

Friday, March 9, 2012 8:26 PM, CST

I suppose there is no sense in me worrying over it for another 2 weeks... I am off of work this week Monday and Wednesday. I have all kinds of weird stuff going on this month...yesterday I had 'spotting'--didn't even know that was POSSIBLE after the whole hysterectomy thing?? I have painful tingling in my right breast. I continue to have insane amounts of bruises all over my body???

Wednesday, March 14, 2012 9:08 AM, CDT

Today was my 'bumped up' appointment with the oncology doctor, to go over all my 'issues' I've been having. The most concerning? The hundred bruises covering my arms, legs and back. Now I even have one on my belly. I have the knowledge that there is a ****slight**** chance of the chemo I had causing leukemia. So of course I freak out. You all know me! And lastly the spotting...yes, I had a hysterectomy, yes it is now a dead end, with no cervix, uterus, ovaries or fallopian tubes. How the FLOCK can I have spotting???

I had called previous to move my 3-21 appointment up to this week, as in no sense in worrying....but I just got a phone call telling me that he is out sick and will have to reschedule to next week the 22nd. The day *after* my original appointment-grrr! Panicking.

Thursday, March 22, 2012 7:32 AM, CDT

Meeting with the oncologist today....please pray for me and my family again today....it has been working for the past year and five months, so why fix what isn't broken, right?? I am very unsettled about this one, though.

I pray: The essence of God is within me, embracing me and surrounding me now in this place and at this time. In the flow of God energy and insight, I quietly go within to know my True Self and to commune with the power of the all Good. I am blessed by the nearness and unconditional love of God. I see the God who is my friend, by my side, abiding with me. I see the God who is my comforter, holding me with tenderness and love. I see the God who is my counselor, communicating with me that I am wise, whole and capable, far beyond my own human understanding. I see the God who is my protector, guiding me in wisdom, showing me the way and surrounding me with powerful insulation from anything that would distract me from my heartfelt desires and dreams. I sit with any feelings of discomfort, discord, worry, doubt, or fear knowing that these are not here to stay, but they come bearing knowledge and insight. I ask them what gift they have to give me. I bless these feelings. I am non-resistant. I welcome all of my emotions knowing that my feeling nature is how I am ever-connected to the God Presence. As I flow with my feelings, acknowledging and blessing all of them, the good and the so-called "bad," I realize that I am steering my life, choosing a thought that feels better in each moment, and always evolving in my Power and Presence as a Child of God. God soothes me, adores me, cherishes me, and lifts me up. I feel this even in this moment and feel totally satisfied in exactly where I am. Truly all is well and I am always in my right and perfect place. And so it is. Amen. Thank You God for carrying me through this strange life I've been living...

Thursday, March 22, 2012 7:29 PM, CDT

Whew. I'm done with onco doc, and ALL GOOD!! Whhewwwwwwww.

The deets? I had to work 9-6 today...but since my rescheduled appointment was at 10:30. I went to work and had to leave an hour later to head to the cancer clinic. My friend Molly volunteered to meet me there, knowing how intimidated I was about this one. When I left work, I headed there, meeting her in the parking lot.

The routine once you get there is to check in at the desk, they give you a sheet listing possible new symptoms, and you are to circle ones that apply. While waiting, you go into the lab, have your blood drawn, and wait for the results to get over to the doc. I of course had like 30 new symptoms to circle and explain...so it took me awhile. Molly and I hung out, making small talk, trying to keep our minds off of where we were & why.

This is also the most intimidating...sitting there waiting, you look around and see all of the sick people. There are usually a handful of bald people in there, looking horribly ill. It is so sad that that was ME a year ago. I can't even fathom that anymore. I see the pictures, read this story, and talk about it...but it doesn't even seem like that was my life anymore. I'm so far removed from that now...

Julie called my name, gave me a big big hug, and took me back. Here we go. Molly got to come with...I have nothing to hide anymore. In the exam room, she goes over all of the things I have circled on the sheet...entering it into the computer. BP and temp were good, then she headed out, and Carol and the PA came in. We discussed in length the issues I have had/having with my plantar fasciitis. They could see the bruising on my arms, noting that as well. They really had no answer to why I was bruising so easily-or where the heck they were coming from. Sara the PA did a physical exam, including a breast exam. She noted that the skin was looking great, and also my scars were healing great. We talked about how I had been feeling, etc. Then I met with the oncologist, he discussed with me that my blood test results were fine. Basically, I left just with an appointment to meet up with him in 3 months again. That was a GREAT relief to hear him tell me that my blood test results were ok...since I was convinced I had leukemia!! He was unsure about the bruises, he actually wasn't too concerned about it. He is always so great at calming my fears-letting me know that it's all 'normal'.

Here I am taking my deep breath, and relaxing for another three months ☺

Thanks again, Molly, for coming with me. What a great person you are! And you look FANTASTIC. Congratulations on all your hard work this past year ! You are an inspiration for sure.

I love all the new friendships I have formed while going through this. There are just so many great people in this world, it's hard to have time to spend with everyone. I hope I didn't freak you out with the appointment...I seem to not have a filter anymore....I so often have to whip my shirt off in front of people and talk about everything from how I am feeling to my bowel movements-LOL-that I don't even think about it anymore. I just open my mouth and it all spills out. Mostly I notice *after* I talk that what I said has made someone uncomfortable......then I trip over my words trying to lighten the mood by making foob jokes, and nervously laughing. But I'll work on that. I swear!

This recent appointment with the oncology doctor showed me that I should not get *so fucking nuts* over everything! Big weird things *can* go wrong without it being cancer again believe it or not. It just has to be time to let things roll off my shoulders. Put the black cloud that has been following me in its place. Easier said than done-I know--better than <u>anyone</u>.

Friday, March 9, 2012 6:22 AM, CST
The End. For now.

Dear friends and family, and those that are both: Whew. I can feel it in my heart-this is the end of my Caringbridge Journal. I have given everything I can to this fight against cancer. I have shared everything I can; everything I know; every painful detail of my journey. I have completed my treatments; my surgeries. I feel that my mental health is finally returning to what it should be at this point in my life. I am gaining back my physical abilities. I am finally working full time out of the home again. I honestly can say it's time to move forward....get rid of the cancer stigma...and just become Shelly again. Or "Mommmy!!!" Or "Babe." I could never ever ever have gotten this far without every SINGLE PERSON in my life. Everyone has touched my life in so many ways. My husband, my kids, my family, my friends, my medical team, my employer, my coworkers, my high school classmates.

Mostly, I'm just so MOVED that everyone even *thought* of me; *prayed* for me. I mean, I'm NO ONE...just another person that you used to know...

Thank you, everyone, for all the amazing support...I love you.

♥Shelly

♥♥

Guestbook Comment: Friday, March 9, 2012 8:52 AM
I am so proud of you Shelly! You are one strong woman! Thank you so much for allowing all of us to share all of your moments good or bad with you. You are an inspiration, and will help many out there in the years to come who fight this battle! Well done girl! Well done! Tina

Guestbook Comment: Friday, March 9, 2012 5:59 PM
Reading your last entry made my heart sink and made me cry. To think about the journey you have been on. From the time you found out, through the worst days of sickness and not being able to move, to where you are now. I am so thankful to God for leaving my friend to be here with me, with your family and so many friends during this battle. I always knew you were feisty and a fighter, now the world knows! You have changed lives; you have changed mine! My life and those that know of you and your story will be inspired by your strength and what you have pushed yourself through! There is sooo much more I could say but...Thank you for being my friend, I love you! Melissa

Guestbook Comment: Saturday, March 10, 2012 8:44 AM
Shelly, thank you sooo much for having the courage and strength to share all those moments good and bad, funny and sad, with everyone. Something tells me that you may never really know just how much your choice to share has impacted everyone that has read your journal. You are an amazing person. To see that you are ending your journal is both a happy time and a sad time for us readers. Happy because that means this chapter of your life is closing and sad because that means we will no longer have those little notes to read that are reminders for all of us. I wish you nothing but the best and all the happiness the world has to offer. God knows you have

earned at least that. I really hope you continue on the journey of writing your book because I really think it will be amazing. Take care and stay strong just like you always have!!! Tammy

Guestbook Comment: Saturday, March 10, 2012 4:39 PM
Shelly, it was great to see this last post in your CB site. I also will just keep in touch in person, email or FB. You have been so strong, truly an inspiration to all of us who have been following your journey. We are all happy that this part of the journey of your life is over and complete, never to be revisited again! You have lots to focus all that energy on now- the house, the kids, the job, the remodeling and decorating, and soon the yard work and landscaping? I'm sure if you're feeling a little bored, you can always become super PTA mom or something along those lines. See you soon, Love ya! ~Ann

DID YOU REALLY THINK I COULD END IT THERE?!?!?

The Bonus Entries...

May 2012

Healing was slow from my reconstructive surgery. But the results were satisfactory. Once the initial swelling was gone...the bruising went away...and things settled-I have to say that it is a miracle that the PS could do what he did. I have seen some AWFUL results of reconstruction after radiation...and I sure am lucky. They aren't perfect-they sure the hell aren't what they used to be! But they are 5,000% better than fucking TISSUE EXPANDERS!!!!! I believe that I was off of work until February 1. It was supposed to only be 2 weeks ☹. The end result is good though. Now that I am past the surgery, past the pain, and past the swelling...they are average. I was disappointed with the size, the TE's stuck out so much further-and even though the implants are bigger and fuller, I feel very flat. They are still a bit lopsided, and the radiated side is still a bit smaller. But honestly, I shouldn't be so vain to criticize! I am so truly thankful that someone was able to put me back together again. I have no pictures of the first time I saw myself after my mastectomy, but I have the image in my head of that FIRST look in the mirror. I will never forget the impact that had on me. I can't even lie-it was horrifying. I hadn't known what to expect, what it would look like-the extent of the incisions...it was BAD. Right now I feel that I am comfortable with how they have turned out.

Going back to work was very difficult. Emotionally, I HATED working there. Physically, I had been very timid in using my arms to lift up

469

and around-in fear of something inside tearing. Once back to work, it was a different story! Everyone was very helpful in lifting things down for me, and reaching things that I couldn't. A lot of the 'uncomfortableness' that was there before I left was finally gone. Everyone was very nice and understanding. I am still left with these horrendous scars. 10" long on each side ☹. I still get twinges on the part of the scar that is the furthest back.

May 1, 2012 A.M.
Once again, I am off of work indefinitely. UGHHHHHHHH. My plantar fasciitis has flared up incredibly. I do not have one single day where I don't cry in pain. Either when I get up in the morning or when I have to walk on it at work, in the breakroom where I sit and ice it for an hour. Once I get home-driving with my heel down and toes up on the gas pedal is EXCRUCIATING. Last night while grocery shopping, something 'gave'. I know exactly where I was when I felt the tear. So, now I am off to rest, since I refuse to have foot surgery. The podiatrist has been nice so far, not pushing surgery too much. I hope I don't get frickin' fired for all this BS going on with me ☹

June 4, 2012 6:00 A.M.
I wish I knew WHO could figure me out. Somehow my autoimmune system seems to be fucked up....It started with eczema showing up on my mastectomy scar. It is moving onto my arms....wrists..hands.. legs. The condition of the skin on my scalp is deteriorating...the 'Seborrheic dermatitis' that causes dandruff has gone WILD, leaving my scalp just one huge unhealthy area. I'm under the assumption that it is now psoriasis. Three weeks ago, I developed a rash on my legs....I noticed it when I was shaving. In fact, I was shaving to go to the foot doctor (wink-it used to be I'd shave my legs for

DATES! Now it's for the doctor!) And when I shaved, these little red spots started showing up on my legs. Looked like razor burn....but didn't go away. It got worse and worse, traveled up my legs, on to my thighs, across the pubic area and my buttocks. WTF???????? The best way to describe it, is it looked like I was bleeding *under* my skin. Remember when you used to get hickeys???? How it looked like little dots of blood under your skin? Not a bruise? Those are the little dots I had all over. I finally broke down and went in to see my family doc. She had no idea what it was!? She recommended that I see the dermatologist. So I made an appointment with the dermatologist in Sheboygan. By the time my appointment came, the red spots had all blistered, leaving me with all these nasty bubbles and sores-mostly on the backs of my calves. Dr. P took one look at my leg...then I saw him hang his head and shake it. (((WTF????? Seriously!))) I tentatively asked ...what..........is it cancer????? And he said that he felt this looked like Leukocytoclastic Vasculitis . WTH is that?!?!?!?!? I asked...he said it's complicated; it can be many, many things. It can be autoimmune. It can be a reaction to medicines. More than 80% of the time they never figure out what causes it. Oh, great. Yep-that'd be me....it could be Lupus, it could be my body reacting to an infection. He said there's only one other thing that visually presents like this, and that is scurvy. ARrrrrr. Laugh all you want. I'd rather have a vitamin C deficiency (scurvy) than LUPUS. So he tells me that they will need to take 2 biopsies. One for the preliminary-yes it is a vasculitis or no it's not....and one to send to Miami to see what *kind* of vasculitis it is. No cure. Just try to figure out causes. Basically it's your white cells attacking your red cells. I was expecting a quick scrape of the skin, or blisters....but no. I was injected with a needle to administer numbing stuff. They cut out 2 biopsies-one of an actual blister, one of healthy skin not affected. They stitched me up and everything. I left numb, bleeding and bandaged up! WTF!!! Poor Melissa had been in the waiting room this WHOLE time....she must have thought I snuck out on her! Prelim reports will be in next week...the conclusive one not until late the week after. Awesome.

Now I am one big sore/flaking/bruised mess. Gross, eh???

Oh yeah, and the bruises that appeared a few months ago? They're back. I am bruising all over again. Where's House M.D. when I need his diagnostic abilities???!!! I didn't catch a picture of all the bruises that were everywhere, but I will guesstimate for you-I bet I had 25+ bruises on each of my legs. No exaggeration.

June 6, 2012
Went to Bay Beach with the kids with the Rosenthal's today. It was soooooooooo much fun, and really an amazing day. I'm not sure who had more fun, Fish or the kids?! Ilyssa braved the Zippin' Pippin' 5 or 6 times. Olivia bribed me on ONCE. FUCK THAT. I am NOT a roller coaster kinda girl. The whole day was very enjoyable. I love my kids! ♥S

June 8, 2012
At this point, I have stopped journaling on a regular basis, I have spent the past few months working on this book. I have been busy living life, and dealing with many uncertainties. I have built up and destroyed some of my self-confidences. I have done some amazing things, and also feel as though I have spent months doing nothing with my life. At this point...3 months later...I don't know where to start. I have been through some crazy stuff! This may all be random or this may make sense...who knows! Right now I am in

Bjorklunden, up in Bailey's Harbor, Door County on an Infinite Boundaries retreat through the Breast Cancer Recovery Foundation in Madison. It is amazing to have the opportunity to be here, to be "living" with other cancer survivors. We have shared a LOT of experiences, stories, tears, and TONS of laughter! I have been outside my comfort zone many times. Anyone that knows me knows I have very definitive boundaries! I order the same things at every restaurant. I do the same activities. I like to go to the same places. These past four days, I have shared things about myself that NO ONE knows, not even my husband. Some are cancer related, some are fears. Some are deep feelings that I don't know who to discuss them with or how to talk them through. It is comforting to know that the other women here have a LOT of the same fears and experiences as I have. They have fears of death, reoccurrence, connecting with others, intimacy issues...spot on for everything that bothers me daily. I know that my support group of friends are there for me, I know that they would sit and listen, and not judge. I know that I could tell them that I once murdered someone and chopped them up and ate them, and they would calmly sit back and listen! (For the record, I have NOT murdered anyone, and I would not even eat you if we were the last 2 people on a mountain!) But there's just something different about me now. There's this whole "BIG" thing I've been through, and not ONE SINGLE PERSON can understand it. Not even me. So it is super hard for me to discuss some of these feelings, and fears. I know the natural response for most is to say, oh, no, you will be fine! You're too strong to die, this is just a test. But that choice is not ours. It's Gods.

June 9, 2012
Here at the BC retreat. Daily we have group discussions, talking

about our diseases, our emotions, our fears. So much emotion in one room!!! 10 people, 10 stories of hurt, and loss, and uncertainty. I find myself compelled to help one woman-who is on her way to eviction after all her medical bills and missed work. I need to share my resources with her-share every little tidbit with her. Any resource she can look up or check into. She is an adult....a grandmother-with nowhere to go. That could easily be us. We have been on that last straw many times, unfortunately. I have typed up a list of the organizations that I know of & given it to her, in hopes of possibly helping her out.

We have started a discussion on how we view ourselves, our self image, both before cancer and since cancer. On a scale of 1-5. I gave myself a 3 before cancer. I like being average, I like to just 'be'. Since cancer, I would say a 2. This really has destroyed all my self-confidence. I don't feel like I have pride in myself; I don't feel 'good' about myself. How can I???? I have been violated by this horrendous thing...this 'cancer'. I have gone through unspeakable things. I have seen my body disfigured. I-worst of all-had to rely on the kindness of others; had to ask for help. That is the biggest blow to my self-esteem.

Sitting here viewing the other women in my circle, I see one woman, who is the closest to my age, who reminds me of what I'd like to be like. She is fit, tattooed, and confident. I like her 'aire'-her way of carrying herself. I soooo need to get that back. I want to be able to hold my head up high, and feel amazing about myself. I don't want to worry about how others' perceive me. I don't want to feel like I don't even belong in my own skin. I want to match the person I am on the inside. I want to be 'that person' that people see and automatically *know* I'm confident. Comfortable in my own skin; I care for my body-and I care enough to "fix" myself for my husband and kids. To be beautiful inside and out.

Things I'd like to do with my life-accomplish 2 dreams:
*finish and publish my book
*start my own cake business.

I also need to work following through. Period. True with parenting, daily chores, meal planning, eating habits, everything. Also make rules for the kids to follow too. No more backtalk, make their lunches the night before, even brush their damn teeth without complaint!

June 11, 2012
Preliminary pathology shows that the biopsies taken from my leg are conclusive with LCCV. But not yet definite. Will be waiting another week or so for that result. Booo. I really wanted scurvy so I could be a pirate. I think I could ROCK an eye patch.....and it would be kinda cool to have a parrot?! Dr. P. told me that it is basically where your body eats through your blood vessels. Awesome. That would 100 PERCENT explain the bruising! At least I know I'm not going crazy...

June 12, 2012
Today is our 13 year wedding anniversary. Wow...who would have ever thought that it would go by so quickly. It doesn't seem that long ago that we were newly in love, dating, going on vacations, and planning our wedding. ☺

Ooooh! Guess what!!!! We won Dells season opener tickets on the radio! I went down to pick them up, and here it was a fold open card with free admission to quite a few places, including Noah's Ark and Mount Olympus. There was also $3 admission for places like Pirate's Cove mini golf, house on the rock, boat tours, the comedy club, etc. Discounts off of dinner, some shopping, etc. The only catch is it needs to be used by July 1. I guess we're heading to the Dells next weekend!

June 19, 2012
All the pathology is back. Definitely is vasculitis. (LCCV). Awesomesauce. Cause unknown.

June 27, 2012
Met with the oncologist today....I discussed a million things with him. He thinks my large bone pain is possibly caused by the vasculitis. That is also where my hundreds of bruises are more than likely coming from. He said my bone and liver numbers were good (that's what we want to hear!) But sent me back in for another blood draw...to check my kidneys, etc. He suggested I see a rheumatologist soon to discuss this disease further. I also talked with him about why he didn't do a tumor marker test last time (or this time) and he told me that number just wasn't all that reliable. WHAT?!?!! He told me a year ago that that was *the* test to follow up on my cancer screening. Now it's just my liver and bone numbers? I'm still not sold. I'd kill for a PET scan. My insurance has repeatedly refused a PET. Oh, and he switched my 5 year pill in hopes of lessening the side effects. Fingers crossed. I'm super happy with my Onco. doc, but I just don't have the brain capacity to understand all the mumbo jumbo that he explains it with. Stinkin' chemobrain. I sometimes feel duped by some of these medical professionals. They will tell me something at an appointment. I will come home, update you all on what happened, etc, and then in 3 months, when I bring back up that ONE thing they told me about...all of a sudden they completely back pedal...oh, no,

that isn't at all what I said, or that has changed or blah blah blah. (perfect example: my PS told me after my surgery in December that if I was unhappy with the outcome of the right breast or in general...we could discuss other kinds of implants, and revise my chest. Now when I met with him this past week-he tells me that I have the biggest implant in that they make, and I would only gain .2cm projection by swapping to a different implant. WTH?!?!?!? Not that long ago he said otherwise...) Therefore, I am utterly confused about this cancer antigen test. I completely get that they are the medical professionals, but do they really think that we completely forget the protocol they told us NOT THAT LONG AGO????????? Whatever. I can only fight for so much! Pick your battles as they say...My blood work has been coming back good for the past year-super happy about that! What a blessing. Also I have no more tissue expanders and all my reconstruction surgery is done. I guess I can deal with that.

June 2012

GUESSSSSSS WHHATTT!!! I just had my meeting with the U.S. Department of Agriculture inspector at the location of my NEWLY RENTED KITCHEN!!! And it is all official! I am all licensed and 'More Frosting Please!' is IN BUSINESS!!! I am so super excited to have this dream finally come true! It has been soooo long since I started looking for a rentable kitchen that I didn't think this would EVER happen! I cannot imagine where this adventure will take me in the future! I have dreamt of this forever. Without cancer, I don't think I ever would have taken the leap to do something like this. I was so 'comfortable' in my job/life before. It's about time I find some motivation and improve myself/life. My employer has been great, but I do hope that someday I can move past being an employee....and become the employer.

I will now shamelessly plug my new Cake Business...

More Frosting Please!

Cakery for All Occasions!

920.980.4360

www.MoreFrostingPlease.com

yeahcake@wi.rr.com

Offering superior cakes for your Perfect Day. All you need to bring are your thoughts and ideas for your cake, and we will work together to come up with your dream come true for your Wedding or any other special event. I love to create unique cakes suited to your liking. And I am very aggressive in my pricing. Being a family of five, I know More Frosting Please needs to be budget friendly. I have been decorating cakes 40 hours a week for over ten years.

More Frosting Please is fully licensed by the state of Wisconsin & insured. And YES, we do deliver! We are considered an on-demand bakery, which means I do not have a storefront, and that the licensed kitchen I rent from does not allow for visitors. I converse with most of my customers via phone or email, and then we go over their needs. Subsequent visits are made in a convenient location for both parties. We do cakes for all occasions....wedding cakes to single cupcakes. I prefer weddings booked to be within a 40 mile radius of Plymouth-but some exceptions can be made. I specialize in unique designs (nothing you'll find in the binder at your local grocery store!) themes that take your cake "outside the box", and also 3D cakes. Of course I also do basic birthday cakes! If you are interested in a free consultation or quote, please call today! Please visit us at www.facebook.com/MoreFrostingPlease to view our full gallery.

Dream # 1 accomplished!

Now, I don't know where I'll be in four years from now. But I do know that I have fought my ASS off to get where I am right now. Health wise-you have all read what I've been through. Business wise-I guess I'll just have to wait and see how far it goes! There are some weekends I can barely keep up and others that I have no orders. I have found this to be my calling-my ONE thing I'm good at. I can decorate the SHIT out of a cake!! Someday I hope to be successful enough to make More Frosting Please a household name-to no longer have to work full time for someone else. Don't get me wrong...I am in LOVE with my career...but I'd like to not get up at 4a.m. and go to work! Ha! Success-wise I can't even lie-I am SO proud of myself for finishing this book! I have spent a year using EVERY SPARE MINUTE working on it! I work 2 full time jobs, and have three kids and STILL brought this book to life! If you truly feel that you can't do something-ANYthing...that is just an excuse to YOURSELF. YOU CAN DO ANYTHING. I'm just a ho-hum girl, from a small Wisconsin town, that loves to say 'fuck' and I have changed LIVES. Seriously. I have people I don't even know come up to me and tell me that I am an inspiration. Tell me that they have prayed for me over the past year. They tell me that they now do self-exams and have gotten mammograms because of ME.

I did this.

I inspire people.

I am nothing special, but I have done some amazing things.

Fuckin' A is THAT an understatement!

THE END.

Dream #2 accomplished. ☺

'Dear Cancer' letters...

While working on putting this book together I had an amazing idea: I asked friends, family, and acquaintances to write a 'Dear Cancer' letter. To put their feelings down on paper, to let go of some things that have been bothering them. To share their experiences with cancer. To just say FUCK OFF to cancer. The following are their amazing thoughts...starting with mine ☺

Dear Mom,
Do you have any idea how much I love and miss you?? Can you see Josh and Ilyssa and Alaina? Do you know I can't even talk about you without tears in my eyes yet now-STILL-after over 16 years? I try to be the best mom I can-I learned that from you. There are many days I don't think I can do this even one more day-be a mom-but you made it-you did it. You would love these little shits-they're just the right blend of crazy! You're my Angel, and I miss you every second. Keep me sane...Love, Shelly

In Loving Memory of Patricia Ann (Phillips) Knowlton
November 18, 1946-January 6, 1996

Lost her fight with Ovarian Cancer. Missed daily with heavy hearts.

{written by me, age 35, invasive ductal carcinoma, stage 3a}
Dear Cancer,
You have put me through HELL. For the last 71 days you have invaded my life; messed up my family; and made me cry. I think you are a mean spiteful bastard that doesn't realize I

already have enough on my plate. My three children are high maintenance; my life is still in chaos from relocating to Plymouth; my husband and I enjoy boring. BUT you have taken that nice, quiet, boring life and changed it into a world of hell. Of running and doctor appointments and nausea and pain and drugs and worry. You have made me afraid to move, bend, think, and even leave the house. You have made me quite knowledgeable in the terminology of all things breast cancer related. The words 'Stage 3A Invasive Ductal Carcinoma' are words I never thought would cross my lips. You traumatized me when you reared your ugly face at my mammogram-turned-biopsy. While I was there all alone-you became my number ONE enemy. It took everything I had to hold it together just long enough to break the news to my husband; my family. You made my husband panic; you made my dad relive every second of my mother's cancer in those first few minutes after I had to tell him. You suck. You have made me go through the absolute hell of a double mastectomy. Pain that no one could imagine. You made me go through the hell of drains and tissue expanders. You have made it impossible to lie on my stomach-and that is one of the only joys in my day. Well, it WAS anyway. Asshole. You took away my happiness; you took away a chunk of my children's innocence. They now are aware of your name; they are aware of words NO CHILD should have to know....things like mastectomy, hysterectomy, drains, incisions, ports, mammograms, menopause, chemotherapy, radiation, and BALD. You snuck your way into my lymph nodes causing more extensive surgery...more scars, more worry-a lifetime of baby-ing that arm. You have made my upper torso a source *of stiffness and pain. You have made me go through a second surgery to remove all my female organs-throwing me into early menopause, causing me MORE rage and mood swings and pain than before. You have scarred up my body more than the pregnancies of THREE children ever did. You have made me go through medical tests/procedures that 90% of people have never even heard of and couldn't imagine. The pain from these procedures is unbelievable. UnFATHOMable. Some of the things I have been put through have damaged my spirit. You have made it necessary to have a port put in so I can receive the "lifesaving" chemo.....which is made from MUSTARD GAS. Seriously. You have made me go on a crash diet. You have made me become a 'hat person' when I have never worn one in my life. You have made me become close enough to the pharmacist that we're on a first name basis. You have introduced me to more medications and prescriptions than I would ever normally put in my body. You have humbled me to have to ask for help from people that I barely know; people that I would never show weakness to. You have made me rely on others for things I would never before do. You have made it impossible to do certain things for myself-simple things like get a shirt on or shower. You interrupt others' schedule by attacking me...making my family and friends take time out of their day or off of work to help out. You made me afraid; made me feel small that first day walking into the 'chemo room'. You took away all my bravado and self-esteem; made me feel meek and sickly. You put me through even more pain every time they access my port. You made me shake and shiver; feel nauseous and unable to be a Mom to my children. So for all of the hell you*

have put me through and all of the hell yet to come all I have
to say to you is "bring it." Go ahead, bring it. See, what
you DON'T know about me, and what not many people know
about me...is that I am a fighter. This is such a small
portion of my life that this isn't going to bother me long. I
may be down right now and beaten up...but my Family has
my back. My Friends 'got my back'. I have this humongous
support group behind me EVERY STEP OF THE WAY. They
are AMAZING. You see, we had this HUGE party this past
weekend, and you weren't even invited. We celebrated my
fight. We brought awareness to the world about you and
your evil-doing and will save at least ONE life telling people
to get a mammogram; to see their doctor regularly for breast
exams; to do their self-exams at home in the shower or in
bed. WE, cancer....are onto you. You will never take these
special people away from me....we will do what we can to kick
you out of our lives permanently. Some of these people have
been in my life since I was 5 years old. Some of them are
brand new in my life and only have popped into it because of
YOU. One more thing to 'thank' you for I guess. You have
brought me new friends; better friends. You have brought my
existing friends closer again; closer than ever before to
stand beside me and fight you. You have brought people back
into my life that I haven't seen in yeeeears. Some as long
as 18 years ago. You see, these people came together to
support me. To cheer me up. To help me. They have started
getting mammograms; they have been brought together to
reconnect with each other. They too are making sure that
you are not part of my life for any longer than necessary. We
surround ourselves with light and laughter...just to keep you

out. I have reconnected with 2 amazing people through all this and the two of them have become a support system beyond ANYthing I could ever have imagined. They have helped us since day one of relocating back to Plymouth and continue to give of themselves to our family. They are selfless in that they have done everything for us-from helping us move, to cleaning our toilets when I just can't. You, cancer have strengthened myrelationship with my Soul Sister, Betsy. You have brought me back to having her in my daily life, and you can bet your ass I thank God every day for her. Not you. So there. You have brought my husband and I closer together than ever before. You have taught him what a Moms job entails. You have taught him patience, caring, and selflessness. You have taught him that not even YOU can keep me down. You have brought out strength in him that I'm not even sure he knew about, much less me! You have brought my love for him to the surface; shown me the exact reasons I'm glad I married him. You may sometimes bring us stress, and strain, and burden. But have you met my KiDs?!?!? You got NOTHIN'on them. They have kicked my ass on a daily basis for years in preparation to fight you. They have hardened me, made me stronger, and made me who I am today.....so I can take you down. You have lifted me up to a place where God is now taking over. You have brought me to His attention and He's 'on it'. You can't go up against Him and win, cancer. Not with this chick. Bring on the chemo, the sickness, the baldness, the radiation, more surgeries.....you name it. I have no other choice than to go through this, so I may as well bring my A-Game.....you know the one.

The one where I beat your ass and you never come back.
Fuck off and Die,
Shelly.

{written by ann bunke, age 37, no history of cancer,
                              she's been in my life for 20+ years}
Dear Cancer,
You Suck! You sneak into people's lives like a thief sneaks
into a home to steal possessions. However, what you try to
steal has much more value than mere purchased or earned
items. You try to steal independence, security, dignity,
humanity and life. You try to take away these things from
your victims who have done nothing to deserve this
unwarranted attack. You try to hurt the families of your
intended target, you frighten, anger, and depress many of
them as well. You try to suck their life savings away, their
careers, their future potential, and their ability to care for
their own loved ones. You try and you try, but so
fortunately you fail often. Too often you have touched people
in my life with your darkness, you have hurt too many people
to ever be of a need to anyone. I have unfortunately learned
from dear friends and family that Cancer is not a surprise
diagnosis any longer, but just another fight. You seem to
appear in our lives when we are the busiest; the most happy,
or the most susceptible to your ills. I want you to know
that you are not welcome in my life or my neighborhood. Don't
come near me or those who I hold dear to my heart. You bring
nothing positive to anyone. You have nothing to share, teach,
or give to anyone, except for heartache. Heartache we do
not need, any more than we need to be robbed by a thief. I
know that thieves can be caught and punished by the law;

but somehow, cancer, you continue to work like you are above all laws. You should know that someday you will be caught and be made to pay for all the crimes you have committed against humanity. We grow stronger and fight you more aggressively, and you lose more often. There is no where you are welcomed in this world, no place for you to find a haven or a home to settle into where you are welcomed or wanted. There is only room in my world for healthy, happy people who are too busy living their lives to have time for you and the darkness you like to bring. My life is for living and celebrating the greatness of all of those in it. Stay away!

Ann Bunke

{written by sara (eilers) block, age 36, cervical cancer}

Dear Cancer,

You are a selfish bastard and you're ruining my family! You took my precious sister when she was just a little 5 year old princess. What the f#%* did she ever do to you? Poor little thing. She should have been playing with her dolls and playing dress up. She should have been playing hop scotch outside with her other sisters and brothers. She should have been playing with her doggies and kitties. She should have just been a perfect little girl. You ruined all of this for her. You took all that away from her and stuck her in a hospital bed and killed her within months. And still taking Paula wasn't enough for you, was it? You still had to take a piece of everyone's hearts that loved her so dearly. You took away a piece of my mom and dad and that piece they will never get back again. You tried sucking off the lungs of my mother but you were a weak bottom feeding bastard and she kicked your ass...for now. I'm sure you have some underlying

scheme to squirm into her body again but I would strongly suggest you go f#%* yourself instead. Oh look, you had the balls to come back! See my big sister with thyroid cancer, see my big sister remove her entire thyroid, see my big sister radiate the shit out of you! Are you dead yet you piece of shit? No, of course not. "Hi, what's your name?" He said. "Hi to you too! My name is Sara, and you?" "My name is Cancer, and I'm back to finally give you a run for your money!" You first came into my life like you do a lot of young female adults, cervical cancer. Enough cervical cancer for extensive surgery and the removal of 30% of my cervix. "You thought getting pregnant was hard before, Sara, think again." For so many years, I tried and tried to have a baby of my own but nothing was working, no pills, no shots, no insemination. What could be wrong with me? Then, my doctor noticed a grape sized lump on my thyroid, just like my sister. I immediately had that tumor removed and 1/3 of my thyroid and thank God! Cancer failed. With blessings from the man upstairs and the love of my beautiful husband, we were able to have two gorgeous babies through in-vitro fertilization. And here I sit, April 2012, with several new tumors on my thyroid just knowing that this is the time that Cancer is back to finally give me a run for my money.
Sara Block

{written by my sister, sandi schneider, age 40}
Dear Cancer,
Shelly had told me about a few days before Halloween that Andy had found a lump. She was making an appointment to see the doctor to have it checked out. The only person I told was Adrian that she had a lump and was going to have it

checked out. This was always in the back of my mind. I kept thinking please not again. Hadn't cancer hurt our family enough? On November first, Adrian had won tickets to the Mike McCarthy show in Green Bay. Dad and Judy were watching the girls so we could go. When we got back to pick up the girls, I could tell something was not right. Dad and Judy were quiet and said that I needed to talk to Shelly. At this point, I did not need to talk to her; I already knew what the tests showed—Cancer. We got home, got the girls settled and made the obligatory call. Shelly told us yes it was cancer and she would meet with the doctors to discuss her options. All of this was happening on Ilyssa's 8th birthday. Shelly had decided she was not going to tell her kids until she knew exactly what was going on. We then decided not to say anything to my girls until her kids had been told. That turned out to be a VERY long week. I tried to wait until the girls were in bed to let my emotions go, but Alex being Alex new something was not right. She kept asking me-What is wrong with my Aunt Shelly? Why won't you tell me what is wrong with her. She is a very persistent little girl. I was also wondering how I was going to tell Brittany. Shelly is like Brittany's second mom. Shelly was there the second Brittany was born and they have always been close. The one good thing is Brittany was 13 and could understand this a little better. Saturday November 6 was the day all the kids found out. Alex and Brittany did very well considering the news. There were a couple questions, but overall they understood. The day Shelly had her surgery, I didn't sleep much. Anyone that knows me knows I am the worrier/emotional one. I kept thinking of our Mom. By the time her cancer was found, it was very far along. I was thinking of our Dad. How can he continually be put through this? First his Dad then his Mom to lung cancer. And in between that, a mother-in-law to cancer, his sister passes suddenly and our Mom. How much is one person supposed to handle? The surgery went well-no surprises. What they thought they would find they did. I didn't get to see her after her surgery because she had the mastectomy and started reconstruction. I went and got her kids after school and stayed with them until someone came to stay with them. I went back the next morning to see her. It was hard to see her in so much pain but I knew she was strong and could conquer this. Shelly is a fighter. I was also worried about the chemo. I remember our Mom being sooooo sick. I was hoping in the 15+ years since our Mom had cancer that they found a way to make that better. The next few months were a blur. Thanksgiving where we (Schneider's) had 2 dinners in one day (can't even remember that ever happening); helping with the kids; getting Shelly to appointments; her second surgery; help plan their benefit; Christmas; Brittany breaking her ankle four days before the benefit; the benefit; the start of chemo; radiation and then the all-important blood test. I was really glad Shelly chose to not wear a wig. Our Mom wore won and I always hated it. It did not look very natural. I know it was a pretty good bet that she would lose her hair. But seeing her without her hair after she shaved it—WOW did it hit me hard. I guess I really don't remember seeing my mom with her bald head so it was like the first time. Maybe I have just blocked it out. I know men in our family have been known to have a receding hair line but not us girls. I know it upset me for a while, but I finally got used to it. I kept saying it was going to come back red and curly (I got the curly right) I was thankful that Shelly did not get too sick from the chemo. The burns from the radiation sucked but I knew Shelly would heal. The most important thing is your mental state. And Shelly had that in spades. The day in June for the almighty blood test was nerve wracking. I was hoping all the Jones' had been through would be worth it. The test was good and showed that the chemo and radiation worked. As I write this it has been over a year since that first blood test. Every 3 months I still ask-When is the blood test? What did it show? The months are ingrained in my head and I am now looking forward to when it is only every 6 months. Baby steps. The big goal is when the test has been good for 5 years. Then the sighing and the wait can get off our shoulders. I know it is always something we will have to live with, but at that point a sigh of relief can be done. Through all of this I have realized that life is short and you should live it to the fullest because you don't know if you or someone you love will be there the next year, month, day or even hour.

The one thing I would like to tell Cancer is PISS OFF!!!!!!!!

^Sandi

{written by betsy (parker) wiltzius, age 37, lost her father to cancer in 2012 and has been my soul sister for 23 years}

Dear Cancer,

I can't tell you which day of the week it was. I can't tell you what I was wearing that day or whether or not it was raining. Were there carefree kids playing and laughing in the

491

grass as I drove home to my family? I didn't notice that either. Some people remember these minute details on one of the most important days in their lives. But this wasn't going to be a blissful celebration. I do know exactly where I was, however — the exact spot on this strange planet — because when Shelly uttered your name it stopped me dead in my tracks. I never understood the fear or confusion or emotional devastation your gruesome name evoked until that moment. But then, in the next heartbeat, I knew what I had to do. I went to her. I went to Shelly to hug her, to hold her, to cry with her, TO LET HER KNOW SHE WAS NOT ALONE. Even though you destroy, devastate, take away, and terrorize, I never realized you are not stronger than what we can build. Despite the rearing of your hideousness, we built love, faith, friendship, confidence, determination, and strength. Yes, most of all Shelly built strength. Strength greater than any Olympic athlete. Strength deserving of a shimmering superhero cape. And that's what Shelly is to me — a superhero. To have stared you in the face and crushed you while life raged on around her is astonishing and monumental. So even though you present yourself as a terrorist-take-all, you never knew that what we were building was stronger and everlasting. I won't lie. I've cried many tears each time you threatened a friend or family member. I cried like any child would when you took my dad too soon from us. But in the past two years Shelly and I have shared more tears of joy and laughter than of fear or sorrow. And that's what I'll remember always. So, Cancer, with this I bid you farewell and good riddance. Should you dare revisit, beware! I have God & a Superhero

492

on my side. In hatred and disgust, Betsy

*{written by ryan rosenthal, age 39, no previous cancer experience
and a friend for over 20 years}*
Dear Shelly,
*You are the 1st person I have known, and loved for many
years, that got Cancer. I knew Cancer was totally awful,
but I REALLY never knew the hell a person goes though for
treatment and the aftermath. First of all, I can't image
what you and Andy went through emotionally. How to handle
living, dying, money, and what is going to happen with the
kids. I would have been a nervous wreck, but I thought you
handled each day with courage. You fought cancer head on. I
never realized the pain and discomfort you went though. It
seemed you went through hell with each treatment and got
totally wiped out. I was happy to see that your family
stayed strong and held it together. I know what kind of
person you are, and I knew you were going to kick Cancer's
ass, but I really got scared when I came over one night to
drop off some supper and saw you wiped out. I saw you in a
state that I had never seen you before. You looked weak and
depressed. I drove home crying and praying for you and your
family. On a final note, I am so happy to see you back to the
old Shelly. You gave me a whole new look at life and what is
important: family, friends, health, and to try not to stress
about stupid stuff. When I think of you and what you have
gone through, you inspire me. Every time I hit a brick wall at
work or at home, I think to myself, "What would Shelly do?"
She would grab it by the nuts, and smash them. "So Ryan,
just get it done."*
Prayers to you and your family, Ryan "Fish" Rosenthal

{written by my niece, brittany schneider, age 15}
Aunt Shelly, I have written a poem about the cancer that has been in our family. So, this is what I wrote instead of a letter. I hope you like it!!!!

Cancer

Breast Cancer,
I'm glad you left my aunt through chemo and radiation.
She didn't deserve what she had to go through.
One good thing that did come
out of this is she became closer to her family.
She also got to spend more
time with her husband and three kids.
Breast Cancer, please don't come back.
I don't know what I'd do if you hit her again!
She is still not feeling well
after what you did to her
and I know she wants you gone
for good now. Cancer,
You also made my Grandpa
relive the effects of cancer.
Don't you know that you took my Grandma's
life! My family has suffered enough
with you around!
You took away a loving person from my mom,
my aunt, my Grandpa, my sister, cousins, and me
that we didn't have around because of you!
I hope you're happy that you made my family miserable
and that my mom and aunt don't have a mother anymore!
So thanks for that!
Just remember what you have done
to us and just stop letting us suffer!

494

Just please go away and leave us alone.

THANKS!!!!!

*Well, I hope you like it & think about putting it in your book!
LOVE YA! Brittany*

{written by Mary, breast cancer SURVIVOR! Whom I met at a BC retreat}
Dear Cancer,
Who invited you to the party of life? Certainly not ME. Not
to MY party! YOU came uninvited and unannounced,
barreling through the door as if you had every right to be
here and overshadow all the festivities and other guests.
How DARE you! You know the song, "It's My Party and I'll
Cry If I Want To"? Well, that should have been playing in the
background after you showed up. I would have preferred
the Beatles or some other music from the 60's. Did you
bring a dish to pass? NO! Instead you gave me an altered
taste and aversion to some foods. Sometimes you made it
even difficult to eat what was contributed! Oh, and when
everyone else was enjoying themselves with fun and laughter,
you cornered me on the couch where I couldn't move because
you blocked my way with fatigue so overwhelming I thought
it would never pass. Oh, and the party apparel. Now there
was something else you spoiled! You had to spoil my hairdo,
taking it away completely, gradually, mind you, so that I was
forced to join in the process and pull it out in chunks. But I
fixed you! My wig was killer. At least you couldn't take
that away from me and most people didn't even know that I
wasn't wearing my own head of hair. Because YOU had to

495

show up, there were all those appointments. So much info to absorb. You couldn't have the decency to give me time to take it all in. NO. You were impatient and demanded that decisions be made and everything be done immediately, leaving no time to contemplate what would be best for me and my loved ones. Remember the nasty beverages at the party? You know. The "Red Devil". The one that turned my pee to orange. Not to forget the others. Cytoxan. There's a wonderful thought; a guest at the party would insist that you take the cocktail, regardless of the fact that it would do nasty things to you. But there was no avoiding it with you hovering all the time around the punch bowl. You had no consideration for the members of my family who stood by watching the party continue while they cried and worried. But, once again, we fixed you. They also prayed, as did many other people at the party, some of whom I didn't even know! Those prayers proved to be much stronger than you. I'll bet you felt the power, didn't you. I'll bet you were a bit uncomfortable and rightly so. You couldn't conquer those. Yeah, you made a good attempt to crash the party, and you might have succeeded. But you didn't know I had extra special guests who wouldn't let you. Did you see all those people with the stethoscopes and needles and IV bags? How about those with the body forms and the radiation machinery? Did you see the concern and compassion in their eyes and on their faces? Did you hear them when they explained what you might try to do, but what they would do to help me fight? You might have missed that, but I didn't. Though they may never be at my party again, I will NEVER forget their presence at this one. Oh, don't forget those people who were there before, during, and who continue to be: My husband, my daughter and son, and his wife and child. My dear friends who sat with me to watch the movies being played in that corner of the party while I couldn't get off the couch. And all the people who brought food so I wouldn't have to do so much preparation for the event. Then there were all the cards, letters, emails, Facebook messages, flowers and gifts. They just added to the comforting ambiance of the party, don't you think? You didn't think you would need to compete with that, did you? But I do have you give you some credit. The guests you brought with you turned out to be some of the most wonderful people I have ever met. New people. The women who laughed and joked in the radiation treatment waiting room. We call ourselves "The Sisterhood of the Radiated Boobs"! Yup, we had fun. Guess what! We still correspond and are meeting for lunch soon. Of course, there were all those women from the YMCA Livestrong program. You know, the ones we sweat with and shared our stories and grew to become physically and emotionally stronger. I'll wager a bet that you didn't think I would connect with them, did you? There are five of us who still meet for spinning (cycling) class every Thursday followed by coffee afterwards. We share our concerns, but also laughter, joy and hope. They would not have come into my life had you not brought them to the party. Then there was the Infinite Boundaries Retreat. I had NO idea you would bring such diverse and wonderful women who would enrich my life so deeply. Most I won't see again, but some will stay in touch, and hopefully we'll be able to meet as well. What wonderful guests they were! Although you might not have intended to

do so, your presence directed me to a stronger relationship with my God. With great joy, I admit that was the most valuable and treasured gift I received. Now I'm moving on and I'm not leaving a forwarding address. Should you ever decide to try to crash another party of mine, I'll be much better prepared for you. But watch out. I fight HARD!
Sincerely, Mary

{written by joey vander schaaf, age 35, no history of cancer, amazing friend for over 6 years}
Dear Cancer,
I never ever in a million years wanted to know anything about cancer, especially breast cancer! I guess being born in Green Bay and being an avid Packer fan it first hit close to home when I heard that Deanna Favre had breast cancer. Then I started to see all the breast cancer merchandise that came out at Kohl's. But the day I heard my good friend Shelly had it, which was 2.2 seconds after she told my sister and they hung up, I was in immediate denial, knowing that there had to be some mistake. Shelly has 3 children that are the same ages as my 3 oldest children. Shelly was supposed to go have another medical surgery-they had to have mixed her results up with someone else. The poor girl lost her own mother at such a young age to cancer. I mean, Shelly had already too much on her plate with moving, her husband's new job, her new job, new schools, new baby-sitters, and a son with Asperger's. I mean God only gives us what we can handle, right? I didn't even want to talk to her, what do you say to someone that has breast cancer? "I'm sorry, I know how you feel, it could be worse....." there is NOTHING right to say. I didn't want to be one of those

friends that said all the wrong things. Every time I would read her blogs, I would start crying and feeling guilty, because I "thought" I had a tough day, but this strong woman is trying to raise 3 small children and keep her head afloat, while fighting cancer and going through chemotherapy. What seemed like "Big" problems to me was nothing compared to what Shelly was going through. Shelly could possibly DIE and she has no mother and her kids could end up without a mother. She is the glue that holds the family together; she is the center of the universe to her children and husband. So what did Shelly do? She went into 'Shelly mode' and started researching everything that was available and ended up in surgery in a few days after she found out. If anyone knows Shelly, she doesn't go turtle speed about anything, she jumps in with both feet and then some, and speeds right ahead to "FIX" the problem. I am proud to say Shelly is the strongest person I know. But, I am sad to say, every time I see any pink, or breast cancer things, I think about Shelly. I did not EVER want to think of such a good friend associated with breast cancer. Shelly inspired me to get a mammogram, after over a year, at the age of 35. The whole time I am sitting in the exam room, I kept thinking, oh my, this is how Shelly found out, please don't let it be me....and after 10 minutes of sweating the doctor came in the room and said, you are good to go. I did have to go back the following week, because they wanted to do another mammogram to take a closer look, but all came back perfect and I know that she has saved so many lives by her inspirational story. Shelly is a breast cancer survivor!!!! And she even has the cute stylish curly hair now ☺ I love

you Shelly! But I HATE that the word C-A-N-C-E-R has to ever be in the same sentence with your name!
Love you girl,
Joanna Vander Schaaf AKA-JOEY

{written by danielle meyer, a neighbor; mom of my sons friend; sister of Amanda-leukemia victim}
Dear Cancer,
I don't know where to begin. Someone so special no longer exists due to your cruel phases of life sucking qualities. My funny, smart, life loving, beautiful, talented, magnificent sister does not get to enjoy watching her three boys grow up. Here is her tale of life, love, and heartache. But you should know-you lived through it with her.

Amanda was the funniest person I knew. She could really hold your attention when retelling a story. She had a way of making you smile no matter how bad things got. She has three beautiful boys that she may only watch from above now. Nicholas, Andrew, and Bradley were her treasures. She lived for those boys. She didn't have the best of marriages though. She lived through much abuse, but stayed because she loved him so much. She always said "it is ok, he loves me enough that I know he will change". When Larry, her husband, cheated on her, she finally stood tall and said "enough". She divorced him and went back to school. She worked so hard and struggled much. She had the smarts to do whatever she put her mind to. Her passion in life was to help people, and that she did! She became a nurse and started working for Aurora Medical Center. She was so happy and we all were so very proud. She had found love again and they planned on getting married. But that happiness was short lived. She had volunteered for some testing when she was in nursing school. They had told her she needed to go to a doctor for further testing. So when she got the final test results they told her she had Leukemia. It was life shattering for all. She had come so far and gone through so much, and then you had to appear. Everyone's hopes and dreams turned into nightmares! She went through many radiation treatments. Her hair was falling out in globs, so she shaved it all off. After her treatments she did go into remission, but the doctors told her you would come back. They suggested a bone marrow transplant. She thought long and hard and said yes to the transplant. She was sent to Ann Harbor Michigan where the transplant would be done. My sister Rachel and I were tested to find out who was the closest match. Rachel had agreed to be the donor since she was the closest match for Amanda. I remember all the exhausting tests they had to perform before the transplant could occur. Amanda held strong though. She had once told me about a little girl who had Leukemia also. She told me how fearless this little girl was and how they kept each other company through each other's struggles. Amanda was a lot stronger because this little one brought so much hope. Her fearlessness toward you was just amazing. She was a fighter, but in the end you overpowered her and she passed away. After she was gone, Amanda's strength started to diminish. She had mourned for her and had many feelings of despair. Amanda couldn't believe this beautiful little girl would never grow up. She loved her little boys and feared for them so much. She had many thoughts of death and how she wouldn't make it through. She had asked us all to make sure her boys would grow up knowing how much she loved them. She talked like there was no hope for her. When that little girl passed, Amanda's flame started to fade too. I had reminded her that she was the wind that made us all soar and we were the boat that would always keep her afloat. But her ship was sinking so fast. There was barely anytime to say good bye.

We were told everything was going to be Okay. But the phone rang that awful evening, it was Jon. He was the man who stayed by her side every minute and took care of her boys when she couldn't. He called to say that we all should get to the hospital because she doesn't have much time left. So that is what we did. We all rushed to the hospital to see how far she had fallen. It was an unspeakable site. My wonderful sister, who gave me so much through our life together, had slipped into the abyss of the unknown. She woke just enough to say my name three times and slipped back into unconsciousness. To this day the color yellow makes me sick to my stomach because that was the color of her skin when I entered her hospital room. Her body had rejected the transplant and was slowly filling with toxins. I stayed long enough to beg and plead with her to hold strong. I had told her that we all love her and life would be miserable without her. I brought up stories of our child hood together. Talked to her about how much we fought but through it all, we could laugh at each other's dumb choices in life. How I loved it when she sang, because her voice was just delightful. She had a talent for everything. I was jealous of

502

her in many ways growing up. But that's what sisters do. We compare, fight, laugh, and love no matter what curveball gets thrown. To this day I hate myself for not staying by her side during the last beats of her heart. I wasn't there when she was born and I just couldn't be there to watch her die. That's what I told myself at the time. I was mad, frustrated, and scared. I had ran from that hospital so fast, a move that I will ALWAYS regret. Amanda only lived 29 years of life. She was born July 07, 1978 and you took her from us February 29, 2008. I hate every form you take! You come into people's lives and shatter everything in your path. But, someday we will find the cure. We will keep fighting to destroy you, just like all the lights you turned out. We are all working to end you Cancer!! We'll NEVER give up the fight. Rest in Peace, Amanda Panda Bear. You are always in my heart and many others. You touched us all in so many ways. Your light will always shine in your boys!!! We love and miss you deeply!!
Love, Danielle.

Amanda Lee Irene (Preston) Alger
July 07, 1978 - February 29, 2008

(Shelly-Sorry it took so long, I miss her so much and cry at every thought of her. I hope this will help with your book. I wasn't sure how to put it together. THANKS for including my sisters' story...I look forward to seeing the end results ....THANK YOU SHELLY!!!!!!!)

{written by candice lueck, breast cancer survivor! Whom I met at a BC retreat}

Dear Cancer, I hate you because you make me sick and in so much pain. Who are YOU to do this to me or furthermore to ANYone especially children. You show no regret. You have taken away all of my abilities to make money, make love; feel love. You have taken many of my friends and family. You have given me a life sentence of pain in my legs, hacked off my chest, and made me feel real ugly. You are that monster under the bed that I always feared when I was a child; but you never reared your ugly face til now. That was your mistake. I have fought you two times now and I won't stop so give it up cause I am gonna win. I have God on my side and He has the greater power than you, cancer. You are the devil and you need to be reckoned with. I met other people who hate you as well and they're not gonna let you continue to let you destroy their lives as freely as you think you can. You will not destroy our faith, courage or ability to endure the disabilities you have inflicted upon us. We will find ways to cope with that. Get ready cancer cause we're fighting back you son of a bitch-because now there are more of us and we're 'Zippin' On'! You have consumed my thoughts, actions and my dreams and hope for a brighter future. Things that now will never come true because of you. I had to beg and borrow just to pay the bills from what you did to me. I had to ask for charity which I would never, ever have done. You make me feel so small when I want to feel normal. You have taken away my smile. I hate you and always will. Some of my friends never thought you would come into their lives but you did. You made my husband look at me in a different way and for that I HATE YOU. We once were very much in love. Now because of you sometimes it is hard to get

out of bed. I wonder how much pain I am going to wake up
with. I must leave pain medications next to the bed so I
can make it up to start a new day to fight you once more.
You have made me crawl to pick the weeds around the
beautiful flowers that give me pleasure in my new life of hell.
I hate you more than the so called devil, cause I haven't had
the pleasure to meet your friend yet. SO, when I do I will be
ready for him, cause you made me strong and hardened
enough to endure almost anything that comes my way. I
have learned to fight harder than I thought possible to. I
have been spreading the word about you to everyone I know
and things that will help them never meet your ugly face. You
are now in the open where everybody can see you now. You
won't be able to hide under the bed anymore. Thank God for
that though. Know what cancer? I have real friends now
and we are so onto you and your friend the devil and all of
your ways of trying to destroy us. We have support groups
to help us get you out of our system. SO get ready we will
never give up til we eradicate you. And when I go to Heaven,
I will never have to deal with you again.
Candice

{written by angie lathrop schroeder, age 36, no cancer history, a
friend for over 31 years}
Dear Cancer, you are a bully! You have been able to sneak
your way into the lives of every single person I know. You
have hurt people I love. You have taken away people I love.
You have destroyed families, lives, spirit, and sometimes even
hope. I hate that you have caused me to fear for the safety,
well-being, and lives of people that are important to me. Do
you see how people pull together to support your victims?

Human beings' ability to pull together to support and protect one of our own is not to be underestimated. I believe one day, we WILL destroy YOU! We get better and better at fighting you. What comes around goes around — what you have done to us you will get back times three. And that day will not come soon enough. Until that day, I will continue to fight you anyway I can. I will help anyone you hurt hold onto hope -- hope in a cure, hope in prevention, hope in the future, hope in all else that is good in the World, and hope that you will not be able to hurt anyone else......ever. I believe in miracles and miracles will be the end of you.

Angie Lathrop Schroeder

{a Poem written by melody schneider, at age 17 after she lost her Mom to breast cancer; sister of a classmate that I have known since I was six. Many memories of their family growing up...}

```
CRY
            death
                    dying
illness...ALL
   cause Harm.              Emotional.
                                Physical
Mental.          They can      wreck        the
foundation              of a  FAMILY.
                 Loss of hair       loss   of
        mind...
HOW    do    you    DEAL???????
        You can't              You won't.
One day          EVERYthing    is      FINE....
(next)      SHE'S SICK.
Telling     (you)   of         her
            struggles
Trying    not
            To  (cry)    show her !!! FEAR !!!
The    last    you                   remember
```

```
              (remember her well)                    is
her saying...                        Don't
                        worry!!!!
        (be happy)
                        I WILL BE ALLRIGHT!

(BUT)      she's    NOT!   She's
                           GONE!
And there's nothing you can do....
               But
                     CRY
                AND...       NEVER,EVER
          FORGET            her!!!!
```

{written by the same melody schneider, 2012, age 32}

Dear Cancer,

How do I start? Is saying I HATE you too much? Was it not enough to see my Mother in emotional turmoil that you had to add physical turmoil on top of it?? I have all these thoughts right now, and yet I cannot seem to figure out how to express them properly. My Mom was, is and forever will be, the greatest Mom to ever be. She was kind, forgiving, generous, funny, beautiful (inside and out!), thoughtful and most of all COURAGEOUS!! I get so pissed off when I hear people say you have to be strong to beat cancer. My Mom was the strongest person I have ever met and yet she did not win the fight. But, some may say, she did win a fight. She is no longer in any pain-physically or mentally or emotionally. She is at peace, riding her horses, and watching her grandchildren grow. It is so frustrating and sad to see my daughter well up with tears, for no other reason than she is sad and misses her Grandma and wishes she could have met her. Not only did you rob us of a wonderful mother, but you robbed our children of a

spectacular Grandmother! I strive every day to make her proud of me and the way I am raising my children. When people tell me that they think I am a good Mother, I say thank you-I learned from the best! My mom was eleven days from being 43 years old when she was taken from us. She didn't get to be there for her youngest child to turn 18 or graduate high school. She didn't get to be at her children's weddings or witness the births of our children. We did not get to have her by our side for all of these things that you so desperately need your mother for. Cancer has made me an emotionally hard person. It is very hard for me to love another adult and I make sure I tell my kids I love them every chance I get! And not only did I have to grow up too fast, knowing she was not going to be there for me, but because you took her when you did, my oldest brother had to grow up too fast also. A 24-year old man should not have to take on the responsibility of raising his little sister-albeit I was almost 18, but he still had to be the parent to me when he should have been able to go do whatever he wanted to! I will never understand why some people make it and others don't. All I do know is that she is watching us every day and one day we will be there to hug her again.
I love you, mom ☺

In Loving Memory of Linda Lou Lawrenz
January 8, 1955-January 7, 1998
♥ Melody

{written by Kaelin, age 7; ...daughter of Melody Schneider ...lost her grandma to breast cancer before she was even born... }

To: Shelly
From: Kaelin
Dear Cancer,
I wish you would have let her live until I was seven, that way I could have met her. I always cry just like I am right now. I love my grandma even though I never met her. I'm very happy that Shelly won. Please keep other peoples family alive for children that want to meet them. Please let people live awhile.

{written by jenny stam, age 36, no cancer history, amazing friend for six years}
Dear Cancer,
I will never forget the day you became a word in my friend's life and mine. Hearing my very dear friend, Shelly, tell me that she has cancer will be a day I will NEVER forget. You started out as a lump that turned into "maybe" an infection, but all along it was really you... CANCER! When I first heard Shelly tell me that she had "you" I couldn't really believe it. I went through all the thoughts everyone who hears that word goes through...maybe they were wrong, run the test again, that can't happen to my friend...but it did!! You changed my friend's life forever, but forever she will be stronger than you. It would seem kind of silly to thank you for coming into my life and my friend's life, but I think I will go out on a limb and say...THANK YOU!!! You have changed not only Shelly's life, but many lives... because of YOU many woman have gotten mammograms, because of YOU many woman do self-breast examinations, because of

509

YOU many lives have been saved and for that I say THANK
YOU!!! Don't get me wrong I don't like you or ever will, but
because of what you did to one of my closest friend's life,
you made me realize that you can be beat and YOU made me
see how very very strong Shelly Jones is!!!! I love my friend
and I am so glad that she IS stronger than YOU!!
Sincerely, Jenny ☺

{Submitted/written by sara lee mayer, sister of my friend, Cory whom
I have known since the 1990's}

Life is too short
Don't waste a minute
Enjoy each day
And Everyone in it
Tomorrow will come
It could be your last
Make the most of today
Life passes too fast.

Cancer is so limited.
It cannot cripple love.
It cannot shatter hope.
It cannot corrode faith.
It cannot eat away peace.
It cannot destroy confidence.
It cannot kill friendship.
It cannot shut out memories.

"In loving Memory" to Miss Makalya Rose who lost her
battle with leukemia at the age of 6

The sun is still shining, the sky is still blue,
But life here still isn't the same without you.
If tears could build a stairway, and memories a lane,
I'd walk right up to heaven and bring you home again.

Miss Makayla Rose March 8, 1997 - Jan 4, 2004

"Makayla Rose is my best friend's daughter. They have been a part my familiy's life for 15+ years. She was the bravest little girl I have ever met, and I am lucky to have called her Mom my best friend. I think about her every day! Sara"

(Author's note: when Makayla was going through chemo, I remember her family coming into the video store where I worked at the time...her smile was infectious, she was such a beautiful soul. I didn't know the rest of her story until Sara submitted this letter...it has been 9 years since I last saw Makayla. Thank you God for keeping her in Your loving arms until her family can be with her again. Everytime I see her Mom at school I just think "what an amazingly strong woman. I am humbled by her strength; she puts ME to shame.")

{written by DeAnna Hadnot, a friend since we were both trying to get preggo with our first kid}

Dear Cancer,

I don't just hate you, I'm terrified of you. You have changed my life forever in ways I never thought imaginable. When I was 19 years old and a sophomore in college, I was having the time of my life. I was living in a dorm with all my sorority sisters and doing all the things college girls do. One night, during my mid-term exams, that life came to a screeching halt. The phone rang and it was my dad. My dad never called at night! He always called early in the morning to make sure

511

I was there. But this night, he chose to call and had some news...news I never thought I would hear. "Your mother had an irregular mammogram. And they did a biopsy today. The results showed it was cancer. She will be having surgery tomorrow...a mastectomy." You know, I can't even remember how I responded other than crying. I was told to get in touch with my cousin who was also at the same school and had a car....and he was to take me to see her the next day after her surgery and bring me back for exams. All I know is that I was in shock and a state of disbelief. I couldn't be losing my mother! Not at this age. I still needed her!

That was my first encounter with cancer involving someone close to me. I was young, bullet-proof and emotionally unequipped to deal with the aftermath. Seeing her in the hospital after surgery, hooked up to all the tubes and wires, in pain and helpless was surreal. What do I do? I don't even remember whether I spoke to her.

My mom came through the surgery fine and did three months of chemo with all the vomiting, etc. while I was at school. I came home between quarters and did what I could but I mostly stayed at school because I couldn't handle it emotionally and had no idea what to do at home. I didn't know how to help my mother or cook. Some of my family think poorly of me to this day for being distant during this time. But I just couldn't. And obviously my father couldn't handle it either because my mother caught him having an affair while she was going through chemo and my family was torn apart. They divorced shortly after. Little did I know, cancer would come to haunt me again… and again.

My father was diagnosed with liver cancer in 2005. My parents were divorced and my dad had remarried by this time. The tumor in his liver was operable and the fantastic doctor he had felt he could get it all. And he did but told us the chance of re-occurrence was 85 percent. My father was never the same after surgery. He lived his life in fear of cancer; he went from being a mid-life crisis, sports car driving, party animal, 60 year old who thought he was 40 to a 70 year old man sitting in a recliner, watching sports and refusing to socialize.

My mom struggled through many years of depression from the divorce after 35 years of marriage but managed to come through on the up end and find her own life doing all the things she loved to do and never having to answer to anyone for doing them. If she wanted to spend her entire day quilting or reading, she did. No questions asked.

The summer of 2008, things took a terrible turn. I got a phone call from my mom. She told me her lymph nodes in her neck had been swollen for several weeks and she'd done two rounds of antibiotics but they were still enlarged. Her doctor was sending her to an ENT. Within a week, she saw the ENT and he wanted to do further tests…a biopsy. My sister Kelly said she would go with her. On July 17th, I got the call that the biopsy results were in. It was cancer. Thus began the journey again.

My mother came to live with us in August of 2008 to get cancer treatment for throat cancer that had metastasized to the lungs. We did chemo....and chemo...until her frail body could take no more. She finally got to the point she couldn't get up anymore. And we stopped. We battled pneumonia a few times; the last time we called for hospice. She made it a few days past one year. She died July 25th, 2009.

The real kicker to all this...when my mom was near the end.... having hallucinations and calling for unknown people, we got the call that my dad's liver cancer was back. He headed down to Gainesville, FL to see a specialist.

His surgeon thought it should all be simple. The surgeon even planned to film the surgery for instructional purposes. My father celebrated his 75th birthday with us in Gainesville on June 1st, 2009, the night before his surgery. On June 2nd, the surgery took place but it was not as simple as the surgeon had hoped. Arteries were involved and repaired but didn't work the way expected after surgery. He was on life support for 15 days before my step mother decided it was time to let him go. He died June 17th, 2009...three weeks before my mother.

I didn't bother to mention the three or four times my dad had melanomas removed. That somehow seems trivial now. Isn't that stupid? How can any cancer be trivial??? And my husband has had two basal cell cancers removed from his arm. I'm told those aren't fast spreading so I take it for granted.

514

But cancer has tested me and I can only say that it has tested me second hand. I haven't had it myself or had to face the thoughts some must go through when they are diagnosed. But it made me an orphan in a three week time span. It left me in the store looking at Father's Day cards for my husband and realizing I don't have to buy one for MY father anymore. It left me holding my phone in my hand in the kitchen realizing I can't call my Mama to see how to cook something. It left me explaining to my two small children that their Papa and Gran aren't coming back. It left me with a void only a Mama can fill.

I've watched friends go through it recently as well and cannot imagine the struggles and turmoil. I just can't. Cancer tore apart my family. Cancer changed me and my life forever. I wish I could better express how, but I'm not sure what to say. I made it through my mother's breast cancer mostly unscathed but her second bout with cancer changed me permanently in so many ways. Some good and some bad. I miss her every single day. And I will never recover.

There just must be a way to overcome this terrible disease. Every time I turn around, someone else has cancer. We have to put a stop to it. It's time....cancer must die.
DeAnna Hadnot

{written by Ilyssa Jones, my oldest daughter, at age 10}
Dear Mom, I can't think of anything to write except that I had to suffer through this with you. And I hated all of it-this was the worst time ever. I had just turned eight and the

next day I had to hear all about stupid cancer. I had just about a million questions about breast cancer.

Will you die? Will you be fine? How long will this last? Why did this happen? When I heard this I hated that you will be in serious pain. I went through this for over a year of my life. {Worst experience ever}

Cancer, you put my mommy through so much pain. Why *my* mommy? The second she started battling cancer, I knew that she could make it through this.

My mom is stronger and so much better than you. She will fight you until you die. I hate you more than anything. I cried every day for my mommy, prayed that she would be alright.

I have just a few more things to add-have I mentioned that you really suck? You have destroyed my family for the past year.

My mom fought you for over a year hoping nothing would go wrong but you made that impossible. My mom has beat you-and is getting stronger every second.

Mommy, you are one of the bravest, strongest people I have ever met. One of the others is my Daddy-he went through it with Mommy every day-he was strong enough to deal with it, where me, on the other hand, I cried at recess just hoping that when I got home the dumb, stupid cancer would have just disappeared and that my Mommy would be okay but that did not happen and it still has not happened. But back to daddy I did not see you cry even once you were really that strong.

I wish that this dumb stupid cancer would have left my mommy alone. There is a slight problem with that though,

516

if you did not come than that would mean today my mommy would not be the slightest bit stronger or braver.

But this stupid cancer has changed the way we do things. Because now my mommy can't run and play and tickle Josh, Alaina, and me.

You must have thought that you were the strongest thing alive, once you met my mommy-you had to have realized that my mommy is ready to kick your stupid butt any day any time. I really hate the fact that you hurt my mom to the point where she could not get up by herself; she could hardly walk or even remember some of the things she promised us we could do (like me not getting a birthday party for when I turned eight.)

At this point tears are just streaming down my face to the point where I can't see what I am typing.

You, mom, are strong, brave, protective, caring, honest, and the best mommy!! And I am-as you call me-your very very very strong baby girl.

I love you so very much and I am so glad that you are okay.

I love you. Your oldest daughter {Lulu}

{written by melissa Schumacher, age 37. No history of cancer; an amazing friend for OVER 25 years!}
Here you go-
I don't believe one ever thinks cancer will touch their lives. Me personally, I believe anything is possible and don't underestimate the possibility of things, good or bad. I think it helps me be prepared for the worst and for all situations. Along with being realistic. I could not have been any less prepared for this to have touched my life not only once but

517

three times in the past year. I've seen three courageous woman fight for their lives, with one, my aunt losing her battle. One of my closest friends, my maid of honor, the person who'd help me with a body, if needed; was diagnosed with stage three breast cancer. I cannot put into words what I felt or thought when she told me, I think I may have even blanked-having a flood of emotions and thoughts overwhelm me; not knowing what to say or do. I knew I would be there for her, even though I wasn't always sure how to without being in the way. There was so much support and I am so thankful that her and her family received that from so many!! As Shelly was becoming an expert on all areas of her cancer, treatments, care, funding etc....I was a novice, starting to dive in and search myself and probably constantly asking her questions wanting to understand. Her Caringbridge site was truly wonderful for getting frequent updates without "bothering her" when she was resting which was so needed! To go through and think about her journey, each stage again, makes my heart cry. To see such an incredibly strong woman be so put out with this disease. The mental and physical anguish that she went through for not only herself but also her family, one can never imagine unless there. To see a true friend fight; fight for her life. Not just for herself but to still be there for her husband and her children. To be able to stay alive and hopefully have a life again! One thing that stands out to me is while she was going through all of this, she still had the strength above and beyond, to be there for me while I went through a divorce. I do not think she will ever understand or know what her example in this has done for me and others that know her and even those that don't! I have done a lot of praying for her and her family throughout this continually. I thank God for her-my friend! Here is a (((((big hug))))) just because you are still here for me to give them to you and for being a great friend! Plus I know how much you like them! I love you Shelly! Melissa

{written by miranda wiltzius, age 16, my friend Betsy's daughter} About 75% of my life was spent uneducated on cancer; the types or effects. It was up until my grandpa got cancer where really, I didn't care. Everyone thinks it won't happen to them. They also don't think it will happen to someone they love. Your life is going normal-until you have to start living it day by day. I feel that's what Shelly and her family had to do. She didn't know what was going to happen; whether she was going to be tired or scared. It was already to the point where Shelly's family felt like my family. Her kids were like my siblings. I babysat so that Shelly could have less worries. Being able to do that for them when I was only 14 makes me proud; I was able to already put others before myself. When you care about someone, you do things for them that you wouldn't usually do! Like dishes. I HATE doing dishes, but I helped them out by doing them. You have to remind yourself-what does 15 minutes of dishes mean to me and what would it mean to Shelly. Having chores of my own and then the Jones' chores on top of them sucked, but that's okay. It really helped her family out, and that means a lot to me. It helped me grow up a lot. I'm 16 now and can look back and I am still proud of everyone who made an impact in their lives. ^M.

{written by candice braun, age 35, a close friend for over 16 years}
Dear Cancer, I often think "how do you pick who you decide
to inflict your disease upon? Why is it not the 80 year old
man who has smoked 2 packs a day since he was 13 years
old? Why did you pick my 35 year old friend who has children
and her whole life ahead of her?? Why didn't you pick me??"
But I do know the answer to that! You chose her because
you knew how strong and determined she is. You knew she
would be a fighter. You knew she could beat you. Cancer...I
am so mad at you. I am so mad you had to choose her. You
made her sick; you gave her more pain that a human should
ever have to go through. You made her life a living hell! Why??
For what reason?? That, I don't have the answer to. Life is
hard enough without your interference. I am mad at you for
hurting her and our friendship. Because you see, when you
were there, I am ashamed to admit...I was a SUCKY friend.
I was scared of you. No not because I was afraid I would
catch you. I ran in the opposite direction...I didn't know how
to deal with you. What if I said the wrong thing? What if I
tried to soothe her but only made her angry because I was
healthy and she was dealing with you?? Is she too tired to
talk? Will she be annoyed with me? Does she want to be
alone? Of course not IDIOT! She needed me, to help her
through this, cry, scream at me if she wanted to. And most
importantly, just be her friend. The friend I should have
been, the friend I was not. I am sorry...so sorry you had to
come along. I am sorry I LET you get in the way of me and
my friend. I am sorry I let you affect me at all. I am
SORRY you scared me away. So cancer...go AWAY. Get
away from my friend and don't you dare EVER come back.
You are NOT welcome. Don't think about coming back

because if you do, she will kick your ass again. She is strong, smart, caring, funny, talented and creative and beautiful. She is one tough woman. A woman I admire and I aspire to be like her every day. SO you can go now. Nobody will miss you or ever wants to see your ugliness again. Oh- and by the way......Thank You. You made me realize a life lesson. A true friend will forgive you for being a jackass. Hold on to your friends tight, be there for them and cherish the time you spend together. Be there in SICKNESS and in health. (Kinda like a marriage, huh??) And love them, even if you think they hate you.

Sincerely, Candice

{{I could <u>never</u> hate you. I love you Candice!}}

{written by Andy Jones, my loving husband, age 37...}

Dear Cancer,

There are thousands of words in the English language to convey emotions, but there are no words to describe the feeling in your gut when your wife calls you and tells you "I have cancer". Your wife, your partner, your best friend, your rock, the mother of your children. The person who makes your life complete has cancer. You don't know what this means. Is she going to live...is she going to die? My drive home that day...those 45 minutes...were the worst of my life. When I got home, she couldn't look at me or speak to me or she was going to "lose it". It took about 20 minutes before she would let me hug her and talk to her about what the doctor said. Those 20 minutes were all that it took for me to hate you cancer. The fear in her eyes broke my heart. For that, FUCK YOU cancer.

521

You were the cause of that fear cancer. A husband protects his family, he fights to defend his family. He works to make sure everything is correct. The 3 words the doctor told my wife "you have cancer" destroyed my ability to protect my wife. There was nothing I could do to help her. I couldn't fight this fight for her. You destroyed a part of me. For that, FUCK YOU cancer!

Telling our children that you had invaded our family was one of the hardest things I've ever had to do. There is NO way to tell them that the world they know is now gone. That mom is sick, that she might die. How the HELL do you tell a child that??? You destroyed a part of their childhood innocence. For that, FUCK YOU cancer.

You made my wife fear for her life. Fear of what would happen to her children without their mother. You destroyed her body. Took her breasts. Burned her skin from radiation. Scarred her body from surgeries. Took her lymph nodes making her more susceptable to other diseases. Made her hair fall out. Forced toxic medicines into her body to fight you. Things that are known to cause cancer and had been used at Nazi death camps had to be used to fight you. You forced her into early menopause with no possibility of hormone treatment to ease the transition. You took her sex drive, her ability to feel like a woman. Worse than all that, you destroyed her confidence, her self-worth, her being. For that, FUCK YOU cancer.

You have done so many things to try to destroy our lives...but I have to tell you...you won't win. Shelly is too strong. You have no idea of the beast you have created. You have brought out the "fight" in her. She has always been a

522

strong woman, but now when you look her in the eyes you can see the fight, the determination simmering inside. She will not lose this fight. This beast you created will win. She has the support of so many people, close friends and strangers. They are all behind her to support her.

She fights you in her body. She fights you by encouraging others to get mammograms early to make sure you can't hurt others. She has cupcake fundraisers to help support others fighting you. She wrote this book to help inform others about her fight against you and to educate them on the process of fighting you to try to make it easier for women in their fight with you.

You have destroyed many aspects of who Shelly was. BUT, what can be destroyed can be rebuilt. Her inner strength is much greater than it ever was before you came into her life. She has decided to fight you and she will win. She has fought through all the treatments and is in the process of getting back her life. She is back to work and has even started her own cake business "More Frosting Please". She may never have been able to do this without her new inner confidence and fire. Every day she moves further away from you. Never to have you come back.

Your days are numbered Cancer. You may as well give up now. You will not beat her. Someday soon you will never be able to hurt anyone again. You will be eradicated from this earth.

So cancer, in the words of my beautiful wife:
FUCK OFF AND DIE!

Love ya Babes,
Andrew Jones

Acknowledgements

Everything in this book is either real or as close to as I could remember. This is my account of what I went through. Some names have been changed, omitted or shouted from the rooftop as requested.

It is not my intention to praise any person(s) above anyone else. Everyone in my life is equally giving and encouraging. I firmly believe God gave me the strength, courage, and humor to get through this hell.

It is also not my intention to put down or leave out any individual(s) or organization. I am an opinionated young woman. Period.

Thank you, Mom, for being my Guardian Angel when I was fighting these demons. You showed me what it meant to stay strong, and never give up.

Thank you Dad, for raising Sandi and I to be TOUGH. And thank you for taking care of me. I'll never forget all the raspberries and grape juice you brought over for us! ☺ I Love You.

Thank you Andy, for picking up where I couldn't within our family. For being BOLD and copping a feel that fateful day. I would be living a much more serious diagnosis if it wasn't for you. Thank you for not showing me your fears-but also for discussing them with me once we were out from under that black cloud. Thank you for saying you will be "fine" with the menopause because I am 5 feet 4 inches of *cRaZy*PSYCHO*MOODY*HOT-FLASHIN' *RAGIN' CAJUN*EMOTIONAL WRECK*!! {even though now that you're living through it you'd rather just jump in front of a bus!}

Thank you also for not smothering me with my pillow! And for backrubs. And for 1,000's of glasses of milk. And for your lobster love.

Thank you Sandi, Adrian, Brittany and Alexandria. You have supported me since Day 1. You have been a key part in my healing. You have been selfless, considerate, helpful and understanding. You have given me four more reasons to stay strong and kick some ASS.

If I had to do this all over again-which I WON'T-I wouldn't change anything about my medical team or healthcare facility choices.

Thank you most of all to my three amazing children. I cannot take away what we all had to go through-all I can hope is that you will forget with time.

I Love You.

1. Me. Looking normal "before"
2. Myself and Andy in the nature center at Parkview School
3. Jenny & Joey visiting Plymouth for the very first time.
4. My beautiful crazy amazing kids: Josh, Ilyssa & Alaina
5. When I see this pic, I think "this is the LAST normal day". This is the last photo Andy & I had taken together before my cancer diagnosis a few days later.
6. These beautiful flower arrangements are all from my stay at the hospital during my mastectomy surgery. They sat on top of the TV to brighten my days!

Top to Bottom:
My new "shortest lived hair cut ever"

<-- Dr. Evil

Once I had my 2nd chemo my hair started falling out in clumps- so we buzzed it off.

Sitting in the 'Big Chair' having poison..er...I mean chemo...pumped into my body.

By this point I was a total cue ball. And may I just say it is DAMN COLD with no hair!